CM01022893

Enlarging Translation, Empowering Translators

Maria Tymoczko

St. Jerome Publishing
Manchester, UK & Kinderhook (NY), USA

Published by

St. Jerome Publishing
2 Maple Road West, Brooklands
Manchester, M23 9HH, United Kingdom
Telephone +44 (0)161 973 9856
Fax +44 (0)161 905 3498
stjerome@compuserve.com
http://www.stjerome.co.uk

InTrans Publications
P. O. Box 467
Kinderhook, NY 12106, USA
Telephone (518) 758-1755
Fax (518) 758-6702

ISBN 1-900650-66-5 / 978-1-900650-66-3 (pbk)

© Maria Tymoczko 2007

All rights reserved, including those of translation into foreign languages. No part of this publication may be reproduced, stored in a retrieval system or transmitted in any form or by any means, electronic, mechanical, photocopying, recording or otherwise without either the prior written permission of the Publisher or a licence permitting restricted copying issued by the Copyright Licensing Agency (CLA), 90 Tottenham Court Road, London, W1P 9HE. In North America, registered users may contact the Copyright Clearance Center (CCC): 222 Rosewood Drive, Danvers MA 01923, USA.

Printed and bound in Great Britain by
T. J. International Ltd, Cornwall, UK

Typeset by
Delta Typesetters, Cairo, Egypt
Email: hilali1945@yahoo.co.uk

British Library Cataloguing in Publication Data
A catalogue record of this book is available from the British Library

Library of Congress Cataloging-in-Publication Data
Tymoczko, Maria.
  Enlarging translation, empowering translators / Maria Tymoczko.
     p. cm.
  Includes bibliographical references and index.
  ISBN 1-900650-66-5 (pbk. : alk. paper)
1. Translating and interpreting. I. Title.

P306.T96 2007
418.02--dc22

                                  2007017191

For my friends and colleagues whose own work made this book possible: A, A, A, A, A, A, A, B, C, C, C, D, D, E, E, E, F, G, H, I, J, J, J, J, J, J, K, K, L, L, M, M, M, M, M, M, M, M, M, N, N, N, O, P, R, R, S, S, S, S, S, S, T, T, T, T, U, V, W, X.

Contents

Acknowledgments

In 2002, after 25 years of working on translation studies, I was invited to give the annual lectures at CETRA, Europe's premiere post-graduate summer research institute in translation studies. It was a great honor to be named CETRA Professor, and the lectures I delivered at CETRA that year form the basis of this book. In fact the subtitle of the book could be "The CETRA Lectures". Each chapter grows out of one of the presentations that I delivered, though they have all been expanded considerably beyond the scope of the lectures themselves. It is with great pleasure that I acknowledge my indebtedness to the faculty at CETRA that year, most particularly José Lambert, as well as Andrew Chesterman, Theo Hermans, Dirk Delabastita, Christina Schäffner, Luc Van Doorslaer, Mona Baker, Reine Meylaerts, Stefano Arduini, Robert Hodgson, and Ubaldo Stecconi, all of whom challenged me in various ways, leading to a running conversation about central issues in translation studies for a full ten days. All the students deserve to be named with gratitude as well, but special in terms of their contribution to this book are Martha Cheung, Stefan Baumgarten, Katrien Lannoy, and Ilse Feinauer.

After delivering the CETRA lectures, I presented some of the material at other venues as well. My thanks to Giuseppe Castorina for sponsoring my lectures in Rome in spring 2003, and to Theo Hermans and Mona Baker for inviting me to be the 2003 annual lecturer at the Translation Research Summer School of University College London, the University of Manchester, and the University of Edinburgh. Much gratitude to Jacqueline Hurtley for her kind invitation to give two lecture sequences in 2004 as part of the doctoral program in Construction and Representation of Identities in the Facultat de Filologia of the Universitat de Barcelona; the sustained teaching in Barcelona was the occasion for which the text of this book began to take final shape. Thanks also to Yvette Torres who invited me to lecture in the Graduate Translation Program of the Facultad de Humanidades of the Universidad de Puerto Rico in San Juan, where several sections of the book were presented.

Chapter 1 initially grew out of the opening lecture of a series on "Western Translation Theory" presented to the M.A. Translation Program at Tianjin Foreign Studies University in Tianjin, China, in 2000; I am grateful to Lin Kenan for inviting me to Tianjin as lecturer in the program and to Jin Di for bringing me to Tianjin initially in 1996 and introducing me to the faculty there. The core of chapter 5 was first presented as a plenary lecture in 2001 at the VIII Encontro National de Tradutores in Bel Horizonte, Brazil; my thanks to John Milton, Adriana Pagano, Fábio Alves, and Célia Magalhaes for the invitation and for their hospitality on that occasion. Each of these opportunities to speak contributed materially to the book, forcing me to confront objections, to sharpen my arguments, and to clarify explanations that were too cryptic.

Many individuals also deserve thanks for specific input, including Antonia Carcelen-Estrada, Georges Bastin, Elisabeth Camp, Daniela Fargione, Elizabeth Fitzpatrick, Naomi Glenn-Levin, Gene Haley, David Lenson, Bruce McCandless, Carol Maier, Marilyn Robin, Ana Rona, James Scott, Mahasweta Sengupta, Linda and Phillip Summers, Julianna Tymoczko, and Else Vieira. I am also grateful to my graduate students whose lively and stimulating work in translation studies continually expands my ideas about the field; my thanks particularly to the students in Translation, Ethics, and Ideology in spring 2005 for their deep engagement with and stimulating thought about issues that motivate this book. Special gratitude to Portia Williams Weiskel, whose careful copyediting has vastly improved the text, and to Mona Baker in her role as editor, whose suggestions were as always extremely valuable. I am most indebted to the University of Massachusetts for granting me a Samuel F. Conti Faculty Research Fellowship for 2006, which provided me a full year of released time from teaching, during which I completed the manuscript of this book.

Warm gratitude to Kevin McCullough and Ann McNeal for their sustained and sustaining encouragement and friendship during the writing, and to my family for their interest and concern. A special blessing on Carrot for keeping me company.

Maria Tymoczko

Introduction

When I was an infant, I lived in my grandmother's house with my young mother while my father served in the United States Army during World War II. I was raised in Cleveland, Ohio, one of the great industrial cities in the north of the United States. Cleveland is situated at a major intersection of the old transportation routes across the Midwest: the geography is such that all east-west traffic in that part of the country passes through the city. During my childhood iron ore came down the Great Lakes to Cleveland on the world's longest boats and coal came up by rail from Pennsylvania; where the two met there were great steel mills and foundries and manufacturing plants. This industry drew waves of immigrants from central and southern Europe in the early decades of the twentieth century, and the city was full of Poles, Bohemians, Slovaks, Lithuanians, Slovenians, Hungarians, Italians, Greeks, Lebanese, and many other nationality groups, as well as people from earlier waves of immigration such as the Germans and the Irish. Cleveland was also a major destination for the Great Migration, the movement north undertaken by so many descendants of the black slaves from the South. The park surrounding Liberty Boulevard in Cleveland had shrines to many of the nationality groups that had settled in large numbers in Cleveland, and there were dozens of shrines to be proud of because more than ninety cultures had formed the city.

My grandmother had come alone from eastern Slovakia to Cleveland when she was 16 years old. She spoke no English when she arrived. She was drawn to Cleveland because many people from her small village were heading there. It was a form of chain migration resulting in a Slovak community on the West Side of Cleveland, which she joined when she arrived. My mother was also born in Slovakia because her parents were of that breed of diasporic immigrants who went back and forth across the ocean, not fully severing their ties with their birth countries. My mother was born during one of the periods when the family was in Europe, and she first came to the United States by ship, passing through Ellis Island with her family when she was not quite four years old. She grew up in a tiny house in a mixed ethnic neighborhood, and it is to that home I was brought as a baby when my father went to war.

The neighborhood was entirely inhabited by immigrants who had not given up their native languages. It was an ordinary event to hear people speaking in Slavic languages and dialects of Italian and I no longer know what else, but probably German at least. No one assumed you would be able to communicate adequately in English, though English accented and inflected in various ways acted as a kind of link language for people. Absent a common language, people used gestures accompanied by disparate languages for communication or they relied on the kindness of others to facilitate transactions through translation or other types of intervention.

Because I spent my first two years of life in my grandmother's house in

Cleveland, I learned to speak in a place where many languages were part of daily life. The house lots were narrow, at most 25 or 30 feet (8 or 10 meters) wide, and many nationalities were packed close together. By the time I was two and a half years old, I had a passive rudimentary knowledge of three languages – Slovak, English, and Italian, probably in that order. My knowledge of Italian was the gift of our voluble Italian neighbors who lived only a few feet away and whose voices could easily be heard in our yard and in our house during the warm seasons of the year. In my grandmother's house any of the West Slavic languages (Polish, Bohemian, or Slovak) could be spoken and understood, and my grandparents spoke to each other in Hungarian when they wanted to communicate privately without being understood by their children. My mother and her siblings used English and Slovak by turns, or both together, depending on the occasion.

When you met a new person during the years I was growing up in Cleveland, the first question you asked after learning the person's name was "what is your nationality?". The question implied both ethnic group and nation-state affiliation. I had never met anyone who answered that question by saying "American" until I went to Harvard University (on a scholarship, of course) for my undergraduate education. In the world I grew up in, we identified ourselves as Slovak and German and Irish and Italian and Scottish and Polish and Russian and French and English (though I hadn't actually met any "English" people before I went to high school). It was a shock when I went to Harvard at age 17 to meet someone for the first time who said he was "American", end of story, no other nation, no other identity, no other language. I knew then I was in a different world from the one I had grown up in.

This world I am describing is a United States that no longer exists, and sometimes I feel swept away by time, stranded in a space-time continuum that is not quite my own. My childhood explains why I never think of myself as simply "American" or "Anglo", even though English is my first language. I am certainly not Anglo-Saxon, just as the Irish are emphatically not Anglo-Saxon or English or "Anglo", even though most of them also use the English language most of the time. Even my father's parents who came from families that had spoken English for many generations, some of whom had been in the United States for more than a century, did not think of themselves as English or even just American, for their people came from the Celtic fringe of the British Isles, mostly Scotland and Wales, and they self-identified as such.

I have begun my introduction by telling my own story because this is the environment in which I first learned about language, culture, and politics. In the ethnic world of Cleveland, Ohio, it was assumed that most people spoke at least two languages; it was normal to hear several languages in a single day, on a single street, at a single market; whole communities lived their lives using the many languages of Europe rather than English; and people were subject to asymmetries of power, resources, and prestige as a consequence of their languages and cultures. This is the context in which I first experienced translation and in which I first began to conceptualize translation abstractly.

Most of the major industrial and commercial cities of the United States had this character in the middle of the twentieth century, as did many rural communities, and innumerable U.S. citizens have been formed by such environments. If you were a child in such a community or such a neighborhood, as I was, you were constantly the beneficiary of translation because your elders always knew and spoke languages that you did not and they passed their transactions on to you via translation. This ethnic life of my childhood is at the core of my conceptualization of translation and it colors the way I think about translation. I am grateful to many people with whom I grew up for their kindnesses in cultural and linguistic mediation.

As I say, this is a United States that no longer exists, and yet it is still possible to find places all around the country with similar character: sections of cities where you can live in Spanish, neighborhoods where Arabic is the dominant language, districts in most big cities where Khmer or Chinese is the norm. There are also many neighborhoods from Boston to Los Angeles where newly arrived immigrant groups mingle and recreate the sort of community I have been describing. The languages are now likely to be Latin American forms of Spanish and Portuguese, Caribbean creoles, Arabic, Hindi and other Indian languages, and various southeast Asian languages. My childhood experience, combined with my perception of the United States as a place where many cultures and many languages have homes, keeps the oral norms of translation foremost in my mind. It is probably my wide exposure to oral translation types – where interpretation between languages can be quite variable, from brief summaries or explanations to verbatim transfer – that leads me to think about translation theory as I do. Translation has been an open category for me since infancy. When I read for the first time the work of translation theorists such as Gideon Toury, Itamar Even-Zohar, and André Lefevere, I discovered words for experiences I had lived and concepts I was reaching for. This is the standpoint from which I speak about translation.

Growing up in a multilingual environment taught me that languages have their own palpable meanings, their own conditions of appropriateness, their own cultural underpinnings, and their own rankings in political hierarchies. I spoke an English saturated with Slovak words and concepts that had no English equivalents. When Carol Maier (2002) speaks of her own childhood experience in the United States as a seamless convergence of two unpaired domains, she speaks to my condition. The wisdom of linguistics is bred in the bone of children who have lived this way, and such children are found everywhere in the world.

My early experiences with languages, cultures, and translation are germane to this book which contests many dominant presuppositions of translation studies that impinge on the theory of translation. In the following chapters I take a variety of approaches to argue that translation studies must de-Westernize its perspectives on the nature of translation processes and products, reconceptualizing many of the fundamental (though often unspoken) assumptions of the discipline. As I see it, a local form of knowledge about translation rooted in European languages and dominant European translation history has been promoted broadly and propagated internationally as a universal framework for conceptualizing translation theory and practice. The impetus to dislodge the way the discipline is imbricated in dominant Western thinking is reified in this volume, but it is not unique to my work. The commitment to rethink translation studies has been gathering momentum for almost a decade and many scholars have participated in the effort. My views are related to the work of those who write about postcolonial translation studies and those who have contributed to several recent collections taking up the theme of moving beyond Western models of translation, including *Beyond the Western Tradition* (2000), edited by Marilyn Gaddis Rose; *For Better or For Worse: Translation as a Tool for Change in the South Pacific* (2004), edited by Sabine Fenton; *Asian Translation Traditions* (2005), edited by Eva Hung and Judy Wakabayashi; and *Translating Others* (2006), edited by Theo Hermans. Individual scholars too numerous to mention here have contributed their own articles and monographs to this development, many of which will be cited in the following pages. In turn these scholarly studies are related to the increasing number of translation scholars who are active internationally in the field and who come from outside Europe and North America. A notable sign of the internationalization of translation studies is the formation of the International Association of Translation and Intercultural Studies (IATIS) which, recognized by UNESCO, has already held two very successful international conferences. My contribution to this development in translation studies is the exploration of the theoretical necessities for and the implications of moving beyond dominant Western discourses about translation.

This interest in moving beyond Western conceptualizations of translation is timely: the increasing push for globalization almost everywhere in the world has put translation at the heart of diverse international cultural, economic, and military enterprises. There are important questions that the nexus of translation and globalization raises for me as a translation theorist, as a postcolonial scholar who has investigated cultural exchange in situations marked by asymmetries of power, and as a politically engaged person interested in justice and equity in the world. Such questions speak directly to issues that have been central to my scholarship and my life since childhood. What types of cultural interface do we envision as a consequence of globalization and how will they differ from forms of cultural interface in the past? Who will define "culture" in such conditions of cultural interface and how will that definition be instrumentalized? To what extent will cultural exchange be multidirectional in the age of globalization, and to what extent will asymmetries of power, resources, and technologies mean that "cultural exchange" will become a euphemism for the acculturation to Western or dominant international standards of many peoples around the world who have heretofore led their lives within local frameworks of knowledge, belief, and values? To what extent will "cultural exchange" become a banner for opening up and exploiting new markets around the world? What roles will translators and translations play in all this? Will translators be instrumental in defining culture and empowered to initiate and shape cultural interface? Or will translators and their translations be implicated in the destruction of the local by the global and serve primarily as instruments of dominant interests and powers? How we define and think about translation will have much to do with the answers to these questions.

Thus far translation studies in international contexts has developed primarily as a Western and Eurocentric discipline, largely because the two most important historical events motivating the development of the field as an academic subject involved Europe and North America in a primary way. First was World War II which initiated the early investigations of translation in terms of linguistics, specifically code switching, and in terms of function, focusing on the ways that translation can influence the reception context and shape the receiving culture itself. These early investigations of translation studies reflect the central preoccupations related to translation during World War II, namely the use of translation for cracking codes in intelligence operations on the one hand and for cultural production related to propaganda on the other. Translation in these spheres was seen as an important element in the victory of the Allies,[1] raising the value of translation as an academic, practical, and theoretical concern. Conversely it is no accident that both Germany and Japan have also had a sustained interest in translation in the last half century.

The second critical historical development that gave an impetus to translation studies was the emergence of the European Union and the decision of the E.U. to retain all its major languages as official ones, rather than to adopt a melting-pot model of political affiliation or even to choose to transact business in a restricted group of dominant languages. The result has arguably been the most extensive translational activity in the history of the world, with a consequent demand for translators and translator training that has required an academic field to meet the constraints of the political context. Although theory and practice of translation in this context have served very local needs and have thus been Eurocentric by definition, meeting the needs of the E.U. is correlated with a great deal of the growth and success of the discipline of translation studies worldwide.

Western perspectives in translation studies have also been privileged because of the dominant roles of Europe and North America in globalization itself as an economic and communicative process. Europe and North America have been key players in the extension of corporate economic activities to multinational

---

[1] Including the Soviet Union which subsequently invested heavily in translation during the Cold War, as part of its ideological program. As early as 1978 Holmes (1994:102) noted the importance of accessing Soviet work on translation theory, a desideratum that remains in the emerging international discipline of translation studies because the story of the development of this branch of translation studies remains to be told in one of the link languages that is used in the discipline internationally.

modes of operation, as well as in the proliferation of international and intergovernmental organizations.[2] Added to these factors is the leading role of North America in the development of the technological and informational vehicles for globalization. Thus, it is perhaps no surprise that Eurocentric and North American conceptualizations of language and cultural interface have been extended internationally by globalization.

In the international discipline of translation studies, these various historical factors have favored the primacy of Eurocentric and North American conceptualizations of translation both practically and theoretically. As a result translation studies has privileged a particularly Western view of translation, namely the view of translation as a 'carrying across', a 'leading across', or a 'setting across', the original meanings of the words in the major Western European languages for 'translation', including English *translation*, Spanish *traducción*, French *traduction*, and German *Übersetzung*. All these words privilege transfer as the basic mode of translation whether that transfer is figured in terms of transporting material objects or leading sentient beings (such as captives or slaves in one direction or soldiers and missionaries in the other) across a cultural and linguistic boundary.[3] Theo Hermans notes that "if the etymology of the word 'translation' had suggested, say, the image of responding to an existing utterance instead of transference, the whole idea of a transfer postulate would probably never have arisen" (1999:52). It's not so much that these Western views of translation are pernicious *per se* but that they constitute only one of many possible ways of conceptualizing translation: they are limited and they are also ideological. I believe that if the theory and practice of translation remain predicated upon and restricted to dominant Western European conceptions of translation, translators will *ipso facto* through their processes of translation, consciously or not, be enlisted in the political aspect of globalization from a dominant Western point of view, that is, the use of globalization to further the carrying across of Western dominance – military, political, economic, and cultural – in the world.

---

[2] Cronin (2003:109-11) discusses the role of the European Union in the increase of translation internationally; he also gives statistics related to the growth of NGOs and intergovernmental organizations since the beginning of the twentieth century. With respect to economic activities, Cronin (2003:134) notes that more than 60 per cent of world economic production is accounted for by the speakers of three languages, namely English, German, and Japanese, and that with French and Spanish, the figure rises to 75 per cent.

[3] See below, chapter 2, as well as Tymoczko (2003, forthcoming b). The conceptualization of translation as a form of 'leading across' may be related to the practice of using captives of native tribes to serve as linguistic intermediaries by many of the early explorers; it can also be seen as a metaphor related to conversion both to Christianity and to European forms of culture. An early instance of the metaphor is found in the writings of St. Jerome where he says, "like some conqueror, [Hilary the Confessor] marched the original text, a captive, into his native language" (Robinson 1997b:26b). Note also the connection of translation as 'leading across' and words for 'education' in many European languages. Lakoff and Johnson (1980) discuss the importance of conceptual metaphors embedded in the meanings of words and in syntax.

Current models used to teach translation, to train translators, and to research the products and processes of translation are generally based on these narrow, dominant Western European practices of and discourses about translation. The problems with Western models are manifold, however. For example, they presuppose outmoded theories of meaning – either Platonic conceptions of meaning or positivist ones. Andrew Chesterman and Rosemary Arrojo observe that "The metaphor 'translation is transfer' . . . implies that something is indeed transferred, something that presumably remains constant throughout the process and is thus objectively 'there'" (2000:153). More modern concepts of meaning, by contrast, view meaning as being constructed by cultural practices and cultural production, notably language, and inflected by the context. As a consequence the target text meanings can never be fully "the same" as source text meanings, nor is there a circumscribed meaning in a source text that awaits transfer or carrying across by a translator.[4] Thus, insofar as a translator is taught to use a specific protocol for determining and transferring meaning, that protocol will narrow a translator's choices and decision making; it will circumscribe the translator's agency, and inscribe the translator within a dominant Western construction not only of translation but also of what counts as meaning.

Moreover, Western conceptualizations of translation can be associated with the metaphor of the translator as standing "between" in the transfer process. The metaphor of between suggests that the translator is neutral, above history and ideology; the translator can even be seen as an alienated figure in this construct, an alienation that can be passed off as the "objectivity" of a professional (cf. Tymoczko 2003). The consequence is the effacement of ideology and the evisceration of the agency of the translator as a committed, engaged, and responsible figure. Thus, the transfer metaphor implicit in Western conceptualizations of translation undermines the self-reflexivity and empowerment of translators, encouraging a sort of amnesia about ideology in translation processes that facilitates the unexamined ascendancy of the values of the dominant powers within a culture and throughout the globalizing world.

There are many other problems with basing translation studies on an implicit and unexamined foundation of Western views of translation. Eurocentric conceptions of translation are deeply rooted in literacy practices (as opposed to oral practices, still dominant in most of world). Indeed, Eurocentric ideas about translation are shaped by practices deriving from biblical translation in particular and by the history of translating Christian sacred texts. Western conceptions of translation are also heavily influenced by the tight connection of language and nation in Europe (which privileges the view that a nation should be united around a single language and that "normal" cultures are monolingual). The history of Eurocentric translation is connected with the practices of empire and imperialism

---

[4] This argument is developed at greater length in chapter 7 below. See also Catford (1965), Nord (1997), Appiah (2000), Davis (2001).

as well. These are obviously not acceptable conceptual bases – much less ideal ones – for founding an international discipline of translation studies, for serving as the basis of translation theory around the world, or for providing international standards of translation practices. Certainly they do not conduce to developing internationalist approaches to translation that can facilitate an equitable relationship among peoples and mutality in cultural exchange predicated on multidirectionality in a globalized world.

The narrow foundations of translation studies as a discipline are also reflected in central pretheoretical assumptions about text, the nature of translation in multilingual cultures, the normal model for translation processes, and so forth. The history of Western European translation privileges an implicit literalism that has been used to disseminate the empires of religion, secular rule, and commerce throughout the last five hundred years. For reasons such as these, I believe that translation studies thus far has taken a very local form of knowledge about translation based on these assumptions and universalized it as a general theory. Insofar as translation studies is intended to serve the needs of the European Union or North American countries, that basis for the discipline may be sufficient, but plainly it will not suffice in the context of globalization, nor does it suffice intellectually as a theoretical foundation for thinking about translation cross-culturally. Translation studies must move beyond Eurocentric conceptualizations and translators must become self-reflexive about their pretheoretical understandings and practices of translation, or else translation in the age of globalization will become an instrument of domination, oppression, and exploitation. When translators remain oblivious of the Eurocentric pretheoretical assumptions built into the discipline of translation studies, they not only play out hegemonic roles in their work, they willingly limit their own agency as translators.

In the simplest terms this book argues that translation studies needs to adopt a broader – in fact, an open – definition of the subject matter at the heart of the discipline, namely translation. Because the field has taken shape around a narrow Western definition of the matter, based on the conceptual metaphors embedded in Western European words for 'translation', and because a local set of knowledges and practices has become the basis of universalist claims about translation, much of what is argued in the field is partial, flawed, and in need of amendment and expansion. In thinking about these problems, I had the intuition that opening the definition of translation to include a larger range of ideas besides those currently dominant in the West, including ideas from beyond the Western sphere, would also lead to insights about the agency of translators and ultimately to the empowerment of translators. As I worked with the materials in the chapters below, I became ever more convinced of this connection. I argue that there is a recursive relationship between the openness of meaning in translation, the empowerment of the translator, and the enlargement of the concept translation beyond Western metaphors related to transfer.

Let me return to the question of my own formation as a translation studies scholar to explain a bit more about how I arrived at my place of enunciation in this volume, challenging dominant and hegemonic pretenses of the Western world as a whole, despite the fact that I am an English-speaking citizen of the United States. My early experiences as a small child in a multilingual and economically disadvantaged context marked by secondary orality were later overlaid with a considerable amount of formal education relevant to translation. It is perhaps worth telling some of this story. My second language is actually French, which I began learning intensively from the time I was six in the Cleveland Public Schools. The school system stressed an audio-oral approach to learning languages that precluded translation and encouraged students to immerse themselves in French as an independent linguistic world, rather than referring everything back to English. We were taught with gestures and enactments instead of English when we needed explanations, and I remember my sixth-grade French teacher doing such things as jumping from his desk and flapping his arms when he wanted to convey the meaning of *voler*, 'fly'. Needless to say, these experiences taught me a great deal about language and meaning, and my English came to be permeated with French words and concepts as well as Slovak ones. French also gave me a mental home unlike that in any other language.

Equally important for the way I think about translation was my university work in medieval European languages and literatures. I was blessed with teachers like A.B. Lord and Louis Solano (himself from a multilingual immigrant family) who stressed the oral nature of medieval culture and the oral base of the medieval vernacular literature that has survived from those times. I was familiar with oral narrative because two of my grandparents were storytellers, and my father's mother was particularly influential on me in this regard. It became clear to me that translation and cultural transfer were intimately involved with the emergence of much of medieval European literature. I spent a great deal of time trying to image precisely the way Celtic, Latin, and Arabic stories had passed into Old French literature, the mechanisms of translation and cultural mediation that allowed the newness and difference from other cultures to be taken up in the forging of a great literature in its first stages of formation. Later when I was a graduate student, Máire MacNeill Sweeney, the former Secretary of the Irish Folklore Society, was teaching Irish folklore in the Celtic Department at Harvard; she provided me tools I needed to conceptualize the mechanisms of and resistances to intercultural transfer in oral conditions, including the transfer of stories and lore in oral traditional cultures. The various strands of my education and my upbringing – both stressing multilingualism, cultural difference, and primary and secondary orality – converged in my thinking to challenge the precedence of the written over the oral in many cultural contexts.

In addition my approach as a translation theorist has been shaped by my teaching of and research in medieval literature, which brought me into repeated contact with extremely diverse text types that resulted from the process of medieval translation or that were indigenous to medieval European cultures. Such text types often do not fall neatly into any of the standard contemporary translation studies grids related to function, for example. The knowledge of medieval texts and translations has provided me another alternate set of standards for interrogating modern dominant Eurocentric norms of translation as I have attempted to theorize translation. The culture gap between the medieval and modern periods has also acted as a way of perceiving cultural difference in translation. For me distance in time has been an analogue to thinking about cultural asymmetries that distance in space provides many, even most, translation scholars. Finally, the irresolvable difficulties and uncertainties of understanding medieval cultures and medieval texts have permanently affected my thinking about difference between cultures, making me both more skeptical of my "certainties" and more respectful of the gulfs that can separate peoples and individuals alike.

It was certainly serendipitous for my understanding of translation to have found my way into Irish studies where I learned so much about the relationship between cultural production, ideology, and power, subjects that are central to thinking about translation. I am particularly grateful to the intelligence and kindness of Thomas Kinsella, at once a great poet and a great translator, who is so articulate about the position of literature and language in a nation that has been colonized and that inherits a dual tradition. My senior colleague in Irish studies at the University of Massachusetts, David Clark, was also a mentor, patiently teaching me much about writing, rewriting, and retelling in the Irish revival. From both I learned a great deal about the role of texts in identity formation and nation building in a bilingual postcolonial country in the nineteenth and twentieth centuries. Here I must also acknowledge the role played by my students and colleagues in Irish studies, many of them Irish and Irish American, who conveyed their thoughts and perceptions about ideology and the political dimensions of texts, rewritings, and translations with great passion and deep feeling. Rarely do cloistered medievalists see the world from perspectives such as those.

The process of actually translating medieval Irish texts into English was formative for me in terms of understanding the complexities of cultural interface in translation. I am grateful to the National Endowment of the Humanities for sponsoring my translations of early Irish stories and to Liam Miller and the Dolmen Press for publishing them as *Two Death Tales from the Ulster Cycle*. What followed was my real initiation into translation studies as a discipline. It was Marilyn Gaddis Rose who first invited me to a translation studies conference and André Lefevere who introduced me to the group of descriptive translation scholars that was beginning to coalesce into what Theo Hermans has called "an invisible college" (1999). These colleagues all enriched my life and my thinking about translation immeasurably. Marilyn's conference started me on what has been a wonderful odyssey of thinking about language, literature, culture, politics, and ideology, as well as the relationship of translation to all of these.

My own personal history has been deeply connected with politics, ranging from work in the Civil Rights movement, radical student activism, and antiwar demonstrations in the 1960s, to feminism and grass-roots politics in the 1970s, to electoral politics in the 1980s and thereafter. The ideological component in systems theory gave me ways to integrate my academic interests with my political commitments. Indeed systems theory became a way of conceptualizing and ordering many things that I had lived but had no way to write about, most especially power, politics, and ideological contestations.

I have been fortunate to teach in the Department of Comparative Literature at the University of Massachusetts Amherst, which has valued translation and has included translation theory and practice in its curriculum from the inception of the program. Warren Anderson and Fred Will were my senior colleagues when I first joined the department, both skilled in the methods of the Iowa workshop approach to translation, both skilled translators; they offered me implicit theoretical models of translation, as well as a great deal of encouragement, as did my other colleagues, all of whom have been translators to one degree or another. When Warren and Fred retired, I was fortunate to be given the graduate translation courses to teach. I am particularly indebted to Warren's help during those first few years of teaching translation; his ideas persist as a thread in my views of translation. Comparative Literature at the University of Massachusetts continues to be a vibrant place to think about and teach translation studies; when Edwin Gentzler joined us as a colleague in translation studies, it became my good fortune to have him as collaborator in both teaching and research.

The account of my journey into translation studies wouldn't be complete without acknowledging the contribution of Thomas Tymoczko, my husband of many years. He and I were graduate students at Harvard when translation was a hot topic, with people as diverse as Roman Jakobson, W.V.O. Quine, and Anthony Oettinger on the faculty. The philosophers were particularly engaged with the topic of translation. Tom's dissertation on Quine's thesis of the indeterminacy of translation and Tom's later work on translation, including his interest in and contact with Eugene Nida, gave my thinking about translation a philosophical edge. Tom was a good teacher, and our discussions of philosophy, language, and translation continue to stand me in good stead; it was he who brought Wittgenstein's thinking into my ambit as well. Tom's lucid accounts of difficult philosophical issues was also instrumental in prompting me to try to teach and write about translation without relying on jargon, using the strengths of ordinary language to make my arguments whenever possible.

As I indicated earlier, I have given a very personal introduction to this book in part because I wish to indicate something about my place of enunciation. If indeed anthropology and translation studies have affinities, as has been so often argued, then perhaps translators and translation scholars will do well to borrow some of the emerging practices of anthropologists and ethnographers by prefacing our scholarship on translation with some account of our own formations, our views of language, our experiences of and attitudes toward cultural difference, our political loyalties, and the like, such that our positions on translation can be more adequately assessed by readers. Although I come from the United States, at present the center of hegemony in the world, and although my languages and outlook are Western, I have tried to suggest why my thinking about translation has been formed by practices and experiences that stand at the margins of or even at times outside the dominant Western ideas that have shaped translation studies thus far. I understand experientially how different and asymmetrical languages are, how they remain unpaired domains for perceiving meaning in the world. My thoughts about translation have been formed by community interpretation and by knowledge of oral translation products and practices that stand outside the focus on the transfer of meaning associated with the words *translation*, *traduction*, and so forth. I have also been deeply involved with the activist use of translation for engaged and politicized purposes. Not least, I was educated in an environment where there was a reigning skepticism about the possibility of perceiving, transferring, or recuperating meaning in the translation process, as well as skepticism about the "sameness" of texts that are iterated by different speakers in different places at different times.

Enlarging Translation, Empowering Translators deals with very large topics and attempts to draw together their implications for translation: among others, the course of modern history, the workings of geopolitical power, philosophical inquiry about meaning, insights from cognitive science about conceptual thinking, the nature of contemporary research methodologies, and understandings of ideology, ethics, and culture. Any one of these topics could be the focus of a book about translation in itself; thus each topic inevitably is treated in a somewhat summary manner. Nonetheless, it is at times useful to stand back and try to see a subject whole. This can only be done by taking on a large perspective in which things sizable in themselves assume their proper proportion in relationship to the subject in focus. In this book I try to present such a large view of translation, acknowledging both the strengths and limitations of my standpoint.

PART 1: ENLARGING TRANSLATION

1. A Postpositivist History of Translation Studies

When the first surviving pronouncements about the practice of translation appear in the records of Western culture – and they appear early, some two thousand years ago – it is assumed that translation is a defined process with a circumscribed domain. This is no surprise: to Cicero, whose comments in *De oratore* (ca. 55 B.C.E.) are generally recognized as offering the earliest Western norms for translation, the circumstances and function of translation are treated as self-evident. The languages (Greek and Latin) and their anisomorphisms are taken for granted; the text types are well known (oratory in Cicero's case) and considered unproblematic as types; the purposes of translation are presupposed (facilitating the formation of a Roman citizen, learning public oratory, developing more powerful models than Latin oratory itself could provide, increasing the vocabulary stock of Latin, defamiliarizing Latin rhetoric so that Cicero would not sound like Ennius); and the cultural context of both source and target text are assumed (Greek city-state rhetoric, public contexts in Rome such as the Roman Senate).[1]

Before continuing, let me say a word about terminology. I am using the term *Western* to refer to ideas and perspectives that initially originated in and became dominant in Europe, spreading from there to various locations in the world, where in some cases, such as the United States, the Americas in general, and Australia, these ideas have also become dominant.[2] I am capitalizing the word to indicate that the term refers to a concept, not a direction. There is an obvious difficulty with the terms *East* and *West*, both of which imply perspective and position. East or west of what? In Chinese tradition where China is the "Middle Kingdom", India is "the West", but for the British India was part of "the East". To the Romans the nations of southwestern Asia were considered "the East", a perspective still encoded in the phrase "the Near East". Moreover, at present, when Western ideas have permeated the world and there is widespread interpenetration of cultures everywhere, the terms West and Western have become increasingly problematic.

Şebnem Susam-Sarajeva (2002:193) discusses difficulties with this terminology including the polar opposite "non-Western", which reduces the rest of the world to being defined (by contrast or opposition) in terms of the Western. She points out as well that the terminology aggregates vastly different cultures outside Eurocentric spheres and effaces great differences within Western cultures (epitomized by differences among Britain and the Celtic fringe – Ireland, Scotland, and

---

[1] Robinson's anthology of Western statements about translation includes the comments of Cicero (1997b:6-12) and his followers.

[2] For a discussion of how Latin American cultures constitute alternate ways of being Western, see Molloy (2005:372, 377n2 and n3) and sources cited.

[handwritten margin note: terminological problems: Western – non-western center – periphery]

Wales – or Switzerland and the United States). Although I basically agree with her assessment of the difficulties, I find her solution of using the discourses of center and periphery problematic. I see knowledge as ultimately local, with life being lived and experienced in a multicentered manner. Reification of some parts of the world as center and others as periphery undermines that the valorization of the multiplicity of perspectives in translation studies that constitutes one facet of the argument I am developing in this book. I believe that every place and every nation is a center of experience, knowledge, and wisdom, where I use *nation* in the oldest sense of the word, namely to indicate a people or a community. There is no ideal solution to these problems of terminology, especially at a time when Western culture is being rapidly taken up all around the world and naturalized to the local. Thus, although I use the term *Western*, I am also avoiding the term *non-Western* which constructs an implied binarism that effaces distinctions of cultures everywhere. Widely varied patterns of cultures are lumped together, particularly in the aggregate *non-Western*, and then collectively silenced.

Let us return to Cicero's statements about translation. These comments by Cicero were not, of course, the first reflections on translation in human history or even in Western history, but they are some of the earliest to come down to the present day because they are among the first associated with literacy practices in the various languages of the world.[3] Thus they have survived the course of time. Before written comments about translation practice, there were certainly oral observations about the practice of translation or interpreting, but they have not been preserved because writing is one of the principal means by which humans transmit culture wholesale to the future. No doubt, however, oral statements about interpreting were equally straightforward, for again the situation of any particular oral practice of cultural exchange was well defined: the languages, the types of utterances, the persons communicating, the purposes of communication, and the cultural contexts were all ostensively apparent.

Like most teachers of translation theory and practice, I dutifully include a unit in my classes in which I have students read surveys of early statements and pronouncements about translation such as those of Cicero, asking students to become familiar with various canonical texts about translation from the earliest period to the twentieth century. What I have realized over the years, however, is that I tend to approach this question of the history of translation theory and practice with a sense of dread. It was in part the investigation of the reasons for that dread that led me to write this book.

Translation is primarily instrumental for many of the early authors, facilitating activities that are themselves worth discussing. As a process translation often seems obvious to early commentators, as does their task as translators,

---

[3] Cheung (2006a) contains early Chinese statements about translation, a number of which antedate Cicero.

which is to find solutions to the problems posed by translation as it is defined in their context. This is true even when the authors are promoting or prescribing a specific approach to translation as a whole. The presupposition that the problems of translation are obvious and that the solutions of the writers are clearly correct and generalizable is what makes most statements about translation before 1900 difficult to use and to teach as translation *theory*. These early statements have a transparency about them resulting from implicit assumptions that the activity of translation is circumscribed by the situations and presuppositions of the several writers; such assumptions thus offer a self-evident bottom line to any particular writer's inquiry about and position on translation.

This transparency in the early record stands in sharp contrast to the current problematizing of translation and the probing into its nature. It is as if before 1900 translation were conceived as a closed field, a field similar to the geography of a single country or even simple arithmetic calculation. One may continue to learn information virtually indefinitely about such a closed field by increasing the delicacy of the inquiry, but essentially the broad strokes of what can be learned and the boundaries of the domain are well defined at an early stage. In such inquiry the task of researchers is to fill in more and more detail on the basis of the given parameters and the structure of the defined domain.

Reading the early history of Western thinking about translation can be both stultifying and disturbing, therefore, because it consists of statement after statement about how to translate, statements that are delivered in positive, declarative, and definitive terms about issues that in modern approaches to translation are complex, open, and often indeterminate. The tone of the early statements is significant: the writers give prescriptive and definitive advice and they proclaim clear norms. It does not seem to matter to the writers that they contradict each other from decade to decade, from century to century, often knowingly.

When my students and I undertake this investigation together, I usually ask in an openended way what the students think about the reading. I am often amazed to hear them say that they find the sequence of statements interesting and useful: they say that the survey gives them ideas about how to translate and they report finding it gratifying to be given definite instructions about the process. The disjunction between my own response and those of my students ultimately caused me to begin to interrogate my own reactions: why *do* I find the early statements so unhelpful and in fact so frustrating? Why *do* I read such statements as I would read journal entries about travel abroad, revealing as much about the viewer as about the viewed? To a large extent I believe that the answers to these questions lie in my unease with and aversion to normative stances that are delivered without any indication of self-reflection and self-reflexivity about the speaker's own place of enunciation and without even minimal acknowledgment of the relationships binding the speaker's beliefs, actions, and ideological context.

By and large the attitudes of most early writers about translation reflect what have come to be known as realist or positivist orientations to knowledge,[4] but since the early decades of the twentieth century such uncritical and transparent approaches to knowledge have been increasingly discredited. The importance of acknowledging position and perspective has become almost universally recognized in academic discourses, and a certain metacommentary and self-reflexivity about the researcher's position and stance are now expected. These expectations are associated with the popular dictum in contemporary literary studies that the task is not to solve the problems but to problematize the solutions. Marilyn Gaddis Rose offers a similar judgement, observing that the history of early statements about translation is "essentially a record of successive guides to pleasing literary taste", and that these statements do not constitute theory *per se* in the contemporary understanding of that concept; instead they are "recommendations for adhering to accepted rhetorical practices as the recommender understands them" (1997:15). Similar issues have led Martha Cheung to title her collection of primary documents about translation in Chinese as *An Anthology of Chinese Discourse on Translation* (2006a), and she discusses in her introduction why she rejected calling these statements "theory" (cf. Lin 2002:162).

Thus, my dis-ease with the approaches of early writers to translation is not merely a matter of personal taste. To a large extent what is troubling about the early statements has to do with the huge shift in how knowledge itself has been viewed since the beginning of the twentieth century. Associated with the demise of positivism in the West, this shift makes it increasingly difficult to enjoin people to translate in any single way or, in fact, to take rigid normative stances toward any social practice and to view any subject from a single perspective exclusively, as the early statements about translation tend to do. Accordingly, it becomes increasingly difficult to use early pronouncements about translation and to recommend them to students without extensively contextualizing the material, showing how each statement served the ethos and logos of its day and how it can be related to its cultural moment. This work has not been systematically attempted in translation studies, and it is certainly beyond my own personal reach, particularly in an introductory course on translation theory and practice or even in a study such as I have undertaken here.

Since World War II and the coalescence of translation studies as an independent academic discipline,[5] thinking about translation has had a definitional

---

[4] Most of the early Western statements about translation in anthologies antedate positivism *per se* in its philosophical sense, but the authors' lack of self-reflexivity about the limitations of their own perspectives is often rooted in an ethos in which knowledge has an absoluteness that converges with the attitudes of later positivists. Some of this ethos is attributable to imperialism, some to Christian views, and some rooted in realist epistemological orientations that go back to Greek philosophy.

[5] I am using the term "translation studies" broadly and somewhat anachronistically to refer to all the postwar developments related to thinking about translation, even before the term was coined in the 1970s. In English the phrase was developed as an analogue to black studies or African American studies, women's studies, Irish studies, and so forth; such terms proliferated after 1960.

impetus that has grown out of and been motivated by postpositivist perspectives on the subject matter. This definitional impetus has increasingly revolved around two points. First, research and theorizing have steadily expanded, thus opening the domain of translation and problematizing many aspects of translation that were earlier taken as obvious or transparent. It is increasingly recognized that there are more and more strands involved in translation, more and more features of translation that vary across time and space and that must be accounted for and understood. Thus, what seemed transparent to early writers on translation because it was assumed (including characteristics of specific languages, anisomorphisms of specific language pairs, text types, cultural contexts, patronage, power relations, and ideology, to name but a few parameters) is not in fact uniform or even obvious across the whole range of translational phenomena. Indeed the elements of translation viewed by early writers as a matter of common sense are often merely a reflection of *idées reçues* associated with particular cultural situations or ideological positions of their own times. As areas associated with translation have become problematized, therefore, translation theory has also shown a continual tendency to expand the purview of translation, with a concomitant expansion of the scope of translation research.

Second, and clearly related to the first point, there has been a steady movement in the field toward greater self-reflexivity as scholars and translators have come to realize that their own perspectives on translation are not universal. That is, scholars have begun to understand that any perspective, even a dominant one, is only one way of looking at translation. This chapter will briefly trace these currents through the various developments and schools of translation studies in the second half of the twentieth century. It is not, of course, possible to deal with the history of translation studies as a discipline in detail in this context. Nonetheless the overview below offers a way to conceptualize both the history and structure of translation studies as a whole since World War II and to suggest ways of characterizing the discipline that can serve as alternatives to stereotypical ways of describing it found in the existing literature.

1.1 Initial Considerations: Beyond Positivism

Although the primary focus of this chapter is a brief survey of the major theories of translation that have emerged since World War II, some background material will be useful before turning to the survey so as to locate the various approaches in a broader pattern. In a sense it is possible to undertake a thematic overview of the field because translation studies has matured sufficiently so that the history of the field can be written. There are several collections of primary documents pertaining to pronouncements about translation through the centuries, notably André Lefevere's *Translation/History/Culture: A Sourcebook* (1992a), Douglas Robinson's *Western Translation Theory from Herodotus to Nietzsche* (1997b), and Martha Cheung's *An Anthology of Chinese Discourse on Translation*

(2006a). There are narrative overviews of such longitudinal views, most of them relatively short, such as chapters in Eugene Nida's *Toward a Science of Translating* (1964) and Susan Bassnett's *Translation Studies* (3rd. ed., 2002). The sequence of translation theories since World War II has been treated by Edwin Gentzler, *Contemporary Translation Theories* (2nd. ed., 2001); Jeremy Munday, *Introducing Translation Studies: Theories and Applications* (2001); and Mary Snell-Hornby, *The Turns of Translation Studies: New Paradigms or Shifting Viewpoints?* (2006). There are also detailed overviews of particular approaches to translation theory in the series titled "Translation Theories Explained" (currently titled "Translation Theories Explored") issued by St. Jerome Publishing: Christiane Nord, *Translating as a Purposeful Activity* (1997) on functionalist theories; Peter Fawcett, *Translation and Language* (1997) on linguistic theories; Jean Boase-Beier, *Stylistic Approaches to Translation* (2006), focusing on cognitive stylistics in particular; Theo Hermans, *Translation in Systems* (1999) on systems theories; Luise von Flotow, *Translation and Gender* (1997) on feminist theories of translation; Douglas Robinson, *Translation and Empire* (1997) on postcolonial theories; Marilyn Gaddis Rose, *Translation and Literary Criticism* (1997) on literary theories of translation; and Kathleen Davis, *Deconstruction and Translation* (2001). Leo Tak-hung Chan's *Twentieth-Century Chinese Translation Theory: Modes, Issues and Debates* (2004) broadens these considerations by anthologizing texts pertaining to modern Chinese translation theory. In addition, there are studies that look at longitudinal questions pertaining to translators and translation in context, such as the volume edited by Jean Delisle and Judith Woodsworth, *Translators through History* (1995). This is only a partial list of available studies, and I refer the readers of this book to these volumes for more detailed considerations of any one approach to translation studies discussed below, as well as for comprehensive bibliographical information.

What is almost universally true of the existing studies, however, is that the preponderance of data about translation processes and products, the overwhelming number of pronouncements about translation retailed, and the theories considered are drawn from Western materials and Western contexts.[6] This is an issue worth pondering. Does it indicate basic ignorance of translation in worldwide contexts among most scholars in translation studies publishing for international contexts? Does it mean that (like some natural scientists) most translation scholars think there is little material worth considering outside Western contexts? Is it tantamount to saying that the only "real" translations and the only "real" thinking about translation have occurred in Eurocentric environments? Is it a sign of hegemonic thinking on the part of scholars in the field who do not

---

[6] Delisle and Woodsworth (1995) stands out in this regard as offering a significant number of case studies that transcend Eurocentric contexts, as do, of course, Cheung (2006a) and Chan (2004). There is also a considerable amount of material dealing with traditions around the world in the *Routledge Encyclopedia of Translation Studies* (Baker 1998), particularly in the historical section.

come from Western traditions? If any of these is true, how can the field improve in this regard? In this chapter I do not intend to 'recapitulate the disciplinary surveys that have been done, nor am I able to ameliorate them, but I will return throughout the rest of the book to historical considerations related to moving the field beyond Eurocentric interests and presuppositions.

Here I begin with a framework from Western intellectual history that may be helpful to schematize and organize some of the developments in translation theory during the last half century. I argue that the field has been gradually expanding to consider more and more facets of translation, more and more perspectives on translation, an expansion that is associated with the demise of positivism. It is an expansion, however, that at present is still severely limited by the primarily Western focus of translation studies as an international academic discipline. Thus, the question of enlarging translation – the primary subject matter of this book – takes its place in a trajectory that has already been established for decades in translation studies yet still remains curiously parochial and limited by persistent Western assumptions.

To understand the implications of the demise of positivism, it will help to give some background on the philosophical movement of positivism itself. Positivism can be defined as "a philosophy asserting the primacy of observation in assessing the truth of statements of fact and holding that metaphysical and subjective arguments not based on observable data are meaningless".[7] Elaborated by Auguste Comte in the 1830s and thereafter, as a philosophical system, positivism recognizes only "positive" facts and observable phenomena, as well as the relations between specific facts, more general facts, and laws, thus privileging the "positive" sciences, principally mathematics and the physical sciences. In his *Tractatus* (1921) the early Wittgenstein is generally recognized as offering one of the most trenchant articulations and defenses of the later phrases of positivism in the early twentieth century. He encapsulated the doctrine in his aphorism, "What can be said at all can be said clearly, and what we cannot talk about we must consign to silence".[8]

Views of knowledge that underpinned nineteenth-century conceptions of the university and university curricula in the West were grounded to a large extent in the philosophical framework of positivism and presupposed tenets associated with Western imperialism. It is not surprising that the central fields of the humanities (including the study of languages and literatures) were constituted during that period as disciplines of their time, thus rooted in both positivism and imperialism. In Eurocentric domains thus far, academic thinking about translation has taken shape principally within humanist disciplines and it has inherited these orientations. In part because of its positivist framework, much research in the humanities

---

[7] Cf. *American Heritage Dictionary*, "logical positivism", s.v.

[8] "Was sich überhaupt sagen lässt, lässt sich klar sagen; und wovon man nicht reden kann, darüber muss man schweigen" (Wittgenstein 1961:2-3).

in the nineteenth and early twentieth centuries was focused on the collection of observable data, including such things as the elucidation of difficult languages, the preparation of editions of primary texts, and the attempt to determine such factors as textual authorship, historical context, and the biographical particulars of specific individuals.

The impact of Western imperialism on academic subjects was not limited to the humanities; indeed presuppositions associated with imperialism affected all branches of knowledge. Academic investigations generally excluded concepts of mathematics, medicine, alternate views of nature, and approaches to scientific questions developed outside Western contexts. The social sciences reduced "non-Western" cultures to primitive curiosities and "non-Western" individuals to objects, institutionalizing aspects of an imperial or colonizing gaze in the protocols of anthropology and other observational disciplines that focused on peoples from beyond the Western ambit. These imperialist premises of academic disciplines were in turn interconnected with positivism, for positivism implicitly and uncritically asserts the dominant (and, hence, Western) perspective as the basis of observation, taking one specific cultural viewpoint as the correct or "objective" perspective for assessing the truth of statements of fact and for garnering positive, observable data. Thus a local Eurocentric perspective was presumed to be the only possible neutral view of the world.

These frameworks began to break down in the first quarter of the twentieth century, eroding rapidly as the century progressed. For example, in his mature work, *The Philosophical Investigations* (1953), Wittgenstein offered shattering examples and arguments that undermined positivism. Wittgenstein began to address issues of perspective, the habits of human communities, the difficulties and arbitrariness in human communication, the incommensurability of life forms, and the importance of convention, among others. His work converged with and extended developments in the natural sciences and mathematics, as well as other fields. As a consequence of these varied developments, positivism as an approach to knowledge and the production of knowledge had been largely abandoned by the end of World War II in most intellectual circles.

In this trajectory the work of three figures stands out '– Albert Einstein, Werner Heisenberg, and Kurt Gödel. Although an exploration of their accomplishments is beyond the scope of the present study, we can note briefly some aspects of their impact. Einstein's challenges to Newtonian physics and his relativity theories, Heisenberg's uncertainty principle (1927), and Gödel's incompleteness theorem (1931) held implications not merely for their own specific disciplines but for the concept of knowledge itself. All of these theories turn on the significance of perspectives and frameworks, as well as loci of uncertainty, in physics and mathematics. Scientists were not the only figures involved in the shift away from positivism. Figures such as Sigmund Freud and Carl Jung played a role, and artists such as James Joyce and Picasso were important as well, problematizing "objectivity" and anticipating in their work discourses about perspective that emerged later in academic fields.

The changing views of knowledge in the twentieth century undermined nineteenth-century epistemological and ideological premises of the traditional humanities and, indeed, of academe as a whole, thus challenging orientations in Western culture that go back to the Greeks. It is no accident that arguments for enlarging the conception of translation can be connected with the postpositivist views of the later Wittgenstein, as we will see below. In the second half of the twentieth century, postpositivist views of knowledge shifted inquiry in the humanities and the social sciences away from research oriented toward digging out and amassing observable "facts", to self-reflexive interrogations of perspective, premises, and the framework of inquiry itself. It is in part for this reason that literary studies have become increasingly focused on theory and metatextual questions, while history has undertaken a reconsideration of the very postulates that have guided the construction of the past.

This intense interest in theory and frameworks has been one of the most extraordinary developments in the humanities and the social sciences during the last quarter century. Connected with the so-called "generation of 1968" – the student radicals in Europe, North America, and elsewhere – theory became the passion of a generation of students who were radicalized by the politics of the period. In turn many of these students became the teachers of today, asking metaquestions not only about texts and language, but about the very disciplines having to do with texts and language. They have turned a self-reflexive eye on what constitutes knowledge, the knowing subject, and the knowing institution, that is, academe.

Changes in the conception of knowledge traceable to the demise of positivism and the erosion of imperialism have been accelerated by the more recent phenomena of globalization.[9] Earlier ideological and self-reflexive investigations of both history and literature had resulted in inclusionary approaches, transforming the canons of literature and admitting alternative histories, as the validity of perspectives other than those dominant in the West has been gradually asserted, and as the inequities, injustices, and violence of colonialism, patriarchal culture, and other forms of oppression have been acknowledged. Nonetheless, globalization has introduced new factors that have furthered these and other changes. Although the phenomena and implications of globalization are hotly debated, it is evident that the interpenetration of cultures, the shrinking of both spatial and temporal distancing, and the ascendancy of new technologies are all having a transformative effect on many aspects of knowledge production, transmission, and preservation in the new millenium.[10]

It is against this large intellectual backdrop that the following discussion

---

[9] Globalization has also undermined other ideologies, notably nineteenth-century views of nationalism.

[10] For example, see the discussion in Cronin (2003).

of the development of translation studies since World War II must be set. What I argue for is a full integration into translation studies of postpositivist understandings of data collection and theory formation. Such understandings recognize that there are multiple perspectives on the natural and social worlds, that such perspectives need to be explicitly recognized and acknowledged, and that perspectives utilized within the field of translation studies should increasingly include perspectives from outside dominant spheres. An expanded framework of this sort will include perspectives on translation that interrogate hegemonic impositions and that will nurture self-definitions of the nature and practice of translation throughout the world. This is a direction that I believe the field has been lurching toward for decades, but in an inchoate and somewhat random manner: a general broadening of perspectives and conceptualizations, including a developing habit of self-reflexivity, has been intertwined with clear retrogressions. In part I am writing to promote a more conscious awareness of the large philosophical issues that translation studies is grappling with, so as to facilitate a greater awareness of and consensus about the direction that the field is taking.

1.2 Periodization and Translation Theory

Let us make a short detour to consider the periodization of writing and thinking about translation proposed by George Steiner in *After Babel: Aspects of Language and Translation* (1992:236 ff.). Steiner divides statements about translation (in the West, of course) into four periods (1992:248-50). His first period runs from Cicero's precept of 46 B.C. to Hölderlin's commentary of 1804; Steiner says that this period is characterized by statements of translators with an immediate empirical focus. The second period, spanning roughly 150 years, from 1792 to 1946, he describes as dominated by hermeneutic inquiry. Steiner's third period begins in the late 1940s; he observes that "in many ways we are still in this third phase" (1992:250), a period characterized by the attempt to apply linguistic theory and statistics to translation and the endeavor to map the relations between formal logic and linguistic transfer. The fourth period Steiner dates from the early 1960s, when translation study had become a point of contact between established and newly evolving disciplines such as psychology, anthropology, sociology, and sociolinguistics.

Periodization is difficult in any field, but Steiner's attempt to schematize the development of translation inquiry is particularly strange, a lopsided and asymmetrical way to divide the development of a field of thought that spans more than two thousand years. Not only do his periods cover vastly different amounts of time but the last two also overlap. Part of Steiner's difficulty in attempting to establish periodization results from mixing together temporal periods properly speaking and movements related to translation methods. Fundamentally, however, I see Steiner's asymmetrical division as motivated by the huge shift in the way knowledge has been viewed since the abandonment of positivism. It is telling that his first two periods cover roughly two thousand years and the last two merely 50 years, the decades in which postpositivist epistemology began to shape thought about translation. In essence, without labeling it as such, Steiner gives us a periodization in which Western thinking about translation is implicitly divided by the postpositivist revolution, confirming the postwar era as the period in which the modern discipline of translation studies was established.

The recognition that knowledge in any field is affected by time and space, viewpoint, immediate context, and long-term history, as well as by factors such as social context, subject position, and place of enunciation (particularly within the humanities and social sciences), has been generally presupposed in recent decades. Accounting for such factors is especially important in a field like translation studies where scholars and practitioners alike grapple with cultural frameworks in an explicit manner. Thus, it makes sense that Steiner's periodization of translation studies should reflect the huge gulf in Western thinking before and after World War II, a convenient marker for the ascendancy of postpositivist approaches within academe and for a major epistemological shift in much of the world.

World War II is a watershed for views of translation in other ways as well. Before the war, during the 1930s in particular, people had begun to exploit the relation of language, cultural production, and social manipulation. Social engineering through textual and cultural production, especially by means of language, was practiced assiduously and dramatically by both fascist and socialist governments throughout the 1930s. This relationship can be seen in the film industry of the Soviet Union, for example, where important figures such as Sergei Eisenstein and Vsevolod Pudovkin viewed film as a means to consolidate and unify the new post-Revolutionary state. They were followed in the West by the film-making of directors such as John Grierson in the United Kingdom and Grierson's followers in Canada, Ireland, and elsewhere (cf. White 2003).

During World War II these approaches to culture became generalized throughout the world and the war brought renewed interest in culture overall. Understanding cultural interface and adjudicating cultural differences were equally critical for maintaining alliances across cultural boundaries and for struggling against enemies. Whether friend or foe, it was essential to understand the culture of the other. Moreover, the war brought greater clarity about the role of power in shaping and defining culture and about the reciprocal role of culture in establishing and consolidating power. This relationship was manifest in the case of people who were subjugated, such as the Chinese during the Japanese occupation or the Jews in Europe. The ideological construction of others during the war also clearly demonstrated how perception, knowledge, and meaning were shaped and controlled by cultural context.

During the war cultural interface and ideological agendas also brought into focus the importance of sign systems as such, building a foundation for the later focus on semiotics in the humanities and social sciences. Interest in linguistic and cultural sign systems moved to the center of many operations around the globe, for such information was central to intelligence on both sides of the global conflict. Radical differences in language and culture across the lines of allies and enemies alike made it imperative to understand how to negotiate sign systems of many types.

Semiotics assumed crucial pragmatic and tactical importance in two critical areas during World War II. First was the widespread awareness of the necessity of understanding the codes of others broadly construed, because understanding and "cracking" codes was a precondition of the success of intelligence operations, particularly for military purposes. During World War II there were many people involved in coding and decoding all around the world and operatives were translating to and from more languages than had ever before been used concurrently for strategic purposes. Because the war had a global scale and reached into normally isolated areas, an awareness of the range and diversity of the world's languages and cultures came to the fore, even as translation among them was necessitated. This awareness coincided with an intensive effort on each side of the conflict to develop and decipher codes and encryption techniques. Experiences with natural languages and artificial codes during the war resulted in radical gains in understanding how languages work and how they relate to one another in translation.[11]

Expertise in and understanding of the workings of propaganda were also at a premium during wartime. Again, both sides of the conflict recognized the necessity of knowing how to design cultural artifacts (including slogans, posters, radio broadcasts, films, images, and representations) in order to shape public opinion, cultural response, definitions of identity, allegiance, and so forth. During the war, therefore, many people were engaged in creating texts and other cultural products to achieve targeted effects on specific groups of people – from recruiting efforts and war propaganda to film making, song writing, and *rapportage*. Translation was central to all of these wartime activities involving intercultural communication and propaganda, with reliable translators at a premium in many phases of the operations.

The demands of the war had tremendous repercussions in the postwar period. Almost every facet of life around the world was changed in some respect by World War II and the effects of the war continue to shape our lives. It was the outcome of the war that determined many national boundaries and divided the world into spheres of influence, domains that continue to motivate geopolitical strife in the twenty-first century. More to the point for the issues at hand, the interest in shaping cultural production fueled the postwar boom in advertising,

---

[11] General interest in natural languages was also heightened by experiences such as the use of the Navajo code talkers who were able to transmit secret messages for the Allies simply by communicating directly to each other in their own little-known language, a strategy adopted after the Germans succeeded in breaking all the codes and encryption techniques of the Allies.

spurring the use of propaganda to pursue capitalist and socialist economic policies and ideological and political aims. Propaganda became central to politics and the shape of the polity itself in the postwar period, prefiguring the present in which elections in most countries have become media events and global advertising is a central economic activity. The war transformed intellectual life worldwide as well. For instance, it was the Strategic Bombing Survey undertaken in Europe and Japan by the United States Army in 1945 that developed the statistical methods – including survey and sampling techniques – that transformed the social sciences after the war and that continue to be the foundation of much academic inquiry and general intellectual assessment.

In such circumstances it is no surprise that insights, attitudes, and practices developed during the war should have influenced the realm of translation – not only the practice of translation but its conceptualization and theorization as well. From the postpositivist awareness of difference in perspective and position, to new sensitivities about the workings of signs and codes, to concrete understandings of how textual production is related to power and ideology, wartime concerns had immediate applications for translation. It was inevitable that these considerations should have stimulated and shaped translation studies in the postwar period. The perspectives on translation that surfaced during and immediately after the war are mirrored in the trajectory of translation studies in the last 50 years.

Thus, ironically, there is something fundamentally perceptive in Steiner's choice of 1946 as the major transition point in the periodization of (Western) thinking about translation and in his view that the last two "periods" of conceptualizing translation actually overlap and are inextricable. It is no accident that the interest in translation exploded in the postwar period and that the main schools of thinking about translation that emerged initially after the war can be related directly to postpositivist intellectual interests that were also central to wartime activities. First were linguistic approaches to translation, a school of thought about translation that inherits the wartime interests in cracking codes, the central concern of intelligence operations. Second were the functionalist schools that inherit the legacy of expertise pertaining to propaganda and the manipulation of target audiences through textual and cultural production, honed to perfection during the 1930s and 1940s.

To summarize, therefore, postwar developments with an emphasis on postpositivist epistemology, a new awareness of the nature of linguistic codes, and new textual practices related to the manipulation of culture are all germane to the strange periodization offered by Steiner and more importantly to the character of the schools of translation theory and practice that emerged after World War II. I turn now to a very brief overview of the history of translation studies, suggesting ways that perspectives from (Western) intellectual history illuminate the development of the discipline translation studies in the last half century.

1.3 Philosophical and Linguistic Approaches to Translation

Many of the initial postwar reflections on and theorizations of translation reflect postpositivist orientations to language and culture in an immediate way. For the purposes of this brief survey, I will discuss the theoretical work on translation of Roman Jakobson, W.V.O. Quine, and J.C. Catford, whose writings in various ways represent postwar philosophical and linguistic approaches to translation and illuminate the concerns being traced here. My intention is not to give a complete survey of all the linguistic approaches to translation that have developed and evolved in the last half century and that remain vigorous in their contributions to translation studies, but to concentrate on the early linguistic approaches to the nascent field.[12]

Despite its brevity Roman Jakobson's short essay "On Linguistic Aspects of Translation" (1959) has remained one of the foundational statements for the modern development of thinking about translation. The essay exemplifies central features of translation studies as it has emerged as an international academic field and thus it is no accident that Jakobson's essay is almost universally taught in translator training programs and quoted ubiquitously by scholars a half century after it was written. This is not merely a pietistic trope, for Jakobson homes in on central features of language, culture, and translation that radically differentiate postpositivist approaches to translation from virtually everything written on translation before World War II. He emphasizes contrastive linguistics, clearly identifying the asymmetries and anisomorphisms of different languages. He argues that different languages provide fundamentally incommensurate frameworks for thought and culture in their obligatory features, but at the same time he remains committed to the proposition that translation as such is a possible activity: "Languages differ essentially in what they *must* convey and not in what they may convey" (1959:236). Jakobson implicitly problematizes the question of language itself as the central feature of translation, and from this problematic emerges his famous definition of three types of translation: intralingual translation or rewording; interlingual translation; and intersemiotic translation (1959:233).[13] He also relates thinking about translation to discourses about the relationship between language and experience in the world, thus raising problems of reference and meaning.

These fundamental arguments stand at the heart of contemporary translation theory, and their relationship to the postpositivist concerns we are tracing is clear. Jakobson works from a postpositivist emphasis on perspective, within which the

---

[12] A more extensive survey of linguistic approaches to translation is found in Fawcett (1997).

[13] Because of questions about the nature of a language as such, this distinction can in turn be seen as problematic. Davis (2001:23) discusses Derrida's critique of Jakobson; cf. Halverson (1999a:13) who also analyzes Toury's objections.

anisomorphisms of codes and the constructivist nature of language are central for thinking about translation. Coupled with his larger linguistic framework of paradigmatic and syntagmatic alternatives that provides for openness and generativity in language,[14] Jakobson's proposition that languages have fundamental asymmetries in their representations of the world epitomizes a central shift in thought about translation in the postpositivist period: the transference of meaning as such is not simple nor can it be a self-evident goal of translation. Jakobson's grappling with ambiguities of meaning and his demonstration of the one-to-many quality of translation are still other facets of his work that illustrate significant shifts in postwar thinking about translation.

The work of J. C. Catford, *A Linguistic Theory of Translation: An Essay in Applied Linguistics* (1965), is closely related to that of Jakobson. Drawing on both generative and transformational grammar, Catford gave the first comprehensive statement on translation by a modern linguist, and it was radical in its implications for the development of translation studies. An indication of his challenging stance is Catford's distinction between translation and transference, with *translation* defined as "the replacement of textual material in one language (SL) by equivalent textual material in another language (TL)" (1965:20) and *transference* as "an operation in which the TL text, or, rather, parts of the TL text, do have *values set up in the SL*: in other words, have *SL meanings*" (1965:43, original emphasis).[15] Catford's very definition of translation undermines the positivist view of translation and constitutes a postpositivist challenge to the emerging discipline. Because Catford stresses that meaning is language specific, he posits that translation cannot be a procedure that aims at preserving meaning; thus, Catford neatly detaches the ordinary operations of translation from the preservation of the meanings of the source language and the source text (Catford 1965:35-42). This is a view of translation that accepts the radical implications that follow from the different perspectives on experience encoded in different languages and cultures, as well as the difficulties posed by the asymmetries of codes and indeterminacies of meaning. It is a fundamentally postpositivist approach that has set the terms for many discourses in translation studies, yet Catford's approach still remains to be fully understood, accepted, and assimilated by many teachers and practitioners of translation.

Catford's work in turn relates to W.V.O. Quine's short essay "Meaning and Translation" (1959), published as a companion piece to Jakobson's essay discussed above,[16] and to Quine's extended study *Word and Object* (1960). It is

---

[14] For example, see Jakobson (1956).

[15] Here and elsewhere below *SL* denotes the source language and *TL* the target or receptor language.

[16] The essays of Jakobson and Quine are clearly in dialogue with each other, taking radically different positions about reference, sense data, the determinacy of experience, and the possibility of translation, among other questions.

not possible to deal here in detail with Quine's views on translation, but Quine is a figure that must at least be mentioned. His radical skepticism about the determinacy of translation is one direction that postpositivist thinking about translation took after World War II and it is a position that continues to engage philosophical thought about translation. Quine stresses the fundamental importance of perspective in the translation process (and in the process of linguistic communication altogether), including individual perspective as well as perspectives associated with different cultural and linguistic contexts.[17] Arguing for the existence of radically different translation protocols that can generate different and even incompatible translations, Quine casts radical doubt on the possibility of a normative or prescriptive approach to translation. In Quine's view translation can only be a one-to-many procedure.

As is apparent from this brief consideration of Quine, philosophical interests in translation in the twentieth century have been motivated primarily by linguistic concerns and, hence, the most prominent philosophical approaches to translation are best considered with linguistic theories of translation. Translation was taken up by Anglo-American analytic philosophers focusing on the philosophy of language; they used translation as a vehicle for investigating larger concerns pertaining to language and meaning. The debates set in motion in the mid-twentieth century continue to the present.

Some additional aspects of the relationship between the translation theories of Jakobson, Quine, and Catford and theories of meaning should be noted, for they relate to the postpositivist trajectory of translation studies. Linguists and philosophers, such as Jakobson, Catford, and Quine, stress fundamental uncertainties about meaning that impinge on translation. These uncertainties stem not merely from differences in people's subject positions, interests, and assumptions about the world, but also from asymmetries of language (that both shape and are shaped by cultural perspectives). In addition, perception of the world itself is both overdetermined and underdetermined, as is clear from the work of these scholars. The implication of these uncertainties for translation is that translation will always be a one-to-many operation and that there can be no single correct or "positive" way to translate. Based in part on the language-specific nature of meaning, these theories about translation are associated with the breakdown of traditional Platonic theories of meaning in favor of theorizing meaning in much broader terms. We will return to this subject at greater length in chapter 7.

I have concentrated here on early linguistic approaches to translation studies, but before turning to the functionalist schools let us note that more recent work in linguistic approaches to translation has amplified the postpositivist emphasis we

---

[17] Quine explicitly indicates that he is primarily interested in translation as a sort of model or analogue for larger questions of communication. See Quine (1960:26-27) as well as the discussion in Tymoczko (1999b:146-62).

are tracing.[18] As linguistics itself has opened up to a greater number of parameters, moving beyond structural questions about language, linguistic approaches to translation have introduced these perspectives into translation studies. Thus, the considerations of sociolinguistics and discourse theory can be found almost everywhere, and M.A.K. Halliday's systemic functional theory of linguistics has also been well represented (see Baker 1992). An important branch of translation studies has also applied the concepts and tools of cognitive linguistics – particularly cognitive stylistics – to translation studies (see Boase-Beier 2006). Of importance as well is the application of relevance theory to translation studies, where linguistic concerns move beyond looking at language as a code, a preoccupation sustained for decades by research interests related to cracking codes during World War II. Relevance theory focuses on the fact that language in and of itself is always incomplete, hence requiring inferences on the part of receivers; communication proceeds largely on the basis of inferences that are drawn primarily with reference to context, an all-important factor in construing the meaning of any utterance (cf. Sperber and Wilson 1995). As a consequence there can be no fully determinate or positive understanding of linguistic production. The implications of this development in linguistics for postpositivist understandings of translation, both as it affects source and receptor texts, have begun to be applied to translation studies (Gutt 2000a, 2000b).

Some literary and cultural studies scholars in translation studies have suggested implicitly or explicitly that all linguistic approaches to translation are myopic and focused on minutiae. This is to misunderstand the fundamental import of the discourses of this branch of translation studies, even as represented by the early figures of Jakobson, Catford, and Quine. Far from being limited in scope by their attention to both the details and the larger workings of language, the studies by Jakobson, Catford, Quine, and many later linguists engage with the deepest issues raised by translation in relationship to language, communication, culture, perception, experience, and the world. Even the early work still has radical and far-reaching consequences for thinking about translation today, consequences that have not been fully plumbed by translation studies. To a large degree these scholars are responsible for moving translation studies beyond the mode of culture-bound prescriptive pronouncements about translation characteristic of statements before the twentieth century. Thus, they can be credited with catapulting the field into a modern intellectual framework and putting the largest postpositivist questions pertaining to translation at the center of inquiry. Jakobson, Quine, and Catford also set a trajectory for an entire branch of scholarship and research in translation studies. This trajectory represents one aspect of the definitional impulse in approaches to translation since World War II, to which we will return below.

---

[18] A more comprehensive treatment of the later linguistic approaches to translation studies can be found in Munday (2001:89-107).

It is important to note the openness of twentieth-century linguistic and philosophical approaches to translation compared with most approaches to translation before the twentieth century. Instead of arguing for a single, unified, prescriptive practice of translation, these postwar translation scholars address translation in a broader way by considering a multiplicity of questions related to source and receptor situations, including specificities related to many cultures and languages. They do not attempt to generalize about translation on the basis of experience with a single language pair or a specific cultural context, and they avoid restricting their place of enunciation by implicit assumptions based on a specific cultural context. Rather they attempt to look at questions about translation from a much broader and more generalized perspective. The broadening of purview may ultimately be traced to the necessity for translating across so many languages and semiotic systems for so many purposes and in so many contexts during World War II. Nonetheless, the work of the linguists and philosophers discussed here moved questions about translation to a theoretical plane instead of approaching the subject in a purely instrumental way. Associated with the rise and development of the modern discipline of linguistics, the best of linguistic thinking about translation has attempted to set translation in the context of language in general, rather than privileging a particular language or language pair, as well as particular cultural and linguistic contexts. The range of linguistic types and linguistic questions introduced to translation studies has expanded immensely through the formulation of these theories of translation. Without this-move to generalization – which rests on a postpositivist openness to varied cultural perspectives as well as a large range of languages – the field of translation studies as we know it would not exist.[19]

1.4 Functionalist Approaches to Translation

Functionalist approaches to translation that emerged after World War II were as postpositivist in their orientation as the linguistic theories discussed in the last section, but they reflected a different set of priorities from those of linguists engaged in "cracking the code".[20] The orientation of functionalist theories and practices of translation emerged directly from the intersection of language, cultural production, ideology, and the manipulation of public perceptions – in short from the interest in and production of propaganda during the 1930s and 1940s. Like the postwar burgeoning of Madison Avenue and the advertising industry, functionalist approaches to translation both grow out of and expand upon the awareness of how cultural production functions to influence and manipulate

---

[19] I have concentrated here on the inquiry into translation of analytic philosophy which focuses on the philosophy of language. For approaches to translation based on other schools of philosophy, see Munday (2001:162-80).

[20] An excellent overview of functionalist approaches is found in Nord 1997; see also Munday (2001:72-88).

people, an awareness that was incontrovertible after World War II.

Thus, the first two schools of modern translation studies – the linguistic school and the functionalist school – are not diametrically opposed or incompatible, yet they are distinct in their overall emphases. In contrast with linguistic theories, functionalist theories stress the cultural function of source texts, the goals of translators and patrons, the functions of translated texts in receptor cultures, and the impact of translators and translations on target audiences. At times postwar functionalist views of translation also reflect committed investments in social engineering that characterized both sides of the Cold War, albeit in different ways.[21]

Like linguists interested in translation, functionalists are demonstrably postpositivist in their theories and practices. In part this orientation results from the functionalist tendency to draw on the research and data of linguists, particularly those interested in translation. Rather than working within a fixed framework of cultures and languages or a fixed set of values related to language and texts, functionalists tend to stress relativistic methods of influencing and affecting target audiences, methods that take into account the specifics of the geopolitical positioning of a specific receptor audience and translator. Functionalist scholars of translation also focus on the social and historical contexts shaping the configuration of source and target texts, including the author of the source text, the initiator of the translation, the translator, and the receiving audience. Both the postpositivist nature of functionalist theories and their relationship to the production of propaganda are suggested by the dictum of Hans Vermeer and Katharina Reiss that "a translational action is determined by its *Skopos* [purpose or function]" and that therefore "the end justifies the means" (qtd. in Nord 1997:29). Similarly Christiane Nord argues that function (related to the perspectives of both translator and target audience) rather than any absolute positive standard is the criterion that defines translation error: "If the purpose of a translation is to achieve a particular function for the target addressee, anything that obstructs the achievement of this purpose is a translation error" (1997:74). These are radically postpositivist positions: in both statements perspective and purpose are determinants, rather than absolute translational "facts" or constraints.

The acknowledgement of the importance of perspective is clearly seen in the work of Eugene Nida, perhaps the most famous and most influential functionalist worldwide. His work exemplifies many of the functionalist approaches to translation under consideration. Author of several important works on translation, Nida's most significant and most complex statement about translation is *Toward a Science of Translating* (1964); in it his distinction between formal equivalence and dynamic equivalence is clearly set out and the techniques of dynamic equivalence implicitly and explicitly argued for. Nida repeatedly emphasizes

---

[21] Fruitful studies along these lines remain to be made of translation practices and patterns in the communist bloc before 1989.

that there is no one single way of translating well, not even in translating sacred texts. Instead he argues that the method of translation must relate to the purpose of the translation, the goals of the translator, the nature and needs of the audience, and the historical and social context. Indeed he encourages the use of multiple translation strategies in proselytizing and missionary work – his specific domain of translation – depending on these diverse factors. At the same time he makes it clear that he sees dynamic-equivalence techniques as most effective for the generation of faith. It may seem strange to link Nida's functionalist theory of translation developed for Bible translation to the production of propaganda before and during World War II and to the burgeoning of advertising after the war, but all these activities have commonalities, not the least being an acute understanding of the effectiveness of controlled and manipulated textual processing for achieving specific social goals.

Despite the postpositivist emphasis on translation in the functionalist aspects of Nida's theory, a significant limitation in his writing is the subtext adhering to conservative theories of meaning that run counter to the overall tenor of his postpositivist and functionalist arguments. Nida probably holds to conservative theories of meaning in part because of his religious beliefs. In a sense for Nida (and most Bible translators perhaps), transposing meaning in translation is possible (even assured?) because of his belief that God acts as the ultimate guarantor for the fidelity of meaning in translations undertaken in the service of faith. Although Nida is well versed in linguistics, although he employs discourses from linguistics that acknowledge the radical implications of meaning as language-specific, and although he seems occasionally to argue for a constructivist view of meaning, these discourses do not penetrate his functionalist theory deeply, nor do they radically problematize the overall enterprise of transposing meaning in translation in his work. Thus, beneath his postpositivist practices, there is a view of meaning that derives from a much earlier era, probably reflecting more Neoplatonic and Christian philosophical traditions than positivism. Nida's epistemological positioning is thus complex and he is not alone among the functionalists in this regard.

There is strong resistance to Nida and his functionalist theories among many Western leftists in translation studies. Nida's association with the American Bible Society and his commitment to proselytizing blinds some people to the intellectual value of his work for translation studies in general and the importance of his postpositivist distinctions for the evolution of translation studies since World War II. Ironically Nida has been much appreciated in China – historically a prime target of missionary efforts and a socialist country that has resisted religious indoctrination – in part for having introduced productive new translation criteria that offer alternatives to China's traditional discourses on translation, such as Yan Fu's *xin, da, ya*, 'faithfulness, lucidity, elegance'.[22] The introduction

---

[22] I am indebted here to Lin Kenan, personal communication. Yan Fu's criteria are discussed in Chan (2002) and Cheung (2006b:94-95).

of Nida's work after the opening of China at the end of the 1970s was productive for translation theory in China and has remained so. A factor in the positive
reception of Nida's theories in China may be their compatibility with the use
of cultural production for the purposes of social engineering, a well accepted
practice in China since 1949.

The most significant school of functionalists in translation studies is the
(principally German-speaking) group of scholars who have developed the functionalist theory known as skopos theory, an approach initiated by Katharina Reiss
and Hans Vermeer.[23] The postpositivist aspects of the work of skopos theorists
are in some ways less obvious than those of scholars already considered. Much
of the work of the German functionalists is couched in a positivist and prescriptive rhetorical style that seems to assert that a translator can make "positive"
and definitive determinations about the purpose and function of a text in society
– both texts from the past and the present. There is seldom sufficient discussion
about the difficulties and indeterminacies of making such determinations (particularly about textual functions of texts from the past or from radically different
cultures), a difficulty that skopos theorists share with Bible translators such as
Nida. Contrary to the beliefs of many skopos scholars, it is not always possible
to determine the function of a text. Any perusal of literary criticism, particularly
pertaining to ancient or medieval literature, will show that there are radically
different interpretations of the meanings of ancient texts and their functions in
the original contexts, a point that remains to be fully factored into functionalist
translation theories.

Similarly there can be multiple and conflicting textual functions that compli-
cate the movement from source text to target text. This postpositivist perspective
is also frequently neglected by functionalists in favor of suggestions that the
dominant functions of a text can be determined, that a hierarchy of functions can
be established, that the intention or purpose of the translator and the function of
the translation generally coincide, that the function established by the translator will be that of the user of the translation, and that (in some formulations of
skopos theory) the function should be the same in the target text as in the source
text (particularly in the case of certain types of commercial translation).[24] Again
these are questions that require additional problematizing. It is plainly apparent that

---

[23] Where *skopos* is a Greek work for 'purpose' (cf. Nord 1997:27). Nord gives an excellent
detailed summary of this school, discussing the work of the founders, as well as extensions
by recent scholars.

[24] Cf. Fawcett (1997:107-11). The correlation between the skopos of a source text and a target
text and the correlation between text type and translation method are particularly stressed
by Reiss (cf. Nord 1997:31). Citing Reiss and Vermeer, Nord notes that "in *Skopostheorie*,
equivalence means adequacy to a *Skopos* that requires that the target text serve the same communicative function or functions as the source text, thus preserving 'invariance of function
between source and target text'" (1997:36). Later functionalists move away from this position
and acknowledge the disjunction of functions between source text and target text in many
cases (cf. Munday 2001:80).

there is no single function for most complex texts, that reader response cannot be fully controlled, and that translations often have radically different functions from their sources.

Biblical texts, for example, often have multiple and even conflicting functions, as "The Song of Songs" ("The Song of Solomon") illustrates. The book is a love poem between a man and woman, perhaps included in the biblical canon because it was attributed to Solomon and hence seen as a holy relic. Its function has been widely reinterpreted as an allegorical statement about God's love of humanity or God's love of the Church, but the text can be read in many other ways as well. This example shows that even in the case of a canonical biblical work there is often no clear agreement about a single skopos or a simple hierarchy of functions that the translator can use to guide the translation as a whole.[25]

In functionalist theories not only is there often inadequate attention to the ambiguous, multiple, and conflicting intentions, purposes, and textual uses varying across source (text and producer), patron, translator, and receptor, but it is seldom acknowledged that these intentions and purposes are not necessarily recoverable, as we will see in the discussion of deconstruction below. Moreover, the textual functions of the writer or speaker of a text, as well as its translator, can be subverted or ignored by the receiver. This potential for subversion is frequently erased in functionalist theories of translation, despite the fact that it is a commonplace for texts to be produced with one intended function but appropriated by users for another function. Examples range from religious myths taken as fantasy by readers in other cultures to "bad" reviews of a book used by the book's publishers as a badge of honor.[26] These ambiguities of function, purpose, and use have been stressed in postpositivist literary theories, but they remain to be fully integrated into functionalist approaches to translation.

There are additional philosophical questions related to functionalist theories that follow from the issues already mentioned. If most texts have multiple functions, how do translators adjudicate among them? How do translators decide on the balance of functions in a text? Indeed, can translators be counted on to perceive and recognize all the functions of a text with respect to the source text, the initiator of the translator, and even the translation itself? Is it possible

---

[25] Nord is a functionalist attentive to these issues, discussing some of the problems in attempting to establish functional homologies between biblical texts and their translations. She concludes that even when the functions of the source texts are clear, it would often make no sense to attempt to recreate the effects or functions of the source texts or the intentions of their authors (2003:93). Note that there are also conflations of authorial intention (a problematic concept in itself) and function in skopos theory, as can be seen in the discussion of literary translation in Nord (1997:85), for example. Criticisms of these aspects of functional translation theories are found in Davis (2001:53-63) and Munday (2001:42-44).

[26] A trivial example of a text whose function has been subverted is *The Rocky Horror Picture Show*, produced as a grade-B horror film but functioning as a humorous cult classic for young people in the United States. See also Kothari (2005:270) who discusses cases in India where translated Western feminist writing has been used for pornographic purposes.

to disentangle the function of the target text from the ideological commitments of the translator? To what extent are functions conscious and to what extent are they subliminal or not avowed? How are different speech acts to be negotiated (including illocutionary and perlocutionary elements)? Such concerns suggest that on the level of skopos there are problems of indeterminacy similar to those that translators encounter at the lower ranks of language, indeterminacies that can only be resolved by interpretation based on the perspective of the translator. All of these questions point to the postpositivist nature of translation that functionalist approaches entail but frequently and ironically ignore. Although some of these questions have been approached recently, to date most functionalist theories continue to rely on fairly simple textual models. Once the text type becomes complex – as most artistic, literary, philosophical, political, ideological, and religious texts are – functionalist theories fail to address fundamental problematic issues faced by translators.

Some functionalists – notably Nida – see their approach as consonant with viewing translation as a science rather than as an art. In evaluating this claim we must understand that by the mid-twentieth century, the very notion of science had changed as a result of the reaction against positivism. This reorientation is dramatically apparent in the work of Einstein, Heisenberg, and Erwin Schrödinger in physics, and of Gödel in mathematics, as we have seen. In a postpositivist framework science and mathematics themselves are activities with uncertainties at their very core. In this sense then, the uncertainties of translation and variation in translation choice and practice are not incompatible *per se* with a claim to a "scientific" approach to translation. The relationship to science claimed for translation studies by some translation scholars is a topic discussed in chapter 4 below in relation to research methods in translation studies. For the moment let us note that one weakness of translation studies is that many scholars continue to believe that naive, positivist, nineteenth-century views of science are still operative, rather than understanding the dramatic shifts that have taken place in the natural sciences and in the so-called scientific method as a result of postpositivist developments. Thus the temptation to dismiss or deprecate schools of translation studies on the grounds of "scientism" is as likely to reflect the ignorance of critics about contemporary science as to be justified by the claims and practices of those being criticized. Functionalist approaches to translation studies have suffered particularly from these misunderstandings about science; criticisms of the functionalists (and others, for that matter) based primarily on their invocation of science as a reference point are thus generally misplaced.

Although functionalist theories are often couched in positivist and prescriptive language, and although some functionalist scholars (seemingly unaware of the abandonment of positivism) assert definitive solutions rather than proposing problematizations, and although functionalists at times appeal to science in a nineteenth-century sense, they must nonetheless be situated in the postpositivist trajectory of translation studies being traced here. Functionalists grapple with the effect of a text on its audience, an effect that is historically and culturally situated and, thus, related to specific and divergent spatio-temporal perspectives. One of the common criticisms of functionalist approaches is that they subscribe to cultural relativism (cf. Nord 1997:122). The importance of this postpositivist recognition and valorization of variation in cultural perspectives should not be trivialized or disparaged (cf. Halverson 1997b:18-19). Despite their own rhetoric at times, functionalist theories of translation are part of the postpositivist revolution in intellectual thought in the twentieth century. Moreover, as in the linguistic theories of translation already discussed, most functionalists have moved away from strictly prescriptive approaches, valorizing the premise that positionality and purpose drive the strategy of translation. As a consequence flexibility must be built into functionalist translation theory such that practices transcend the dominant orientation of any single culture. The movement has also utilized work in sociolinguistics that itself is fundamentally postpositivist in orientation; thus functionalist theories of translation account for social differences pertaining to language, literacy, textual practices, and many other cultural factors. Functionalists acknowledge the postpositivist implications of general linguistics as well.

These orientations also mean that most functionalist theories of translation are compatible with or subscribe to constructivist approaches to meaning typical of postpositivist views. Indeed it follows from a functionalist orientation that the problems and uncertainties of meaning in translation go far beyond the level of the word, phrase, or sentence and apply to the text as a whole. Functionalists generally seize on the larger levels of the text as a way of adjudicating meaning on the subordinate levels. Although some functionalists assume a positivist rhetoric in their pedagogical texts, they use textual function as a guideline through the web of acknowledged uncertainties on the subordinate levels of the word, phrase, and sentence. For functionalists it is the chosen function that controls register, appropriate collocations, politeness conventions, decisions about "equivalence", and the like, rather than a fixed esthetic rooted in a single cultural framework.

Clearly all functionalist theories of translation leave unanswered questions, most of which lead away from positivist views of translation, despite the cheerful or arrogant prescriptive surface of many functionalist statements. Functionalists end up (sometimes despite themselves) raising as many problems as they solve and signaling as many indeterminacies of meaning as they resolve. This (at times inadvertent) raising of problems has been an important postpositivist contribution of functionalism to translation studies. A weakness of this branch of translation studies is that there is relatively little exploration of the ways that translators have particular frameworks or perspectives that affect perception of function and specific translation practices, notably ideological commitments that get written into the definition and execution of any translation project. It is also unfortunate that functionalists are rarely sufficiently self-reflexive about their own cultural and ideological positioning and their role in social systems as they advocate certain approaches to particular functions that translation can or should assume. This is true of functionalists ranging from Bible translators to proponents of skopos theory.[27] Nonetheless the postpositivist implications of functionalist theories of translation are obvious, manifest most clearly in the relativizing of both the source text and target text in these theories. Nord politicizes this postpositivist aspect of functionalist approaches to translation in stressing that "the anti-universalism of functionalist approaches is meant precisely to avoid one-sided purposes or cultural imperialism" (1997:122). Despite the critical problems that remain, it is clear that the functionalists pushed translation studies in directions that moved the field away from the positivist pronouncements before World War II. Even the weaknesses of their approaches have caused the field to move toward more open and more self-acknowledged postpositivist positions.

1.5 Descriptive Translation Studies

Many of the elements of functionalist theories that can be problematized are precisely those addressed in descriptive translation studies. It is significant that most of the scholars who developed descriptive translation studies were trained originally in literary studies; thus they brought to the study of translation complex and well articulated textual models that could be used to interrogate the work of both linguistic approaches to translation and functionalist ones as well.

The development of descriptive translation studies, particularly systems approaches, has been well canvassed by Theo Hermans (1999), so here I will focus on the postpositivist strands of this school and briefly indicate some of the major stages of its development. Much of the earliest work emerged in Belgium and the Netherlands. James S. Holmes, a pivotal figure in descriptive studies, stressed the context of translation; he moved beyond binaries to various forms of multilevel mappings of the translation process, demonstrating the one-to-many relationship between the source text and its translations and indicating the relationship between translation and many other types of textual practices.[28] In case studies Holmes documented the highly flexible practices and broad range of techniques of translators, illustrating how these practices relate to the goals of the translators. He also began the process of unpacking the relationship between translation and other sorts of metatexts: criticism, prose summary, and so forth (see 1994:23-33).

Other important early contributions to descriptive translation studies were made by the Czech school, including Anton Popovič and Jiří Levý. These writers forged a connection between descriptive studies and Russian formalism, stressing formal aspects of translated texts and translator choice. They also developed the

---

[27] Nord (1997:119) is an exception who acknowledges that translators work from their own point of view in time and space and that no one can claim to have a totalizing view of the source text.

[28] Holmes's papers are collected in *Translated! Papers on Literary Translation and Translation Studies* (2nd. ed., 1994).

concept of shifts as an alternative to prescriptive language for evaluating translations. Most important for the full emergence of descriptive studies is the work of
the Israeli scholars Itamar Even-Zohar (1978, 1990) and Gideon Toury (1980,
1995). The Israeli group of translation scholars brought to the fore the notion of
translation as part of a literary system, with the literary system in turn embedded
in other cultural systems – including economic and political ones – thus setting
translation in much broader cultural contexts than had been done earlier (cf.
Hermans 1999:110). The ideas of Even-Zohar and Toury were quickly taken up
by scholars in the Lowlands and elsewhere in the world, and the emerging school
of descriptive translation studies began to coalesce internationally.

The linguistic and functionalist schools were essential antecedents to the
emergence of descriptive translation studies. These earlier approaches problematized the process of translation sufficiently such that it seemed necessary
to describe any given translation or group of translations in order to define and
characterize the specific processes involved.[29] One way of understanding this
relationship is to say that the scholars involved in descriptive translation studies
recognized that the insights of linguistic and functionalist translation approaches
were not only germane to the process of translation, but that they could also
be used to assess existing products of translation, namely translated texts.
Translations could be approached as a record of past translation choices, elucidating the relationship between translator, translated text, and context, as well
as functions and linguistic and cultural asymmetries. Descriptive scholars were
well positioned to undertake such analyses because most were literary scholars
trained in complex textual models and skilled in critical textual analysis. Thus,

Descriptive translation studies is the complement to the functionalist and
linguistic schools. Here it is useful to note the structure of translation studies
outlined in James Holmes's seminal essay of 1972, "The Name and Nature of
Translation Studies" (see 1994:67-80). Holmes makes the distinction between
process and product in translation, noting the distinct roles of description, theory,
application, and practice. Whereas the functionalist and linguistic schools focus
primarily on translation processes, descriptive translation studies constitute a
set of postpositivist approaches to translation products. In a sense if the scholars
named here had not invented descriptive translation studies, others would have
done so. It was a movement waiting to happen. In fact many of the people who
published essays in the groundbreaking collection of the school edited by Theo
Hermans, *The Manipulation of Literature* (1985), had generated some form of
descriptive analysis on their own independently. To some extent, therefore, the
school is characterized by polygenesis, but it gained immense strength and articulation when these translation scholars came together in what Hermans (1999)
has called an "invisible college".

The linguistic and functionalist schools were essential antecedents to the
emergence of descriptive translation studies. These earlier approaches problematized the process of translation sufficiently such that it seemed necessary
to describe any given translation or group of translations in order to define and
characterize the specific processes involved.[29] One way of understanding this
relationship is to say that the scholars involved in descriptive translation studies
recognized that the insights of linguistic and functionalist translation approaches
were not only germane to the process of translation, but that they could also
be used to assess existing products of translation, namely translated texts.
Translations could be approached as a record of past translation choices, elucidating the relationship between translator, translated text, and context, as well
as functions and linguistic and cultural asymmetries. Descriptive scholars were
well positioned to undertake such analyses because most were literary scholars
trained in complex textual models and skilled in critical textual analysis. Thus,

---

[29] Hermans (1999:24, 29, 32, 37, 39) documents some of the interrelationships between descriptive studies and functionalist approaches.

almost all the scholars in the emergent school of descriptive translation studies drew on or assumed knowledge of linguistic theories of translation, as well as functionalist ones, but they brought other skills to the task as well. A presupposition of this branch of translation studies is that translations can be examined as one might examine cultural artifacts intended to shape culture (such as propaganda, as well as literature), thus illustrating how descriptive translation studies also reflect intellectual preoccupations traceable to World War II. Moreover, like both linguistic and functionalist approaches, descriptive studies reinforced the emerging postpositivist consensus that translation is a one-to-many process.

A central concern that reveals the postpositivist nature of descriptive approaches is the emphasis on the particular historical and cultural context of any translator, any translation event, and any translation movement. Scholars in this school emphasize that it is not possible to understand translation products (or processes) without understanding the particular perspectives of the translator (including the translator's subject position), the target culture, the specific patronage system entailed, and so forth. Both diachronic and synchronic differences of perspective are seen as operative as translators mediate between or among systems. Moreover, descriptive studies demonstrate that correlations between actual translations and cultural perspectives diverge radically from time to time and place to place, thus challenging all normative, prescriptive, and positivist pronouncements about translation. Clearly, thus, the systems articulations of descriptive studies emphasize differences in frameworks and perspectives, consonant with postpositivist thought.

In this paradigm of translation studies, equivalence is a relationship constructed by the translator; it is a similarity relationship – involving both likeness and difference – and as such it is contingent on many cultural factors. The result is that many translations are possible of any given text, and equivalence has an *a posteriori* nature, rather than a positivist or absolutist value.[30] Although some descriptive scholars have been criticized for their binary thinking and the "scientism" in their search for laws, in terms of the overall development of translation theory, the school of descriptive translation studies must be set within postpositivist perspectives that stress translation as a multivalent, one-to-many process, in which translation is affected by the specifics of the spatiotemporal location of both the source and target texts. Thus, despite the seeming rigidity of their call for laws, both Toury and Even-Zohar also subscribe to the necessity

---

[30] See the discussion of the work of Toury in the next chapter. Van den Broeck (1978) also demonstrates the divergence of the term *equivalence* in translation studies from its use in mathematics and most sciences. Note that the view of equivalence that emerged in descriptive translation studies is consistent with the positions of linguists (such as Jakobson and Catford), philosophers (such as Quine), and many functionalists as well. Cf. Fawcett (1997:53-63). Other discussions of equivalence are found in Baker (1998:77-80), Halverson (1997), Munday (2001:35-64), Chesterman (1996, 1997, 2004), and Tymoczko (2004). See also sources cited in these studies.

of minutely describing the actual data of translation, particularly with reference to the target culture, insisting that conclusions be based on the specificity of such historical and cultural data.[31] The analyses of translations by Even-Zohar and Toury stress the specificity of perspectives and frameworks typical of intellectual work since the demise of positivism; moreover, they test the abstraction of their laws by insisting on historically detailed data and case studies. We will continue to explore the postpositivist nature of descriptive translation studies in the next section.

1.6 The Cultural Turn in Translation Studies: The Power Turn, Postcolonial Translation Studies, Translation and Gender

Most early practitioners of descriptive translation studies were a generation younger than the pioneers in linguistic and functionalist approaches. Most were members of the postwar generation, often the "generation of 1968", the so-called European student activists of the period, rather than people who had experienced World War II directly. Despite the politicization of this postwar generation, early descriptive studies were generally oriented to literary questions because systems approaches in the humanities had been developed primarily by literary scholars. Early descriptive investigations focused principally on standard literary questions such as features of the literary repertory, including genre, style, and other elements of form; issues pertaining to the sociology of literature, such as patronage, publishing practices, and the like; and the role of translation in the development and shifts of literary systems. Although some early descriptive studies raised questions about ideology and politics, most early descriptive research had a focus that was more literary than ideological.[32]

More recent descriptive studies of translation, by contrast, have been invested in questions pertaining to ideology and politics. In a sense these movements represent the political coming of age of translation studies. By the late 1960s historical events associated with the Cold War had begun to deepen the understanding of power as a motivating factor in cultural domains such as translation, and somewhat naive ideological frames of reference – whether based on materialist theories or more diffuse liberal political theories – began to implode. Moreover, during the two decades after World War II, the defeat of Western imperialism by one center of colonial resistance after another all around the globe brought huge geopolitical shifts and realignments, and a widespread rethinking of ideologies. The Vietnam War, protests against it, and the defeat of the U.S. challenged expansionist ideologies of all types. At the same time, within virtually all cultures,

---

[31] The significance of Even-Zohar's and Toury's emphases on laws is discussed below in chapter 4.
[32] Lefevere (1982) offers an early example of a descriptive study that takes up ideological questions.

disenchantment with dominant ideologies resulted in the reconceptualization of society. Such shifts are manifest in the resistance to racism and ethnic oppression (seen in the Civil Rights movements in the United States and elsewhere), the rise of feminism, the protests during the 1960s in many places in the world, and resistance in the Soviet bloc countries. The result was a growing consensus that however important materialist issues might be, more fundamental were structures of power in societies, both implicit and explicit, formal and informal. These interests have accelerated since the disintegration of the Soviet Union, the end of the Cold War, the rise of postcolonialism, and the globalization of the economies and cultures of the world. Thus, the focus on ideology and power in more recent descriptive translation studies relates to larger political trajectories since the 1960s.

A major development of this second phase of descriptive translation studies, dating from the end of the 1980s, has been dubbed "the cultural turn". The term gained currency with the publication of the collection of essays edited by Susan Bassnett and André Lefevere, *Translation, History and Culture* (1990).[33] The growth of this phase of descriptive translation studies relates to the political context sketched above, but it also reflects the development of cultural studies during the last two decades of the twentieth century. Clear commonalities between the cultural turn in translation studies and the rise of cultural studies are evident. For a variety of reasons, translation is an excellent way to get at some of the large questions raised by cultural studies. Translation is usually textualized; thus products of translation leave traces of cultural interactions that are open to consideration by scholars. Translation normally involves the interface of languages, semiotic systems, cultural products, and systems of cultural organization, and it makes manifest the differences and similarities of these features of systems across cultures. Like many aspects of cultural production of interest to cultural studies, translation reveals the impact of ideology, but its slight displacement from the centers of ideology often makes it more transparent as a vehicle for investigation of ideological issues. Like many objects of interest to cultural studies, translations often are culturally marginalized, at times bridging the domains of so-called high and low culture, folk culture and mass culture, and so forth. The economic matrix of cultural production is also often particularly apparent with respect to translation, thus allowing for materialist analyses that reflect another center of interest in cultural studies. Finally, systems of cultural patronage and power are frequently evident in translation processes and products.

All these interests are visible in the cultural turn of translation studies. Many scholars writing in this paradigm continued to explore literary questions, but they began to emphasize ideological aspects of translation, including ideological aspects internal to the discipline of translation studies itself. The second phase

---

[33] The book in turn emerged from a landmark conference held at the University of Warwick in 1988 at which most of the essays in the book were initially presented.

of descriptive studies was more centered on perspective and much more self-reflexive than earlier scholarship in translation studies, and it often highlighted alternate or even dissident perspectives on culture. Specific studies do not simply investigate texts and contexts but subtexts as well, with more weight given to subtexts pertaining to ideology, political valences, and hegemony in particular. As a result, a greater understanding of the relation of translation to those factors began to emerge in the 1990s. Although most studies of this movement continued to be essentially descriptive, some began to take up self-reflexive theoretical perspectives on the discipline of translation studies itself. Such metainvestigations are found, for example, in Lori Chamberlain's essay "Gender and the Metaphorics of Translation" (1992). The work of Lawrence Venuti (1992, 1995, 1998a, 1998b) can be situated in the context of the cultural turn as well, touching its various diverse strands and combining a descriptive approach to translation with a focus on ideology and power, as well as self-reflexivity about the discipline. Venuti, moreover, exemplifies yet another trend of the cultural turn, namely a committed stance toward an engaged practice of translation.[34]

A postpositivist emphasis on perspective and alternative viewpoints is apparent in virtually all the studies constituting the cultural turn in translation studies. It should be noted as well that the cultural turn presupposes a recursive application of functionalist approaches to translation, where the questions asked move beyond surface or structural analysis of text and text type in context to analyses of the ideological functions of the processes and products of translation. As a result of the cultural turn, descriptive translation studies deepened the analyses of what counts as the positionality of the translator, the source culture, the target culture, the translation product, and the researcher. Positionality came to be seen not merely as a matter of history, geography, material culture, or the literary system, but also a question of the relation to power structures, ideology, politics, and ethics.

The interest in the relationship between translation and power began to be articulated during the early phases of the cultural turn, but increasingly it became an independent discourse within descriptive translation studies throughout the 1990s. Edwin Gentzler and I have dubbed this development "the power turn" in translation studies, and we privileged these concerns in the collection titled *Translation and Power* (2002).[35] The power turn has focused on issues of agency, the ways translation can effect cultural change, and the relation of translation to dominance, cultural assertion, cultural resistance, and activism. Translation scholars have examined many facets of the relationship between translation and power, including political control and subversion, the power of translation to construct political discourses, and the power of the translators as agents, as well as ideological aspects of culture governing translation such as discourse

---

[34] Tymoczko (2000a) offers an overview of this development.
[35] See also Tymoczko (forthcoming a).

structures and censorship. Descriptive studies in this paradigm avoid simplistic views of power and challenge dominant and hegemonic views of power, arguing that power is not simply "top down", invested primarily in political institutions, but exercised as well by those seeking empowerment and engaging in resistance. Work in this branch of translation studies also tends to avoid simplistic polarized models of power, in which some have it and some don't. Within a more complex paradigm of power, translation is seen as an activity where discourses meet and compete; translation negotiates power relations, shifting in complex ways to meet the imperatives of specific historical and material moments. In such complex negotations, as perspectives from historical studies of translation illustrate, no single strategy of translation has a privileged position in the exercise of power or resistance.

An important strand of the second phase of descriptive studies is post-colonial translation studies, which also poses important questions related to ideology and power.[36] This theoretical framework will be discussed at length in chapter 5 below, but for the moment we can notice that postcolonial translation studies consider translation within contexts in which differences of perspective are heightened and often polarized by highly asymmetric power relations, as well as radical linguistic and cultural differences. Thus, the postpositivist nature of most descriptive studies, particularly in relation to ideology, is perspicuous in postcolonial translation studies, for radical differences in perspective are normally at the heart of translation events in such contexts. Central concerns of postcolonial translation studies include semiotic differences across cultures and languages, as well as the use of text for social construction and manipulation, thus revealing the debt of these approaches to earlier linguistic and functionalist theories of translation.

Interest in perspective as it is played out in translation is central to studies of gender and translation as well, represented by the feminist work of Nicole Brossard, Susanne de Lotbinière-Harwood, Barbara Godard, Sherry Simon, Luise von Flotow, and others.[37] As in postcolonial translation studies, scholarship on translation and gender often combines description, theorizing, self-reflexivity, and activist programmatics characteristic of the second phase of descriptive translation studies, examining power and ideology in both translation processes and products.

The most recent movement in the second phase of translation studies can be called "the international turn", related in many of its concerns to postcolonial translation studies. Currently still gaining momentum, this movement is marked by the increasing role of translators and translation scholars from beyond Europe

---

[36] An overview of postcolonial translation studies is found in Robinson (1997a); see also Tymoczko (1999b).

[37] The feminist strand of translation studies is well charted in Simon (1996) and von Flotow (1997). On the intersection of translation studies and gay theory, see the discussion in Munday (2001:188-89) and sources cited.

and the Americas, and it is signaled by the formation of the International Association of Translation and Intercultural Studies (IATIS) which has held two meetings thus far. The interventions of this movement have begun to propel translation studies beyond dominant Western perspectives on translation, thus reexamining and putting into question all aspects of the field that have been developed implicitly and explicitly on the basis of Western data and Western translation history. As a result basic ideas about translation and dominant translation practices are being reconceptualized, broadening perspectives on translation far beyond those provided by Eurocentric thinking and insisting on local knowledges about translation.[38]

This brief characterization of the sweep of descriptive translation studies over a period of more than 25 years indicates that postpositivist inquiry came of age with this approach. Focusing on frameworks of all types and explicitly acknowledging perspectives associated with source texts, translators, target texts, patrons, and audiences, as well as perspectives within the discipline itself, the various phases of descriptive translation studies signal the full commitment of translation studies to postpositivist intellectual inquiry.

1.7 Deconstruction and Poststructuralist Approaches to Translation

Although poststructuralist approaches to translation are not fully separable from those included in the cultural turn and the other movements subsumed under the second phase of descriptive studies, it is useful to give them consideration as a separate grouping within translation studies. Almost by definition poststructuralist approaches to translation are also postpositivist, because poststructuralism in general and deconstruction in particular emphasize such things as multiplicity, semiotic openness, and permeability rather than convergence of meaning. These approaches to translation illustrate how descriptive translation studies at the turn of the twenty-first century have moved increasingly away from positivist views of translation typical of statements before World War II.

If we think of the cultural turn and the power turn in translation studies as attending to cultural and ideological subtexts involved in translation, as well as to the relationship of texts and contexts, we might say that poststructuralists and deconstruction scholars are interested in layers of text that are even less apparent than most ideological subtexts. These include, for example, the *non dit*, sublated ideological discourses, and culturally assumed structures of knowledge embedded in language and texts, the unlimited semiosis behind texts, inconsistencies and fragmentary elements that reveal slippages of thought and belief, polysemous language, and the play of words. Neither these elements nor the working methods

---

[38] Collections of essays are found in Rose (2000), Fenton (2004), Hung and Wakabayashi (2005), and Hermans (2006).

of this wing of translation studies can be subsumed within positive "facts" or the implications of "facts". Poststructuralist translation scholars and critics expose additional parameters to be considered when thinking about translation, but they similtaneously uncover the uncertainties and indeterminacies of translation processes and products, as well as the ideological pitfalls of scholarship that is not itself self-reflexive.

A major project of deconstruction has been to show the ideological sub-structures of much received language. In translation studies poststructuralism has exposed the workings of dominant ideology and hegemony pertaining to knowledge and positionality in traditional translation processes and products. This branch of translation studies has interrogated the notions of "correct" trans-lations or "correct" equivalences, exposing such ideas as inevitably culturally and politically engaged. Built into these deconstructive projects implicitly and explicitly is an awareness of perspective and, indeed, conflicting perspectives. Poststructuralism in translation studies is a movement that demands self-reflexivity on the part of translators, readers of translations, and translation scholars.

In accordance with basic tenets of poststructuralism, deconstructive transla-tion studies have focused on the "specificity of context" that is "essential to the very existence of meaning" (Davis 2001:2-3), where context is understood as temporal, spatial, historical, and linguistic in nature. Much of the application of deconstruction to translation follows the work of Jacques Derrida, who "warns against attempts to sever meaning from context, and persistently emphasizes the importance of history to deconstruction" (Davis 2001:2-3; cf. 25). For Derrida historical structures themselves are never fully closed nor can they have absolute meanings, and "meaning cannot be extracted from and cannot exist before or outside of a specific context" (Davis 2001:9). As a consequence the antipositivist tenor of poststructuralist approaches to translation is patent.

Deconstruction builds on the postpositivist implications of linguistics, specifically the work of Ferdinand de Saussure, so deconstructive approaches to translation have a filiation to linguistic approaches to translation.[39] Derrida's arguments rest on the "effacement of essentialism" and a view of meaning as an effect of language; together these characterize the developments of modern linguistics, and with the linguists he "rejects the idea that meaning is before or beyond language" (Davis 2001:18). It is thus ironic that many self-proclaimed poststructuralists in translation studies have been among those who have most loudly decried linguistic approaches to the field.

A particular irony of deconstructive translation studies is that many decon-struction scholars have relied on and drawn heavily from Walter Benjamin's essay, "The Task of the Translator" (1923).[40] Aside from its somewhat mystical vein,

---

[39] Davis (2001:12-18) provides a summary.
[40] For example, see Derrida (1985), de Man (1986), and commentaries on these readings in Niranjana (1992) and Davis (2001).

the essay suggests theories of reference and meaning that are not fully compatible with mainline poststructuralist thought. Benjamin's approach to language involves a curious mixture of Platonic views of meaning and more modern attitudes, of positivist and postpositivist elements. One of the most problematic aspects of the essay is Benjamin's appeal to "pure language", *reine Sprache*, language that somehow stands above the concrete anisomorphisms and semiosis of actual human languages. This concept of a pure language suggests an absolutist language that can provide essentialist access to Platonic forms or an absolute reality. Clearly this is a fairly retrograde concept of both language and meaning that is not compatible with the framework of deconstruction.[41]

Benjamin's essay appeals to deconstruction scholars principally because of other more modern ideas, including the instability of texts, encapsulated in Benjamin's notion of the afterlife or survival (*Überleben, Fortleben, Nachleben*) conferred by translations on a source text (cf. Weber 2005). Benjamin takes the view that no text has a fixed meaning; meaning changes over time as culture changes and as perspectives on the text change. As a consequence translations confer (renewed) meanings on source texts and without translation texts die. Kathleen Davis points out that Benjamin's thinking here inverts the normal relationship that obtains in translation studies between source and target texts: "the translation is not dependent upon the original for its existence; rather, the original depends upon the translation for its survival" (2001:40).

Benjamin's work is also attractive to deconstruction scholars because he uses the image of a shattered vessel, tentatively reconstructed from fragments (some of which are usually missing), as a figure for the way that a translation recreates form and text out of fragments of language and meaning. These fragments can be compared – as they are by poststructuralists – with language that is always itself in transition, emerging from a play of differences, simultaneously looking backward and forward in time semiotically, rather than constituting a stable presence. Benjamin's formulation of this image has been very productive for translation studies and it is compatible with many of the basic tenets of deconstruction. It is all the more ironic that Benjamin's thought here goes back to nineteenth-century discourses about literary fragments that were often invoked by colonialist scholars who attempted to "reconstruct" the lost texts of bygone civilizations or the golden past of the "degenerate present" of colonized nations.

Like most movements of the second phrase of descriptive translation studies, scholars using deconstruction and other poststructuralist approaches have focused on ideological questions. This tendency is consistent with the general alliance between deconstruction and leftist thought in the West. This strain of deconstruction

---

[41] Davis (2001:45) sees Derrida as critiquing Benjamin's notion of pure language in "Les tours de Babel", but she gives no argument or analysis supporting her position aside from recognizing that the idea of pure language contradicts other positions Derrida takes on language. Weber (2005) offers another reading of Benjamin's thought on this question. Cf. Lianeri (2006:77-78).

in translation studies is most notably represented by the work of Gayatri Spivak. Her seminal essays look at the relationship between translator, translation, and ideology, and they stress the play of perspective entailed in the work of the translator in relationship to source text, source author, and receptor context (see especially Spivak 1992, 1995). Like deconstruction scholars in general, Spivak consistently interrogates totalizing and universalizing perspectives that mask the role of dominance in the world. As a translator herself, Spivak (1995) has also helped to move translation studies beyond Western perspectives by working with the texts of the Indian writer Mahasweta Devi and moving deconstructive theory into activist practice.[42]

It follows that poststructuralism in general and deconstruction in particular undermine normative and prescriptive attitudes to translation. Not only are such attitudes incompatible with the complexity and openness of language stressed by poststructuralists, but prescriptive views sanctioned by a culture and a pedagogical establishment must of necessity be implicitly formed by dominant ideologies, ideologies that poststructuralists would argue must be at the very least interrogated and in the main contested. This sort of acute awareness of perspective occurring on multiple and recursive levels in deconstructive translation studies is paradigmatically postpositivist in outlook and methodology, extending the postpositivist trend that has characterized the development of translation studies since World War II.

It is evident from this survey of the second phase of descriptive studies that the logical implication of a postpositivist orientation and a postpositivist epistemology is not merely recognition of the importance of perspective for the construction of knowledge about translation, but ultimately an activist assertion of the value of alternate perspectives on translation in relation to those of dominant cultures. Postpositivist approaches in particular seem ultimately to entail ideological and ethical assertions about culture and cultural production, leading to activist stances within translation studies. It is telling that in her summary of the relationship between deconstruction and translation studies, Davis highlights the obligation and responsibility toward "the other" that follow from a decision to undertake translation within the frameworks that she traces (2001:91-106).[43]

---

[42] An advocate for the tribal peoples and dalits of India, Mahasweta Devi herself is from a middle class, literary Bengali family. She was educated in the school founded by Tagore in Santiniketan, following which she took an M.A. in English at Calcutta University. A journalist and English lecturer at Calcutta University in her professional life, she bases many of her literary works on research among the tribals and lower castes of India. She has produced her own draft translations for reference and has collaborated in other ways with her translators (Mukherjee 2004:160). Devi has been awarded many prizes for her writing, including the Jnanpith award (India's highest literary award) and the Magsaysay award (the Asian equivalent of the Nobel Prize). Thus, ironically, as her activist translation gesture, Spivak has chosen to translate a writer who is a highly acclaimed, highly literate English professor in an Indian university, who herself writes in English, and who could plausibly be a candidate for the Nobel Prize. Cf. Bassnett and Trivedi (1999:11).

[43] Following Spivak, Davis also notes that in the 1980s Derrida turned to a "call to the wholly other" (2001:91).

1.8   The Definitional Strand in the History of Translation Studies

A brief summary of the history of translation studies since World War II cannot possibly do justice to the scope of scholarship on translation during the last half century. It is not even possible to include every major working group in translation studies in a framework of this brevity, and those movements discussed have been considered in a very abbreviated fashion.[44] Despite the manifest limitations of this historical overview, a narrative account of the development of translation studies highlights three features. First, contemporary translation theory as such developed in the context of the decline of positivism. The emergence of the academic field of translation studies is connected with the abandonment of pretwentieth-century positivist and prescriptive views of translation that reflected only a specific and narrow immediate cultural context. Modern perspectives on translation incorporate from the beginning the possibility of alternate perspectives on language, culture, and text that make it possible to move beyond self-involved, dominant Western assumptions about translation. The survey indicates that translation studies has become steadily more postpositivist over the past fifty years, as it has come to terms with and validated an increasing number of perspectives from which translation can be viewed.

Second, discourse about translation in the last fifty years is correlated with preoccupations about text and language during World War II: the interest in cracking codes, converging with developments in modern linguistics that stress anisomorphisms of language and the language-specific nature of meaning; and the use of texts as forms of propaganda to shape and mold cultures. Both of these concerns have motivated the development of the field of translation studies and influenced the directions that the field has taken. Their affinities are apparent in contemporary linguistic investigations of translation that continue to see language as a code and also in the work of scholars and voluntary associations of

---

[44] An important approach to translation studies omitted altogether is the translation workshop movement in North America. Mainly developed by poets and other writers, these workshops have been important in furthering the postpositivist development of the field, in part by demonstrating through their exercises the one-to-many nature of translation and the importance of translator perspective, choice, and agency. Primarily undertaken to illustrate the art and creativity involved in translating, the workshop approach has been instrumental in establishing the constructivist element of meaning in translation and the metonymic nature of translation. Gentzler (2001:5-43) offers an extended discussion of this movement, including the role of Ezra Pound whose work likewise contributed to postpositivist discourses about translation. We will return to this approach to translation studies in chapter 7 below.

Another significant omission is an account of discourses and research about machine translation, which manifestly grew out of the intelligence operations of World War II and the Cold War. Ironically the failure of early attempts to develop machine translation themselves pointed to the failure of positivist approaches to translation. Similarly, contemporary developments such as the localization industry and its theorization are omitted here; many of the implications of such contemporary movements are discussed in the following chapters, however.

translators who stress translation as a functional activity or who use translation for ideological purposes (cf. Baker 2006a, 2006b).

Third, the survey reveals an evident paradox. Translation studies has been expanding for the last half century, considering more and more features and parameters of translation and incorporating discourses about these features into the field. At the same time translation studies has been moving steadily away from positivist attitudes about these parameters, acknowledging uncertainties and indeterminacies – including those pertaining to language, cultural difference, and meaning – and admitting radically different perspectives on translation associated with time, place, subject positions, ideology, and power. More and more perspectives have been opened; fewer and fewer facts or certainties have resulted. These simultaneous expansions and increased uncertainties in the field have of necessity brought greater self-reflexivity to translation studies as well.

A way to characterize these developments is to say that scholars in translation studies have been preoccupied in diverse ways with the task of defining translation. This definitional impulse is not trivial: in any academic field definition is an essential element. It is not possible to proceed with research when scholars do not define or delimit the object of study. Paradoxically the emerging definition of translation is increasingly open rather than delimited, and the openness is related to the indeterminacies of the field: the definition of translation resulting from the expansion of translation studies does not have closed or clearly delineated boundaries.

Moreover, looking back at translation studies from the perspective of the postpositivist and postwar themes traced here, we see that movements often characterized as oppositional can be viewed as contributing in complementary ways to the attempt to define translation, approaching a common problem from different directions. Thus, early research on translation centered on linguistic aspects of translation, exploring the nature of translation in relation to language. As such it looked at linguistic asymmetries and anisomorphisms in translation interface, the language-specific nature of meaning as a factor in translation, and the nature of communication in general and its relationship to the limitations of translation, all of which tended to delineate the (open) boundaries of the linguistic aspects of the task of the translator.

Literary and poetic approaches to translation (including early descriptive studies) constitute another cluster of attempts to define translation, focused on the parameters pertaining to literary questions and questions raised by complex and extended texts, as well as their intertexts and contexts. Thus, this school of research investigated issues such as how translation gets shaped or determined by the nature of literature; what practices translators use when translating different literary modes, forms, genres, and text types; how translated texts relate to literary traditions; and how translations and their source texts relate to their cultural, social, and historical contexts. Variation, difference, and openness were again the result.

Still another research cluster attempting to define translation has concentrated on the investigation of cultural dimensions of translation. These approaches ranged from early functionalist perspectives and systems approaches to the cultural turn in translation studies and other strands of the second wave of descriptive studies. It became clear early on that translation could not just be defined in terms of language or text type, but that it was also essential to consider culture in broad and deep ways. Such cultural approaches cannot be fully separated from either linguistic or literary approaches to translation because language is central to constituting any human culture and literature in turn is rooted in both language and culture.[45] Investigations of cultural questions in translation studies have introduced a range of parameters into the definitional strand of translation studies not merely related to material culture but to the largest frameworks of cultural systems including social aspects of language use (such as are treated in sociolinguistics or discourse theory) and ideological dimensions ranging from gender to politics and power.

Often the definitional and postpositivist dimension of translation research has been obscured by the prescriptive packaging of the results, packaging that can be attributed at times to the pedagogical orientation of researchers. Nonetheless, if we look at the various schools that have emerged in translation studies since World War II less as antithetical and more as engaging in a dialectic about the nature of translation *per se*, less as holding opposing positions about translation than as allied in a common enterprise of trying to understand and define translation, less as coming from divergent directions than as sharing some seminal epistemological and pragmatic motivations, it becomes easier to understand the flow of translation research through time and also to know how to position the various contemporary schools that have descended from the early endeavors. The result, of course, is that translation studies is "an interdiscipline".[46]

Failure to understand how all the branches of translation studies relate to postpositivist epistemology and how they represent complementary aspects of postwar investigations of language and text has contributed to the tendency of some translation scholars to position themselves rigidly within one domain or another and to see their approaches as antithetical to those of other branches of the discipline. This is detrimental to the health of the entire field. Whether focused primarily on translation processes or translation products, most theorizing and research about translation since World War II has been motivated in part by the definitional impulse that is inherent in attempting to characterize specific aspects of translation processes and specific translation products and then to generalize these particulars to translation as a whole. Whether operating on the microlevels

---

[45] In fact cultural facets of translation get raised early on by the linguists discussing translation (consider, for example, the discussion of cheese in Jakobson 1959), and many early systems studies consider cultural and even political factors.

[46] See Snell-Hornby (1988); Snell-Hornby et al. (1994). Cf. Tymoczko (2002).

of language or the macrolevels of cultural systems and cultural power, the results form a continuous field that is mutually enriching rather than oppositional (cf. Tymoczko 2002). Teasing out the definitional strand in the history of the discipline has two concrete benefits: it facilitates a greater understanding of the current structure of translation studies and it illuminates the dialogic nature of the development of the discipline and its discursive field.

Most translation scholars would like to believe that the stage of defining translation is essentially over; it would be satisfying to think that the big parameters regarding translation have been sketched out. This view is attractive in part because it would allow translation scholars to get on with their own particular specialized interests – for example, instructing students about how to do commercial translations or researching a very comfortable corner of translation history (translation in Ireland in my case). In thinking about trajectories of translation research in the future, however, I suggest that the task of defining translation is not finished and that it will continue to be a central element of translation research in the foreseeable future.

Whether translation research takes the form of investigating the work of translators and the processes of translation or describing actual translation products from various times, places, and cultural contexts, scholars continue to learn fundamental things about translation as a whole that cause the purview of the field to expand even as the field becomes more open and permeable. This paradox associated with the definitional impulse in translation studies – that as more parameters of translation are identified, more openness is generated in the field instead of closure – is a function of the nature of translation itself as an open concept. The openness of the concept is particularly apparent when translation is approached within a postpositivist framework and when it is viewed cross-culturally. I turn directly to the openness of the concept translation in the next chapter.

2. Defining Translation

If asked to define *translation*, most ordinary people and even most translation experts would probably say that the answer is straightforward: a translation is the process or result of transferring a text from one language into a text in another language.[1] That is, as it is conceived in ordinary language, translation involves the presence of source and target texts and transmission between two languages. In a sense this is where the history of thinking about translation begins in Western tradition and perhaps in many other cultures as well. As we have seen in the previous chapter, however, the trajectory of translation studies since World War II has been to consider an increasing number of features that constitute and define the processes and products of translation.

Moreover, even the simplest definition of the concept of translation from ordinary language must be immediately problematized, because the concepts used to define translation are themselves problematic, including the concepts language and text. Most people have an intuitive sense of what language is, but defining language is not at all simple. What is meant by "a language"? Are all communicative systems to be counted as languages? If so, is the dancing of bees that communicates the location of flowers a language? Do animals in general have languages? Should the songs of chickadees be counted as a language insofar as they indicate the type, distance, and number of potential predators? Should the vocalization pattern of dogs be considered a more complex language than that of wolves in view of the fact that dogs have a greater number of distinct calls and more varied ways of vocalizing than wolves do?[2] Must communicative systems be conscious or intentional to be languages? Are pheromones a form of language, broadcasting gender and sexual readiness to other members of the species? Are the physical gestures shared within human cultures forms of language? What about the many human facial expressions that seem to be cross-cultural and specieswide?[3]

There are even more questions about language that must be considered when we turn to human language. How do languages relate to semiotic systems in general, including codes and other systems of signs? Are artistic codes (such

---

[1] The question of defining translation has been discussed by many translation scholars. Provocative approaches are found in Hermans (1996, 1999:46-54) and Chesterman and Arrojo (2000). The latter resulted in a lively two-year debate ("Forum" 2000, 2001a, 2001b, 2002) that repeatedly touched on the question of defining translation as writers grappled with attempts to delineate shared ground in translation studies. The fact that opinions were so diverse and divergent, even though most of the contributors wrote entirely within Western discourses about translation studies, instantiates and substantiates the necessity of approaching these subjects as advocated in this chapter. See also Halverson (1999a, 1999b) and sources cited.

[2] Comparison of vocalizations among dogs and wolves is found in Feddersen-Petersen (2000).

[3] See Gladwell (2005:197-214, cf. 18-34) and sources cited.

as the conventions used in painting or film) forms of language? Is music a form of language? Is mathematics? How should drumming used as signals be classified? Or the signals of traffic lights? And antecedent to all of these questions, what types of signs and symbols are there and how do they function?

These are merely some of the questions to consider in attempting to define language. Even assuming one could satisfactorily narrow the definition of language to the conscious oral communicative systems of human beings (a definition that would exclude the sign languages of the deaf, incidentally), many questions remain. How are the boundaries between languages to be drawn? What is the difference between a language and a dialect? (Does the aphorism that a language is a dialect with an army really satisfy?) How are dialects to be distinguished from creoles? On what basis should boundaries be drawn in the historical development of languages between distinct states of the language? Should Vulgar Latin, Old French, and Modern French be recognized as three languages or as one? (If these are the same language, then how can Italian, Spanish, and Portuguese make claims to being independent languages? If they are different languages, should Chinese be viewed as constituting a single language during the past two thousand years?)

Is a language determined by mutual intelligibility and are borders between languages defined by the lack of intelligibility? If so, does that make Spanish and Portuguese the same language? What about Swedish, Norwegian, Danish, and Icelandic which are also mutually intelligible to many speakers? Because many so-called dialects of English lack mutual intelligibility, is "English" actually a cluster of languages instead of a single language? Should Mandarin and Cantonese be classified as different languages because they are not always mutually intelligible? How narrowly can one limit the group speaking "the same" language? Can a family have its own language? Can twins have their own language (as the concept of "twin talk" suggests)? Can an individual?[4]

All of these questions are relevant to defining language, and they do not even begin to raise questions about specific characteristics of language or languages. Nothing has yet been said about phonetics, phonology, lexis, morphology, syntax, semantics, writing systems, and all the other features of language and languages at the heart of modern linguistics and sociolinguistics that pertain to translation.

Similarly one can problematize the concept of text that is assumed by ordinary language definitions of translation. What precisely is a text? Clearly it cannot be taken simply as a written document or else most translation events in the world past and present – namely instances of oral interpreting – would be eliminated. Thus oral utterances must be included in the ordinary sense of texts

---

[4] Davis (2001:20 ff., 70-71) discusses some of these problems of defining language as they pertain to translation from the perspective of deconstruction and summarizes Derrida's views about the nature of language, the impossibility of closed boundaries for a language, and the resulting implications for the identity of languages and for translation between languages. Fairclough (1989:21) problematizes the concept of language in still other ways. See also Anderson (1991).

in translation studies. But what other types of texts are to be included? Are we to understand images, paintings, films, and music as texts? Where are boundaries to be drawn between texts that are translations and those that are not? Does translation include abridgments, rewordings, adaptations for specialized audiences (such as children or the newly literate), and texts that have paratextual commentary as an integral feature?

These are not recondite matters: they all follow immediately from and are entailed by the ordinary-language sense of translation, and they are all questions subsumed by or antecendent to the common-sense notion of translation. It is no accident that they are also the questions that lie immediately behind one of the earliest postwar technical definitions of translation, namely that of Roman Jakobson, who distinguishes the following:

> (1) Intralingual translation or *rewording* is an interpretation of verbal signs by means of other signs of the same language.
> (2) Interlingual translation or *translation proper* is an interpretation of verbal signs by means of some other language.
> (3) Intersemiotic translation or *transmutation* is an interpretation of verbal signs by means of signs of nonverbal sign systems. (1959:233)

Notice that Jakobson has made an implicit decision that translation in some way must involve *verbal* language. Moreover, Jakobson's category of intralingual translation responds to the problematic of the nature of language, while his category of intersemiotic translation addresses the problematic of the concept of text.

Not surprisingly, the sense of the word *translation* in ordinary language that we began with accords reasonably well with the second definition of the English word in the *Oxford English Dictionary* (hereafter *OED*): "the action or process of turning from one language into another; also, the product of this; a version in a different language".[5] Interestingly, however, this is not the first definition of the word *translation*. According to the *OED*, the primary definition of the English word is "transference; removal or conveyance from one person, place, or condition to another". We can note here that the English-language sense of *translation* as a form of transfer between languages is preceded by and derived from an older concept, namely the physical conveyance of something material between persons and places. This older sense of translation that permeates the English understanding of the concept at the heart of translation studies is thus connected with the etymological meaning 'carrying across' associated with the Latin roots that supply the English word. This is not a trivial observation because the older and primary meaning of the word is specifically associated with the

---

[5] Citations of the *OED* are from *The Compact Edition of the Oxford English Dictionary* (1971) unless otherwise indicated.

movement of religious relics in the later Middle Ages in Europe, as well as with a specific form of processing religious texts into vernacular languages associated with Bible translation. That is, the current *English* word for the concept of linguistic transposition of texts at the heart of the discipline translation studies is *not* a neutral word: it is saturated with Western history, Western ideology, and Western religious meanings and practices.[6] In general Western European words for 'translation' and the history of translation practices in Western Europe indicate that dominant Eurocentric conceptions of translation are deeply rooted in literacy practices (as opposed to oral translation practices still predominant in most of the world). They also suggest that Eurocentric ideas about translation are shaped by the practices of Bible translation. Western European conceptions of translation are heavily influenced by the close connection between language and nation, and the history of Eurocentric translation is also closely associated with imperialism and its ancillary belief in a hierarchical relationship of languages and cultures. As we have already observed, these are obviously not satisfactory conceptual bases for defining translation as a cross-cultural phenomenon, for founding an international theory of translation, or for establishing an international discipline.

Thus, even if we begin with an unproblematized intuition about *translation*, the task of defining the concept of translation within translation studies becomes immediately much more difficult than it first appeared. First, the basic concepts upon which the concept translation rests – the concepts translation is defined in terms of – are themselves open terms whose definitions are not obvious. Second, it is plainly insufficient for an international discipline to limit itself to or to frame itself within conceptions of an activity and its products that can only be situated within Western frameworks and associated with Christian religious and textual practices. This is particularly the case at this juncture, as the history of translation studies sketched in the first chapter indicates, when for more than fifty years the postpositivist discipline has increasingly considered parameters and features of translation that go far beyond the practices, products, and perspectives of a single culture.

It is time for the discipline of translation studies to come to terms with the implications of the definitional impulse inherent in translation research and theorizing since World War II. Although many individual scholars have contributed to the expanding purview resulting from the definitional strand in translation research, the problematic of defining translation should be explicitly acknowledged and the nature and implications of that problematic more clearly understood in the field of translation studies as a whole. Unlike many earlier scholars who have attempted to define translation and who have sought closure on the question, I am interested in exploring the openness of the definition and the implications of

---

[6] Cf. Tymoczko (2003b:189-92 and forthcoming b); see also the discussion in chapter 3 below. Sandra Halverson (1999a, 1999b) has also analyzed the significance of the metaphor translation as transfer, the conceptualization embodied in the English word *translation*.

that openness for the emerging international discipline.

It is relatively easy to say what a translation is and is not at any particular time and place, but it is not so easy to define a theoretical concept of translation that can be used with confidence to ground the development of translation studies as a discipline. This is largely the case because the practices and products of translation have varied so greatly from culture to culture and from epoch to epoch. What would have been considered an excellent translation during the period of *les belles infidèles* in seventeenth-century France would not have been considered a translation at all in the middle of the twentieth century in the United States, when poets were careful to call their poetic renditions of a source text *imitations* or *versions* rather than translations.[7] This sort of disjunction is even more apparent when one looks further afield – beyond Western nations to cultures elsewhere in the world, beyond the conditions of modern Western literacy to conditions of oral translation, and so forth.

In coming to terms with this problematic, it is helpful to turn to the work on concepts in cognitive science. Such work will serve as a reference point in what follows. At the same time very little of the research in cognitive science has focused on complex social concepts such as translation, and almost none of the research has tried to define cross-cultural social concepts. Most research on concepts by cognitive scientists has been conducted either in terms of simple physical categories (such as birds, chairs, and the like) or in terms of artificial categories (such as dot patterns).[8] A social concept such as translation that has many different inflections across time, space, and cultures raises questions that cognitive science has not yet investigated extensively.

Moreover, some cognitive scientists remain locked into a positivist or realist philosophical framework, seeing concepts as mental representations of "objective" categories of actual entities in the world. Thus they underestimate the significance of language and culture as mediating forces in the construction and perception of concepts and categories, and, hence, of "reality" itself. This blind spot makes research on social categories almost impossible.[9] It is a commonplace in linguistics and textual studies that cultural perspectives embodied in language construct and shape perceptions of the world, including categories and concepts. This postpositivist position is essential in attempting to define translation as a general concept and it is congruent with the historical trajectory

---

[7] These are the terms used by Robert Lowell (1961) and Seamus Heaney (1983), for example.

[8] Murphy (2002) gives a broad survey of research in the field and, hence, illustrates a large sample of the concepts researched.

[9] For example, Murphy holds that "a concept is a nonlinguistic psychological representation of a class of entities in the world" (2002:385) or, alternatively, a "mental representation" of a class in the world (2002:1, cf. 385-441). Lakoff by contrast argues against this realist view of concepts, holding that categories reflect human embodiment and cultural shaping and that concepts and categories reflect a perceived world rather than a world without a knower (1987:50 ff., 196-218).

of translation studies since World War II. Thus, the discussion below will both employ cognitive science and also at times of necessity push beyond current findings about concepts within cognitive science.

Before turning to these questions, let me say a word about terminology. Often it is the practice in discussions of concepts to mark off concepts by using a special type face such as small caps or italics. This convention allows the researcher to distinguish the concept (e.g., *dog*) from actual members of the category to which the concept refers (e.g., dogs). In the case before us, the English word *translation* can refer simultaneously to the concept, the activity of translating, and the products of translation. In his recent survey of contemporary research on concepts, *The Big Book of Concepts* (2002), Gregory Murphy (6) notes that in most cases it will be clear to readers whether the category or concept is being discussed; moreover, there are also instances when the concept cannot be fully disentangled from the category and, thus, a usage that tries to separate them rigorously is problematic. Following Murphy, I forgo using italics or a special typeface to distinguish the concept translation from the category or activity of translation. In what follows, however, I do frequently mark out the intercultural concept at the heart of translation studies from a local English-language concept of translation by prefacing the English word *translation* with an asterisk in order to indicate the cross-cultural understanding that translation studies must move toward: *translation. I realize that this usage may be distracting to some readers, but perhaps that is all to the good. It is a way of reminding people (including myself) of the necessity of defamiliarizing (or foreignizing) the concepts currently used in translation studies. As translation studies emerges as a global field, it becomes increasingly essential to interrogate the basic premises and assumptions that underlie the things everyone thinks they know about translation.[10] Acknowledging the problems of terminology, Saliha Paker (2002:128) observes that it is nonetheless possible to have a multilingual scholarly conversation about the meaning of translation internationally. My usage of "*translation" is an attempt to facilitate such a discussion. The convention is intended to remind the reader that the cross-cultural concept at the heart of the international discipline of translation studies is different from the more narrow English-language (and Western European) concept of translation that is linked by semiosis to notions of carrying across, the movement of Christian relics, and biblical translation.

As we will see below, the words used to indicate the practices and products of translation in languages throughout the world do not actually mean *translation* as such. They have a wide range of image-schemas and semiotic associations that diverge radically from those of the English word *translation* and indeed from those of words for 'translation' in all Western European languages. These

---

[10] These terminology problems in designating cross-cultural social concepts are discussed by Hermans (1995:220-22), who opts for "*translation$_2$*" to designate what he calls the "supralingual category".

distinctions are very difficult to signal with the textual conventions of scholarly discourses. Ironically, if we accept the idea that meaning is strictly speaking language specific, then the Chinese term *fanyi*, for example, will not actually *mean* 'translation'. Any theoretical formulation of *translation as a cross-cultural concept must be able to accommodate the varied semiosis associated with and the wide-ranging set of meanings indicated by all the words used internationally for the practice and products of translation. Translation studies must move beyond presuppositions about the concept *translation associated with and limited by specific Western words.

2.1 Varieties of Translation Types

[handwritten: oral traditions / medieval]

Let us begin by reviewing briefly a variety of translation types so as to understand the difficulties faced in crafting a definition of *translation that can transcend dominant Western conceptualizations. Counterexamples to definitions of translation as a closed and circumscribed concept are immediately apparent in descriptive translation studies that have appeared in the last three decades. Evidence from research pertaining to folklore and other oral traditions, for instance, makes it apparent that in situations where primary and even secondary orality persists, ideas about and procedures for translating generate oral and written texts that show radical differences from their sources, differences that are not currently tolerated in mainstream definions of translation.

In my article "Translation in Oral Tradition as a Touchstone for Translation Theory and Practice" (1990b), I draw attention to three such cases. Perhaps the most striking is the amusing yet very significant account by Laura Bohannan of her attempt to tell the story of *Hamlet* to a traditional gathering of African elders. In the process of her oral translation, she herself recognized the necessity of adapting Shakespeare's "universal" text to the social and material culture of her audience. Thus, in Bohannan's telling Hamlet speaks to Gertrude in her "sleeping hut", Hamlet and Laertes fight with machetes, and Shakespeare's scholars become "people who know things", the equivalent of witches. Bohannan adopted the traditional formulas of her audience's story-telling conventions, beginning "Not yesterday, not yesterday, but long ago, a thing occurred". Even so, as she told her story, the audience became restless, for there were so many interferences with the beliefs, values, and customs of their own people that they began to take issue with Bohannan over her voicing of the story. They began to reshape Shakespeare's tale to suit their culture, making interventions and taking over aspects of the telling itself. Plot and character and relationships between the characters all shifted: the audience approved of Claudius and Gertrude marrying soon after the death of Hamlet's father because it was the local custom for a brother-in-law to marry his brother's widow; they attributed Ophelia's death to witchcraft; and so forth. At the end of their interventions, the audience was satisfied with having heard "a good story", and they congratulated Bohannan for having told it "with very few mistakes", but to Bohannan the resulting translation "no longer seemed quite the same story".[11]

In oral situations the practice of translation has a performance-based esthetic and pragmatic. As a consequence the primary criterion of a good translation is a story well and truly told, rather than close verbal or cultural fidelity, largely because there is generally little or no value accorded to a fixed text *per se* as there is in literate cultures. Similar radical translation shifts can be charted not just when the source is a well-known fixed text such as *Hamlet* but in situations where material is translated from an oral source to another oral text in a second language, or in situations where written texts are based on oral materials (Tymoczko 1990b). In an oral communication an audience must be able to apprehend rapidly and clearly patterns of language, discourse, material culture, and features of the natural and social worlds, as well as genre, tale type, plot, characters, and motifs, to name but a few parameters.

Translation in an oral environment is in certain respects rather like translation for the stage: it is heavily oriented toward the semiotic networks of the receiving audience because of performative constraints on the speakers and perceptual constraints on the receiving audience. Moreover, it is often highly condensed, with materials simply omitted that are not easily apprehensible to the audience. Though translation scholars might be instinctively inclined to reject evidence about oral translation in thinking about translation theoretically (perhaps in part because of the lack of written evidence at every stage of the process), it must be remembered that most human cultures are still oral to a considerable extent and the process of translation in oral contexts is the norm of what *translation has been through most of human history. Evidence comes not only from comparisons of Western international folktales that are inherited from the depths of time and from written works that reflect oral environments, but from the research of contemporary scholars such as Bohannan. It is substantiated as well by evidence about community translation around the world. Thus, Michael Cronin's (2002) arguments for moving studies of interpreting closer to the center of translation studies must be part of the programmatic for readjusting dominant definitions of translation in the current international environment of translation studies.[12]

Examples of translation during the Middle Ages in Europe can also be very different from contemporary conceptions of or norms for translation. Myriam Salama-Carr (2006:123, 125) rightly observes that medieval European translation practices have been largely ignored in Western discourses about translation that constitute the genealogy of translation studies. In Europe there was a divided culture during the Middle Ages, with segments of the population highly literate,

---

[11] Bohannan (1966) gives a detailed account of the session.

[12] My examples are drawn primarily from Western frameworks, but many of the case studies in Hung and Wakabayashi (2005) offer excellent analyses of the effects of oral culture on translation practices in Asia.

highly oriented to written texts, and highly interested in close textual fidelity; Latin-speaking clerics and scholars involved with education, the transmission of classical learning, doctrinal interpretation, and the preservation of scripture would have fallen into this category. At the same time there was an oral basis to most of vernacular life in medieval Europe right up through the fourteenth century. Those involved in literary creation, even when literate, usually served patrons who spoke the vernacular and who remained primarily oral in their orientation; moreover, authors wrote for contexts dominated by an oral esthetic and standards of oral performance in which reading aloud remained the norm.[13] For most patrons verbal fidelity and the stability *per se* of a (written) text in medieval vernacular translation were of little interest.

Thus, translation practices during the European Middle Ages were divided, such that close literal translations coexisted with very free translations, often from the same period and the same locale, even with respect to the same type of source texts. An example is the translation of medieval Latin saints' lives into Old French. In some cases these early French translations of Latin saints' lives are so close that the Latin sources can be identified from the translation itself; this is particularly the case of prose texts, where the fidelity of the Old French translation is sometimes so close that the Latin source text is obvious behind the vernacular surface. These translations reflect textual standards related to biblical exegesis. At other times translations of saints' lives into Old French vary considerably from a "word for word" standard, taking the form of a very loose restatement of the story that makes it impossible to determine precisely what the source text was. Such retellings are generally in verse, and twelfth-century examples include texts that are new literary creations such as Benedeit's *Voyage of Saint Brendan*, a fairly free adaptation of the Latin text involving abbreviations and additions, probably prepared for a royal bride coming to England, and Wace's *Life of Saint Nicholas*, a conflation of several Latin sources, probably associated with the Norman promotion of the cult of Saint Nicholas among the laity. There are other examples where the Latin source is fairly certain but gets manipulated in significant ways, such as Wace's *Life of Saint Margaret* which departs from the Latin source text principally in adding Old French prayers at strategic points.[14] At times the variation in translation practice can be correlated with function, including public oral recitation versus private devotional use, secular versus monastic reception, and so forth.

Translations from Latin into early Irish illustrate some of the radical shifts characteristic of many medieval vernacular translations. The poetry of Blathmacc, an eighth-century Irish monk, offers examples. Blathmacc is credited with several

---

[13] Oral reading stands in contrast to silent reading which only came to the fore very late in the Middle Ages and in the Renaissance. Practices of reading aloud remained central modes of textual dissemination and reception as late as the nineteenth century, until literacy became widespread in Europe.

[14] See the introductions to Benedeit (1928) and Wace (1932, 1942).

surviving narrative poems in Irish, one reflecting the life of Jesus and another an Irish version of the *Gospel of Thomas*. In both cases Blathmacc translates his material into heptasyllabic riming quatrains, the requirements of which turn prose narrative into highly allusive and epigrammatic poetic accounts; the poems are typical of long Irish poems of the period, though they have a more definite narrative thread than is customary. They are so far from the narrative texture of the source texts, however, that a modern reader finds it difficult to consider them translations.[15]

A similar unapologetic subordination of the content of a source text to the standards of the receiving audience is found in an early thirteenth-century Irish translation of the story of Ulysses, called *Merugud Uilix maic Leirtis*, literally 'The Wanderings of Uilix son of Leirtes'. Based on Latin sources including the *Aeneid*, the text is a nine-page (288 lines) version of the adventures of Ulysses. Though it derives ultimately from accounts like the *Odyssey*, the story may have passed from Latin through Irish oral tradition before being written down, for it has been partially restructured on the basis of an international folk tale. The most recent editor notes that "there is very little of the classical version of the story left" (Meyer 1977:xvi; see also Hillers 1999). The text is part of a wave of translations into Irish of continental and classical materials, an Irish outgrowth of the international movement known as the "Renaissance of the Twelfth Century".[16] Irish storytelling of the period favored relatively short narratives, and the Irish writer conforms to this standard in giving a very abbreviated account of the story of Ulysses to suit the vernacular conventions of his day. He calls his text a *merugud*, literally 'wandering, going astray',[17] assimilating it partially to a contemporary Irish genre known as the *immram*, literally 'rowing around', a story about a hero's adventures as he travels the sea, rowing from island to island. The charming use of Ulysses' patronymic to identify the hero in his Irish guise – Uilix mac Leirtis – is another manifestation of the cultural domestication in this medieval translation.

One way of looking at these variations in the fullness of translation types documented in descriptive translation studies is to say that translations can vary radically with respect to the rank at which they operate. In some cultural circumstances translations proceed at the rank of the word or the rank of the sentence. But in other cultures the process of translation occurs at the rank of the text or the entire story. In cultures where oral standards persist, translations often

---

[15] See the discussions in Williams and Ford (1992:77-78) and Carney (1964).

[16] There is a parallel wave of translations from Latin literature into most European vernaculars in the twelfth and thirteenth centuries, an example of which is the twelfth-century *Roman d'Eneas* in Old French, a translation of the *Aeneid*. I have written on the French translations of the period as a factor in the emergence of medieval romance in "Translation as a Force for Literary Revolution in the Twelfth-Century Shift from Epic to Romance" (1986-87).

[17] The title is from Old Irish *merugad*, 'wandering, going astray; erring, confusion, error' (*Dictionary of the Irish Language* s.v.).

operate at the higher ranks of text or story. In such circumstances radical changes may occur not just at the level of word and sentence, but also at higher levels of language and text. Thus, cultural information or plot or textual conventions (such as length, formal patterning, and the like) may shift radically as the text itself is accommodated to the reception standards of the target audience. All these types of translation practices must be accommodated within the cross-cultural concept *translation in the development of translation studies as an international academic discipline.

Examples challenging dominant ideas about the nature of translation can be found in the modern period as well, including contemporary practices of written translation. Even at a single point of time, a modern culture can produce very diverse types of texts that are equally regarded as translations. The coexistence of such different types of translation and different translation norms came home to me when I was researching translations of early Irish literature during the Irish revival for *Translation in a Postcolonial Context: Early Irish Literature in English Translation* (1999b). As I indicate in that study, the Irish translations are quite polarized in their strategies. On the one hand are assimilated literary translations, of the sort that Lawrence Venuti (1992, 1995, 1998a, 1998b) calls domesticating translations. These are marked by significant adaptations of the source language (e.g., Augusta Gregory's free transpositions into the Kiltartan dialect or translations using Tennysonian English), the plots (including the development of consistent chronology and biographical framework for the stories), and literary forms (where the Irish narrative form is represented variously as Homeric epic, folktale, dramatic poems, and so forth). Many of these translations shade into original literary creations, including Standish O'Grady's *History of Ireland*, Augusta Gregory's *Cuchulain of Muirthemne*, and Eleanor Hull's *The Cuchullin Saga in Irish Literature*.

On the other hand there are translations that are almost tortuous in their discursive strategies, having as their translation unit the word, the clause, or the sentence at most. This is the case with many philological translations, not just those of the nineteenth century but scholarly treatments in the second half of the twentieth century as well.[18] When I was initially researching the situation, I thought these were antithetical types of documents, but later came to see that they were polarized elements of a single translation system. In a sense each translation type depends on the existence of the other; they are divergent yet symbiotic. The early domesticated translations capitalized on the taste for Celtic narratives that Macpherson's popular eighteenth-century texts had initiated and the Irish cultural revival demanded, even as the scholarly and literal translations authenticated the fact that there were genuine Irish texts behind the translation movement, thus deflecting the risk of recapitulating the Macpherson controversy

---

[18] For example, the translations of Cecile O'Rahilly (1967, 1976) or the translations of Irish poetry by Gerard Murphy (1956).

in an Irish context. Both translation practices were motivated by and contributed to a nationalistic ethos in different ways: the domesticated translations were part of building a national literature, even as the philological translations documented Ireland's glorious cultural past. Both translation traditions were also united in a shared sense of decorum and public morality, unified in suppressing sexual, scatological, and antiheroic episodes.[19]

Here I've only given a small sample of translation types from Western tradition, but once one begins to be alert to the varied and capacious nature of the cross-cultural and cross-temporal concept *translation, one finds that examples of radically different translation types abound everywhere. In the last hundred years there are literary translations that diverge radically from the content of the source text, ranging from the translations by Ezra Pound that were motivated by a desire to remake English-language poetics to the translations of Catullus by Celia and Louis Zukofsky that transpose the sounds and metrics of Catullus's poetry through their choice of English words, irrespective of grammar or continuous semantic meaning. At the other extreme are very close gloss translations done by philologists breaking new ground in translating ancient texts or contemporary oral texts that have never been written down before. There are radical abridgments of texts from distant cultures and there are painfully literal translations of instructions for electronic equipment produced in factories outside Europe and North America. Translations of legal, medical, scientific, and business documents are often thought of as relatively unmarked, but they are in fact full of summary, paraphrase, additions, and various strategies of dynamic equivalence that result in significant semiotic shifts between the source and receptor texts in order to adjust to cultural differences in these (technical) domains (cf. Gambier 2002:211).

There are translation types with quite different purposes but similar surface characteristics, and translations with similar purposes but very different surface structures. There are also texts that are classified as translations (even legally) that have only a tenuous relationship to the "sources". Such is the case discussed by Itamar Even-Zohar of an advertisement on a cereal box that was clearly intended to satisfy legal requirements for bilingual packaging in a bilingual country; in fact the "translation" was a new text altogether, a replacement of and supplement to the "original", thereby efficiently imposing two advertisements rather than one on the bilingual target audience (Grähs et al. 1978:348-49). The recent collection of articles on advertisement translation edited by Beverly Adab and Cristina Valdés (2004) exemplifies the complexities of translating multiple semiotic systems in advertising, often necessitating the creation of new texts altogether. Advertisement translation also illustrates the theoretical challenges of multimodal and multimedia texts for translation studies, as well as the difficulty of drawing clear lines between source text on the one hand and target text on the other. Clearly going beyond transfer alone, the translation of advertisements

---

[19] A full discussion is found in Tymoczko (1999b:122-45).

also raises questions about deliberate effacement of meaning and text type.[20] Jonathan Abel also offers Japanese examples of translating – notably translations of *The Tale of Genji* into contemporary comic books – that challenge dominant definitions of both translation processes and products, for in these works style is always foregrounded, change is assumed, and the original text is far from sacred (2005:155).

Still other divergent types of translation are emerging as a consequence of globalization and contemporary technology. The term *localization* has been coined for translations that are naturalized to the target culture in the extreme, often diverging radically from whatever template can be defined as the "source text" and thereby destabilizing traditional distinctions between "original" and "translation". Anthony Pym remarks on the significance of the "social logic by which the concept of translation itself is changing as its very name is being re-placed" (2000:192). The significance of the emergence of these new names for translation is that increasingly contemporary translation is moving away from the transfer hypothesis that has dominated thinking about translation in Eurocentric cultures since the end of the Middle Ages. Ernst-August Gutt (2000a:166; cf. 2000b:209-11) notes that [in the West] translation has traditionally been conceived as an interpretive activity: the relevance of translation lies in informing addressees of what someone else has said, written, or thought. He observes (2000a:166; cf. 2000b:47-68, 215-20) that at present increasingly the term *translation* is used for communication that constitutes a descriptive use of language. Localizations, advertisement translations, and other types of contemporary commercial translations exemplify this shift.[21]

There is little need to multiply examples further. The situation is obvious to anyone willing to consider the wide range of translations that have been produced through history and across cultures and that are also now being produced. There are also many borderline cases of translation that must be accounted for theoretically in a definition of translation, for example translations that are denied as translations *per se,* such as the official documents in the many languages of the European Union that all stand equally as "originals". The same is true of the French and German versions of the constitution of Switzerland that are both considered primary and "equal" documents, where differences in wording cannot form the basis of a legal argument.[22] Additional unusual and borderline cases of translation have been compiled by G. C. Kálmán (1986), who lists such types as

---

[20] Munday (2004) discusses these and other challenges that advertisement translation poses for traditional conceptualizations of translation.

[21] In a personal communication Andrew Chesterman has observed that Western metaphors for translation as transfer also bring with them a preoccupation with equivalence. By contrast words for *translation in other languages often open up the question of equivalence. It is not an accident therefore that as translation shifts away from interpretive activity and transfer, questions of equivalence will also be reconceptualized in translation studies.

[22] A good case study of this type of translation is found in Schäffner (2003).

(case 1) a target text with no source text, (case 2) a source text with a target text that is identified as an original, and (case 3) a source text that has no target text.[23] Kálmán also discusses autotranslation (case 4), where the writer is bilingual, writing in two languages and translating back and forth between them; in such cases both versions of a single text are also often treated as if they have equal status as originals. The French and English texts of Samuel Beckett's *Waiting for Godot* are cases in point, differing substantially in wording and even having different stage directions (in part because they grow out of different productions of the play); each is normally read as a self-standing original, despite the fact that the English text is later than the French. Multilingual texts (such as macaronic poetry or James Joyce's *Finnegans Wake*) constitute Kálmán's case 5a, where the same text can be read in two or more languages with, presumably, very different effects. Although these cases are marginal, they must not be forgotten in defining and theorizing the international concept *translation.[24]

   All of these diverse types serve as translations from a scholarly point of view, moving and transmitting source materials from one cultural context to another and from one language to another. To distinguish between the wide variety of translation types – even just within Western cultures – scholars have proposed all sorts of proliferating terminologies, including the familiar dichotomies of word for word and sense for sense, literal and free, formal equivalence and dynamic equivalence, adequate and acceptable, and foreignizing and domesticating.[25] There are also gloss translations (Nida 1964:159), as well as phonological translations and graphological translations (Catford 1965:23). Eugene Eoyang in *The Transparent Eye* (1993) distinguishes three additional types of translations: surrogate translations that substitute for the source text and presuppose that readers have no access to the source; contingent translations (such as scholarly facing translations) that constantly refer the reader back to the primacy of the source text; and coeval translations that can stand on their own as literary works but are aimed at bilingual readers who have access to the source text as well. Finally, Moradewun Adejunmobi (1998) proposes a classification specific to postcolonial translation. And yet these diverse terminologies do not describe all the types of translation that have been documented in descriptive studies, nor do they account for all the features and characteristics of translation that have been

---

[23] Kálmán's case 1 is normally known as a *pseudotranslation*, while case 3 is often called *zero translation*. Rambelli (2006:183) points out that pseudotranslations do not refer to an individual source text but to a whole class of texts that share a number of features, with Gouanvic (2000:108) observing that pseudotranslations reveal the collective nature of relations between two cultures.

[24] See also Bassnett (1998) for a discussion of these and other marginal cases.

[25] St. Jerome makes the distinction between word for word and sense for sense (see Robinson 1997b:25); Nida (1964) distinguishes between formal equivalence and dynamic equivalence; Toury (1980) initiated the discourse of adequate and acceptable; and Venuti (1995, 1998a, 1998b) discusses domesticating and foreignizing. Still more binaries are inventoried in Wilt (2003:6-7).

taken up by translation studies scholars in the last half century. The inadequacy in conceptualizing *translation cross-culturally may be causally related to the "overabundance of terminology" that some see as a weakness of translation studies (cf. Munday 2001:46).

2.2 Conceptualizations of Translation Worldwide

Even more suggestive of the broad scope and diverse nature of the cross-cultural concept *translation are words used in languages around the world for the activity of translation. A hint at the realignments of translation theory that may be necessary in moving beyond dominant Western conceptualizations of translation is offered by words from around the world for *translation, whose etymologies, cognates, image-schemas or metaphoric meanings, lexical fields, histories, and specific practices are extremely diverse. Obviously a definitive exploration of this question is a matter of considerable collective work, going far beyond my own capabilities and the constraints of this study. What follows, therefore, are merely a few intriguing and suggestive examples.

In India two common words for *translation are *rupantar*, 'change in form' and *anuvad*, 'speaking after, following', both of which derive from Sanskrit.[26] Sujit Mukherjee (1994:80) argues that neither of these terms implies fidelity to the original and that the concept of translation as faithful rendering came to India with Christianity, a translation practice obviously rooted in the concept of transposing a sacred fixed text. Mukherjee also indicates that Indian words for *translation do not necessarily imply a change from one language to another; they can also indicate a process called *transcreation* in Indo-English (2004:43, 140).[27] These Indian words suggest that alteration in form and variation are to be expected in a translation, and they may be associated with oral standards of evaluation. *Anuvad* derives from a root meaning 'speak', and Udaya Narayana Singh specifies that the term emphasizes *parole* and the performance of a text, rather than literal rendition; insofar as translation is derivative in this paradigm, it has this status solely because it comes after the source text, and the temporal relationship does not impute its value as a creation.[28] The concepts of translation associated with these words may also suggest a negative view of translation enterprises that seek to replace sacred source texts with an "equivalent" text; paradoxically transcreative practices of translation in India recognize and preserve the sole authority of the sacred source texts by not presuming to replace them. G. Gopinathan (2000:165) indicates that Sanskrit was considered "Deva

---

[26] Trivedi (2006:110-16) specifies that *anuvad* originally had the meaning of ritually exact repetition associated with incantation. *Rupantar* by contrast is a more modern word, formed as a new Sanskrit compound; because *rup* means both 'form' and 'beauty', the word suggests a change in form that retains the esthetic effect of the source text.

[27] Gopinathan (2000:170-72) also discusses the practices of transcreation.

[28] Communication at the conference "Asia in the Asian Consciousness", Tejgadh, India, 2005.

Bhasha" (God's language) and that ancient Vedic texts were considered the words of God, forbidden to be translated, an idea that prevailed until modern times.[29] Harish Trivedi observes that as a temporal metaphor *anuvad* contrasts with the spatial ones of Western European words for translation (2006:113). The temporal metaphor may be motivated by oral practices of translation, but it may also reflect the precedence of the sacred before the profane.[30]

A number of scholars have inventoried a broader survey of words used in India for the concept *translation than those discussed here.[31] Another suggestive word for the concept is *chaya*, 'shadow' or 'counterpart' (Gopinathan 2000:166; Mukherjee 2004:65). As a Sanskrit gloss of a Prakrit text, *chaya* suggests that a translation should follow at the heels of the source text, not deviating or departing from it in form or content; at the same time the metaphor suggests that like a shadow, such a translation will appear quite different, depending on the angle from which the translator illuminates and interprets the source text (Gopinathan 2000:166). The shadowy nature of *chaya* also suggests to me that such a close translation is seen as having a sort of lifeless quality in Indian culture.

Interestingly enough, according to Trivedi (2006) the most striking aspect of the history of translation in India is the absence of translation from foreign languages as a textualized practice (cf. Gopinathan 2000:165). Although the words *rupantar* and *anuvad* suggest oral interpreting and oral translation norms, Trivedi indicates there is an absence of significant translated texts from outside India in the historical and literary record until the period of European colonization. He attributes this absence in part to multilingualism in India, including types of multilingualism in which different forms of a single language are mutually intelligible, as Sanskrit and Prakrit were, a linguistic divergence associated with class and gender. In part the lack of translation as a literacy practice can also be attributed to the existence of a single standardized written language across a large culture area, reflecting the cultural role of Sanskrit as a sacred and learned language serving to unite the different parts of the sub-continent (Trivedi 2006:111-13) and its status as a language associated with power as well.[32] As Trivedi suggests, it is possible that cultural sufficiency or enclosure also played a role in the absence of translations from outside India (2006:105-6).

Trivedi indicates that until the modern era no translations have survived

---

[29] In this regard it is suggestive that Hindus and Catholics in particular derided nineteenth-century Protestant Christians in India because of the existence of different and competing translations of the Bible (Israel 2006:456).

[30] Bermann (2005:269) argues that a "translator elicits an echo not only of a *different* but also of a *previous* language", reminding readers that Benjamin sees translation as a temporal affair in addition to a spatial one. Clearly these views have affinities with the image-schemas associated with *anuvad*.

[31] See Ramakrishna (2000:94), Mukherjee (2004:45), Gopinathan (2000, 2006), and Trivedi (2006).

[32] This question remains to be investigated more thoroughly. Obviously Persian and Arabic also served as languages unifying large segments of India during specific political eras.

into Indian languages from non-Indian materials, only translations out of them, notably into Chinese, Arabic, and Persian. He observes that India "presents a starkly different historical model for translation studies to contemplate" (Trivedi 2006:106). Moreover, among Indian languages new versions of the old Sanskrit texts were not regarded as translations but often as the greatest original works in the emerging vernacular literatures, thus putting into question whether the concepts of "original" and "translation" themselves may be Western rather than universal (106-7). Ganesh Devy (1999:187) argues that textual elements and signficance in India can be used again and again because Indian metaphysics is based on repeated rebirth and does not lay undue emphasis on originality. The true test of a writer is thus to revitalize; hence, literary traditions in India are essentially traditions of translation.[33] Like Mukherjee, Trivedi concludes that there is some question as to whether the very concept of translation as understood in the West existed in India before colonization. In evaluating the nature and similarity of concepts, it is essential to consider what status concepts have, not just what their identities are (Lakoff 1987:322), and thus Trivedi rightly insists on the significance of the fact that the status of translation was very different in India from that in many other parts of the world.

By contrast, the current Arabic word for *translation is *tarjama*, originally meaning 'biography', connected perhaps with the early focus of Syriac Christian translators on the Bible, patristic texts, and lives of saints in the third to fifth centuries of the common era. The association of the word for translation with a narrative genre, biography, indicates to me that the role of the translator is seen as related to that of a narrator. In turn this suggests the powerful potential of the translator's agency, because the translator is one who "tells" and hence frames the material being translated. The early Syriac translators eventually turned to other subjects, becoming primary conduits of Greek science and philosophy to their contemporaries. This learned movement underlies the later great translation tradition into Arabic initiated and patronized by the Abbasid caliphate, as well as the subsequent production of mathematical and scientific texts and translations in Arabic.[34]

This broader range of translation activity is perhaps related to a second meaning of *tarjama*, namely 'definition'.[35] This second meaning is relevant to the

---

[33] Note the valorization of free translation involving additions, embellishments, and other creative departures from the source text in Turkish translations associated with nationalist discourses (Paker 2002). The early texts transposing Sanskrit materials into "new originals" in Indian vernacular languages might similarly indicate regionalist cultural assertions, particularly those in Dravidian languages.

[34] A full discussion of these translation movements is found in Montgomery (2000:60-137); see also Faiq (2000), Salama-Carr (2000, 2006). For other words for *translation in Arabic, see Salama-Carr (2000:102, 2006:128).

[35] This meaning of *tarjama* is current in the Arabic of Iraq; in Orissa, India, the word can also mean 'in depth analysis'. I am indebted here to Abdulzahra Muhamad and Sachidananda Mohanty, personal communications.

involvment of Syriac translators with Greek learned texts, especially scientific and mathematical ones, as well as the flowering of Arabic translations related to these subjects, for such texts are heavily oriented to defining and explaining objects of the natural and conceptual worlds. In this light it is important to understand actual Syriac and Arabic translation practices, for translators did not merely transmit Greek learned texts unchanged. When scientific and mathematical knowledge had expanded, the translators augmented the Greek texts with their own culture's supplementary frameworks and advances, merging and recasting the Greek material so that the subject matter became better articulated and better defined in the translations than in the source texts.[36] Salama-Carr shows that translators were viewed as scholars in their own right, and they were expected to demonstrate "the same level of knowledge as the author" being translated (2006:124). It is perhaps the translation practices associated with such scientific and learned translations – practices linking translation to definition – that also illuminate the prohibition in Islam on translating the Qur'an. If to translate is to define in this tradition, then to translate the Qur'an is to delimit it, to turn an open and numinous religious text into a biography or into a closed intellectual and scientific text that defines the source text and that updates the source with contemporary frameworks. Clearly this cannot be desirable treatment for a sacred text.[37]

Words in other languages for *translation also stress the importance of translation as a form of storytelling. In the Nigerian language Igbo, the words for translation are *tapia* and *kowa*. *Tapia* comes from the roots *ta*, 'tell, narrate', and *pia*, 'destruction, break [it] up', with the overall sense of 'deconstruct it and tell it (in a different form)'. *Kowa* has a similar meaning, deriving from *ko*, 'narrate, talk about' and *wa*, 'break in pieces'. In Igbo translation is an activity that stresses the viability of the çommunication as narration, allowing for decomposition and a change in form rather than one-to-one reconstruction. The freedom of translation in this paradigm is illustrated by the naturalization of the story of Adam and Eve in Nigerian tradition as a story in which Adam becomes a great farmer.[38] This conceptualization of *translation and its practices is related to the necessities and freedoms of translation in oral contexts, and there seem accordingly to be some commonalities of conceptualization with the medieval European vernacular translation practices discussed earlier.[39]

---

[36] See Montgomery (2000:61-137). Salama-Carr indicates that in this translation movement, translation was seen as "retrieving and explicating" the scientific knowledge (2006:124); moreover, she says (126) that the trajectory of translation was toward the interpretive.

[37] Robinson (1996:65) and Salama-Carr (2000:103-4) also offer suggestive historical and theological perspectives on this prohibition. See as well the entry by Hassan Mustapha on translating the Qur'an (in Baker 1998:200-4).

[38] I am indebted for this information about Igbo to Isidore Okpewho, personal communication.

[39] To these Igbo words (as well as the narrative implications associated with Arabic *tarjama*), we might compare the Ojibwe word for translation *aanikohtamowin*, combining a prefix for 'link' with a stem for 'story', suggesting that translation makes a connection by telling a story (Godard 1997:57).

Still another conceptualization of *translation is indicated by the most common Chinese locution for *translation, *fanyi*, which includes the sense 'turning over'; the term is represented using the character for *fan*, which means 'turning [a leaf of a book]' but also 'somersault, flip', and the character for *yi*, which means 'interpretation', but is also a homonym of the word meaning 'exchange'.[40] The two terms, *fan* and *yi*, were both used independently for the activity of translation, but by the twelfth century they were "completely interchangeable" (Cheung 2006a:202). The concept *fanyi* is linked to the image of embroidery: if the source text is the front side of an embroidered work, the target text can be thought of as the back side of the same piece. Like the reverse of an embroidery – which typically in modern Chinese handwork has hanging threads, loose ends, and even variations in patterning from the front – a translation in this conceptualization is viewed as different from the original and is not expected to be equivalent in all respects. At the same time, of course, the "working side" of an embroidery teaches much about its construction. Both images – embroidery and turning [a page] – suggest that in China text and translation are related as front and back of the same object. They can also be thought of as positive and negative of the same pattern if the embroidery or weaving technique imaged is brocade which is smooth on both sides but the pattern appears in obverse colors and opposite directions. This is the image proposed in the tenth century by Zan Ning commenting on the meaning of *fan*: "the meaning . . . can be conveyed by likening it to turning over a piece of brocade – on both sides the patterns are the same, only they face in opposite directions" (Cheung 2006a:177). If one considers the implications of the homonym of *yi* meaning 'exchange', it is clear that translation in China is also linked to trade, commerce, and mutual interactions, a meaning that is reflected in etymological stories about the origin of the practice of translation as ancillary to the invention of intercultural exchange and trade. Together the images behind *fanyi* suggest exchange in which the resulting figures turn to face each other, facilitating their cultural communication and interchange.[41]

Translation has a long textualized history in China, epitomized by the translation of Buddhist scriptures into Chinese beginning in the second century C.E. and continuing for almost a thousand years. Traditionally some translation of the scriptures is associated with the Great Wild Goose Pagoda in Xi'an at the eastern end of the Silk Road, a pathway for exchanges of all sorts between China and other peoples. The importance of translators as culture heroes in China is signaled by the popular tale about bringing the Buddhist scriptures to China to be

---

[40] Additional Chinese terms for *translation, their image-schemas and implicit metaphors, and their theoretical implications are discussed in Cheung (2005).

[41] I am indebted for some of this material to personal communications with Martha Cheung and Liu Xiaoqing. Note that the image or metaphor of translation as a form of turning is also found in some European languages, including Latin *convertere* (Tymoczko forthcoming b), Old English *wendan* and *awendan* (Halverson 1999b), and Spanish *convertir* (Rafael 1993:xvii). For a discussion and critique of translation as exchange see Cheung (2005) and sources cited.

translated, known in its most famous redaction as *Journey to the West*. All these meanings associated with translation history and practice in China must be folded into the international concept *translation used in translation studies.

We can also note an aspect of the configuration of translation in China that is more an absence than a presence. The development of characters rather than phonetic symbols as the dominant form of writing in China can be looked at as a textualized embodiment of translation. Because a text in characters can be read, understood, and utilized by speakers of many different languages, this practice of writing becomes a form of translating that circumvents or bypasses the action of translators *per se* and the production of textualized translations. Judy Wakabayashi (2005:24-25) argues that the use of characters across linguistic boundaries induces forms of "mental translation" in readers. In a sense this form of writing can be compared to machine translation without a machine: the characters themselves serve to generate the translation for speakers of other languages using the same writing conventions. This is a potent literacy practice that also obviates intralingual translation necessitated by linguistic evolution: texts from other areas of China or from the past can be read despite dialect differences or even more radical historical changes that might cause regional varieties of Chinese to be mutually unintelligible in spoken form, as Cantonese and Mandarin are for many speakers at present. It is, of course, much more difficult to learn to read characters than phonetic representations of speech, but the use of characters is an extremely efficient means of communicating in writing across language boundaries and, hence, an efficient means of handling translation in a multilingual empire.[42]

Thus, the use of characters is a powerful way to insure cultural continuity, obviating both interlingual translation and intralingual translation within the cultural sphere sharing the same literacy practices. Characters insure fidelity which becomes predicated solely on textual survival.[43] Although translation itself is

---

[42] For more extensive considerations of the conceptualization, history, and practices of translation in China, see Chan (2004), Hung (2005b), Wong (2005), and Cheung (2005, 2006a). The implications for translation of the Chinese form of writing *per se* are discussed in Wakabayashi (2005) and Semizu (2006), particularly as they pertain to Japan, Korea, and Vietnam. See also the article "Script in Translation" by Gordon Brotherston in Baker (1998:211-18).

[43] Consider the following thought experiment. If the Romans had used characters instead of phonetic symbols and if Western Europe had retained that writing system, the works of Roman authors would continue to be transparent to modern readers without the need for translation. This follows because characters are ideograms and hence not subject to phonological evolution or even linguistic disparity (cf. Cronin 2006:25). At a minimum, thus, speakers of all the Romance languages, as well as speakers of English, would be able to read Latin literature. But users of other European languages employing the same character set would be able to read the texts as well (including no doubt German speakers who inherited the mantle of the Holy Roman Empire in the Middle Ages, and the Celts who conserved Latin literacy for Europe in the Middle Ages). Moreover, if literacy in Europe were tied to characters rather than phonetic symbols, the linguistic divergence of Italian, Spanish, Portuguese, and French

internalized or rendered unnecessary by the use of characters, this writing practice makes it difficult to theorize about translation.[44] In a language that uses characters, it is more difficult to develop discourses about specific translation issues such as phonological asymmetries, asymmetries of lexical fields, anisomorphisms of grammar, and divergent cultural nuances of words or phrases, because many of those linguistic features of translation are effaced by the script itself. Aspects of meaning are also effaced, particularly in the use of a common character set for different temporal states of the same language, different dialects, and unrelated languages sharing a common writing system; thus both synchronic and diachronic differences in language and culture requiring adjudication in translation are obscured. As a consequence linguistic and cultural aspects of translation become less transparent and more difficult to explore and to theorize. At the same time, these effacements of differences in meaning constitute powerful ideological vectors and vehicles of cultural dominance. Charles Holcombe observes that "to the extent that . . . [Chinese characters] are tied to a particular set of ideas – to a specific vocabulary – [the characters] bring with them the vocabulary of Chinese higher civilization [and] . . . [create] an 'empire of ideas' . . . which simultaneously circulates and reinforces Chinese concepts and excludes other ideas or at least makes their expression difficult" (quoted in Wakabayashi 2005:19). This means of extending an imperialistic and hegemonic worldview through "mental translation" is potent indeed.

A final intriguing conceptualization of translation is exemplified by the Malayo-Polynesian subgroup of the Austronesian languages, including Tagalog and Malay, as well as various other Indonesian languages. The word for translation in Tagalog is *pagsalin*, from the root *salin*, which means 'to pour the contents of one container into another container' (Barbaza 2005:250); related to *pagsalin* is the Malay word *tersalin* from the same root (Hung and Wakabayashi 2005:2). The action of pouring signified by *salin* contrasts with transferring solid materials from one place to another place (where solid materials remain unchanged in the transfer process). *Salin* is used only for the transfer of materials requiring a container, such as liquids or small granular solids, such as rice. Such materials change form depending on the shape of container holding them. A conceptualization of translation imaged in terms of pouring from container to container excludes fidelity as a central attribute of the translation process. Raniela Barbaza (2005:250) argues that translation thought of this way implies taking control and reshaping

---

would be obscured because they would all continue to generate very similar and mutually intelligible texts in the same characters. Thus translation across the Romance languages would be obviated and the linguistic differences and even mutual incomprehensibility of the spoken languages would be effaced.

[44] This point is discussed by Red Chan in "Currency of Translation Theories: Reception and Transformation of Western Translation Theories in Contemporary China", an unpublished paper delivered in Tejgadh, India, in 2005; cf. Wakabayashi (2005:54). See Cheung (2005, 2006b) for a reappraisal of Chinese translation theory.

the source text to one's needs and interests; function becomes the primary value of translation processes and products. The conceptualization also seems to imply the possibility of esthetic and cognitive reshaping, suggesting affinities with the processes of translation in oral reception contexts discussed above with respect to Igbo, as well as medieval texts in European languages.

Doris Jedamski (2005:213) surveys a variety of words related to translation in Malay, concluding that the closest to 'translated' is *tersalin*. Interestingly enough she notes that used in its active form, the word means 'to give birth' in Malay. Birth is obviously connected both with liquid (the amniotic fluid) and shape-changing (where in the process of birth a young mammal takes its proper shape after being a round bump in its mother's belly). The semiotic associations of translation in this group of languages are clearly very powerful: translating is associated with bringing new life into being and pouring a fluid substance into a container that will give it a new shape. Note also that if there were a substratum of belief in rebirth, reincarnation, or transmigration of souls in this group of cultures, the connection between translation, birth, and the reshaping of a fluid substance is also suggestive. Similar associations could derive from one of the most significant aspects of the traditional religions of insular cultures in southeast Asia, namely the immanence of all life, in which "life is evident everywhere in a multitude of forms" and there is "a recognition of the oneness of the individual with the whole in the commonality of life" (Eliade 1987:13.524). Scholars of comparative religion have concluded that "the result is an essential openness to life, a basic acceptance of life's many manifestations, and ultimately a celebration of spiritual differentiation" (Eliade 1987:13:526). One manifestation of this openness may be the fluidity associated with words for translation (*tersalin*, *pagsalin*) and the acceptance of the many potential forms that a translation can take. Because *translation in this group of languages is not conceptualized as transfer or iteration, but as birth and reshaping in another form, this cluster of associations is reminiscent of Walter Benjamin's (1923) concept of translation as ensuring a text's survival and afterlife.

This is merely a small number of words for the international concept *translation, but the words illustrate distinct conceptualizations, histories, and practices of translation that go beyond Eurocentric understandings of translation. They stand for many, many more alternate views of the processes and products of translation that exist throughout the world, and all have radical implications for theorizing *translation as a cross-linguistic, cross-temporal, and cross-cultural concept in the emerging international discipline of translation studies.

All of these words for *translation suggest aspects of the concept and norms for its praxis that differ considerably from those currently dominant in the West. Not one of these words is fully synonymous with *translation*; one need only think of the chains of semiosis associated with such words synchronically and diachronically to understand the point.[45] The embedded presuppositions about translation in these words, as well as the translation histories and practices associated with them, suggest meanings that are as valid for understanding the international concept *translation as those of the English word *translation*, yet they have not been fully researched or theorized, nor have they entered common discourses about translation in the international discipline of translation studies. Neither the meanings and practices associated with the English word *translation* nor those associated with other words in European languages for the concept *translation should have a privileged position in the theorizations of translation studies. If the international discipline of translation studies had been initiated and had gained strength in a context where the dominant language was Arabic or Chinese or Igbo, the recommended practices for and the theories of translation would obviously be considerably different from those that have emerged in Eurocentric contexts.

Developing such an argument cannot, of course, rest solely on the etymological meaning of words for *translation, and I am actually only sketching out a hypothesis here. A full demonstration of this point would require much more data and a deeper investigation of current terms for translation used around the world. Both cognates and lexical fields of words for *translation would have to be considered. There would also have to be extensive explorations of local practices and products of translation and local histories of translation, with careful attention to diachronic shifts in all of these. In turn the histories and practices of translation would be interrogated in light of the early meanings of the words for *translation in each culture. The ideological implications of all these aspects of translation in various cultures would also have to be investigated; like associations of Western words for translation, suggestive ideological aspects of some of the translation traditions considered above can already be discerned in my small survey. Etymologies and word meanings can thus only be considered as a stimulus or starting point for inquiry, but they are nonetheless suggestive of conceptual orientations toward translation, the growth of local concepts of translation, and, hence, the growth of local forms of knowledge about translation.[46]

If reference is fixed directly by acts of naming rather than indirectly via properties, as Saul Kripke (1980, cf. Lakoff 1987:239) argues, then how are

---

[45] Trivedi argues that the words for *translation used in India "are not and cannot become synonymous and optional words for the English term 'translation'": to list these words for *translation in India "as alternative terms for 'translation' is actually to enlist them under the flag of Western 'translation'" (2006:117). Legrand cautions that scholars must "rebut any attempt at the universalization of singularity under the guise of ascribed similarity" (2005:41).

[46] Halverson (1999a, 1999b; cf. sources cited) argues that etymologies provide key evidence for the meanings of translation in given cultural contexts, in part because they suggest inherited image-schemas and metaphorical frameworks behind the conceptualizations. See also Lakoff and Johnson (1980).

categories to be construed cross-culturally when both their names and their properties vary around the world? This is the case of the words used internationally for *translation, as indicated by the various terms discussed above, but it is also the case for most social concepts.[47] George Lakoff argues that when there are multiple ways of understanding or framing a situation, knowledge becomes relative to those understandings (1987:300), thus suggesting a radical relativism in the nature of cross-cultural social concepts. One can see the implications of these questions for future work in translation studies, but they also point to the necessity of extending and deepening the research on concepts within cognitive science. Inclusion rather than relativism is one possibility for the solution to the conundrum of such concepts, but there are additional issues to be considered, as we will see below.[48]

Contemporary Western norms for translation began to coalesce more than a century ago to meet the needs of emerging forms of imperial and commercial bureaucracies, of empires and capitalism. More recently these Western norms have spread throughout many parts of the world because of globalization. Disseminated through pedagogical practices governing translation in the literate segments of many cultures worldwide, these norms are largely generalizations of the translation history, practices, and theory in the West. Yet it should be clear from this survey of international words for translation, that Western views of the cross-cultural concept *translation are in many ways extremely narrow, culture bound, and culturally specific, incapable even of modeling past practices of translation in the West itself. Thus, the uncritical dissemination and adoption of Western translation norms and practices in other parts of the globe becomes highly problematic; it is a prime example of a hegemonic form of knowledge. If a more adequate international theory of *translation is to be developed, a theory that does not merely serve as a vector for Western culture and Western power, translation theorists must consider a much broader field of examples in defining *translation and in developing translation theory for use in international contexts than they have done heretofore. The international concept *translation must be reconceived to encompass a wider range of examples and more diverse practices across time and space throughout the world.

2.3 Approaches to Defining Translation in Translation Studies

In turning directly to the question of how to define the cross-cultural and cross-temporal concept *translation, let us begin by revisiting the relationship between concepts and categories. The two have been viewed as closely interrelated, even at times synonymous, in traditional realist approaches to concepts. Gregory Murphy,

---

[47] Are we to understand the problem as a metainstance of the indeterminacy of translation, to use Quine's terminology?

[48] Halverson (1999a) offers interesting considerations on relativism in translation studies.

for example, indicates that "the most basic assumption of traditional views of concepts is that they are summary representations of a class of entities" and, alternatively, "whatever my concept is, there is a category of things that would be described by it" (2002:73).[49] Classical approaches to defining concepts have their roots in Greek philosophy and logical thought; for centuries, indeed right to the middle of the twentieth century in many quarters, concepts were seen as being defined in terms of the common properties of the class of entities identified by the concept and, by extension, the necessary and sufficient conditions related to concept membership.[50] In the case of the concept *translation, such conditions would identify all objects in the world through time that are translations and would simultaneously exclude all objects that are not translations. Recent research in cognitive science has superseded these classical views of concepts, as we will see in the next section. Nonetheless, even without the results of the research in cognitive science, the various complex parameters of the concept *translation identified in the last half century of work in translation studies, coupled with the many types of translations characterized in descriptive studies, made it clear early on to translation scholars that classical approaches to defining translation would not work.

Let me emphasize the implications that follow for translation theory in defining *translation: *there are no necessary and sufficient conditions that can identify all translations and that at the same time exclude all non-translations across time and space.* In part this is the case because different cultures have had different and even contradictory criteria for translation as a process and for translations as products; moreover, cultures also have different and even contradictory criteria for distinguishing languages and for constructing texts. Even supposing that minimalist conditions such as those used by speakers of ordinary English for *translation* – namely interlingual movement of text, as reflected in the *OED* definition that we began this chapter with – could be used to identify all translations, the real challenge begins when a person attempts to specify conditions that distinguish translation from other types of interlingual transmission. Though the two generally accepted conditions for translation remain problematic as necessary and sufficient to identify *all* translations, it is clear that they are completely inadequate to rule out all *non-translations*. This is the case because the minimal characteristics of interlingual transfer and movement between source and target texts are shared with and pertain to many types of interlingual communication

---

[49] Note that Murphy goes on to refute this view of strict identity between a concept and a category; cf. Lakoff (1987:xii). Lakoff discusses other bases for concepts besides categories (see, for example, 1987:286).

[50] Murphy (2002:12) summarizes these conditions by indicating that *necessity* refers to the parts of the definition that must be in the entity for it to be a member of the category; *sufficiency* indicates that if an entity has all the necessary parts mentioned in the definition, then it must be a member of the category. Properties that are both necessary and sufficient would definitively delimit the boundaries of a traditional category.

besides translation, including summaries, scholarly articles on source texts, film adaptations of texts, and so forth that are distinguished from translation in most cultures. But narrowing the conditions for *translation cross-culturally any further is effectively impossible: almost any condition used to exclude types of interlingual and textual transmutation as not being translations will also exclude certain forms of translation that are attested in the historical record.

How can translation studies move beyond this impasse? How can theorists define the cross-cultural concept *translation and delineate the relationships that bind different types of translation without including non-translations as well? Conditions that are necessary for translation in one cultural context are not always required in another; conversely, characteristics that are sufficient for translation in one culture may define an adjacent text type in another. Faced with these problems, some scholars are tempted to circumscribe theorizing about *translation by considering only the types of translations that are familiar or dominant in their own cultures. This is a somewhat shabby and self-defeating intellectual move. As Louis G. Kelly wrote in *The True Interpreter* more than a quarter century ago, "the critic must be one who crosses the frontiers of time and space – who needs a largess of vision – something indispensible if we presume to sit in judgment on colleagues of the past", and he reminds the reader that modern attitudes about translation should be tempered by an understanding of past criteria (1979:227).

It has also become increasingly problematic to base an international scholarly field on Western standards in a world that is challenging and pushing beyond such standards. Because most scholars active internationally in translation studies are still from Western countries, restricting the purview of the emerging international discipline to dominant contemporary Western norms will *de facto* construct translation theory as the theory of modern Western practices of translation. In a field devoted to cultural interchange and intercultural communication, as translation studies is, it seems obvious that scholars should not limit their ideas of the cross-cultural concept *translation to practices and ideas developed in Western Christian (imperialist) contexts. It is offensive to think that Western scholars are content to delimit their understanding of *translation using conditions typical of their cultures alone and that they thus become agents of Western dominance by blindly promulgating Western presuppositions about translation processes and products. Equally troubling is the blind acceptance of implicit Western norms and definitions by teachers and scholars of translation in countries worldwide, who thus inscribe themselves willingly in a hegemonic manner within Western discursive structures.[51] Şebnem Susam-Sarajeva (2002:195-96, 199) offers an eloquent account of how scholars outside Eurocentric contexts often begin their

---

[51] Hung (2006:156-59) and Gopinathan (2006:244-45), for example, document some of the perturbations caused by the extension of dominant Western ideas about translation to contemporary cultures speaking languages other than European ones.

careers by internalizing Western theory; they then come to (dis)regard their own cultures' concepts of and thinking about translation as old-fashioned, irrelevant, and simplistic, setting them aside in favor of Western views, even though tools originating in Eurocentric contexts do not necessarily prove useful when extended beyond the Western. She notes that self-colonization "is the state a large part of the world finds itself in today" (198). In a similar vein Martha Cheung warns that for scholars outside Eurocentric domains to be content with modern translation theories inspired by Western scholarship is tantamount to "cultural self-disinheritance" (2005:38).

Translation studies has been struggling with these problems for decades. Though the conversation has been protracted, the definitional impulse in the field is not trivial, as we have seen, for it is difficult to have a field of inquiry if the subject of inquiry is not well identified. In this quandary about the very substance of translation studies, the work of Gideon Toury stands out. An important watershed in the definitional strand in translation studies is Toury's proposal that a translation is "any target language text which is presented or regarded as such within the target system itself, on whatever grounds", a definition he put forth as early as 1980.[52]

Toury here follows J.C. Catford who refers to translation in an open-ended way as "an operation performed on languages: a process of substituting a text in one language for a text in another" (1965:1). We have seen that Catford defines *translation* formally as "the replacement of textual material in one language (SL) by equivalent textual material in another language (TL)" (1965:20). For Catford "translation equivalence is an empirical phenomenon", discovered *a posteriori* by comparing the source language and target language texts and by investigating the underlying conditions of and justifications for translation equivalence (1965:27). Catford famously formulates his definition leaving out the question of meaning and omitting normative criteria for the relationship between the texts in part because his definition of translation presupposes the linguistic theory of anisomorphisms of meaning itself across languages. We will return to the question of meaning in translation in chapter 7.

In contrast to Catford's view that stresses the production of translations, Toury's definition of translation explicitly focuses on the reception conditions for translation products in the target language as the decisive factors in identifying translations empirically. For Toury it is the receptor culture that sets criteria for translations rather than, say, some abstract decision-making procedure by scholars or even by translators themselves. Presumably Toury would say that the intercultural concept *translation is the aggregate of all the decisions about

---

[52] See Toury (1982:27; cf. 1980:14, 37, 43-45). As soon as this definition was proposed, some of its problems were recognized. For example, Toury's definition of *translation includes pseudotranslations as translations and conversely excludes plagiarism in which actual translations are passed off as originals. Nonetheless, Toury's gesture here was a milestone in the development of translation studies as a truly international discipline.

receptor texts made by the various cultures of the world severally. By accepting any text that is considered to be a translation in the context that receives it, Toury broke with the tendency to limit the objects of study in translation studies to those consonant with dominant, modern Eurocentric models and definitions of translation. His definition is, therefore, inclusive of all translations *ipso facto*, and in his formulation Toury opened the way for cultural *self-definition* within the emerging international discipline of translation studies. This must be underscored: Toury's move is critical in decentering translation studies as an international field, in moving the field beyond Eurocentric positions, in offering sufficient conditions for a transcultural concept of *translation rather than attempting to define arbitrary necessary conditions, and in permitting *self-representation* regarding the basic data of translation by people who know it best in their own cultures.

It is significant that Toury's definition of *translation is an *a posteriori* definition rather than a prescriptive definition or a definition depending on necessary and sufficient conditions. For Toury, whatever objects function as translations within a receptor culture and are recognized as translations by members of that culture must therefore be studied by scholars as translations, however different such objects might be from scholars' own expectations of and norms for translation in their own cultures. Toury's definition of translation acknowledges that there is a somewhat arbitrary aspect to the definition of translation in any given culture, which only empirical investigation can discern. Bassnett captures this arbitrariness in her observation that translation is "a set of textual practices with which the writer and reader [or interpreter and audience] collude" (1998:39). Toury's move is essential to incorporating translation history and practice worldwide into translation theory, but it is also critical for understanding the nature of the cross-cultural concept *translation and for recognizing the type of concept that *translation is, as we will see below. Significantly Toury's open definition is still resisted and even disparaged by some Western translation scholars, a resistance that speaks to their own investment in dominant Western norms of translation.

A second important development pertaining to the definitional impulse in translation studies is related to and perhaps even implicitly entailed in Toury's *a posteriori* definition focusing on the target system. This is the theory of rewritings formulated by André Lefevere (1982, 1985, 1992b), or the theory of refractions as he first called it. Because of my work with translations of varied text types and radically divergent discursive strategies in a number of different cultural contexts, I have come to prefer Lefevere's earlier term "refractions" rather than his later term "rewritings", because *refraction* suggests more clearly the partial, fragmented, and metonymic nature of all translations and all cultural transfers (including even simple lexical borrowings).[53] We will return to Lefevere's work in the next chapter where it offers a pertinent model for investigating the boundaries

---

[53] The metonymic aspects of translation are discussed at length in Tymoczko (1999b:41-61, 278-300).

of an international conceptualization of *translation.

Although Lefevere's ideas had antecedents in translation studies, it was he who first posited that translation is a form of refraction or rewriting and then worked out the implications of that relationship. He demonstrated that there are commonalities to all forms of rewriting, including anthologies, abridgments, histories of literature, works of literary criticism, and editions, as well as specialized versions of texts such as children's versions, film adaptations, cartoon versions, and so on. Like other forms of rewriting, a translation is a metatext, a text about a text.[54] All types of refractions including translations are forms of representing and processing source texts, and hence they all have ideological valences. Lefevere argued that the lines between types of rewritings are blurred and that the characteristics of the various kinds of rewritings reveal a great deal about the nature, function, and social position of all of them. In a sense Lefevere demonstrated that the boundaries between translation and many other categories of metatexts are permeable; his framing of translation in terms of rewriting or refraction, showing the commonalities of all types of rewritings, was instrumental in validating the wide range of translation types discussed in descriptive translation studies and in having them accepted by translation scholars in general.

Together the arguments of Toury and Lefevere imply that it makes little sense to argue about whether a particular text is a translation, version, imitation, adaptation, summary, and so forth. In other words, Toury cut through a great deal of irrelevant argument about whether a certain text is or is not a translation, and Lefevere showed that whether defined as a translation or not, any text representing another text has much to teach about the intercultural category *translation *per se* and that all such texts have a great deal in common. It follows that investigations of the various types of rewritings and refractions are instructive for understanding the nature of translation, and translation in turn provides important perspectives on other kinds of refractions. To some extent this recognition is implicitly operative in the use of the concept translation by anthropologists, ethnographers, cultural studies scholars, and postcolonial theorists as a metaphorical way of speaking about their own subject matter that "rewrites" and represents source cultures. Unfortunately, very few who use the concept translation in this way have actually taken the time to read the literature of translation studies and to understand the problematization of translation that has emerged since World War II. Anthropologists and cultural studies writers often continue to act as if the concept translation were transparent or obvious, remaining roughly at the level of sophistication about translation as the ordinary language definition that we began with.

Toury's contribution to the definitional strand of translation studies is significant in part because he points to the necessity for the cross-cultural concept *translation to be open in nature: any formulation of a definition of *translation

---

[54] Here Lefevere follows the essays of Holmes (1994) and Jakobson (1959), among others.

must make room for all the types of translations that have actually existed and been recognized as translations in human cultures around the world through time and all the types that may come to be recognized in the future. In turn Lefevere begins the work of indicating where some of the boundaries of the concept *translation are to be found – namely in adjacent forms of rewriting or refraction (even though those boundaries are permeable and vary across cultural contexts) – and he begins to explore how those boundaries are to be drawn.

Ultimately, however, in defining the concept *translation in the emerging international discipline of translation studies, Toury's approach is not fully satisfying. We would like to know more about the nature of the concept *translation and to be able to say more about its (open and permeable) boundaries. We would like to be able to survey the range of features associated with translations and correlate them with different translation types. We might also like to know more about the range of translational phenomena within specific contexts, the sorts of things that enter into decisions by various cultures to identify certain phenomena as translations and reject others as not translations, the types of correlations that exist between these identifications and other cultural processes and products, the correlations that exist between such determinations and social conditions, and the like. Work in philosophy, linguistics, and cognitive science helps to push beyond Toury's inclusive definition, suggesting ways to approach some of these outstanding questions.

2.4 Wittgenstein, Concept Formation, and the Definition of Translation as a Cluster Concept

It should be clear by now that when I talk about defining the cross-cultural concept *translation, I am not talking about agreeing on a dictionary definition for the word *translation*, though even that is a great deal more problematic than most people might think.[55] I am also not talking about specifying the necessary and sufficient conditions for translation as either process or product. The question before us is whether it is possible to move beyond Toury's definition and to come to deeper understandings of the nature of *translation as a transcultural concept that can ground the international discipline of translation studies without retreating to a culturally chauvinistic and limited point of departure for theory or to a prescriptive stance for practice, both of which reject the cultural production of other peoples. Similarly we would like to be able to arrive at theoretical formulations that apply to translational phenomena cross-culturally rather than retreating from theory altogether, focusing only on culturally specific observations. I propose to begin by unpacking some of the philosophical implications of the milestones in translation studies set by Toury and Lefevere and by attempting

---

[55] Lakoff (1987:75-76) indicates that different dictionaries stress different paradigms of a complex category, offering salient examples. Cf. Murphy (2002:11).

to extend their insights. We must start by asking several questions. First, if it makes sense to think that there is a complex cross-cultural concept *translation, what sort of concept is it and what are its features? Moreover, what methods can scholars use to deepen knowledge about a cross-cultural concept such as *translation? Finally, if a better understanding of the concept *translation is achieved, what are the implications that follow for research in translation studies?

One way to progress beyond the contributions of Toury and Lefevere – and for that matter Catford – is to supplement their work with the insights related to concept formation by philosophers, linguists, and cognitive scientists. We have seen that concepts and categories are closely interrelated and at times have even been treated as synonymous. Thus, frequently a concept can be identified with a category, and a category with a concept, provided we view both as being cultur-ally constructed. In the case before us, the concept *translation is closely linked to the inclusive category of translations found around the world, as well as the category of activities that produce translations. Accordingly, in what follows I will use the terms *concept* and *category* somewhat interchangeably.

As we have seen, in defining a concept or category, traditionally scholars have attempted to identify the necessary and sufficient conditions that pick out all entities that are members of that category and at the same time exclude all entities that are not members. In the case of the concept *translation, however, this approach leads down a blind alley because of inconsistent and contradictory practices of translation within and across cultures. Fortunately, work in cogni-tive science, linguistics, and philosophy in the past several decades has shown that such traditional approaches to concepts and categories turn out to be much less productive in general than people for centuries had thought, and alternate approaches have been proposed.

The development of new approaches to concepts and categories involves the work of many scholars,[56] but much of the seminal thinking can be traced to Ludwig Wittgenstein. In his *Philosophical Investigations* (1953), Wittgenstein engages in skeptical consideration of the concept language. Using an adapta-tion of the Platonic dialogue, Wittgenstein observes: "You talk about all sorts of language-games, but have nowhere said what the essence of a language-game, and hence of language is: what is common to all these activities, and what makes them into language or parts of language" (1953:section 65). Answering his own objection, he continues, "this is true. Instead of producing something common to all that we call language, I am saying that these phenomena have no one thing in common which makes us use the same word for all, – but that they are *related* to one another in many different ways. And it is because of this relationship, or these relationships, that we call them all 'language'" (1953:section 65, original emphasis).

As the work of Toury and Lefevere suggests and the results of descriptive

---

[56] Lakoff (1987:12-57) offers a convenient summary of important milestones.

translation studies confirm, the answer to the riddle of how to define *translation as a cross-cultural concept is that like language it cannot be simply defined in terms of necessary and sufficient features that hold across cultures or even that hold normally within specific cultures. As in the case of language (itself a concept upon which *translation rests, we must remember) discussed by Wittgenstein, there is "no one thing in common" that entails the use of the world's various words for all the exemplars of the category or concept *translation. Translations do not cohere as a category in virtue of sharing one or even a few characteristics that can be used to identify all translations but only translations. Rather translations are "related to one another in many different ways", to use Wittgenstein's phrase, forming a category determined within cultures and cross-culturally by many partial and overlapping similarities. Within a cultural practice, examples of translation can normally be identified and frequently described relatively easily, but as a category that transcends particular times and places, translations cannot be defined by closed boundaries such as those characteristic of categories defined within the formulations of classical logic.

Open concepts or categories, such as Wittgenstein proposes for language and such as I am proposing for *translation, are common in human culture – kinship relations and number and tool being among the most well known and most notorious of this type of concept. Here I will refer to such open concepts and categories as "cluster concepts" and "cluster categories" (cf. Gleitman et al. 1983:91). One of the cluster concepts that has been most thoroughly discussed is the concept game, treated at length by Wittgenstein in his *Philosophical Investigations* (1953:section 66 ff.). In discussing the concept game, Wittgenstein canvasses the many types of games that people play: board games, card games, dice games, ball games, games based on skill, games based on chance, games involving competition, games involving cooperation, games played in teams, games played alone, and so forth. He observes that in passing from group to group, many common features drop out and others appear; he concludes that a concept such as game is comprised of "a complicated network of similarities overlapping and criss-crossing: sometimes overall similarities, sometimes similarities of detail. . . . I can think of no better expression to characterize these similarities than 'family resemblances'" (section 66-67). He concludes that games form a family. Wittgenstein also uses the metaphor of a thread to characterize such concepts: "we extend our concept . . . as in spinning a thread we twist fibre on fibre. And the strength of the thread does not reside in the fact that some one fibre runs through its whole length, but in the overlapping of many fibres" (1953:section 67).

In his discussion of game, Wittgenstein enjoins, "Don't say: 'There *must* be something common, or they would not be called "games"'" – but *look and see* whether there is anything common to all. – For if you look at them you will not see something that is common to *all*, but similarities, relationships, and a whole series of them at that. To repeat: don't think, but look!" (1953:section 66, original emphasis). Here Wittgenstein points to the fact that membership in a cluster category is not a matter of logic but rather a function of *practice* and *usage*. Membership is an empirical question, not one based on theoretical criteria; this is why he says "don't think, but look!". Cluster categories such as language or game or *translation differ from many other types of categories because of their essentially pragmatic quality: they are deeply connected to cultural practice and hence must be understood through observation and description. Although logically it might be hard to indicate how to distinguish a translation from, say, "cluster bombs or potato peels",[57] in actual *practice* the terms for the concept *translation in the world's languages are not applied to such objects. A given speech community has surprisingly little trouble deciding what a translation is and in distinguishing a translation from a potato peel or a cluster bomb – or even for that matter an adjacent form of textual refraction – based on its communal practices. If a translation scholar *looks* at the objects identified as translations by people in any given culture, a researcher will also have relatively few difficulties distinguishing translations from potato peels.

Wittgenstein explicitly considers this problem of identifying the members of a cluster category with reference to game:

> How should we explain to someone what a game is? I imagine that we should describe *games* to him, and we might add: "This *and similar things* are called 'games'". (1953:section 69, original emphasis)

The term *describe* is key here. It suggests the importance of *a posteriori* observation and characterization rather than *a priori* stipulation or definition in understanding a cluster concept. It also follows that the ability to recognize and describe any given member of a cluster category such as *translation will turn on the ability to understand the culture being observed.

There is, thus, an even more fundamental requirement than definition for understanding a cluster concept implied in Wittgenstein's emphasis on telling the questioner to look for "similar things". Recognition of members of a cluster category requires the ability to perceive and comprehend similarity, which is at the heart of perception of concepts and categories in general – a basic human capability not yet fully understood – and the ability to perceive the variety of criteria

---

[57] In a personal communication Theo Hermans whimsically offered these examples as part of an objection to my argument. Hermans has actually taken positions on the nature of the concept *translation that are congruent with the argument I am making here. He observes, "the term 'translation' has no fixed, inherent, immanent meaning" and he sees translation as a self-reproducing practice in which change occurs through autopoiesis (1999:144). Moreover, he notes that "the most central and powerful tenet of descriptive translation studies has been that translation cannot be defined a priori, once and for all" (1999:158-59). He sees translation "as a label attached to a number of practices"; accordingly, "it is important . . . to map out what the term covers and what other terms are conceptually near" (1999:155). See also Hermans (1996:42-48).

that can be used to judge similarity in the objects under consideration.[58] In fact Murphy (2002:481) indicates that one could start with theories of similarity and use them to motivate various theories of concepts. The implication here is that if members of the cluster concept *translation are related by family resemblances, then similarity in translation procedures and products will also be characterized by family resemblances.[59] Investigation of types of similarity in translation will in turn illuminate the concept *translation as a whole. Wittgenstein argues explicitly that "giving examples is not an *indirect* means of explaining" a cluster concept such as game "in default of a better"; it *is* the way that such concepts are learned and communicated, setting a framework for how such examples are to be employed as well (1953:section 71, original emphasis). Thus, examining examples of a cluster concept like *translation and exploring their similarities and differences lead to understanding the concept itself.

Wittgenstein acknowledges that a concept such as game is not precise and is not known "exactly", "but this is not ignorance", he writes, for "we do not know the boundaries because none have been drawn" (1953:section 69). He suggests that a concept such as game – or *translation – is a concept "with blurred edges" and might even be called "a blurred concept" (section 71). Although Wittgenstein argues that for a special purpose it is possible to draw a boundary for such a concept, a boundary is not required to make the concept usable (section 69). In fact it may not be an advantage to replace an indistinct or blurred concept with a sharp one, because, as Wittgenstein notes, an indistinct concept is often "exactly what we need": it may sometimes be better just to be told to stand "over there", for instance, rather than to be given more precise coordinates (section 71). He discusses at length how we operate in many circumstances with concepts with blurred edges, not to mention language that is vague or imprecise in various ways. Indeed Wittgenstein points out at greater length than I can possibly do here how such language serves human beings very well in ordinary life.

I have unpacked Wittgenstein's comments about cluster concepts in some detail partly because he is so succinct and so good at expressing in ordinary language the characteristics of cluster concepts and at answering the objections that many people make to this form of categorization. More importantly, his work is not yet fully superseded. Unlike most scholars working on concepts and categories, Wittgenstein considers issues relevant to complex social concepts of the type rarely studied by cognitive scientists.[60] Indeed, the concepts and categories

---

[58] Similarity is currently the subject of intense research in cognitive science; for comprehensive collections of papers, see Vosniadou and Ortony (1989), Cacciari (1995), and Gentner et al. (2001). The question of similarity and translation was taken up at a groundbreaking conference at the American Bible Society in New York City in June 2001, which issued in the collection of papers in Arduini and Hodgson (2004). See also Chesterman (1996), Halverson (1997), Tymoczko (2004), and sources cited.

[59] See below 4.2 for additional consideration of this point.

[60] Lakoff (1987) is another writer who discusses such complex social concepts.

Wittgenstein uses as examples (language, game, number) are some of the most complex and important categories for human life and human cultures around the world. Moreover, the power of some of his insights – for example, the *a posteriori* nature of cluster concepts and their connection with cultural practice – has not been sufficiently appreciated or understood by cognitive scientists and other critics, including translation scholars who have attempted to use Wittgenstein.[61] To date cognitive scientists have not yet come to terms with Wittgenstein's insights about complex social and cultural concepts; instead he has been used and even misused in a relatively shallow manner.

Wittgenstein's insights are by no means exhausted in what has been said thus far; indeed there is a great deal more relevant to translation studies that could be derived from his formulations. For example, Wittgenstein asks, "What does it mean to know what a game is? What does it mean, to know it and not be able to say it?" (1953:section 1). Much the same can be asked about *translation. Knowledge of a cluster concept is a puzzling philosophical matter. Moreover, his emphasis on the blurred nature of cluster concepts and their blurred edges – as well as the obvious conclusion that it is not possible to give fixed criteria for category membership in cluster categories – indicates that such concepts are not fully amenable to explanation with classical logic. Instead it appears that they might be more productively approached through so-called fuzzy logic, a field developed since Wittgenstein's time. If this is the case, then a thoroughgoing application of fuzzy logic to *translation might be very instructive and might have much to offer the discipline of translation studies. Such an investigation is, however, beyond the scope of this book.[62]

Wittgenstein's arguments suggest that cluster concepts such as language or *translation also have similarities to the types of concepts that cognitive scientists call *ad hoc* or goal-derived concepts and categories. Such concepts are not based on fixed features but instead on holistically structured activities and on goal structures that are a function of cognitive models (Murphy 2002:62-63; Lakoff 1987:21, 45-46). Such concepts and categories include, for example, things one will need to pack for a camping trip, activities that make good entertainment on the weekend, or good foods to eat on a diet. Such *ad hoc* or goal-derived concepts are not based on common features shared by the members of the category. Moreover, they cannot be derived from observing examples and noting the features that occur most frequently (Murphy 2002:63), and they cannot be predicted by logical argument. They can only be described on the basis of observed practices that differ

---

[61] See the discussion in 2.5 below of the misunderstanding of Wittgenstein's concept of family resemblances in cognitive science.

[62] Cronin (2003:115) also maintains that fuzzy logic will be important in understanding translation and machine translation. Lakoff (1987:13-30) discusses these questions at greater length, noting that some categories have membership gradience, degrees of membership, and no clear boundaries. Lakoff (1987:30) observes as well that fuzzy set conditions vary from culture to culture.

from person to person, situation to situation, culture to culture. In addition, they are related to larger structures of cultural knowledge and practice (cf. Murphy 2002:63). Not surprisingly translation has many of these features in any given cultural context, because the goal of translation as a form of cross-cultural communication can involve adventitious, improvisational, and *ad hoc* strategies.

Exploration of cluster concepts – including *translation – takes us deep into the realms that Pierre Bourdieu (1977) has discussed related to cultural practice and cultural knowledge. Such concepts are imbricated in Bourdieu's notion of the habitus of a culture, and they depend on the nexus of ideas, beliefs, cognitive structures, knowledge, and practice.[63] Clearly, therefore, such concepts and categories will differ cross-culturally. As Bourdieu has argued, moreover, there is a problem defining or explaining cultural practices from the perspectives of both internal members of a culture and external observers. In the case of translation, it follows not only that there may be problems in understanding or explaining the nature of translation practices from within a cultural domain but also that there is likely to be a metaproblem in defining the culture's concept of translation, even when there may be relatively little problem engaging in the practice of translation or in identifying examples of translations in any particular context. These difficulties are increased geometrically when one attempts to define a concept such as *translation cross-culturally. Thus, translation studies requires recursive forms of self-reflexivity to define and understand its object of study.

It was in part through the exploration of concepts such as language and game that Wittgenstein was led to consider the limitations of the role of logic in human culture, human language, and human conceptual formations. Such concepts as language and game contribute to informing Wittgenstein's powerful repudiation of positivism and his interpretations and defense of "ordinary language", which serves the needs of pragmatic communication and grows out of specific cultural praxis. In the context of Wittgenstein's arguments about concepts such as game, we might see Toury's definition of *translation in a new light. Toury can be viewed as arguing for the importance of attending to ordinary language in translation studies, as well as giving an implicit defense of ordinary language in translation studies projected across time, space, cultures, and languages. In such a framework, the ordinary language of all cultures not just Western ones holds authority for defining *translation theory and practice. In this sense, then, local terms for *translation around the world are important to attend to and to explore.

We should note that Toury's thinking about *translation as an open and *a posteriori* category was shaped by the work of Wittgenstein, whom Toury cites (1980:17-18). Although openness (and ambiguity) may be a problem for some

---

[63] Bourdieu defines the *habitus* as "a system of lasting, transposable dispositions which, integrating past experiences, functions at every moment as a *matrix of perceptions, appreciations, and actions* and makes possible the achievement of infinitely diversified tasks" (1977:82-83, original emphasis). Chapter 6 contains a more extensive discussion of the implications of Bourdieu's thought for translation studies.

scholars who like controlled intellectual domains, including bounded or closed definitions, it is the openness of the concept *translation and its lack of precise boundaries that have allowed translation practice to adapt to diverse cultural conditions, to diverse social functions, and to changing technologies as well – including the transition from orality to literacy and the contemporary technological requirements of translating for global capitalism and the modern media. Having flexible or blurred boundaries for a social concept can be an advantage; it facilitates change and adaptation and allows for innovation as the need arises.[64] It is, moreover, the blurred nature of *translation cross-culturally rather than its sameness or precision across cultures that makes translation such a fascinating concept to study in its infinite variety and its complicated criss-crossing relationships to language, text, culture, and history. I can only agree with Peter Fawcett (1997:73-74) who observes that it is a mystery "why theorists are so determined to defuzz the discipline" of translation studies.

Exploration of the varied relationships between the blurred cross-cultural concept *translation on the one hand and language, text, and culture on the other demands sophisticated analysis of historical and cultural context, analysis undertaken with acuity, specificity, and precision. Translations must be identified and analyzed with respect to local criteria, not with respect to cultural criteria imposed by an external observer or another (dominant) culture. Wittgenstein's analysis of cluster concepts underscores the importance of descriptive studies of translation in unraveling theoretical issues within the field of translation studies, sustaining the points discussed in the previous chapter. It is the descriptive branch of translation studies that is most alert to the characteristics of actual translational phenomena that can be seen ("look!") and observed *a posteriori*. Here Wittgenstein also implicitly offers a warning against the presumption of *a priori* scholarly judgments based on logical or prescriptive criteria. Wittgenstein's arguments about blurred concepts illuminate facets of the philosophical and conceptual strength of the positions of Toury and Lefevere, indicating the power of their views for understanding *translation transculturally. Wittgenstein's work also suggests reasons for the directions that have been taken and that are currently being taken by the emerging international discipline of translation studies.

2.5 Limitations of Viewing Translation as a Prototype Category

Wittgenstein's arguments about cluster concepts are related to many of the most powerful findings about concepts in the last half century. They are germane to the development of prototype theory, one of the foremost theoretical approaches to concepts in cognitive science. Prototype theory was pioneered by Eleanor Rosch,

---

[64] Cf. Wittgenstein (1953:section 83). Examples of the current need for translation to adapt to technologies are found in the comments of Gentzler in "Forum" (2001:1.163-64) and Cronin (2003).

who appropriated Wittgenstein's term "family resemblances" to describe how concepts cohere in cognitive perceptions.[65]

Classical views of concepts and categories stress necessary and sufficient conditions for category membership, as we have seen. In such a view all category members have equal status, because the features defining category membership pertain equally to all members; thus no member of a category can have special status or be a more central exemplar than any other member of the category. The experiments of Rosch and her associates provided the first full-scale empirical challenge to these classical views of concepts and categories. Rosch's research demonstrated that contrary to the predictions of classical theories, certain features of a given category are often seen as more central than others and, moreover, some category members are seen as more typical and more central to their category than other members. As a result Rosch concluded that categories must be understood as having an internal, asymmetrical structure in which some members constitute better examples of the category than other members. Rosch's experiments dealt with a number of different category types including colors, animals (including the category bird), and material objects (including the category chair).

So-called prototype effects are widespread and impact upon learning, memory, and judgment of similarity pertaining to category members. Experiments have shown that subjects view certain members of categories as more representative than other members. Thus, North American subjects see robins as more representative of the category bird than chickens or penguins. Similarly, wooden kitchen chairs are seen as more representative of the category chair than rocking chairs or stuffed armchairs. Such prototypical members serve as cognitive reference points, and their features are more likely to be generalized to other members of the category than vice versa. In some experiments prototypical members of categories have also been shown to be easier to learn and to remember.

Prototype theory continues to be one of the leading approaches to concepts and categories in cognitive science, despite the fact that it has been subject to a variety of criticisms and shown to be insufficient to explain many phenomena pertaining to concepts and categories.[66] Other principal approaches include exemplar theories of concepts (in which concept formation is based on actual exemplars encountered by people) and knowledge approaches to concepts (in which concept formation is seen as inextricable from broader frames of cultural

---

[65] My discussion of prototype theory follows Lakoff (1987) and Murphy (2002); Murphy presents a contemporary view of prototype theory as it has been developed since the ground-breaking work of Rosch. Both Murphy and Lakoff include comprehensive bibliographies of Rosch's work, and Lakoff (1987:39-57) gives a good summary of the salient stages of her work. An earlier version of the argument in this section as it relates to corpus translation studies appears in Tymoczko (1998).

[66] Systematic summary criticisms of prototype theory in regard to the principal topics of concept research are given in Murphy (2002). See also criticisms in Vosniadou and Ortony (1989).

knowledge). A full discussion of all these approaches to concepts is beyond the scope of this study, but it should be noted that at present no one of the leading theories of concepts can explain all the experimental data pertaining to concepts and categories. Thus, all the principal theories continue to play a role in the field. Gregory Murphy sums up his comprehensive overview of concept research by concluding that any emergent view of concepts will have to incorporate aspects of all the current theories (2002:477-98).

Before proceeding with a discussion of prototype theory, let me offer a cautionary note. In appropriating the term "family resemblances" from Wittgenstein, cognitive scientists have misunderstood and in certain ways underestimated the power of Wittgenstein's perceptions. In prototype theory categorization is probabilistic; concepts are represented by descriptions of their common components, and category membership is based on a certain number of features, weighted by importance (Murphy 2002:235). Although no particular feature or set of features is defining for category membership in prototype theory, family resemblances are seen as features that are usually, though not always, found in category members, and the theory considers that some features are more important than others (Murphy 2002:42, 44). Prototype theory says that there are few features that all members of a category have in common, but the representation of a concept involves a general listing of features that most or many of the members have; such a list is a description of the category as a whole, not of particular members (Murphy 2002:73).[67]

These are precisely the sorts of views that Wittgenstein contested. Wittgenstein perceived that certain concepts are decentered. Rather than sharing (aspects of) a defined pool of common traits, members of concepts (such as language) cluster in groups. Each group has features overlapping with other groups, but there is no common core of features delineated as family resemblances that could be used to form a summary representation of the concepts Wittgenstein discusses, no "one fibre" as he puts it or even a group of common fibres. To the contrary, he indicates that as one passes from group to group of games, "one can see how similarities crop up and disappear" (1953:section 66). Wittgenstein offers a model of concepts in which such groupings or clusters of members (as are found with respect to the concept game) have relatively equal weight. Thus, in Wittgenstein's perception about game or language, no prototype could be found for the category as a whole. Divergent views of favorite or central instances of the concept game could be held by individuals, families, certain groups of sports enthusiasts, whole cultures, and so forth, but in his model the clusters are so disparate that the notion of a common core or a general pool of traits or a summary representation

---

[67] Murphy (2002:42) indicates that a prototype is not the "best example" but rather "a summary representation that is a description of the category as a whole, rather than . . . a single ideal member". At other times, however, family resemblances are equated with average properties of the category members or features that occur most (cf. Murphy 2002:63).

becomes meaningless. It is, of course, an empirical matter as to whether this is the case, but it is telling that in promoting their views prototype theorists have not used the categories or types of categories that Wittgenstein discussed. The differences between Wittgenstein's notion of family resemblances and the notion of family resemblances used in prototype theory must be carefully distinguished, particularly in approaching a complex social concept such as language or game or the international concept *translation.[68]

Not surprisingly, given the definitional impulse in translation studies and the difficulty of defining the concept *translation, some translation studies scholars have become interested in cognitive science approaches to categories and concepts. Prototype theory in particular has been embraced by a number of scholars with interests in corpus translation studies, research methods in translation, and translation theory. Mary Snell-Hornby (1988) and Sandra Halverson (1999a, 1999b) have argued most forcefully for the view of translation as a prototype category, exploring the implications of prototype theory for understanding the structure of the concept translation and for the theory of translation.[69] My proposal that the cross-cultural concept *translation is a cluster concept, therefore, contravenes current work in translation studies that utilizes prototype theory as a way to think about the concept translation. In what follows I suggest some reasons why prototype theories of concepts and categories cannot solve the dilemmas and difficulties posed by the conceptualization of a complex social concept like *translation, particularly when one wants to look at such a concept from transnational, transcultural, and translinguistic perspectives. In fact I suggest that the questions about categories and concepts that translation studies scholars must grapple with in order to understand *translation as a cross-cultural concept have not yet been dealt with in any of the major theories about concepts developed in cognitive science thus far.

As indicated above, in prototype research it has been found that for many concepts there are exemplars considered to be better representatives or more typical members of the concept. A person is usually more inclined to generalize about an entire category on the basis of typical or more representative exemplars than on the basis of atypical or less representative ones, using the prototype itself as a point of reference for the entire category. Such central exemplars are not stipulated by scholars; they are determined on the basis of empirical research that indicates what category members can be correlated with prototype effects. (Remember that Wittgenstein tells us to look!)

But what can be used as a prototype of the cross-cultural concept *translation?

---

[68] Note that Lakoff (1987:42) also blurs the distinctions regarding family resemblances as the idea was developed by Wittgenstein and as it has been appropriated by prototype theorists.

[69] Halverson (1999a) also serves as a valuable introduction to cognitive science in general and category research in particular. See also Laviosa (1998) and Chesterman (1998) for other approaches to the application of prototype theory to translation studies, as well as sources cited in all these studies.

Indeed, what exemplars of translations can even be used to test prototype configurations empirically? In adapting the framework of prototype theory to translation
studies, scholars cannot simply decide in an arbitrary way, on the basis of opinion
or their own cultural contexts, what the central exemplar(s) of the field should be.
At the very least research would have to be undertaken to determine the answer to
the question of representative examples of translation. Halverson has done such
research with European subjects and reports prototype effects (see 1999a), but
to understand the concept of *translation in a fully cross-cultural context, such
research is clearly not sufficient. First, in order to be significant, such research
would have to be conducted on at least two levels, because cognitive scientists
have shown that concepts within any given domain take different forms depending on whether subjects are experts or ordinary members of society.[70] Thus, to
determine prototype effects of the cross-cultural concept *translation, it would
not be adequate to canvass translation studies scholars or translators or even
translation students alone. One would also have to poll a broad and representative
sample of the social spectrum, including, for example, people who are highly
literate and people who read infrequently, people who know many languages and
people whose principal exposure to translation is community interpreting. One
might even have to identify different groupings of "experts" in different areas:
sophisticated readers, multilingual persons, legal scholars in certain situations,
and so forth, as well as translators and translation scholars. The problems here
are obvious, and Murphy cautions that the more subjects know about a domain,
"the less our experiments apply to them" (2002:482).

Even if such research were undertaken, however, the resulting prototype
would merely serve as an index for the cultural group that served as the basis
of research (say, U.S. or European residents in the early twenty-first century).
In principle, to determine the prototype(s) or representative example(s) of the
international concept *translation, such research would have to be undertaken
in many diverse countries and culture groups. Finally, supposing such research
were in any way feasible, it would still not generate one or more prototypes that
could be useful for generalizing about translation as a whole and for constructing a general theory of translation, because the theory of translation must serve
as a framework for the cultural production of the past as well as of the present
and the future. Obviously there is no way to conduct empirical research that will
generate secure data for prototypes of *translation in different cultures in the
past, let alone the future.

To understand these points it may help to have a concrete example from
a domain that all readers are familiar with, namely the nature of cooking and
food as two concepts partially interrelated as process and product. If one were
to attempt to define a prototype of cooking, research would probably show that

---

[70] The differences between concept usage by experts and by ordinary members of a culture
are discussed by Lakoff (1987:32-38) and Murphy (2002:211, 229-33).

in Europe, the United States, and Canada, the prototype would involve cooking on a (gas or electric) stove, using a covered metal pot. Other types of cooking would probably emerge as less typical exemplars (frying, baking, and so forth). But it is clear that this prototype cannot serve for all the cultures of the world, for there are other local prototypes of cooking that involve different heat sources (open fires, coal braziers, ovens) and different implements as well (roasting spits, woks, griddles, cauldrons). When history is factored in, even more prototypes for cooking must be supposed for other eras and cultures, including cooking pits filled with water and warmed by heated stones and the direct use of embers. Clearly the prototype of a covered metal pot on an electric or gas stove has few features in common with the earliest forms of cooking, which go back at least 200,000 years.

Similar problems arise in attempting to establish a prototype for food. In Europe, the United States, Canada, and elsewhere, research might show that the prototype of the main meal of the day is shared on a general level: a protein serving, some starch, and some vegetables. But that prototype would immediately have to be differentiated if one were to undertake research about prototypes of the meal in specific countries. Thus, the prototypical protein (and rankings of the favored proteins) would vary: perhaps beef steak in the U.S., lamb in Greece, fish in some Scandinavian nations, pork cutlets in Germany or Austria, and so forth. The starch would also vary, perhaps pasta being favored in Italy, potatoes in Germany and the U.S. Certainly the specific vegetables and the amount of vegetables would differ radically from culture to culture. Moreover, outside these relatively homogeneous Western cultures, prototypes of the main meal would diverge even more radically, with many cultures not even having a main meal shared by a family grouping.

The problems of trying to establish prototypes for *translation suitable as the basis of research and theorizing in translation studies illustrate the difficulty of doing research on and constructing theories about social concepts in general that extend across temporal, spatial, linguistic, and cultural boundaries. This is part of the reason that such concepts have not yet been extensively researched by cognitive scientists. Examples of *translation (or food, cooking, language, game, and so forth) as manifest in cross-cultural contexts are indicative of the difficulty of trying to extend the results of research in cognitive science based on concepts that are relatively simple (such as the concepts chair or bird, or concepts related to abstract dot patterns) to complex social categories pertaining to cultural production across time and space.[71] Thus, in thinking about how to approach the cross-cultural concept *translation, translation scholars are not only approaching a difficult problem specific to the field of translation studies, they are breaking

---

[71] There are even issues pertaining to conceptualizing and categorizing natural species that have not been adequately addressed by cognitive scientists, as Lakoff (1987:31-37, 118-21, 185-95) rightly argues.

new ground that will shed light on many other concepts of central interest to the humanities and social sciences.

With respect to most social and cultural concepts, it is apparent that one culture's prototype is seldom that of another. Moreover, simplifying a cross-cultural social concept by representing it with a single prototype (derived from one culture at one point in time) can result in a thin understanding of the concept itself: the prototype gives no information about the variability of the category in question or the richness of the concept (Murphy 2002:42). Indeed Lakoff (1987:82) cautions that prototypes may hide most of the richness of cognitive models of categories. This is a particular peril to avoid in a field like translation studies that valorizes diversity and promotes international exchange of ideas, values, material culture, and so forth.

The points we are exploring can even be illustrated with respect to the relatively simple concept chair, a concept that has frequently been used as an epitome of a concept that shows prototype effects. Thus, the current prototype of chair in Western culture (a wooden chair with four legs and a straight back, rectilinear, of simple design, typical of a "kitchen chair" or a freestanding chair in a school) would have been very unusual and eccentric in Western countries during the Renaissance or even in the seventeenth century, when the prototype of chair was probably a relatively low three-legged (carved) wooden object (with a relatively small back), suitable for the irregular dirt and stone floors of the period, similar to those seen in some old castles or museums.

In general prototypes of human social and cultural concepts are culture specific. A particular prototype is normally central to conceptual and categorical thinking only with reference to a particular cultural setting at a particular time. Such concepts can even have more than one prototype in a complex differentiated society, varying, for instance, by gender, class, region, or level of expertise. Thus, the use of the prototype of one segment of one culture at one point of time as the basis for theorizing about a cross-cultural concept like game or *translation always risks implicit assertion and imposition of cultural dominance or hegemony. This is an especially unfortunate way to approach translation studies and the concept *translation which predicate cross-cultural communication and interchange.

Still another way of indicating the difficulties of identifying a single prototype for the concept *translation is to say that conditions of translation have been so variable through human history that it is no easier to delineate a prototype for the concept than it is to delineate necessary and sufficient conditions that can identify all translations and only translations. It seems very unlikely that a single prototype could serve for both oral translations of stories in preliterate cultures and contemporary professional translation of written commercial documents, just as there are no necessary and sufficient conditions that identify translations (but only translations) in both of these cultural contexts.

Viewing translation as a prototype concept is sometimes satisfactory as a first-order approximation to the understanding and practice of translation at a single time and place, in a single context, where the prototype will correspond roughly to the dominant notion of translation in that specific context. In fact this is essentially the approach of Halverson's (1999a) research and arguments. Such an approximation necessarily assumes a synchronic and rather static way of modeling the translation system. Even in such restricted contexts, researchers must be careful to make allowance for the divergence of views of ordinary subjects and experts (such as translators or translation scholars) in making determinations about the nature of the prototype. In addition, an attempt to delineate a prototype of translation can only be feasible for a cultural context where there is a relatively uniform translation practice and a relatively homogeneous social structure. Homogeneity notwithstanding, there may still be a need to account for counterpractices in such a situation.[72] A prototype approach may not even be pertinent where there is a bifurcated practice of translation, such as those discussed above in section 2.1 with respect to the European Middle Ages or Ireland at the turn of the twentieth century. In cases like these researchers will need to delineate a minimum of *two* prototypes consonant with a bimodal statistical distribution of translation products. In view of the fact that many cultures in the last two thousand years have had a literate culture coexisting with oral culture, a bimodal distribution is perhaps more common than one might at first suppose.

Thus, approaching translation from the perspective of prototype theory is not particularly advantageous in advancing theoretical analyses of the cross-cultural concept *translation, where translation processes and products must be considered in the broadest and most general sense possible rather than in ways that are culturally specific and culturally restricted. Indeed, discussing *translation as a prototype concept is likely to muddy the waters in any broad theoretical context, requiring, for example, the exclusion of empirical data from the past or from situations that are not Eurocentric. It does not seem to be an approach that can respond to the widely divergent image-schemas of translation suggested by the words used for translation around the world, such as those discussed above in section 2.2. A prototype approach to translation will risk effacing philosophical and cognitive implications of the data as well as the richness of the concept.

By contrast, looking at the cross-cultural concept *translation as a cluster concept allows for the inclusion of widely varied types of translation processes and products, even specific translations that are divergent or eccentric with respect to properties common to most groups of translations. We can illustrate this point by returning to the concept game discussed by Wittgenstein. Some games are competitive (chess) and some are not (ring-around-the-rosy). Some

---

[72] Gentzler (1996), for example, discusses the counterpractices in the (relatively uniform) U.S. translation system related to one of the most significant cultural crises in U.S. history in the twentieth century, namely the repression of the left associated with the McCarthy hearings. This cultural crisis was particularly disruptive of the arts and impacted directly on writers in particular.

games are team sports (soccer) and others are not (solitaire). Some games are entertaining (bridge) and others are maddening (social one-upsmanship). Some games are fun and others are exquisite forms of torture. And so forth. Because of these vast differences, it is impossible to find a prototype of game that would hold cross-culturally; the concept might even vary widely with respect to smaller subgroups, say families. Approaching *translation as a cluster concept allows for similar inclusion within translation theory of translations that are very close to the source text as well as those that are very free, translations that operate at the rank of the word and others that operate at the rank of the entire text, and so on. Moreover, viewing *translation as a cluster concept permits translations of all cultures and all times to be worthy of equal consideration in the construction of translation theory, as opposed to positing a cross-cultural concept of *translation as a prototype concept with an asymmetrical and hierarchical structure in which some cultures' concepts of translation are marginalized. Thinking of *translation as a cluster concept allows for self-definition of translation as a central form of cultural practice in each society, and it accommodates the incommensurability of terms for *translation in the world's languages.[73] The result is a view of translation that is congruent with Toury's definition, facilitating a decentered and truly international approach to translation studies as a field that is open to all players in the world.

     Because of the diverse nature of translation, it is more productive for scholars to talk about norms of translation rather than attempt to identify prototypes of translation. The idea of a dominant norm for a particular context and practice of translation would seem to offer the principal advantages of prototype discourses without the theoretical problems incurred by using prototype theory. This productive direction has been taken by many scholars, including Toury (1980, 1995), Hermans (1991, 1993, 1996, 1999:72-101), Andrew Chesterman (1997:51-98), and the scholars whose work is included in *Translation and Norms* (1999), edited by Christina Schäffner. Exploration of norms fits well with the nature of *translation as a cross-cultural cluster concept. As an approach to *translation, norms also leave room for the agency of individual translators who can decide to improvise, to innovate, to depart from norms, or even to flout them.[74]

     The interest in norms may seem simplistic to some, but in fact it distills a central axis of the postpositivist development in translation theory in the past three decades, as the dates of the publications cited indicate. The interest in norms is intertwined with and responds to the problematic of defining translation. A sublated sense of this relationship may have in fact contributed to the shift in translation studies toward a focus on norms and an exploration of the connection

---

[73] Seeing *translation as a cluster concept also helps to circumvent some of the ethnocentric double binds that Hermans (2006:44-48) outlines.

[74] Crisafulli (2002:30-37) argues that descriptive scholars must remember the "individual factor", namely, that individual translators can choose to depart from norms or flout them; thus there must be a balance between theoretical attention to both collectives and individuals.

between norms and contexts. The concept of norms in relationship to translation is deceptively simple, in part because it paradoxically signals a movement away from prescriptive stances in both descriptive analyses and pedagogical practice even as it describes the existence and operation of (prescriptive) standards, il-luminating their culture-bound nature.

The danger of effacing the role of norms in explorations of the concept *translation – as can occur in all prototype approaches – is that translation theory risks becoming essentialist. Bourdieu argues:

> "Essentialist thought" is at work in every social universe and especially in
> the field of cultural production – the religious, scientific and legal fields,
> etc. – where games in which the universal is at stake are being played
> out. But in that case it is quite evident that "essences" are norms. That is
> precisely what Austin was recalling when he analysed the implications of
> the adjective "real" in expressions such as a "real" man, "real" courage
> or . . . a "real" artist or a "real" masterpiece. In all of these examples, the
> word "real" implicitly contrasts the case under consideration to all other
> cases in the same category, to which other speakers assign, although
> unduly so (that is, in a manner not "really" justified) this same predicate,
> a predicate which, like all claims to universality, is symbolically very
> powerful. (Bourdieu 1993:263)

This essentialist move is familiar in scholarship about translation and some formulations of translation theory, where some scholars have found it so easy to use the term *real* in the sense Bourdieu discusses, giving themselves permission to dismiss particular texts (especially those from other times and other cultures) as not being "real" translations.

Lakoff argues that people tend to reason on the basis of typical examples (1987:41-42, 86-87) and that in general people find it difficult to hold in mind simultaneously more than one model for a phenomenon (118-21). He argues that the idea that there is a "real" sort of entity seems to require a choice among models in situations where available models diverge and there is a strong pull to view one as most important (1987:75). Although models can provide cognitive reference points, they are context dependent (Lakoff 1987:89), a factor that is easily effaced even though it should not be forgotten. Here it is worth noting Halverson's (1999a:21-22) view that internalized models of translation, expec-tancy norms, and correctness notions actually constitute an implicit concept of translation. Clearly, in theorizing a subject such as translation within a truly inter-national framework, scholars cannot forget that norms and typical translations may be very different in diverse social contexts and diverse cultures; essentialism is antithetical to good thinking about the subject. Moreover, as Lakoff observes, functioning scholars in their everyday work must be able to shift from one con-ceptualization to another (1987:305). Translation scholars in particular must be able to shift among different conceptualizations of the cross-cultural concept *translation as it is expressed in varied translation processes and products through time and space. Seeing *translation as a cluster concept where different types of translation processes and products are governed by different norms facilitates such mental flexibility.

The focus on norms is also more easily reconciled than are prototypes with the necessity of recognizing that translation is an open category, not only histori-cally and cross-culturally, but even at a given locus in the present. However strong a culture's norms, a translator is not logically (or even practically in most cases) utterly precluded from choosing to translate in any of the many ways already attested in the historical record or even from inventing new strategies of transla-tion. Particularly at present, in an age of migrations and diasporas, there is a high potential for the divergent international norms for translation to interpenetrate, with the result that the actual products of translation in any particular context have the possibility of presenting a very broad field. This is especially the case with respect to minority and minoritized languages and literatures.[75] The resulting field of study is much more easily theorized in terms of norms than discourses pertaining to prototypes.

2.6 Conceptual Knowledge, Ethnocentrism, and Ethics

Using their understanding of linguistic and cultural difference, translation stud-ies scholars have begun to define the problematic of intercultural concepts in various domains, interrogating the concepts of scholarship itself. Working in this vein Alexandra Lianeri (2006) has shown that the academic concept of history has been constructed on Western bases rather than in ways that would include other conceptualizations of the memorialization, organization, (re)construction, and analysis of the past. She indicates that the development of the concept his-tory used as the foundation of the international discipline of history is inscribed within specific discourses of identity and affiliation that make it a very Western concept. She raises questions about the inherent ideological aspects of history as an academic discipline and the possibility of investigating and valorizing the past of all cultures within its framework. Following Fredric Jameson, she argues that when the implicit ethnocentrism of such contemporary academic concepts is not understood, scholars merely presuppose what is to be demonstrated (2006:76).

As translation studies becomes an increasingly internationalized discipline, particularly a discipline that espouses the value of difference, it becomes essential to turn a self-reflexive eye on the academic terminology utilized in translation studies and to recognize the ideological implications inherent in the construction of the field to date. This is especially the case when a single language – English – is becoming dominant as a link language within the discipline. In the introduction

---

[75] Cf. Venuti (1998b), Branchadell and West (2005), and Cronin (2003, 2006).

to *An Anthology of Chinese Discourse on Translation* (2006a, cf. 2006b), Martha Cheung illustrates such an approach, interrogating the cultural and ideological bases of English words such as *philosophy*, *science*, *theory*, *religion*, and *history*. She shows that they cannot be used in any simple, transparent, or unproblematized manner with reference to the history and practice of translation in the Chinese culture area without distorting the materials of study and imposing a hegemonic grid on the subject matter.

   I have argued in this chapter that the concept at the heart of translation studies – the cross-cultural and cross-temporal concept *translation – falls into this domain, requiring conceptual and ideological rethinking. It is very easy for those of us who are translation scholars or translators to slip into thinking that we understand translation in general, based on our own personal experiences and our cultural presuppositions about the subject. The difficulties discussed above epitomize the problems of defining *translation at present, but at the same time they point to the necessity of continually problematizing any definition of *translation as it takes shape. The recursive problems in approaching a definition of *translation illustrate the difficulties of exploring social concepts in general, especially social concepts that have transcultural and diachronic extensions, that turn on meanings in many languages, and that serve as the focus of academic disciplines. Thus, the attempt to understand and conceptualize *translation stands with other self-reflexive inquiries in the field of translation studies at the cutting edge of both concept research and academic self-definition.

   In the last chapter I traced the steady growth of translation studies as more and more features of translation were investigated, an enlargement associated with what I have called the definitional impulse in the field. The counterpart to this growth is the expansion of the cross-cultural concept *translation itself, signaled in Toury's definition of a translation as "any target language text which is presented or regarded as such within the target system itself, on whatever grounds" (Toury 1982:27; cf. 1980:14, 37, 43-45). Toury's definition is consistent with an understanding of translation as a cluster concept. In demonstrating an increasing number of factors that must be considered in translating, as well as in describing and assessing a broader range of translations and their ideological import, translation studies has steadily enlarged its knowledge of the types of choices translators make. Each realm of choice that a translator exercises can also be thought of as indicating a type of relationship that translations can have with their source texts, thus signaling one feature among the many family re-semblances that constitute the cross-linguistic, cross-cultural, and cross-temporal cluster concept *translation. Awareness and acknowledgment of the variety and scope of these family resemblances will help translation studies consolidate as an international field by providing a framework for the continued growth of the field and by pointing to additional translation types, translation strategies, and dimensions of translation that remain to be investigated.

   Although translation must be viewed as an open concept, this does not mean that for particular purposes a person or group (a scholar, a patron, an employer, a consumer, a government, and so forth) cannot propose a limited or even prescriptive definition of translation. Indeed this happens all the time. Let us return for a moment to Wittgenstein's remarks about the boundaries of a cluster concept, here in reference to the concept number.

> I *can* give the concept 'number' rigid limits . . . that is, use the word 'number' for a rigidly limited concept, but I can also use it so that the extension of the concept is *not* closed by a frontier. And this is how we do use the word "game". For how is the concept of a game bounded? What still counts as a game and what no longer does? Can you give the boundary? No. You can *draw* one; for none has so far been drawn. (But that never troubled you before when you used the word "game".) (1953: section 68, original emphasis).

Wittgenstein continues,

> We do not know the boundaries [of game] because none have been drawn. To repeat, we can draw a boundary – for a special purpose. Does it take that to make the concept usable? Not at all! (Except for that special purpose.) No more than it took the definition: 1 pace=75 cm. to make the measure of length 'one pace' usable. And if you want to say "But still, before that it wasn't an exact measure", then I reply: very well, it was an inexact one. – Though you still owe me a definition of exactness. (1953: section 69)

It may on occasion be advantageous or necessary to define translation narrowly, say for particular experimental purposes where data are being gathered or for venues where translation products and practices must be standardized. But such *ad hoc* definitions should not obscure the openness of the cross-linguistic, cross-cultural, and cross-temporal concept *translation as a whole, nor the cultural constructions behind any particular bounded definition, particularly in theorization.[76]

Within particular cultural frameworks and for specific stipulated purposes of research, pedagogy, or practice, therefore, it is possible to propose narrowed definitions of cluster concepts based on a restricted number of features and on groups showing a particular configuration of family resemblances. In certain

---

[76] Similarly it is possible to give a restricted definition of the concept brother in terms of Western culture, leaving aside cultures where kinship terms group together as 'brother' a broader range of relations than males who are the children of the same parent or parents (cf. the first definition of *brother* in the *OED*). A definition formulated in terms of Western standards will obviously exclude cultures that count the male offspring of aunts and uncles as members of the same category as the male offspring of one or both of one's parents, just as Western standards will also exclude the conceptualizations of cultures that do not differentiate siblings by gender.

circumstances a prototype model of the subset of the full cluster category in question might be useful as a working tool, particularly in relationship to a specific temporal, geographical, and linguistic context. In such a situation a prototype model of translation could facilitate investigation of specific types of translation products or processes, or facilitate translation practices in a specific situation, or allow exploration of the local structure of the concept of translation, illuminating central examplars. Nonetheless, any such narrowed definitions must be formulated with the awareness that a controlled and limited definition is only useful for the particular purposes for which it is created.[77]

A major problem with using a restricted definition of most intellectual concepts that are foundational for translation studies is that the research based on the restricted definition will only have limited utility for and transferability to broader contexts. The same is true for the generalization of the conclusions of such research to theoretical discourses. Therefore, such a theoretical formulation will be not only exclusionary but also self-limiting. This is a critical problem in a field focused on translation, a practice that involves cultural interface. Translation types that have cropped up at different times and in different cultural contexts always have the potential to reappear elsewhere or at other times because of cultural intersections. Translation involves a constant cross-cultural juxtaposition of text types, communication patterns, and values, as well as decision strategies by individuals, adjudicating and resolving such cultural disjuncts. The result is the continual possibility of inventing new translation strategies and reinventing old solutions that transcend the boundaries of locally dominant definitions and practices of translation. For these various reasons, the best research is conducted within the broadest possible conception of translation. When a limited definition is used, a researcher must also be careful to restrict the conclusions to a similar limited domain and to remain alert for the relevance of the excluded data.

Murphy observes that a concept "is formed within the constraints of one's understanding of the world" and that "background knowledge affects not only inital acquisition of a concept but also later categorization judgments" (2002:139, 173). As a result, he indicates that "people tend to positively categorize items that are consistent with their knowledge and to exclude items that are inconsistent, sometimes even overruling purely empirical sources of knowledge" (Murphy 2002:173). These observations are as true of translation as of other facets of

---

[77] As a concrete example, we might say that if professional translators working in Brussels for the European Commission were chosen as the prototype in a specific research project on translation, then the results of the project would probably be restricted to translation in this context or contexts very close to it. Quite different results would emerge from having chosen as prototype the professional translators who worked in the official translation bureaus of the People's Republic of China after 1949, where team translation was the norm and teams included at least one member whose duty was oversight of ideology and another whose responsibility was to be polisher of the target text (often a person with no knowledge of the source language).

life, despite the explicit attention to cultural difference in the field of translation studies. The importance of background knowledge for categorization judgments and empirical understanding is yet another intellectual reason to investigate and teach a wide range of translation types, including a substantial sample of historical and international examples. Only broad knowledge and intellectual openness can avert a narrow understanding of the nature of the cross-cultural, cross-temporal concept *translation, as well as hegemonic thinking within the emerging international discipline of translation studies. In this regard contemporary scholars in the field are fortunate to be able to benefit from the international turn that the discipline is currently taking.

In addition to the intellectual imperatives for recognizing the interrelation of culture and concept formation are ethical imperatives. Kathleen Davis addresses these ethical necessities directly:

> an arrival at theoretical closure would preclude response to the otherness necessarily posited in the establishment of the theory's own categories, and would by definition preclude responsibility. For instance, a claim to define the unique characteristics of translation . . . forms a concept of "translation" – its essence and its boundaries – through the exclusion of that which is other to this essence or is outside those boundaries. An ethics of translation theorized according to such a definition would be irresponsible to that which it excluded in order to define itself. (2001:92)

Thus, under purely local conditions when one uses a tighter definition of translation than the one Toury has given, it is always important to think about what is excluded in ethical as well as intellectual terms, for such exclusions lead to a hierarchical and exclusionary view of the world. Ironically they often eliminate and erase perspectives with more merit than the theories privileged.

Following Derrida and writing in terms of philosophy, Lianeri amplifies these ethical considerations, observing that inclusion of other conceptual bases of translation across time, culture, and language is not sufficient in itself:

> if one wants to proclaim "the right of all" (men and women, Western and non-Western) to the constitution of thought, one would need to consider the history of thought, to refuse the temptation to simply pronounce the expansion of philosophy to include the "other" and deliberate, instead, on the special and privileged relation between the philosophical and the European vocabularies. (2006:81)

Voicing similar concerns, Doris Bachmann-Medick emphasizes the necessity of attending to issues of "power and interpretive authority" (2006:35-36), and Şebnem Susam-Sarajeva observes that "what matters at this point is no longer the intrinsic quality – relevancy, efficiency or usefulness – of the models, tools or theories exported by the centre, but rather the authority and power which accompany this process" (2002:198). These ideological and ethical considerations underscore the importance of the questions raised in this chapter about the definition of the cross-linguistic, cross-cultural, and cross-temporal concept *translation. The concerns addressed by Lianeri can be extended to translation theory, translation studies in general, and institutionalized knowledge as a whole. Indeed the ethical and ideological implications of expanding translation are the subject of the second half of this book: they are entailed in and implied by the intellectual imperatives to expand conceptualizations of translation. If negotiated well, I believe they can lead to increased agency for translators around the world.

Wittgenstein's cluster concept model is essential for addressing the ethical and ideological concerns raised by diachronic and transcultural investigations of *translation. It provides an inclusionary framework for understanding the typologies and relationships of only marginally overlapping types of translations. Within a cluster concept approach, translation studies can affirm and investigate such distinct clusters as translations in oral contexts, so-called "natural" translations, translations in commercial and globalized contexts, literary translations, translations in multilingual contexts where all texts of a document will have the status of "originals", close literal translations of sacred texts, translations that coordinate word and image, and so forth, as well as new clusters of translation types that will inevitably emerge as a result of changing technologies. The cluster concept approach to *translation also gives a framework for an ethical internationalization of the field of translation studies, allowing for self-definition of translation by all cultures, thus decentering a field that has thus far been dominated by Western logocentrism.

In this chapter I have principally discussed *translation as a concept and category in terms of translation products – actual translations found in the historical record. This fits with the notion from cognitive science that concepts are associated with a class of entities, as we have seen. But the terms for *translation often refer to more than a class of entities. They also refer to a class of activities, actions, and processes, and such processes are essential to contemplate with reference to interpreting, probably the most common type of translation activity across time and space. Although the argument that *translation is a cluster concept can be made in a congenial fashion in terms of translation products, ultimately it must also be explored in terms of the processes that generate those products. In some circumstances it is interesting to investigate the two separately, but process and product cannot be fully separated in a discussion of the nature of the concept *translation.

Minimally we can observe that if translation products constitute a cluster category, it follows that translation processes must also constitute a cluster category. The notion that translation processes form a cluster category has radical implications for translation pedagogy, however. Just as all translation products must be considered within the history and theory of the cross-cultural concept *translation, it follows that so must all translation processes. In applying this theoretical insight to pedagogy, one can see immediately that it undermines and in fact detonates prescriptive attitudes toward teaching and assessing translation in a global context. Again, one can circumscribe the concept *translation as a process or an activity, thus prescribing certain aspects of the activity, *but only as this applies to locally limited and locally specified situations*. A scholar or teacher engaging in prescriptive injunctions about translation should be conscious of how limited those pronouncements are and *owes it to students to specify the limitations explicitly*. Students are entitled to know that what they are learning are local norms for translating and that these norms are not absolutes or human universals, if only because translation norms are likely to change during the course of the student's working life. Such disclosures also have ethical correlatives, striking the heart of logocentrism.

The implications of seeing *translation as a cross-cultural cluster concept are therefore profound practically, intellectually, and ethically. The openness of the concept (the understanding of which in turn is formulated in terms of other open concepts, including language and text) indicates that the definitional impulse will be an ongoing strand of translation research as the field moves beyond its Western focus and as it contends with the challenges of contemporary and future conditions of translation. At the same time the openness of *translation is at the root of the richness and vitality of the concept, enabling its processes and products to adapt to the specific and varied needs posed by human communication and interactions across the most diverse cultural boundaries. Without the many forms of *translation documented cross-culturally, it is hard to see how human life could thrive either at the level of the individual or the group. The blurred boundaries of *translation ensure the flexibility needed to facilitate interchange, growth, learning, and friendship as required by individuals, groups, and cultures through time and space.

3. Framing Translation: Representation, Transmission, Transculturation

Any entity – human beings, objects, events, social constructs – can be looked at in many different ways and, as such, fit into many categories. A dog is a dog, but it is also a mammal and an animal, and it can be a pet or a yellow Labrador retriever as well. A shoe can be a fashion statement or a tool if it is used to hammer something flat. A person can be a woman and also a European, a scholar, a mother, and dozens of other things. A party can be an entertainment and also an occasion for a business transaction. A government can be a provider of benefits to its citizens but also an agent of imperialism in the wider world. Sometimes the entity is equally and simultaneously in several categories; sometimes a member of one category is a member of another category in virtue of its place in a conceptual hierarchy or taxonomy (a dog is a mammal); sometimes an entity becomes a member of other categories because of the functions it serves or because it is included in an *ad hoc* category (a shoe can be a tool or something to take on a camping trip). Sometimes a shift of category has to do with differences in human perspective, both individual and cultural.[1]

As we have seen in the last two chapters, defining the cross-cultural concept *translation is not an easy task, and a continuous definitional strand can be traced in the history of translation studies since World War II. Part of the reason for both has to do with the many perspectives that can be brought to bear on translation and the multiple ways that specific translation products and processes can be conceptualized. Thus, a translation might be conceptualized or categorized as a literary text, a linguistic construction, an example of cultural interface, a commercial venture, a sign of power, a feminist statement, and even perhaps a revolutionary tactic. This sort of complexity increases geometrically when translation is investigated as a cross-linguistic, cross-cultural, and cross-temporal concept. One way to think of the history of translation studies, as well as the relationships among current scholarly approaches to the subject, is to say that different schools of translation studies have applied different frameworks to the cross-cultural concept *translation, permitting scholars to see translation from a number of different conceptual perspectives.[2]

---

[1] Murphy (2002:199) gives an even more elaborate outline of the multiple categories that an entity can be part of; the same point has also been made by cultural studies scholars interested in identity formation.

[2] A word about terminology. I am using the terms *framework*, *framing*, and *frame* as they are used in ordinary language, rather than in any of the various technical meanings that have developed in linguistics or the social sciences. Thus, I am referring in a non-technical manner to the use of a frame of reference (such as a textual, cultural, or intellectual frame of reference) to assess a topic or activity, here to assess translation. All the principal concepts used here as frames of reference for translation – representation, transmission, and transculturation – have been extensively explored in other critical contexts and also in ordinary language contexts. I am arguing that ordinary knowledge pertaining to each can serve as a useful frame of reference for explorations of translation. Cf. Wilt (2003:43-59) on framing.

Translation studies scholars have framed translation in terms of language and linguistics, social systems, functions, textual and literary questions, ideology, and a broad range of other cultural issues; the history of translation studies can be read as a record of framing translation in diverse and often divergent ways. In his discussion of concepts, George Lakoff observes that "when . . . we have multiple ways of understanding, or 'framing', a situation, then knowledge, like truth, becomes relative to that understanding" (1987:300). Such a pattern of multiple frames of reference is advantageous as a means of exploring complex social categories, particularly cross-cultural ones, because such categories usually have multiple roles and relationships within any culture, and those roles and relationships shift across cultures as well. Thus, a variety of frameworks can provide useful perspectives on different aspects of the social concept, opening up complementary ways of understanding the phenomena. These benefits notwithstanding, a field that uses multiple frames of reference to conceptualize its subject matter can be difficult to understand as a coherent discipline.

One advantage of employing frames of reference in translation studies relates to the nature of cross-cultural cluster concepts. As discussed in chapter 2, a cluster concept can be thought of as a "blurred concept", having "blurred edges", to use Ludwig Wittgenstein's terms (1953:section 71). A survey of the range of members of a cluster category such as *translation reveals that attributes and similarities crop up and then disappear as one moves from one group or cluster to another within the category. Thus, it is not possible to delineate necessary and sufficient conditions for category membership or even to identify a prototype. In addition, although it may be relatively unproblematic in practice to distinguish a translation from a potato peel, the blurred edges of the cross-cultural category *translation mean that in many respects it is no easier theoretically to define what is *not* a translation than to define what *is* a translation. This is one reason that for decades there has been (fruitless) contention about the boundaries between translations, adaptations, versions, and imitations both in the discipline of translation studies and in larger social contexts, particularly in Western culture. Frames of reference help to delineate or demarcate the blurred edges of a cluster concept without imposing closure or boundaries on the concept itself.

This chapter will explore the blurred borders of the cross-cultural concept *translation. Because *translation is a cluster concept, groups of translations share features that are also typical of other closely related activities and concepts. In specific social circumstances delineation of the blurred edges of the category *translation is a pragmatic one. A decision about whether a text is a translation may depend, for example, on the function of the text within the society (e.g., a text will form part of a recognized anthology of translations). Alternatively the decision may rest on the practices of a culture that determine whether certain texts are or are not translations. But there is more that can be said about these blurred boundaries: ostension is not the final method for determining what a translation is, nor is pragramatic sorting the end of explorations about translation types, the boundaries of translation, and the contours of the cross-cultural and cross-temporal concept *translation itself.

Framing is a good strategy for exploring the characteristics of a cluster concept, particularly a complex social concept such as *translation in cross-cultural and cross-temporal perspectives. The principle can be illustrated by considering the types of frameworks that might illuminate the characteristics of the cluster concept game. The concept might be framed in terms of the objects used (cards, dice, balls, nets, strings, stones), the number of players (single player, pairs, teams), the function (entertainment, group affiliation, physical exercise), the degree of competition versus cooperation (single-person competence, individual rivalry, group rivalry), the degree of chance versus skill (roulette vs. chess), the relationship of games to developmental stage (infant games, children's games, adult games), the relation to gender (boys' games, girls' games, women's games, men's games), venue (home, school, public space), and so forth. Thinking about and doing research on the parameters suggested by these frames of reference would reveal a great deal about the nature of the concept game within individual societies and cross-culturally as well. One would learn a great deal about specific games, as well as the nature of games in general, even though the cluster concept game would remain open and unbounded.

A second advantage of approaching a cluster concept from the perspective of frames of reference is that looking at other activities that fall within those same frameworks but outside the concept being investigated also contributes to understanding the concept by illuminating differences as well as likenesses. In the case of the concept game, one could look at situations involving competition in other social contexts and one would learn how competition in games is both like and unlike competition in trade or commerce, for instance. Thus, frameworks enable the deployment of comparison in the fullest and most powerful sense. The comparative perspective offered by a framework also tends to circumvent myopic disputes about a subject matter and to promote self-reflexivity, an essential attitude in exploring cross-cultural concepts as we have seen.

Although the history of translation studies can be understood as a series of attempts to frame translation in productive ways, the scholar who was perhaps most explicit and deliberate about using a frame of reference to investigate translation was André Lefevere. His exploration of the concept rewriting (or refraction) must be understood as a means of framing translation within a larger conceptual perspective. Recognition of the importance and utility of exploring the permeable boundaries of translation was one motivation for Lefevere to think about rewritings as a whole. He saw that many features of translations are shared with editions, anthologies, rewritings for specific audiences, and the like. Thus, Lefevere reasoned that by exploring the nature of various types of rewritings, the nature of translation would also be illuminated. Investigating the superordinate category rewriting not only could help in understanding the category translation, it could also make investigators more aware of their own pretheoretical assumptions and stereotypes that might interfere with formulations in translation theory.

Thus, the obverse of the exploration in chapter 2 – exploring translation by considering the heterogeneous types of translation and by describing the range of translations attested historically – is to explore the cross-cultural concept *translation by using as frames of reference other concepts that include many (though not necessarily all) translations and that have characteristics similar to or shared with many (though not necessarily all) translations. The strategy of trying to define types and attributes of the concept *translation approaches the problem of definition from *within* the boundaries of the category. By contrast, a strategy using a larger or adjacent category as a frame of reference that (fully or partially) subsumes translation or that overlaps the category translation, encompassing some of the permeable boundaries of translation, is a way of approaching the definitional problem from the opposite direction, so to speak, from *outside* the cross-cultural category *translation. Such a bidirectional method of defining a blurred category or cluster concept can be thought of as a sort of mini-max strategy, delineating the permeable boundaries by approaching them as a limit simultaneously from within and without the conceptual structure. It is a way of approximating the map of the conceptual territory, even if the tactic does not generate the sort of closed figure that results from establishing necessary and sufficient conditions for concept membership.

One type of category that can be used as a frame of reference for translation is adjacent and partially overlapping categories of texts, such as postcolonial narratives.[3] This is in fact a strategy that has been used productively to investigate postcolonial translations in particular, a project to be discussed at greater length in chapter 5. The use of postcolonial literature as a reference point for translation illustrates how framing can be conducted in terms of specific text types that share border areas with (some types of) translation and how such framing helps to illuminate the characteristics and boundaries of translation. Although adjacent categories have much to teach about translation, I believe that more powerful insights are obtained by investigating the permeable boundaries between translation and superordinate categories that include many or even most (although not necessarily all) translations. This is partly the strength of Lefevere's choice of the superordinate category rewriting (or refraction) that includes almost all translations.[4] Interestingly enough, as he elaborated it, Lefevere's tactic of framing actually also depends on using adjacent types of rewriting as standards of comparison: he explores in turn commonalities between translations and other specific forms of rewriting including editions, anthologies, historiographies, and literary criticism, as well as the overall insight gained about translation from

---

[3] An example of the use of this frame of reference is found in Tymoczko (1999a).

[4] Note that rewriting as a superordinate category does not include translations that all have equal standing as originals, such as official documents of the European Union, nor does it include a number of the types of translations considered in Kálmán (1986), including many autotranslations and pseudotranslations.

looking at the larger category rewriting in general (see Lefevere 1992b).

In this chapter I propose to look at three broad categories whose properties are linked to those of translation. They are all categories so broad that they in fact include most translations. Translations as product and process constitute subsets of the three different forms of cultural interface designated in English by the words *representation, transmission* (or *transfer*), and *transculturation*. Following contemporary terminology in literary studies, I will refer to these three categories as "modes" of cultural exchange.[5] These three superordinate categories (or concepts) are explored here for insights into the nature of translation. Because of the nature of the family resemblances that link the cross-cultural concept *translation, most individual translations fall within each of these related modes of cultural exchange, even though the entire concept *translation cannot be fully subsumed in or delimited by any one of the concepts being used as frames of reference. Nonetheless, as in the case of Lefevere's category of rewriting, through exploring what is signified by the modes representation, transmission, and transculturation, translation scholars can come to understand more clearly the boundaries and attributes of the cross-cultural, cross-temporal concept *translation, as well as the category *translation as a whole.

As modes of cultural interface, representation, transmission, and transculturation illuminate the nature of specific clusters or types of translation. These three modes also show the relationships that different clusters of translation have with each other within the larger category *translation and the ways specific translations are linked through partial and overlapping correspondences related to these modes. Moreover, an exploration of these modes also offers language for speaking about differences that distinguish specific types or exemplars of translation. Thus, consideration of the modes representation, transmission, and transculturation is instructive about some of the factors that enter into the translation strategies employed by specific translators and favored by specific cultures, as well as being useful in characterizing particular types of translation products and translation processes found across time and space.

3.1 Representation

Representation is a large and capacious concept, and, thus, a full discussion of the issues pertaining to representation and translation is far beyond the scope of this book. Nonetheless, any consideration of the nature of translation must include representation, if only in a cursory manner, for almost all translations are representations: translation as a category is by and large a subset of representation

---

[5] In literary studies, for example, comedy and tragedy – both of which can be expressed in a number of formal types and genres including narrative, drama, or lyric – are often referred to as modes.

and most individual translations fall within the larger category representation.[6]

The definition of *representation* in the *Oxford English Dictionary* indicates the broad scope of the concept. Below are elements of the definition that pertain to the nature of *translation as a cross-cultural concept:

> . . . an image, likeness, or reproduction in some manner of a thing;
> . . . the action or fact of exhibiting in some visible image or form;
> . . . the fact of expressing or denoting by means of a figure or symbol; symbolic action or exhibition;
> . . . a statement or account, esp. one intended to convey a particular view or impression of a matter in order to influence opinion or action;
> . . . a formal and serious statement of facts, reasons, or arguments, made with a view to effecting some change, preventing some action, etc.; hence a remonstrance, protest, expostulation;
> . . . a clearly-conceived idea or concept;
> . . . the operation of the mind in forming a clear image or concept;
> . . . the fact of standing for, or in place of, some other thing or person, esp. with a right or authority to act on their account; substitution of one thing or person for another . . . [7]

Note the significance of these aspects of representation for the understanding of translation. As a representation, a translation offers an image or likeness of another thing. It exhibits that thing in a tangible manner. It has symbolic significance. It is a statement intended to convey a particular aspect of a subject so as to influence its receptors. A representation has a formal standing in society, presenting evidence or argument for a particular purpose, and translations must be considered in this light. Translation is also involved in achieving mental clarity. A translation stands in place of another entity and has authority to substitute for or act in place of that entity. These statements capture only some of the implications that follow from regarding translations as representations.

These various aspects of representation are rarely all characteristic of any single translation of course, but the definition indicates why representations in general and translations in particular are weighty; the power of representation is palpable in the various aspects of the definition. The definition of *representation* and the use of representation as a frame of reference for translation make manifest some of the reasons why translation itself is so powerful an act, why translations

---

[6] Lewis is an example of a critic who positions translation "as a form of representation that necessarily entails interpretation" (1985:39). We should observe, however, that some translations fall outside the category of representation, including pseudotranslations, translations that masquerade as originals, and translations that have the status of originals (e.g., E.U. documents).

[7] This list is a partial summary of the definition in the *OED* s.v.

have played significant and transformative roles in many cultural contexts throughout history. The definition of *representation* illuminates why translations are constitutive of reality and why the process of translation is associated with textual manipulation. Using representation as a frame of reference for translation is also suggestive of many issues pertaining to the ethics of translation, including the commissive aspect of translation.[8]

As the definition of *representation* indicates, representations involve a "particular view or impression of a matter", and this is one reason representations participate in ideological or polemical contestations. Another factor in the ideology of representations is the role of discourse in the formation of representations. Not only do representations involve perspectives and (sometimes hidden) agendas, they also reflect and are structured by preexisting discourses that inform the views of those making the representations. Like other representations, translations are shaped by ideological discourses.[9] In the last few decades postcolonial theory has been preeminent in exploring the textual role of overt and covert discourses in cultural representations pertaining to both colonized peoples and the colonizers, but such discursive aspects of cultural representations in texts are not limited to postcolonial contexts. The role that discourse plays in shaping translations and translation movements in general is highlighted by focusing on translation as a form of representation. Descriptive translation studies have addressed issues pertaining to discourse and representation, particularly but not solely in postcolonial contexts and other situations of asymmetrical power. We will return to this topic in chapter 5.

Not all representations pertain to cultural interface; many – probably most – occur within specific cultures and relate to negotiations and struggles in local circumstances. In part because of the intertwining of representation and power, representation has been much discussed in the social sciences. In fields devoted to cross-cultural representations such as anthropology and ethnography, there has been a crisis of representation since World War II, as scholars have questioned the positivist premise of "objectivity" to which their disciplines have traditionally aspired and as they have acknowledged their own potential role in the assertion of cultural power.[10] In a postpositivist paradigm the constructivist aspect of social representations must be acknowledged. Thus, anthropological or ethnographic representations *ipso facto* cannot be "objective", for they depend

---

[8] The commissive aspect of translation is discussed in Tymoczko (1999b:110-13, 137-38, 259-60, 268-69) and sources cited.

[9] Fairclough (1989:49-55 and passim) discusses these issues at length and gives salient examples. The relationship between ideology, representation, and translation is discussed by Arrojo who links ideology in translation with the "system of representations" underlying the social subject's lived relation to "the real" (2003:167n3).

[10] Essays on this topic are found in Clifford and Marcus (1986), and Clifford (1988:21-54). For the relevance of these issues to translation, see Sturge (1997), Wolf (2000, 2002), Staten (2005), Bachmann-Medick (2006), and sources cited.

on the viewpoints and perspectives of the describers, and those describers have usually been members of dominant cultures. Ethnographic representation is a form of definition, creating or constructing a tangible image of the culture represented, shaped by the language and discourses of the ethnographer. Increasingly it has also been recognized that such constructed images have ideological and ethical aspects; as with representation in general – indicated in the definition above – there is an implicit or explicit social purpose, a claiming of authority, an intent to effect action, and an appropriation of the right to speak for another culture in all ethnographic representations, even if these facets are effaced or unacknowledged by the ethnographer.

Since the 1970s translation studies scholars have increasingly come to see that these aspects of representation are also characteristic of translations and that the ethical concerns and intellectual problems pertaining to representation must be faced in translation studies, whether it is a case of commercial, legal, medical, media, or literary translation. Earlier linguistic views of translation, in which the task of the translator was modeled primarily as linguistic transformation, have been superseded accordingly. In exploring rewriting as a framework for translation, Lefevere was instrumental in demonstrating the representational aspect of most rewritings and refractions, including translations. Translation is not only a principal form of intercultural representation, it is one of the oldest and most continually practiced forms of representation in human culture. Many aspects of the constructivist dimension of translation have been explored, largely in descriptive translation studies. The symbolic nature of translation has been examined, particularly in relation to the type of image cast by a translation. Cultural issues pertaining to the power, authority, and social agency of translations, as well as the relationship between translation and ideology, have been forcefully raised in case studies and theory alike in translation studies in the last quarter century. These questions about representation are central to the second wave of descriptive studies, as we saw in chapter 1.

Translation studies focusing on gender, race, politics, ideology, and, of course, postcolonial contexts must contend with issues of power, and they must also address representation. Whether directly named as such or not, all these studies turn on the recognition that translation is a form of representation. Scholars have shown that some translations and some translation strategies are explicitly motivated by the impetus to represent for good or for ill. Ideological representation *per se* is sometimes the primary goal of translations, and it can be an overt aspect of a translator's decision-making process as well; in such translations the image cast of the source material can be demonstrated to be the controlling determinant of particular translation decisions and strategies, as well as the shape of the entire translated text. The result can be seen in colonialist and anticolonialist translations alike, but the tendency is also clear in contemporary translations of advertisements, for example. Representation in translated texts can be the motivating factor for additions, deletions, compression, zero translation, and other major departures from the source text.[11] But representation can also be an implicit and subliminal element in the translation process. Receptor discourses can be the vehicles for such covert representations, coded subliminally and obliquely in subtle choices of language, or they can be established in paratextual materials. Silent representations are sometimes revealed by slippages in the target texts and by narrative analysis (cf. Baker 2006a). In some ways such covert representations are even more insidious than more overt ones, as postcolonial translation scholars have demonstrated.

Representation is paramount in many historical cases of translation having to do with empire, but it is a significant factor in almost all translation types, including contemporary commercial translations, media transpositions, news reporting, and the like. It follows that translation shares boundaries with many other human activities that fall wholly or partially under the rubric of representation. Whether it is a question of legal advocacy or travel literature, ethnography or history writing, documentary film making or theatrical interpretation, the writing of advertisements or political speeches, activities involving representation are related to translation processes and products along the axis of representation. Translation studies must continue to explore and investigate these domains for what they reveal about translation, particularly in globalized contexts. Clearly translation studies scholars must also keep abreast of theories of representation as they exfoliate, for the topic is key to understanding central aspects of the processes of translation and the practices of translators. Representation impinges directly on knowing how to construct, read, and deconstruct translation products.

3.2 Transmission and Transfer

A second mode of cultural interface that can be used as a frame of reference for translation is indicated by the English words *transmission, transfer,* and *transference*. These three words are treated as synonyms in the *Oxford English Dictionary*, and in the discussion that follows, I will use them interchangeably. *Transmission* is defined as "the act of transmitting or fact of being transmitted; conveyance from one person or place to another; transference". Essentially the same definition is given for *transference* ("the action or process of transferring; conveyance from one place, person, or thing to another; transfer") and *transfer* (vb. "to convey or take from one place, person, etc. to another; to transmit, transport; to give or hand over from one to another"; n. "the act of transferring or fact of being transferred; conveyance or removal from one place, person, etc. to another; transference, transmission"). As with representation, transmission (or transfer) is not confined to activities between cultures. Most transmission occurs intraculturally, indeed very locally, as exemplified by the case of one person handing an object to another person.

---

[11] See the examples in Tymoczko (1999b).

Transmission, *transfer*, and *transference* are all very general terms in ordinary language; they do not normally presuppose particular procedures or protocols, nor do the outcomes normally constitute specific or circumscribed types of cultural products. To be sure, certain forms of transfer are legally recognized, prescribed, regulated, and sanctioned in many cultures – for example, wills and legacies, the transfer of real estate, deeds, sale and purchase agreements, and marriage agreements in societies where a daughter is the property of her father until she is transferred as property to her husband. But most types of transfer and transmission are based on *ad hoc* arrangements and possess *ad hoc* characteristics. As a mode of cultural interaction, transfer is broad, and as a category it has edges that are blurred in the extreme.

The cultural means of and procedures for most forms of transmission and transfer are indeterminate and unspecified, their methods and forms multifarious. Almost all types of writing and texts involve the transmission of knowledge or information, if only minimally. As a consequence most types of rewriting (including those discussed by Lefevere) are also forms of transmission or transfer of knowledge, whether they take the forms of anthologies, summaries, commentaries, critical works, or editions. Similarly, almost all educational materials are examples of transmission or transfer, including lectures, textbooks, encyclopedias, educational television shows, and films. Obviously most of these particular forms of cultural exchange are also forms of representation, but such is not the case with all or even most types of transfer or transmission (say, physical transfer of objects).

The scope of the category denoted in English by the word *transmission* is indicated by its use for the broadcast of modern media, including both television and radio broadcasts. Here transmission is quite a different process from the other types of transfer already considered, for it involves radical changes in the form of the content or material being transferred: from live performance to electromagnetic waves to electronically generated sound and image. Transmutations in the products of transfer are also suggested by the results of bank transfers. I can deposit dollars in my bank account and have the deposit appear in euros in the bank account of another person far away; this form of transfer turns on a symbolic process involving transfer of value through a change of form, and it does not depend on actual material changing location.

Representation is primarily a semiotic mode, expressed in linguistic signs or other visual and auditory signs. Transfer, by contrast, tends to be material, issuing in physical and concrete effects, paradigmatically exemplified in an object changing hands as it is transferred from one person to another. Indeed, the results of a successful transfer are often material even when the transfer process is symbolic, as in the case of a bank transfer or a transfer of deed. Transfer can involve physical relocation and change, therefore, as well as symbolic or semiotic processes. In Western European languages this is the primary meaning of words related to English *transfer*.

In Western cultures translation has been conceived as intimately connected with transfer, as discussed in chapter 2. In fact the English words *transfer* and *translation* both derive from the same Latin roots, *trans*, 'across', and *ferre*, 'to carry'.[12] By interrogating translation from the perspective of the framework of transmission, we get a broader view of the notion of translation as transfer. Like other forms of transfer, translation can take many forms. It can involve the transmission of substance on the macrolevels of the text, most commonly semiotic meanings, discourses, or elements having to do with the content or structure of the source text or utterance. But translation can also involve transfer on the microlevels of the text; J.C. Catford discusses ways of setting up values and meanings of the source language in the target language text (1965:43-48). Even more obvious forms of transfer on the microlevels of a translation take the form of word-to-word transference, including borrowings, which import (some of) the meanings of source language words into the translated text. Such linguistic and lexical transfer has historically been a significant function of and motivation for translation, because it is a principal vehicle for the development and extension of languages.[13]

The examples of transmission considered above are reminders of the wide range of products and the many types of processes that can be involved in or result from transference. Contemplating the range of activities included in the category transmission facilitates an appreciation of the diverse relationships link-ing the types of translations attested in the historical record. The diversity of the activities that constitute the mode of transmission offers a cautionary note against prescriptive approaches to translation strategies even when the goal of translation is transfer. Summary translations, translations that diverge markedly from the lin-guistic features of the source text, and translations that add significant contextual or supplementary materials are all examples of translation types that privilege transfer, manipulating the source text in different ways so as to transmit the con-tents to the targeted audience most effectively and most efficiently. Attention to the variety of forms of transmission in attested translations permits a scholar to decenter the privileged Western view of translation that has developed since the late Middle Ages, in which the premium on transfer has valorized close textual transposition (Tymoczko forthcoming b). Such views continue to be promulgated

---

[12] *Translation* derives from the past participle of *ferre* and *transfer* derives from the infinitive. Halverson (1999b:9-10) suggests that the two English verbs *transfer/translate* diverged and that *transfer* was primarily reserved for the physical domain whereas *translate* was used for mental and speech act domains. This is not fully the case because transfer in English is not always a physical process (indeed contrary to her views, it often involves abstract "objects", while *translate* retains its primary physical meanings in many circumstances, as indicated by that sense as the first definition of the word in the *OED*). Whatever one's view of the English words, however, the question "are all translations transfers?" takes on radically different mean-ing in the context of the international repertory of words for *translation that do not derive from an image-schema signaling transfer.

[13] Examples are found in Delisle and Woodsworth (1995:25-63).

in pedagogical approaches that stress close textual fidelity and that privilege transfer in a narrow sense. Awareness of the broad range of activities constituting transmission as a mode of cultural exchange offers a corrective to narrow discourses about transfer in translation pedagogy and descriptive translation studies.

Particularly when the primary purpose of translation is transmission or transfer on the macrolevel, translation products are often quite various and diverge considerably from their sources. Understanding the ways that translation overlaps with transmission helps to explain why translation is a cluster concept, because the forms and procedures of transmission vary so much cross-culturally.[14] The concrete and material aspect of many types of translation is also signaled in the connection between textual translation and the earliest meaning of *translation* in English, a meaning reflecting Latin *translatio* – the transfer of power, learning, or the relics of saints from one location to another. These concrete aspects of translation as transmission also suggest the connection of translation with trade and commerce indicated by the Chinese term for translation, *fanyi*, as we saw in chapter 2.

If it is possible to say that almost all translations are representations, is it equally the case that almost all translations are examples of transfer or transmission, even if minimally so? Is it possible to conceive of a translation involving little or no transfer? Here Catford's definition of translation seems to suggest that such a view of translation is indeed possible and perhaps even logically necessary. He writes "translation is an operation performed on languages: a process of substituting a text in one language for a text in another" (1965:1). He later qualifies this definition by saying that translation can be defined as "*the replacement of textual material in one language (SL) by equivalent textual material in another language (TL)*" (1965:20, original emphasis). These definitions indicate the possibility of seeing minimal transmission in translation, depending on the meaning of *equivalent*. In the case where *equivalent* is understood solely in terms of text of equal length in the target language, for example, without consideration of semantics, meaning, or other forms of semiotic equivalence, a translation might involve almost no transfer or transmission of content. Such a situation might seem fanciful at first consideration, but this type of equivalence is found in the case of the cereal advertisement discussed above in section 2.1. Similarly, radical dynamic equivalence (of humor, for instance) might involve virtually no transfer of content or meaning, preserving at best the function of the text. Thus, Catford's definition of translation – as well as concrete examples – allow for zero transfer as a limit in the process of translation.[15]

---

[14] These variations are signaled in the image-schemas and metaphors grounding many international words for translation.

[15] Toury hedges on this point of transmission, insisting in his definition of *translation* on some relationship between source text and receptor text, but leaving criteria for that relationship totally open (1982:27). It would seem that Toury also recognizes the theoretical possibility of translations that do not involve transmission or transfer.

Translations with minimal or radically unexpected transmission are actually well attested in the historical record. One might cite the famous example of the translations of the poems of Catullus by Celia and Louis Zukofsky (1969), where only the sounds and meters of the poems are transferred and the semantic and semiotic correspondence is omitted. Similarly Edward Fitzgerald's translations of the poetry of Omar Khayyam might fall into the category of minimal transmission, signaled by his comment that it were better to have a live sparrow than a stuffed eagle (cf. Bassnett 2002:73-74). More to the point for theoretical purposes, descriptive translation studies have shown that zero translation of texts or segments of texts occurs all the time. Such zero translation or failure to transfer part or all of the source text is almost always of great significance for understanding the nature of the particular cultural interface in question and the nature of specific translation products and translation strategies. If the phenomenon of zero translation is seen in terms of the mode of transfer, it takes on additional theoretical interest for translation scholars as a limiting aspect or a limiting type of translation (cf. Kálmán 1986).

The relationship between translation and the mode of transmission is one of the principal parameters that distinguishes translation practices cross-culturally. Norms pertaining to the fullness of the transmission of semantic elements, the closeness of grammatical and lexical transfer, the explanation of cultural context, and the permissibility of various types of adaptation are all axes of transmission along which translation traditions of different peoples have varied in particular sociocultural and historical circumstances. Many things influence the extent of cultural and textual transfer in translation practices: linguistic anisomorphisms,[16] translation technologies, literacy practices, economic factors, cultural sufficiency or enclosure, cultural receptiveness to difference, esthetic norms, taboos about certain types of content, asymmetries in power and cultural prestige, and ideology, among others. By framing translation in terms of transmission, it is possible to understand why translations of certain types and translations in certain contexts carry over specific aspects of the source text but not others to the receptor context, or why they carry over so few aspects. Just as transfer can be an extremely minimal operation in various non-translational circumstances, so can the mode of transfer in translation be minimal. Norms requiring the completeness or closeness of transmission become defining characteristics of translation practices in some cultures, such that distinctions on this basis are made between translation, imitation, adaptation, and summary. In other cultures such distinctions seem to be scarcely relevant at all. Attention to the role of transfer and transmission in translation practices illuminates the wide variability of translation methods and processes worldwide throughout history.

From the standpoint of theory, it is important to reiterate that translation

---

[16] For example, asymmetries in phonology or naming practices might influence the transmission of proper nouns.

scholars, teachers of translation, and translators themselves must understand that dominant contemporary professional norms about transmission – whether of content, language, function, or form – are not universals, nor are they uniform or value free. Transmission as a mode of ordinary cultural exchange varies widely in its practices, methods, means, and results. Insofar as the cross-cultural cluster concept *translation shares boundaries with transmission, translations can also vary widely in all these ways. Using the mode of transmission as an index for assessing translation types and as a frame of reference in translation scholarship highlights these variations in the concept *translation in cross-cultural contexts, as well as the variations with respect to transfer in specific translation circumstances.

3.3 Transculturation

A third mode of cultural interface that can be used as a frame of reference to illuminate the nature of many translations and the boundaries of the cross-cultural concept *translation is represented by the English term *transculturation*, defined as "acculturation" in the unabridged *Oxford English Dictionary* (1989) and as "the transmission of cultural characteristics from one cultural group to another" in the 1974 edition of the *Encyclopaedia Britannica* (12.65). We will return to a consideration of these definitions below. For the moment, note that the word *transculturation* came into English from the Spanish *transculturación*, indicating the exchange of cultural elements between Europeans and indigenous populations in Latin America. The word is generally used to denote the creolization and cultural mixing characteristic of most Latin American cultures, processes that have resulted from cultural flows in more than one direction. In Spanish the term *contrasts* with the process of acculturation which is seen as a one-way flow of culture, a distinction that is not always observed in the English usage of the term (as we see from the *OED* definition). In Anglophone literary studies *transculturation* has gained widespread currency since the publication of *Imperial Eyes: Travel Writing and Transculturation* (1992) by Mary Louise Pratt.

As with representation and transmission, transculturation is a very broad category. It is similar in breadth to the other two but indicates a very different mode of cultural interface and exchange. It is obvious from the definitions already given that transculturation, like transmission, goes far beyond the exchange of verbal materials. It includes such things as the transmission and uptake of beliefs and practices related to religion, social organization, and government from one people to another, as well as the spread of artistic forms, including music, the visual arts, literary forms, and even tale types. The concept of transculturation covers many aspects of material culture: the uptake of technology and tools, agricultural practices, clothing, food, housing, transportation, and more recent cultural domains related to the modern media. The popularity of Chinese and Mexican food, reggae music, and Japanese anime in the United States are examples of transculturation. Transculturation can become so naturalized that cultural practice shades into hybridization; what was transculturated ceases to be perceived as "other". Most forms of Westernization in countries outside Europe are instances of transculturation, and they characteristically exhibit domestication and hybridization.

Unlike representation and transmission, transculturation requires the *performance of the borrowed* cultural forms in the receptor environment. When transculturation is operative, forms from one culture are appropriated by another and integrated with previous practices, beliefs, values, and knowledge. They become part of the life ways of those on the receiving end of transculturation. This is the significance of the *OED* definition of transculturation as *acculturation*. In textual domains transculturation often involves transposing elements that constitute the overcodings of a text, including elements of a literary system (poetics, genres, tale types, and other formal literary elements); textual technologies including literacy, printing, and electronic media have also been transculturated. Elements expressed in or carried by language can also be transculturated, such as discourses and worldviews. Such elements then become part of the performative repertory in the receiving culture's speech, literature, music, politics, economic system, religion, and so forth.[17]

An interesting feature of transculturation is that it does not necessarily entail representation as a component of the process of cultural uptake. In some cases of transculturation, the dimension of representation may be so minimal as to be essentially nil. Insofar as there is an overt dimension of representation, it may even be misleading and incorrect. For example, it is easy to see that a person can receive and incorporate into life patterns a particular cultural form with little or no awareness that it has originated in another cultural context and has been transculturated into the receiving context. That is, the form may have become so completely naturalized in the receptor culture that it is not seen as "other" or as being representative of the source culture in any way. The transculturation may also have proceeded in such a way as to obscure the point of origin of the cultural element, or the transculturated practice may even come with an incorrect attribution. Pizza is an example of cultural uptake of this latter sort in much of the world: it is often not experienced as specifically Italian at all nor does it stand as a representation of anything Italian to the (literal) consumer as it does in the United States. Ironically, pizza is usually associated with the United States more than with Italy among its fans in China. Most ironic of all, pizza achieved its current popularity among Italian Americans in the United States earlier than in Italy itself as a consequence of transculturating Italian food to America. Its popularity spread as a sort of back formation to the "home country" in the second half of the twentieth century. However pizza is interpreted or represented, the *eating* of pizza is a perfect example of the necessary *performative* aspect of transculturation.

---

[17] An interesting case study is found in Ohsawa (2005).

The concept of transculturation began as a neologism, *transculturación*, coined by Fernando Ortiz, a Cuban ethnologist. Ortiz introduced the term in his 1940 publication *Contrapunteo cubano del tabaco y el azúcar* (*Cuban Counterpoint: Tobacco and Sugar*, 1947) to describe the cultural give and take in Latin American colonial contexts, specifically in Cuba (97-103). The concept passed into English and the term *transculturation* was eventually included in the unabridged second edition of the *Oxford English Dictionary* in 1989, where its first attribution refers to the 1941 text of Bronislaw Malinowski's "Scientific Theory of Culture" (Malinowski 1944:14).[18] Malinowski (1947:ix) acknowledges that he adopted the term from Ortiz, whose work he admired. In 1940 he wrote an introduction to the English translation of Ortiz's work, published as *Cuban Counterpoint* in 1947.

The *OED* definition "acculturation" noted above is therefore problematic because acculturation is usually used to indicate a one-way cultural flow, a process we might think of as assimilation. By contrast Ortiz developed the term *transculturación* to distinguish the two-way processes of cultural interchange that characterized Latin American culture and that resulted in new cultural formations neither fully foreign nor fully indigenous. As Ortiz demonstrates, Cuban culture is in fact a palimpsest of many cultural contributions from the Americas, Europe, Africa, and beyond. Ortiz also wanted to disengage cultural flows from power *per se*, and acculturation is not only generally perceived as a one-way process but is associated with asymmetries in power and influence. Malinowski writes that *acculturation* is

> an ethnocentric word with a moral connotation. The immigrant has to *acculturate* himself; so do the natives, pagan or heathen, barbarian or savage, who enjoy the benefits of being under the sway of our great Western culture . . . . The "uncultured" is to receive the benefits of "our culture"; it is he who must change and become converted into "one of us". . . . It requires no effort to understand that by the use of the term *acculturation* we implicitly introduce a series of moral, normative, and evaluative concepts that radically vitiate the real understanding of the phenomenon. The essential nature of the process being described is not the

---

[18] The word is found in Malinowski (1944:14) with no reference to Ortiz; however in his earlier essay dated July 1940, which became the introduction to the 1947 English version of Ortiz's work, Malinowski writes "Dr. Ortiz told me at the time [1939] that in his next book he was planning to introduce a new technical word, the term *transculturation*, to replace various expressions in use such as 'cultural exchange,' 'acculturation,' 'diffusion,' 'migration or osmosis of culture,' and similar ones that he considered inadequate. My instant response was the enthusiastic acceptance of this neologism. I promised its author that I would appropriate the new expression for my own use, acknowledging its paternity, and use it constantly and loyally whenever I had occasion to do so" (1947:ix). Both of these Malinowski publications appeared posthumously and their publication dates are later than the dates of composition probably because of the disruptions of World War II.

passive adaptation to a clear and determined standard of culture . . . . Every
change of culture, or, as I shall say from now on, every transculturation,
is a process in which something is always given in return for what one
receives, a system of give and take. It is a process in which both parts of
the equation are modified, a process from which a new reality emerges,
transformed and complex, a reality that is not a mechanical agglomera-
tion of traits, nor even a mosaic, but a new phenomenon, original and
independent. (1947:x-xi)

Ortiz himself indicates that the process of transculturation involves several
stages:

transculturation better expresses the different phases of the process of
transition from one culture to another because this does not consist merely
in acquiring another culture, which is what the English word *acculturation* really implies, but the process also necessarily involves the loss or
uprooting of a previous culture, which could be defined as a deculturation.
In addition it carries the idea of the consequent creation of new cultural
phenomena, which could be called neoculturation. (1947:102-3)

A complex example of transculturation that illustrates the interchange and
amalgamation of cultural characteristics such as occurred in Latin America is the
cultural give and take in Ireland. One sees an example in the use of Irish literary
forms and myths in the work of James Joyce. Like Latin America, Ireland is a
locus of cultural interface: a rich and deep Celtic culture going back 2300 years
on the island has become interwoven with many other cultures including Latin
Christian, Viking, and Norman French culture. Most recently English-language
culture has made its contributions, associated with the repeated waves of conquest
of Ireland by England.[19] Joyce recuperates formal aspects of early Irish literature
in his writing, particularly in *Ulysses*. For instance, he integrates native Irish elements in his epic form, including humorous elements; he showcases placelore,
lists, and onomastic elements similar to those found in early Irish literature; he
appropriates Irish poetic conventions of beginning and ending a work with the
same sound or the same word; he privileges sound over sense as Celtic poetry
does; and so on.[20] What is significant for our purposes here is that Joyce performs
– thus, transculturates – these Irish literary elements in English without indicating
their Irish origins to his readers. As a consequence he has been credited by many
critics with being the inventor of these formal features of his modernist texts.

---

[19] The first conquest by England occurred in the twelfth century and brought with it Norman
French culture; the so-called Tudor conquest occurred in the sixteenth century; the Cromwellian
conquest occurred in the seventeenth century; and the following centuries saw their own forms
of conquest including the Penal Laws, the Act of Union, and the Great Famine.
[20] An exploration of many of these issues is found in Tymoczko (1994).

Moreover, Joyce fused his performance of Irish formal conventions with English patterns of narrative that had become dominant in Ireland, thus transforming the English novel and illustrating the two-way effect of transculturation.

Ulysses is a new form of narrative in part because of the central role that transculturation plays in it, merging Irish and English literary and cultural elements. Like many postcolonial writers, Joyce is renowned for formal innovations, but the relationship of many of his "innovations" to literary features of the Irish-language half of his cultural heritage is rarely recognized.[21] The appearance of innovation in Joyce's work is heightened by the absence of overt indications that there are transculturations of Irish materials in the texts; the transculturations seamlessly blend with features derived from classical sources and literature in English, French, and other continental languages. By contrast, W.B. Yeats is explicit about his transfer, representation, and transculturation of Irish literary materials, overtly retelling Irish myths in English and incorporating aspects of Irish prosody into his poetic forms. Because Joyce covertly transculturates the Irish aspects of his heritage, borrowing overcodings and mythic structures rather than stories as such, he is seldom perceived as a performer in English of Irish literary and cultural elements. Paradoxically Joyce's transculturations occurred within the larger context of transculturation in Ireland itself, where cultural flows between native Irish and English cultures led to the transformation of both in Ireland over the centuries and to the emergence of a new cultural amalgam.

The transculturations that shaped culture in Cuba and Ireland are similar in many ways to the massive transculturation currently occurring around the world as a consequence of globalization. At present there are cultural flows in most countries of the world, changing rich and poor, powerful and subaltern alike. One sees striking examples of the process in the arts (particularly film and music), the media, and Internet-based information.

As these examples indicate, transculturation differs from transmission in what happens after the cultural exposure. Transmission does not necessarily entail the uptake of the material transferred to the receivers: children may be taught but not learn; a message may be sent but not received or believed. An imperial society may read the literature of its colonies but refuse to recognize the wisdom, beauty, and power of that literature, instead relegating the texts to the imperial archive or using them to serve the imperial project of domination. In this sense not all translations result in transculturation, nor do all translators aim at transculturation. Here we might compare the functionalist distinction between documentary translations which aim to represent the source text as a document of the source culture and instrumental translations which are intended to operate

---

[21] Nord (1997:98) notes that expected textual features give an impression of conventionality, whereas unexpected features provide an effect of originality. Joyce's readers have generally been unfamiliar with literature in Irish; thus they read his transculturations as unexpected textual elements and interpret them as features of Joyce's originality.

effectively within the receiving culture without necessarily being recognized as translations at all.[22]

For translation studies the concept of transculturation is important because it illuminates certain performative types of translations that function primarily to insert elements from one culture into another. Examples of translations that involve transculturation might include the *Hamlet* performed in Africa by Laura Bohannan (with the help of her audience); the emphasis was on telling the story within the receptors' cultural framework so they could appropriate it, even if the process meant adjusting the story to local performance norms and cultural mores (Bohannan 1966, cf. Tymoczko 1990b). The interactive process of storytelling that Bohannan reports produced a translation that epitomized transculturation, with both the source and target cultures being altered. The process involved much more audience participation than would be the case for a translation having as its primary goal the transmission or representation of *Hamlet* as an artifact of its own system. Similarly, Ezra Pound's translations of Chinese poetry have many of the same qualities, as do the translations of Western works into Chinese by Lin Shu and Yan Fu at the turn of the twentieth century (Lin 2002:165; Wong 2005). All these cases might be looked at as translations that stress transculturation more than transmission; the aim was to perform new literary types for the purpose of shifting the receptor literary and cultural systems toward the models being translated. Translations of songs, plays, or opera librettos whose primary purpose is performance in the receptor language might also be looked upon as privileging transculturation over transmission or representation, particularly in cases where close fidelity to the words of the source lyrics is of secondary interest to the performability of the target text.[23]

In a similar way dynamic-equivalence translations and other forms of functionalism in translation are sometimes more oriented toward transculturation than toward transmission or representation. It is not necessarily the exact representation of the source text or even the transmission of its literal message that is paramount in such forms of translation, so much as the creation of a translation that will insert the text operationally into the system of the receptors. Transculturation more than representation and transference is the goal of a great deal of contemporary commercial translation, particularly translation of advertisements and multimodal translation (cf. Cronin 2003). Transculturation is in fact often the dominant motivating factor in many performative translations that are most exasperating to translation scholars whose own priority is close transfer

---

[22] This distinction is summarized in Nord (1997:46-52).

[23] The Igbo words for translation (*tapia* and *kowa*, both indicating an overall sense of 'deconstruct it and tell it in a different form') discussed in chapter 2 suggest the importance of transculturation in that translation system. One can also discern the goal of transculturation in the translation processes of the Arabic translators of Greek science discussed in chapter 2, where the source text changed the target culture, but the target culture also modified and updated the source text in translation.

of textual language and content. By contrast many scholars have promoted this sort of transculturating translation since the beginning of the second wave of descriptive translation studies (see above, section 1.6).[24]

If we return to Ortiz's concept of the tripartite process in transculturation (acculturation, deculturation, neoculturation), we can see the give and take of transculturation at work in translations where the source text is acquired by a receptor culture, yet its understanding is modified or deculturated by reception into the new cultural context; in turn the received text plays a role in modifying the receptor culture through a process of deculturation and neoculturation. Transculturation is operative, for example, in cases documented in descriptive translation studies where enthusiastic reception of translations of the work of a literary figure in turn raise the status of that writer in his source culture; this sort of reciprocal cultural effect is evident in the careers of Jorge Luis Borges, Julio Cortázar, and Gabriel García Márquez, which were significantly affected by the translation of their works into French and English. Transculturation offers a way of understanding Walter Benjamin's (1923) insight that translations are shaped by their source texts, but that in turn translations shape their "originals" by providing an afterlife for them. The two-way nature of transculturation as a mode of cultural interface thus offers a framework for exploring and understanding many sociological and cultural aspects of translation. It serves as well to illuminate certain international conceptualizations of *translation and the nature of some translations that are marginalized in the discipline of translation studies at present.

Unlike representation and transference which usually occur within single cultures, a commonality between the superordinate mode of transculturation and most clusters in the cross-cultural concept *translation is that they normally involve interchange and interaction *between* or *among* cultures. There are exceptions of course that involve cultural interface and transculturation in heterogeneous cultures comprising multiple languages and multiple cultural patterns. In the case of translation, intralingual translation between two states or two dialects of a single language also occur within a single cultural framework. Nonetheless, such instances represent limiting cases where translation is used for intracultural or self-referential purposes, including defining the self, nation building, movement of tradition across time, and the like. Aside from such cases, translation and transculturation both usually involve exchange across linguistic and cultural boundaries. By contrast, representation and transfer most often occur within cultures, and it is the cross-cultural cases of representation and transmission that are more exceptional. For many reasons, therefore, what can be learned about cultural interchange from exploring transculturation is

---

[24] Within the framework of deconstruction, Davis (2001:84 ff.) discusses translation strategies that value the disseminative, syntactic performance of language evinced in Derrida's work; this performative aspect is precisely what she thinks tends to get erased in translation, but she sees it at work in the translations of Derrida's own texts.

potentially of great significance for understanding the cultural mediation effected
by translation. Transculturation provides a frame of reference for translation that
deserves more sustained attention in translation studies. It offers exciting possibilities for future research and theorization of aspects of translation that have
heretofore been neglected.

3.4 Representation, Transmission, Transculturation, and Translation

The preceding sections are a preliminary survey of the complex topic of framing
translation in terms of three other modes of cultural interface, but several conclusions are nonetheless apparent and bear summation. It is clear that translations
usually are examples of representation – constituting in fact a specific type of
representation – in virtue of the fact that they normally stand in lieu of a source
text. As such, in a sense translation is a type of speech act, the act of standing in
for or representing a source text. As we have seen, since Jakobson (1959) translation studies has generally recognized translation as a form of metatext, involving
reported speech, both of which (metatext and reported speech) constitute forms
of representation. Even if only minimally, implicitly, indirectly, or meretriciously,
translations almost always construct a cultural image of a source. Thus, whatever
can be learned from representation theory, including implications related to the
ideological nature of representations, will be relevant to and even essential for
translation studies, and it will apply to most translations.

Most translations also involve transmission or transfer of some elements
of a source text. As we have seen, however, the relationship of translation to
transfer can vary considerably: transfer can be minimal in the case of a very free
translation or a very restricted translation strategy, and there are even limiting
cases where the element of transmission in a target text is essentially nil. In the
vast preponderance of cases, however, what is known about constraints on or
processes of transmission or transfer will be relevant to translation theory. Thus,
for example, research in information theory about information load, interference,
redundancy, and so forth in linguistic transmission will be highly relevant not
only for the processes of translation but for the assessment of translation products
as transmissions.

At the same time the discussion has shown that translation scholars must
come to understand more clearly that there are many types of strategies and processes of transmission. This understanding will contribute to the ongoing process
of moving beyond pretheoretical Western assumptions about the cross-cultural
concept *translation, as well as narrow prescriptive approaches about transfer in
translation that do little to benefit either the field or practicing translators. There
is an immense range of approaches to transfer and transmission in translations
across time, space, and languages, as descriptive studies have demonstrated with
respect to Eurocentric contexts and as they are beginning to demonstrate with

respect to other cultures as well. Moreover, the role of transmission and transfer in translation is in rapid transition as new types of translation are developed relating to globalization and technological change. All these types of transfer must be surveyed and legitimated in translation studies, both in praxis and theory. Rethinking the role of transmission in translation will contribute to decentering translation studies, to internationalizing the field, to moving beyond limited Western conceptualizations of translation as transfer, and to meeting current demands for translation in which the norms of transfer are shifting.

A smaller number of translations privilege transculturation, the performance of cultural characteristics of a source group so that those characteristics become incorporated into the receiving culture. Literary translations often are examples of texts promoting and privileging transculturation, but so are many translations of religious scriptures and political texts that are adopted by their target audiences as important models or foundational documents. Increasingly contemporary translations serving the purposes of globalization privilege transculturation in multimodal contexts and the information network. As a concept, transculturation offers a framework for exploring various theoretical concerns pertaining to translation, including the commisive aspect of translation and calls for foreignization. Transculturation and transmission are linked in translation processes, but paradoxically the nature of transculturation is such that it can occur without representation, suggesting that the equilibrium in translations between representation and transculturation merits investigation.

Note that each of these modes of cultural interchange is found in translations in a wide variety of forms. There are many types of representation, many forms of transmission, many kinds of transculturation embodied in translations. Translation is always a metonymic process (Tymoczko 1999b:41-61, 278-300), and the ways in which a translator represents a source text, transmits it, and attempts to transculturate it will all be metonymic. Although translators are the agents of the construction of translations, some of the metonymic features of a translation have cultural determinants related to translation norms and specific conceptualizations and image-schemas of translation, as well as other cultural values. Other metonyms result from translators' decisions, interpretations, values, goals, and interventions. Thus, in specific translations the three modes of cultural interface explored here – representation, transmission, and transculturation – are found in varied, fragmented, and partial forms. Because the cross-temporal, cross-cultural, and cross-linguistic concept *translation is a cluster concept, it follows that there are few if any constraints on the types of representation, transmission, and transculturation entailed in translation procedures and products overall. The constraints on how translators negotiate these three modes are not abstract or theoretical; only specific cultural and historical contexts impose such constraints, direct how these modes of interface will be negotiated and balanced, and determine which will be in the ascendancy in any particular situation. Even so, translators have remarkable agency in negotiating and resisting such cultural directives in their specific translation choices and acts of textual creation. Exploring in greater depth how translation fits within these frameworks is a matter for descriptive translation studies to decipher and translators themselves to articulate.[25]

The conclusions that follow from framing translation in terms of representation, transmission, and transculturation as three distinct modes of cultural interchange are augumented by looking at translation from the perspective of all three at once and by investigating the intersections of the four concepts. The strong commonalities of translation with each of the three modes of cultural interface and the fact that almost all translation products fall in at least one of these domains underscore again that the investigation of translation must extend far beyond linguistic concerns. Investigations of representation, transmission, and transculturation fit, therefore, with the consensus in translation studies since World War II that the field must theorize cultural factors and cultural contexts that condition translation, including effects having to do with reception, ideology, and power.

Framing translation in terms of its intersections with these common modes of cultural interface – modes that are part of ordinary human transactions and exchange – also brings new insights about research methodologies in translation studies. The topics of transfer and representation have frequently been discussed with reference to translation, but in the past they have generally been discussed as *properties* or *attributes* of translation. What this discussion indicates – in tandem with the exploration of the nature of *translation as a cluster concept – is that modes of cultural interface are best seen as larger frameworks or matrices within which translations as a category can be (partially) situated.

Viewed as an attribute of translation, transfer has often been identified as the central element in the task of the translator; because this premise has been interrogated so little, consideration of transfer has generally been pragmatic and subordinated to pedagogic concerns. As an attribute of translation, transfer is often approached from a prescriptive point of view, and translators have been instructed in *how* particular sorts of transfers *should* be undertaken so that particular translation products will have the approved transfer results. This manner of treating the relationship between translation and transfer contains hidden presuppositions: that transfer of a particular sort (namely transfer of the content and semantic transfer) is *ipso facto* the primary attribute of the category translation and that transfer is a self-evident process. All of this might seem plausible in a Western context (though it requires the exclusion of a good deal of Western data both from the past and the present), but it is radically inadequate as a theoretical approach to the transtemporal, transcultural concept *translation.

The idea of translation as transfer (of content and of words specifically) became dominant in Western European culture toward the end of the Middle

---

[25] An excellent approach to translation in China using these frames and others is found in Cheung (2005).

Ages. It is associated with the emergence of the words currently used in Western European languages for 'translation': *translation, traduction, traducción*, and so forth.[26] They stand in contrast to earlier medieval words for translation and to medieval translation practices associated with oral contexts discussed in chapter 2. The words emerged concomitantly with the ascendancy of literacy in vernacular Western European cultures in the late Middle Ages. The emergence of these words signaled the development of new canons of translation associated with literacy among the laity and asserted in the context of growing demands for the Bible to be translated into European vernaculars. These canons of translation can be identified with a narrow concept of transfer, actualizing discourses about (literal) biblical translation into the vernacular languages.[27] The new concepts of translation also served the more complex needs of the emerging governmental and commercial bureaucracies characteristic of the period. The valorization of and focus on the transfer of the word was also fueled by semiotic associations of words with the Word (Verbum) of God in the Vulgate version of the Bible used in Western Europe, where the Word signified not only the intentions and purposes of God, but was also personified in Jesus (cf. John 1:1): the word was both grammatical and numinous. Implicit in the Eurocentric image of transfer is the idea that languages stand in an unequal relationship in a hierarchy of worth. These presuppositions about translation and transfer facilitated later imperialism and Western epistemological domination during the European age of discovery, conquest, and expansion.[28]

The historical Western determinants associating translation with literacy, the movement of sacred texts from privileged languages into vernaculars, the focus on the word as a (sacred) symbol of power and authority, and the assertion of power gradients and cultural hierarchies resulted in a very restricted notion of transfer in legitimized dominant translation processes. Such Western discourses implicitly circumscribe the type of transmission that translation should enact. They serve as a foundation for norms whose ascendancy can be traced to the period when the modern words for translation emerged in Western European languages at the end of the Middle Ages, on the brink of European imperialist expansion. The presuppositions and associations about transfer embedded in dominant Eurocentric perspectives on translation studies also block the ability to recognize and valorize alternate types of transfer that have been the norm in translation elsewhere in space and time.

Thus, presupposing that transfer is an attribute of translation (and supposing

---

[26] Cf. also the archaic German *translatieren*, a Latinate word that dates to the fifteenth century (Snell-Hornby 2006:27).

[27] The earliest citation of *translation* in the *OED* is suggestive: in 1340 in the prologue to his translation of the Psalms, Hampole writes, "in the translacioun i folow the lettere als mykyll as i may" (Mod. Eng., "in the translation I follow the letter as well as I am able"). Halverson (1999b) includes an excellent study of the development of the vocabulary for translation from Old English to the modern period.

[28] A more extensive consideration of this topic is found in Tymoczko (forthcoming b).

that the nature of that attribute is established and understood) extends Western epistemological dominance in translation studies. By contrast, using transmission or transfer as a frame of reference makes it easier to recognize other types of transfer than those that have been canonical in Western translation. Transmission used as a frame of reference facilitates the interrogation of Western discourses built into the implicit metaphor "translation is transfer". Examining the cross-cultural concept *translation from the perspective of the framework of transmission as a superordinate category also makes it possible for scholars and translators to deconstruct Western presuppositions about transfer built into translation studies. The result is increased receptivity to the full range of transmission and transfer types documented in translation practices and histories worldwide.

Representation has similarly been approached in translation studies principally as an *attribute* of specific translations or of translation as a process rather than as a superordinate concept within which translations are located. Representation has been discussed primarily by descriptive translation scholars who have demonstrated how particular types of representations are at work in specific translations and specific translation movements; they have deconstructed representations related to power asymmetries and enjoined and celebrated activist representations. Again, however, the focus in such discussions is on representation as a *property* of translation, and there has been little systematic attempt to look at larger frameworks of representation within which the patterns of representation in translation can be positioned. Transculturation, by contrast, is rarely discussed explicitly at all in translation studies. As a mainspring of an anthropophagic view of translation, transculturation figures implicitly in the work of Else Vieira (1994, 1999) on the twentieth-century Brazilian translation movement associated with Haroldo de Campos.[29] It is also implicit in the activist agendas of Lawrence Venuti (1992, 1995, 1998a, 1998b). Using transculturation as such as a frame of reference for translation and as a tool for assessing specific translations, however, remains to be explored in depth in future translation studies.

When representation, transfer, and transculturation are approached as attributes of translation, discussion tends to be prescriptive, stressing how they should occur rather than using these categories as theoretical tools for conceiving of alternate possibilities for the process of translation or for understanding the cross-cultural category *translation. Here I have investigated representation, transmission (or transfer), and transculturation as superordinate categories that intersect with and (partially) include the category *translation, informing specific translation products and processes. Each has been looked at as a potential matrix within which translation can occur or be conducted, though the necessity of each has been interrogated. To see these three types of cultural interchange as larger, intersecting, and complementary modes, to which (some or most) translations

---

[29] This view of translation can be traced to Goethe, who states "The force of a language is not to reject the foreign, but to devour it" (qtd. in Berman 1992:12).

belong, recasts the significance of the concepts and also the ways in which their relation to translation is approached. By extending inquiry beyond evidence provided by translations and translation studies alone, exploration of a frame of reference such as those discussed here helps to guard the field of translation studies against intellectual enclosure. These three frames of reference expand the conception of translation, moving it beyond dominant, parochial, and stereotypical thinking about translation processes and products. Consideration of the range of forms of representation, transmission, and transculturation facilitates broader perspectives on translation and allows for greater understanding of specific translation effects; both are important facets of internationalizing the field of translation studies fully and of empowering translators as well. Only by looking at these concepts as large frameworks that intersect with, partially encompass, impinge upon, and illuminate translation can translation scholars use these modes of cultural interface most effectively to theorize translation and to infuse translation pedagogy with understandings that prepare students to translate in a globalizing world demanding flexibility and respect for differences in cultural traditions.

The difference in approach between using representation, transmission, and transculturation as frameworks rather than attributes can be seen by looking at how translation studies has utilized other superordinate categories that (partially) include translations. Such categories include, for example, language itself, ideology, and discourse. It is *not* that language is simply an attribute or characteristic of translation, but that translation must be theorized within the entire framework of what is known about the larger category of language, of which all translations involving natural languages are a specific subset.[30] Similarly ideology and discourse are larger intellectual frameworks that impinge upon texts and, hence, upon translations. Again, both ideology and discourse are more than properties of translation, though they are of course realized through specific features of texts, including features of translated texts. Setting translation within the frames of reference of the broader concepts of language, ideology, and discourse has been enormously useful in assessing the data of translation studies. In a similar fashion translation has been productively discussed within the frameworks of textual studies and literary systems, both of which are also superordinate categories within which translation processes and products can often or even usually be situated.

The most conscious and deliberate attempt to use a superordinate category to explore the nature of translation in this fashion has been Lefevere's investigations of the superordinate category rewriting. The benefits of his approach for translation studies have been incontrovertible. Similar benefits have come from situating translations within larger theoretical frameworks supplied by postcolonial

---

[30] There are many types of translations that are not restricted to movement between natural languages, notably those Jakobson refers to as intersemiotic translations (1959:233).

studies, gender studies, and the like. I am suggesting that attention to modes of cultural interface such as representation, transmission, and transculturation as frameworks for investigating translation will be equally useful for expanding conceptualizations in the field. Consideration of the modes of representation, transmission, and transculturation are particularly important because the cross-cultural concept *translation is a cluster concept or, to use Wittgenstein's terms, a "blurred" category with "blurred edges". *Translation is a blurred category that intersects with and sits at the junction of other blurred categories, not only the category language discussed by Wittgenstein but also representation, transmission, and transculturation. Where those junctions exist for *translation as a concept and for particular translations is of enormous interest.

This chapter has demonstrated that not all representations are transmissions, nor are all transmissions representations, nor are the members of either of those categories all transculturations. All possible combinations and permutations of these modes can and do occur in translation. The investigation of these intersections and permutations promises to be an exciting venture. Representation, transmission, and transculturation as modes of cultural exchange are complementary and interconnected. Groups of translations identifiable within the cluster concept *translation can be subsumed by each and most translations fall within at least two of these three categories. These modes function as general orientations for translation strategies and rarely are fully separable. They indicate that translation is not simply a form of rewriting or refraction. Rather it shares characteristics with a much broader set of activities having to do with intracultural and intercultural interface, interchange, and interaction. These are frameworks that translation studies scholars will find worth exploring at greater length and in a more deliberate manner in part because they emphasize how central the enactment of cultural interface (and hence translation) is to human life. Just as Lefevere's concept of rewriting has become a general tool in translation studies, contributing to the understanding of the nature of translations as a whole and specific translations as well, so should the concepts explored here become part of the general repertory of frames of reference that facilitate discourse about translation.

Greater clarity about the distinctions between representation, transmission, and transculturation, as well as greater clarity about the relationship of all these modes to the cross-cultural concept *translation itself, will allow teachers and scholars of translation to speak more precisely about various aspects of translation theory and practice. Assessment of the manner in which translations instantiate these three modes will facilitate the descriptive analysis of particular translations, allowing researchers to see how the three modes compete and cohere in specific translations, specific translation strategies, and specific translation programs. Teasing apart these frameworks within which translation proceeds will also aid in establishing typologies of translations existing within the cluster concept *translation and in discerning affinities between translations from very different contexts as well as differences between translation orientations within a single translation tradition. Finally, using these three frameworks as guides provides a way of speaking about the metonymics of particular translations and whole traditions of translation practices, thus giving translators themselves ways to conceptualize and articulate their own orientations to translation.

3.5 Framing Translation: Theoretical Implications

In a sense each frame within which the large and diverse cross-cultural concept *translation can be situated provides a lens for viewing translation, a lens that filters perception of particular phenomena and permits clarity of focus and description. As we saw in chapter 2, in talking about games in particular and cluster categories in general, Wittgenstein enjoins his readers, "Don't say: 'There *must* be something common, or they would not be called "games"' – but *look and see* whether there is anything common to all. – For if you look at them you will not see something that is common to *all*, but similarities, relationships, and a whole series of them at that. To repeat: don't think, but look!" (1953:section 66, original emphasis). Wittgenstein points to the fact that membership in a cluster category is not a matter of logic but rather a function of practice and usage. Membership is an empirical question, not a theoretical one; this is why he says "don't think, but look!".

It is difficult, however, to know what to look for in observing a large collection of diverse objects and difficult as well to know how to see them. Moreover, perception is overdetermined. In speaking about the difficulty of perception alone unsupported by language, Jakobson observes

> There is no *signatum* without *signum*. The meaning of the word "cheese" cannot be inferred from a nonlinguistic acquaintance with cheddar or with camembert without the assistance of the verbal code. An array of linguistic signs is needed to introduce an unfamiliar word. Mere pointing will not teach us whether "cheese" is the name of the given specimen, or of any box of camembert, or of camembert in general or of any cheese, any milk product, any food, any refreshment, or perhaps any box irrespective of contents. (1959:232)

Jakobson reminds us here that it is not clear how to analyze raw empirical data unless one has indices to judge the data by and language to use for the analysis. Frames of reference and superordinate categories focus perception and enable observation and analysis even when they do not encompass the entire cross-cultural concept *translation. They provide both interpretive perspectives and vocabulary that allow researchers to look and see, and then to speak. These are particularly important functions in research on a cluster category where definition of the object of study itself is problematic solely in terms of shared or privileged properties. Representation, transmission, and transculturation are frameworks that can serve as lenses for the perception of translation, but they are not the only superordinate categories to which (some or most) translations belong. There are many others. Some of these have already contributed to work on translation theory and practice, but many remain to be articulated.[31]

An important function of frames of reference is that they mobilize some of the most important powers of human cognition, namely powers of comparison. Comparison activates human perceptions of similarity, which are complex, sophisticated, and flexibly attuned to specific contextual settings. Similarity judgments are also at the heart of analogical reasoning. But comparison uncovers difference as well; indeed because similarity and identity are not the same, similarity relations inherently entail both likeness and difference. Thus comparison induced by a frame of reference for an object of inquiry establishes a context for perceptions of likeness and difference that facilitates scholarly analysis. It is a particularly useful methodology for approaching social cluster concepts such as *translation where likenesses and differences crop up and then disappear as one moves from group to group (or cluster to cluster) within the concept itself, particularly with regard to data drawn from many times and cultures. The use of frameworks as it has already occurred in translation studies is therefore not an accident, but the technique remains to be more deliberately developed.

There are important implications for research in the field entailed in taking seriously the nature of *translation as a diachronic, cross-cultural concept. We have seen that scholars cannot expect to define the attributes or properties of *translation as a whole or of all translations through the determination of necessary and sufficient conditions or even to characterize translation in terms of a general list of common features, as occurs in prototype theories of concepts. Frames of reference, by contrast, help to identify the types, clusters, and groups of translations that together constitute the cluster concept *translation. In particular, frames of reference that subsume one or more groups of translations allow the exploration of features that characterize specific types of translations, thus facilitating perception of the structure of the concept *translation as a whole. Relying on cognitive science in her explorations of translation, Sandra Halverson observes that "it is important to note . . . that the issue of taxonomic relationships, while related to internal category structure, is also linked to the question of how one category relates to others. The means used to structure systems of related

---

[31] Pym (2000), for example, discusses cooperation as a fruitful framework for understanding translation, and his analysis, like those above, could be extended as well. As with the other frameworks explored, cooperation does not of course include all translations (translation as part of intelligence operations during war is an obvious counterexample; cf. Arrojo 1998). The concept transcreation, characteristic of translation in India and also used in Brazilian discourses about translation, might be another productive frame of reference, illuminating many though not all translations.

categories must be related in a principled way to those used to structure a category internally" (1999a:24). Using frames of reference to explore *translation enables perception of such correlations.

The importance of framing is sustained by research on concepts and categories. It has been shown that people do not spontaneously notice concept or category structure. People need the properties of categories to be related; moreover, the presence of knowledge, even in small amounts, results in the construction of realistic categories (Murphy 2002:131, 134). In addition, when people have prior knowledge that relates properties of categories, they are less likely to focus on a single property and more likely to notice category structure (Murphy 2002:131, 133). Framing is one way to highlight clusters of properties in a cross-cultural concept such as *translation, thus leading to a clearer view of the concept as a whole and to greater understanding of the structure of the concept that relates disparate materials from many eras, cultures, and contexts. Framing can also help scholars and translators avoid inappropriate fixation on a small number of properties of translation, particularly those properties taken as natural and beyond question because the properties are typical of the scholars' or translators' own cultural contexts.

Cognitive scientists have also shown that if perception of a concept or category remains limited to one type of setting, it is impossible to see the influence of factors that are constant within that setting (Murphy 2002:482). Comparative approaches based on frames of reference (such as representation, transmission, and transculturation) are useful in evaluating *translation cross-culturally in part because they implicitly shift the setting of the investigation. They permit perception of elements that become invisible when the elements remain constant in a single context. Finally, it has been found that the features of concepts that can be explained and integrated into structures of knowledge are more influential in concept representation than those that are not (Murphy 2002:381). Framing is, therefore, an aid in going beyond those properties at the center of dominant Western translational phenomena, explaining a broader range of international properties of *translation and integrating them into structures of knowledge emerging in the international discipline of translation studies.

I have tried to demonstrate in this chapter that it is possible to go beyond Toury's definition and to stipulate more about the concept *translation than his open (and minimalist) definition would suggest. This is not accomplished by looking for further criteria that limit the definition of translation and contain it, but by looking at superordinate categories that can subsume particular translations or groups of translations. By enlarging the focus in exploring the cross-cultural concept *translation, it is possible to say a surprising amount about the cluster category as a whole without seeking closure of the concept. We must remember, however, that the definition of *translation as such is not the goal of translation research. The goal is understanding: understanding the range and nature of translation data, as well as understanding how the parts that scholars are familiar with relate to the whole, how the subject matter relates to different contexts, and how scholars' individual contexts shape their own perspectives on products and processes of translation. It is also a central goal to communicate these understandings to practicing translators, thus facilitating translation praxis. Being explicit about frames of reference is an essential part of reaching such understandings, because lack of attention to frameworks leads to limited, stereotypical, and culture-bound thinking. Awareness of the diverse and partially overlapping characteristics of translations, as well as of their many though partial relations to various superordinate and adjacent concepts, affords means of conceptualizing *translation as a whole across time and space.

The history of translation studies demonstrates that the understanding of translation has expanded periodically by adopting frames of reference from other areas of intellectual inquiry and other academic disciplines. The first impetus to modern research on the topic came from using frameworks from linguistics to examine translation, followed by frameworks facilitating functionalist and textual analysis of translation. Other large frameworks have included sociolinguistics, systems theories, discourse theory, and cultural studies. Examples of more specific frames of reference for investigating translation are Lefevere's concept of rewriting or refraction, postcolonial theory, and gender studies. Although no absolutes emerge from such inquiries about a cluster concept, it is possible to illuminate characteristics shared by significant clusters of translation processes and products by approaching those clusters of translation from the point of view of a superordinate category or an adjacent and partially overlapping category. No single framework can suffice to illuminate all translations, but a well-chosen frame of reference will illuminate significant types of translation, a significant grouping of translations, significant facets of the process of translation, or the nature of translation in specific contexts. A well chosen array of frameworks will be even more productive. Approaches of this type will thus of necessity continue in translation studies.

As other fields develop new intellectual frameworks in the coming decades, additional frames of reference relevant to translation will emerge, and they will provide new research opportunities within translation studies. This sort of development will be a continual impetus to research in the field. The key to productive use of a particular frame of reference or a specific superordinate category is understanding that translation is only one instance of the larger category rather than viewing the category as an attribute of translation. This sounds obvious but not all examples of research using frames of reference for translation have observed the distinction. Whether the superordinate category is language, discourse, or representation, it is the application to translation of insights from the larger frame of reference that is productive for illuminating aspects of translation, rather than the use of the framework as a index of a specific property of (all) translation processes and products in general.

Frames of reference change dramatically from culture to culture, time to time. The frameworks explored here are examples of that change. They have been signified by English words – *representation*, *transmission* and *transfer*, and *transculturation* – but they are not static Anglophone concepts whose usage now is the same as it was a century ago. One of the words, *transculturation*, did not even exist as an Anglophone concept until it was brought into English from Spanish after World War II. Another, *representation*, was not problematized at the height of the positivist era and the heyday of anthropology at the turn of the twentieth century. Only since the reaction against positivism in the social sciences and humanities has the interrelationship of representation and cultural dominance come to be a central concern, a concern underscored by the postcolonial voices that emerged in the second half of the twentieth century. Even *transfer* – the central sense of translation in Western European languages for five hundred years – and *transmission* have changed their meanings considerably in the last decades. Technological shifts since World War II associated with the electronic revolution, the information age, and globalization have made types of transmissions and transfers commonplace – from FAX transmissions to live television reporting to email and electronic transfer of documents – that could not have been foreseen or theorized half a century ago. These developments have opened up the scope of transfer to new applications in translation studies, suggesting new paradigms for old ways of thinking about the topic.

More such unforeseen frames of reference will emerge during the coming decades and there will be similar shifts in old concepts. Some will come from new scholarly disciplines. More important for the themes being traced in this book will be frameworks for translation and translators that scholars will introduce from cultures beyond the West. New ways of assessing and valuing translations and new modes of cultural interface will be introduced, moving from local knowledge to international consideration. Translation studies can only thrive as a cross-cultural discipline in a global context if it is receptive to frameworks that reflect inherited views of translation worldwide, frameworks that exist for the concept *translation in languages other than European ones. These frameworks constitute the ideational reserve that the field needs to meet future challenges of cultural interface.

Şebnem Susam-Sarajeva (2002:193, 196-97) observes a deadly pattern in academic fields in which theory is seen as something supplied by the center and consumed by the periphery; the periphery in turn supplies the "raw material" in the form of data that are processed by dominant theories and that are used to test those theories. Following Gayatri Spivak, Susam-Sarajeva observes (2002:202n5) that the epitome of this dynamic is seen in the native informant of ethnography who supplies raw data which are then interpreted and analyzed by the "knowing subject" from a dominant culture. It is especially important that translation studies avoid this trap. A first step is using frameworks for translation derived from concepts for *translation from cultures throughout the world, concepts such as definition, narration, following after, turning over, and (re-)birth explored in section 2.2 above. It will also be productive to attend to categories overlapping with translation worldwide that are used to theorize and valorize translation.

An enduring feature of translation studies, investigations based on the framing of translation will become more systematic, more deliberate, and more self-reflexive in future research as the field becomes more self-aware, more able to articulate its own nature, more perceptive about the internal structure of the concept *translation, and more cognizant about the implications of viewing *translation cross-culturally and cross-temporally as an open concept. Frames of reference will be at a premium in structuring research as translation studies increasingly internationalizes. For any group of translation scholars, part of what can be learned from larger concepts such as representation, transmission, and transculturation is not merely (new) ways of looking at and understanding the translation products and processes of other people. Perhaps most importantly, no matter who the scholars are, such frames teach us about ourselves, our own conceptualizations and practices of translation, and our own norms about translation products. Using superordinate concepts such as representation, transmission, and transculturation as frameworks for evaluating and interrogating our own translations and our own imperatives about translation fosters self-reflexivity. This is important in any scholarly field, but it is essential in translation studies where difference and otherness are at the heart of the inquiry.

4. Research Methods in Translation Studies

After canvassing historical practices of translation in several areas of the Chinese cultural sphere – specifically Japan, Korea, and Vietnam – Judy Wakabayashi concludes that there must be "a reconsideration of the nature and definition of 'translation', which cannot in its narrow and conventional sense encompass all the ways in which texts have been reprocessed and reconfigured in East Asia" (2005:61). Writing about translation in the present and future contexts of globalization and thus coming from an almost diametrically opposite direction, Michael Cronin also argues that conceptions of translation and the translator must be reconfigured because of the phenomena associated with the impact of the technologies of globalization; he concludes that translators "can no longer be conceived of independently of the technologies with which they interact" (2003:112). The comments by Wakabayashi and Cronin reify the importance of the definitional trajectory of translation studies since World War II, as well as the implications of the fuzzy boundaries of *translation as a cross-cultural cluster concept. Both translators and translation must be reconceptualized because of different effects caused by the increased networking of the world. It is clear that translation studies must use frameworks from other cultures and other disciplines to interrogate its own discourses and to develop broader conceptualizations of translation.

Translation scholars are currently operating in shifting contexts and they must expand and deepen research if the discipline of translation studies is to stay abreast of its own needs. This is particularly the case if research is to maintain sufficient scope to respond to translation issues emerging in global contexts and to come to terms with the enlargement of the cross-cultural concept *translation. This chapter offers a brief overview of the implications of these shifts for research methods in translation studies and attempts to assess fundamental questions about research that must be faced by the discipline in the near future. The chapter is in some ways a metaexploration of translation research, focusing less on the content of research than on the structures of and conceptualizations about research that require readjustment as a result of the expansion and reconfiguration of ideas about translation.

A central problem with research in translation studies is that so few scholars are fully trained in the research methods necessary for the field. This is not surprising. Because the cross-temporal, cross-cultural concept *translation is a cluster concept and because the concept is so diverse and open, the skills required for translation research are themselves enormously diverse and open. Clearly translation scholars must be grounded in language study and linguistics and must be able to analyze texts. Depending on the particular research subject, a scholar may also need to be competent in the methods of history and historiography, any of the social sciences, cognitive science and neurophysiology, literary analysis, or experimental research pertaining to bilingualism, language acquisition, pedagogy, and the like. Translation research on a particular subject matter (biology, physics, medicine, law) will require knowledge of that field as well. This brief listing indicates that skills associated with each of the three traditional divisions of knowledge – the humanities, social sciences, and natural sciences – might be pertinent to translation research. Translation studies is an open field with connections to many other academic disciplines; this is one of its strengths as an academic subject and part of its excitement. It is an evergreen field for intellectual challenge, but the same breadth makes translation studies a challenging field in which to be active as a practitioner, scholar, or theorist. Stressing the breadth of knowledge required of translators and translation scholars, Cronin concludes that those involved in translation must be characterized by "disciplinary nomadism" (2003:112).

Although translation studies could be considered a social science as easily as one of the humanities, the majority of students and scholars come to translation after humanist training. Many people are excellent analysts of texts but may find it difficult to understand some of the technical linguistic aspects of the field or to master methods of empirical research. Others come to translation studies with training primarily in language study – often language pedagogy – which leaves them ill prepared to deal with the broader questions in the field about culture and ideology. Most translation scholars have been attracted by the almost physical delights of translation itself, yet as practitioners are often myopic about theory, confusing their own practical preferences for universal principles.

To stay abreast of the ever-growing blurred margin between translation studies and other areas of scholarly inquiry, therefore, everyone in the field must commit to a broad reading program that reaches widely into the humanities, social sciences, and natural sciences in search of material relevant, even essential, to their own specialties in translation. A particular stumbling block for many scholars in the field is an adequate understanding of scientific concepts and methods and the ways in which they intersect with research on translation. In essence many translation scholars continue to live out C.P. Snow's notion of the "two cultures" (described in his *The Two Cultures and the Scientific Revolution*, 1960), even though his warnings against the crippling effects of the isolation of humanist and scientific disciplines are now a half century old. People in translation studies with a broad general education are fortunate indeed. Those without such a background must play "catch up": self-study about many fields is a necessary commitment to sound research in the discipline. A mastery of the basics of scientific inquiry is essential. Student translators and student translation scholars must be encouraged to become more well educated culturally and intellectually than ever before.

In order to achieve verifiable conclusions, all research – whatever the field – rests ultimately on observation of the world of experience and the collection and assessment of data resulting from those observations.[1] Data that can be observed, tested, analyzed, and replicated are the bedrock of research. In turn adequate collection and assessment of data rest on fundamentals associated with the so-called scientific method. In a field such as translation studies that is not devoted primarily to the natural sciences and that draws a preponderance of scholars from the humanities, researchers may not be well educated about the fundamentals of research. Some may have to reach back to their secondary education to remember learning anything at all about scientific methods. If this is the case, there is a problem, because in secondary schools science is often taught in a fairly primitive or naive way by teachers who are themselves not actively engaged in or conversant with contemporary research principles and methods. Often what passes for science and experimentation in secondary schools is essentially a nineteenth-century positivist approach that has long been superseded in the scientific research community. Clearly translation scholars cannot practice or promulgate obsolete ideas about research methods. Research must be consonant with postpositivist premises, reflecting the broad trends of intellectual history in the last century and contemporary views of research.

Moreover, if a person's grasp of scientific research principles derives only from exposure in secondary school, it is imporant to realize that some forms of secondary education cover the basic content of the sciences but omit actual laboratory experiences involving student experiments, collection and analysis of data, and write ups of the results. Thus, some humanists lack basic training in hypothesis formation and testing, recognition and determination of margins of error or uncertainties in research conclusions, protocols facilitating replicability of results, and interrogation of the researcher's perspective and presuppositions. All these elements characterize contemporary practices in the social sciences and natural sciences, and they are key to research in any field, translation studies included. Cronin (2006:20-21) observes that former distinctions between the natural and social sciences are breaking down; with its affinities to the social sciences, translation studies will be implicated in this slippage as well. Understanding and working within such frameworks will thus become increasingly important in the coming decades.[2]

Even thinking about research methods in such a context may be a problem

---

[1] Of course, I do not mean that one must necessarily have to collect the data oneself to do research; a scholar may be fortunate enough to have access to materials already gathered by earlier scholars. Indeed assessment and theorization of preexisting data are essential research activities. I am also not giving a definition of *research* as it is or should be understood by institutions assessing their research staff: clearly theorizing and new analyses of existing data fall well within the scope of research in such circumstances. But if there are ultimately no data, it is hard to conceive of being able to proceed with research at all.

[2] Chesterman notes that regarding hypotheses and hypothesis formation, "there is no difference . . . in principle between hard or soft sciences, nor even between empirical and hermeneutic approaches" (2000:21).

for some translation scholars, for there is widespread prejudice against scientific thinking in many humanistic quarters. Ill feelings are not entirely without reason, but sometimes they can actually be traced to a kind of reaction formation based on ignorance of science rather than on substantial knowledge of and informed objection to the sciences. Similarly many who decry the role of science in contemporary life lack an understanding of the links between research in the sciences and research in other domains. Before proceeding to a general discussion of scientific methods and their relevance for research in translation studies, I wish to state plainly that I am not uncritical of the natural or social sciences. Any body of knowledge has an ethical and ideological aspect, and researchers in every discipline have ethical responsibilities. Scientists have not always been mindful or respectful of these dimensions of their practices, nor have they always been held accountable for their work. Alas, neither have all humanists, including those in translation studies.

Any field can be used for good or ill. What goes by the name of science has at times been used to pollute the earth, to exploit natural resources, to make war, and to enslave people. People operating within a positivist framework have used the name of science as a means of uncritically asserting truth or seizing power, obscuring their own partisan interests in the results. There are similar dangers in all academic disciplines, no less in translation studies, particularly in the context of globalization. Fortunately many translation scholars are actively raising ethical questions, concerned that translations studies not abandon social responsibility at this critical time. In any field researchers have an obligation to interrogate the ethical basis of their work; neither the natural sciences nor translation studies is exempt. In my view, therefore, to say that something is scientific is not to valorize it or to say that it is necessarily good. At the same time, to say that a thing is scientific is not to say that it is necessarily bad either.

Whatever your position on science, I suggest that insofar as your research in translation studies involves gathering and interpreting data – assembling a corpus, undertaking numerical analysis, offering an explanation, or recommending translation practices – you will be operating in a domain that cannot be dissociated from what has traditionally been called the "scientific method". Any descriptive study of translation will have to come to terms with methodological problems related to gathering and analyzing data, and any statements about practice, unless they are pure opinion not backed by information and data, will have to do the same. Even if you believe that you can offer valid insights in translation studies without using standard research methods and that there should be a devalorization of science, I offer a reminder that "a moratorium on science is as impracticable as a moratorium on sin" (*Encyclopaedia Britannica* 1974:16.392e). Because so many translation scholars will continue to conduct research and make arguments on what may broadly be called a scientific basis, it behooves all scholars in the field to understand something about sound research methods, if only to be able to evaluate and critique the work of colleagues.

4.1 General Considerations about Research Methods

Let us begin with a very general definition of the scientific method that dates from the middle of the twentieth century. I am citing the *Encyclopaedia Britannica* (hereafter also *EB*) not because it is "correct" or "objective", but because a compendium of this sort represents a type of cultural consensus and reflects widespread thinking of its age about a broad range of subjects. In this case, moreover, by comparing successive editions of the encyclopedia, it is possible to see how attitudes toward the scientific method have changed in the postpositivist climate of the postwar period in which translation studies has taken shape as an academic discipline.

In the 1947 *Encyclopaedia Britannica* there is an entry for "scientific method" stipulating that "any mode of investigation by which . . . impartial and systematic knowledge is acquired is called a scientific method" (*EB* 1947:20.127g). This statement retains a somewhat positivist orientation, asserting the "impartiality" of scientific methodology and hinting at the notion of the "objectivity" of scientific research. Thirty years later the definition of the scientific method had expanded considerably and had become much more elastic: "once considered to be a rigorous procedure that included the study of scientific hypotheses, induction, theories, laws, and methods of explanation, [the scientific method is] now regarded as a family of methods each of which differs according to the subject matter involved" (*EB* 1974:VIII.985 s.v.). One sees here the impact of the postpositivist trajectory discussed in chapter 1 in the emphasis on perspective and flexibility. According to this later definition, the core of this family of research methods is two-fold: experimentation or repeated observations, and the measurement of phenomena (*EB* 1974:VIII.985 s.v.). Though simple, this common core has important implications: research conclusions should be testable, replicable, and verifiable, and they should have a certain precision that corresponds to the concept of measurement.

The notion that scientific methodology is specific to subject matter (and hence perspective) became even more central in the 2005 *Encyclopaedia Britannica*. In this edition the entry "scientific method" disappeared altogether, and one must look in separate entries related to specific disciplines in order to read about the methodologies of mathematics, physics, chemistry, and the biological and social sciences. Moreover, the article on "philosophy of science" asserts that "once it is recognized how different are the kinds of questions arising within such diverse fields . . . the goal of formulating a single scientific method – with a universally applicable set of procedures and criteria for judging new theories or ideas in all fields of science – may come to appear a mirage" (*EB* 2005:25.659).

The pluralism inherent in the "scientific method" can be demonstrated in the domain of physics, where there is wide variability in methodology. Physics has evolved and continues to develop without any single methodological strategy: advances come from careful refinements in measurement to uncover anomalous behavior, mathematical extrapolation of existing theory, critical reexamination of apparently obvious but untested presuppositions, argument by symmetry or analogy, esthetic judgment, accident, and hunch (*EB* 1974:14.427h). From a contemporary point of view, then, the task of translation studies is not to take up a research methodology from another discipline or to develop a single approach to research, but rather to define methodologies appropriate to its own subject matter that will nonetheless retain the basic characteristics of research, namely measurement, verifiability, and replicability.

A helpful perspective on these questions of methodology comes from Charles Sanders Peirce. Peirce argued that the scientific method is one of several ways of fixing beliefs; beliefs in turn are essentially habits of action. According to Peirce it is characteristic of the methods of science that it makes its ideas clear first in terms of the sensible effects of the objects of the science and second in terms of the habits of action adjusted to those effects. An example of this progression is the mineralogist who makes the idea of hardness clear by indicating that the sensible effect of x being harder than y (say, diamond being harder than glass) is that x will scratch y and not be scratched by it. In turn, believing that x is harder than y means habitually using x to scratch y (say, in dividing glass with a diamond-edged cutting tool) and keeping x away from y when y is to remain unscratched.[3]

Applying these criteria to translation, one can see that insofar as scholars attempt to define types of translations in terms of sensible effects and to outline habits of action in terms of those effects, scholars and teachers of translation are implicitly appealing to scientific reasoning in translation studies. Because such arguments permeate all translation studies, it is not, therefore, a matter of injecting scientific thinking into the field or fighting to keep it out, but rather a question of better understanding the particular characteristics of scientific reasoning in translation studies and honing methodologies in order to improve research protocols already used in the discipline. It is also clear that at a time when both definitions of translation and translation praxis (i.e. habits of action) are shifting, questions about research are critical.

In turning to general aspects of contemporary thinking about research methods that relate to this task, it is important initially to recognize that research is *empirical* but that does not make it *objective*. The *American Heritage Dictionary* defines *empirical* as "relying upon or derived from observation or experiment"; by contrast, *objective* is "of or having to do with a material object as distinguished from a mental concept, idea, or belief", "having actual existence or reality", and "uninfluenced by emotion, surmise, or personal prejudice". A good account of these distinctions as they relate to translation has been given by Sandra Halverson (in "Forum" 2000:2.356-62). She points out that belief in a "world out there" entails a commitment to empirical investigation, but not necessarily to "a belief that all parts of that world are observer-independent or that there is one 'true' way

---

[3] See the discussion of Peirce in *EB* (1974:13.1109).

of describing it" (357). She argues that it therefore follows that "an attempt to argue against empirical work . . . by arguing against objectivism . . . is fallacious. The one does not entail the other" (357). The detachment of empiricism from objectivism has been a key element in postpositivist research.[4]

In fact all research, including research in the natural sciences, is subjective, influenced by ideas and beliefs related to subject positions, frames of reference, interpretations, mental concepts, and received meanings, such as theoretical frameworks and disciplinary paradigms. Remember that Peirce argues that the scientific method is a means of "fixing beliefs", not a means of establishing truth. This distinction is central to the postpositivist developments discussed in this book. Because objectivity is impossible, it is all the more important that beliefs and intellectual perspectives should be well grounded in an empirical sense, namely, consistent with observation of the world of experience and experiment. Research methods must result in conclusions that have this character, even though self-awareness about the limitations of intellectual frameworks makes it impossible to claim "universal" validity for the results of research. Obviously what is established empirically will be reexamined when theoretical paradigms or subject positions shift and in fact this sort of reexamination is currently being demanded precisely because of shifting paradigms in translation studies. Observation of the world of experience is nonetheless the foundation of all data, even if observation and description cannot be considered strictly speaking neutral, objective, or completely free of interpretation, ideological assumptions, and value judgments. Moreover, observation becomes critical when intellectual frameworks are being reconsidered, as they are at present in translation studies.

There is widespread agreement that all disciplines that can be said to use aspects of a scientific methodology have three components (*EB* 1974:16.382 ff.; *EB* 2005:658-60, 664). First are empirical data and their theoretical interpretations. Second are conceptual elements and modes of explanation: each discipline has terminology and abstractions, including classifications; such "conceptual elements are the intellectual keys by which phenomena are made intelligible" (*EB* 1974:16.382f). Third, every discipline has formal elements, such as ways of calculating or methods for conducting experiments.

These three elements that are characteristic of any research area can be illustrated by examples from translation studies. One of the classes of data recognized in the field is the repertory of translation products throughout history, and systems theory is one theoretical framework used to interpret these data. Abstractions and terminology in translation studies include ways to classify translation (adequate/acceptable, dynamic equivalence/formal equivalence, and the like). Formal elements in translation studies are exemplified by techniques

---

[4] The disjunction between empiricism and objectivity as it relates to translation studies is also discussed in Chesterman (2000:21), Crisafulli (2002), and Tymoczko (2002:22-23), as well as sources cited.

of establishing and interrogating translation corpora.[5]

It is obvious that research in any field is facilitated by greater clarity about the three basic elements of research. Noting that methodological issues are at the forefront of translation studies, Edoardo Crisafulli asks, "what counts as adequate evidence in translation studies?" and "which features of translation behaviour should we single out as relevant or meaningful?" (2002:27-28). We can pose still more questions related to the basic elements of research. What modes of data collection are being employed? How do scholars use and manipulate data? What types of theoretical and explanatory interpretations have been incorporated into the field? What types of explanatory interpretations are accepted by scholars and what types are contested? What range of conceptual elements is the field working with? What methods of calculation are considered acceptable? How are frameworks and formal elements established and admitted to the field? In translation studies deliberations about these methodological issues have begun, but the field is far behind most of the natural and social sciences in these enterprises, and this type of inquiry must continue and deepen.[6]

It has been generally accepted that to recognize a class or category is the simplest method of science, for it is tantamount to recognizing the unity of central or necessary attributes in a multiplicity of instances (*EB* 1947:20.129b; *EB* 1974:16.384c ff.). Because classification is a precondition of research methods, the theory of classification is an important area in many fields, illustrated in translation studies by the discussions in the earlier chapters of this book. Nonetheless, categorization and classification in and of themselves are not normally the final goals of research. The power of establishing classifications is that category knowledge and its applications permit induction and inferences, as Gregory Murphy (2002:243-69) indicates. Murphy argues that categories whose members are extremely similar provide stronger inductive power than those whose members are less similar, and more specific categories allow stronger inductions than general categories (Murphy 2002:244).

These issues are particularly relevant to translation studies and we will return to them again in the next section. In fields based on cluster concepts, such as linguistics, literary studies, and translation studies, researchers not only face difficulties in establishing classifications, they are limited in their ability to draw conclusions. They can only engage in inductive reasoning based on categorization carefully and cautiously, because the properties of different groups of the cluster category are diverse and dispersed. Classification is made possible by central cognitive skills that allow data to be processed on the basis of similarity, likeness and difference, analogy, and so forth. Questions about similarity are critical in

---

[5] Discussions of corpora in translation studies are found in Laviosa (1998) and Olohan (2004).

[6] For general approaches to research in translation studies, see Pym (1998), Olohan (2000), Hermans (2002), and Williams and Chesterman (2002).

any field, but especially so in a field like translation studies where the center of inquiry is a cluster concept.

Problems of classification have been a perennial issue in many disciplines. In fields where researchers have scientific training, the importance of questions about classification is generally explicitly recognized and addressed. Problems of classification do not end with definitions; even when a discipline has an established classification system, the units to be classified may not have a clear-cut or precise identity. In most fields basic classifications depend on statistical distributions of variable characteristics rather than on constant criteria (*EB* 1974:4.693e). Thus, an investigator will frequently have to develop a decision procedure or elaborate a classificatory scheme rather than being able to appropriate one from an established, preexisting theory or model (*EB* 1974:4.693e).

Another general consideration relevant to research methods is the interdependence of empirical elements (or data) and theoretical ones. Positivist approaches to science viewed empirical data as objective and, hence, independent of theory. Postpositive approaches acknowledge the interrelationship of theoretical perspectives and data. The empirical and the theoretical cannot be kept distinct in any discipline: as the *Encyclopaedia Britannica* asserts in 1974 (16.384c ff., 386c ff.), evidence collected loses its pure and theoretically neutral character. Hence, it is important in scholarly disciplines to be aware of the theoretical framework being employed, because that framework will shape and define the data used in research in various ways. The interrelationship of data and theory has been recognized and addressed in translation studies by several scholars,[7] but the issue must be underscored again. Crisafulli observes that "empirical facts do not exist independently of the scholar's viewpoint; indeed, it is the scholar who creates the empirical facts of the analysis by making observable . . . data relevant to his/her perspective" (2002:32-33). Moreover, he indicates that value judgments influence the selection of data and the categories of analysis, as well as the explanatory theories used to organize the data and the categories (32-33). Noting that categories of analysis cannot be neutral because they imply political and ideological assumptions, Crisafulli concludes that "the process of selecting data – like the ensuing textual analysis itself – is a complex interpretative act" (2002:33, 39; cf. Halverson 1999a:19.). Failure to understand how theory and data are interrelated and interdependent will interfere with the transferability of the results and the soundness of the conclusions of any scholarly research.

Questions related to transferability and the acceptance of conclusions take us to the more general question of how research is validated. Validation is normally constructed in terms of two factors: prediction on the one hand or coherence and scope on the other. Assessment of validity based on prediction is considered an empiricist approach to the issue, while assessment based

---

[7] Toury (1991), for example, argues this point with reference to translation studies, indicating that theory influences how data are interpreted but that data in turn interrogate theory.

on coherence and scope is called a constructivist or rationalist orientation (*EB* 1974:16:387h).[8] In any field principles of validation must to some extent be considered anew with respect to any particular case study or research problem, for each new situation presents its own specific demands related to validation (*EB* 1974:16:388f). Researchers must therefore think through not only how to articulate their *arguments* but also how to make appeals for the *validity* of their frameworks, their data, and their conclusions.

The validation of research in any field depends on the quality of the data collected. A major consideration relevant to the selection of data is that data not be one-sided or biased (*EB* 1947:20.132g). This is a problem in the humanities or social sciences when researchers attempt to assert universal conclusions based on data from a single culture, for example. In this regard the size of the sample is considered less important than the variety of the data, if variation in data exists (*EB* 1947:20.132g). The reliability of data is also correlated with sampling techniques; reliable data collection in the social and natural sciences often involves techniques such as random sampling. Because conclusions resulting from analysis of data depend on induction, the conclusions of research are only as good as the data they are based on. Biased data lead to circular reasoning and undermine the validity of the conclusions.

Still another general feature of research is experimentation and the construction of experiments. One of the differences between observation and experiment is control (*EB* 1947:20.128c): beginning with a hypothesis, the researcher devises ways to test the hypothesis, such as by varying conditions or introducing new variables. An advantage of experiment over mere observation is that experiment makes possible more reliable analysis of complex phenomena and more reliable inferences about their connections (*EB* 1947:20.128c). It is also possible to explore and test specific aspects of interesting phenomena by means of the research design, such that the research reveals more detailed information than observation without intervention or experiment can do.

A final general issue pertaining to research is the question of models, which are often essential to data collection and analysis in research. Translation studies is no exception in this regard, with research on translation practices and descriptive studies of translation products depending equally on models. A model is a simplifed represention of some aspect of the world of experience, and, as such, it includes only those variables relevant to the problem at hand. In certain circumstances a model might not even include all relevant variables because a small percentage of the variables might account for most of the phenomena to be

---

[8] Closely related to coherence is the concept of "elegance" in which simpler explanations with the same coherence and scope are preferred to more complex ones covering the same data. Moreover, the wider the scope of the data and the more coherent the material in relationship to the simplicity of the model, the more elegant the form of validation is considered. Elegance is generally seen as more persuasive than explanations lacking elegance.

explained (*EB* 1974:13.596b). Simplifications produce some error in predictions derived from the model, but these errors can often be kept small compared to the benefit in terms of explanation or improvements in process derived from the model (*EB* 1974:13.596b).

There are several steps common to research methods utilizing models. First the problem must be formulated and the system analyzed to identify relevant controlled variables, uncontrolled variables, and constraints. Second, the model must be constructed and articulated. Third, the model must be used to derive a solution. Fourth, both the model and the solution must be tested. Finally, the solution must be implemented and controlled.[9] Obviously not all of these stages are relevant to every type of research, but the question of models in general is germane to any discipline, including translation studies.

Traditionally the goal of research – paradigmatically so in the natural sciences – has been to find regularities and order in phenomena and to connect phenomena in significant ways (*EB* 1947:20.128e). To discover order in any class of phenomena has been viewed as a way of making the phenomena clearer and more intelligible, namely, of explaining the phenomena under investigation (*EB* 1947:20.133a). In turn, to explain something is to show its place in a larger system (*EB* 1947:20.133a). Because research in translation studies subscribes to these basic goals (insofar as any social phenomena can be said to have order in light of their complex, heterogeneous, and often fragmentary nature), the general principles of research methods discussed here have relevance for the field. It is therefore important to understand them clearly and to articulate their specific qualities in actual translation studies research.

At the beginning of this section, we observed that the scientific method is currently regarded as a family of methods, each of which differs according to the subject matter and field involved, rather than a single unified approach to research. If it is true that to a certain extent every discipline must develop its own methodologies, it follows that it will be useful to explore issues that are particular to research methods in translation studies and to characterize those methods relative to research methods in other fields, especially as the field grows and expands. Such explorations identify strengths of research methods in translation studies and areas in which research methods in the field need to be expanded or augmented. This sort of exploration is particularly important for a discipline in rapid transition, as translation studies is at present as a result of globalization and the increasing internationalization of the field. In what follows, therefore, I look at the ways that the general characteristics of research pertain specifically to translation studies as it is being reconfigured at present.

---

[9] An extended discussion of these aspects of models is found in the entry on "operations research" in *EB* (1974:13.594-602).

4.2 Classification in Translation Studies Research

If conceptual elements "are the intellectual keys by which phenomena are made intelligible" (*EB* 1974:16.382f), then classification and definition are key elements for translation studies to address. Adequate methods of classification are a prerequisite for formulating translation theory, but conversely operative translation theory is not possible unless it serves as an adequate framework for the various classes of data in the field, both cross-cultural and cross-temporal. Thus classification and definition constitute the motor that makes the entire research enterprise go. It is largely for this reason that in the previous two chapters I considered at length the nature of *translation as a cross-cultural, cross-temporal concept and category and that I discussed ways of framing *translation that contribute to understanding and exploring the fuzzy boundaries of translation. These enterprises advance an improved articulation of the conceptual elements in the field.

As we have seen, it is urgent at present to revisit questions of classification in the discipline and to build new approaches to classification into research methods. Adequate classification is not only foundational for the research enterprise, it is a precondition of enlarging the field of data consonant with the increased internationalization of translation studies and with shifts associated with technological change and globalization. Current conceptualizations of both translation and translators must be reviewed to accommodate translation in these new contexts for purposes of praxis as much as research or theory.

There are many questions about classification to be considered in translation studies. For example, if *translation cross-culturally constitutes a cluster concept, what sorts of clusters can be identified within the concept as a whole and how are they affected by data emerging from larger international contexts? What new clusters must be distinguished to accommodate new data in the field and how can they be characterized? Which translation clusters are restricted to individual cultures and which ones transcend (and link) cultural domains? If frameworks provide an important way of investigating translation data, what sorts of classifications do they lead to with respect to old data and emergent data as well? How do new technologies and globalization affect classifications in translation studies? If translation refers to both processes and products, how are these twin systems – each requiring classification – related to each other?

We have seen that it is generally agreed at present that there is no single "scientific method" applicable to all fields, but that each field has the task of defining its own research methodologies. Despite the broad scope of translation studies, some methodological features can be identified as characteristic of the discipline. Many of these features follow directly from the problems of conceptualizing and classifying *translation cross-linguistically, cross-culturally, and cross-temporally. That is, they are singularities that result from having the specific cluster concept *translation at the heart of the discipline.

Halverson (1999a:11) attributes significant disagreements in theoretical discourses about translation to disagreements about the nature of the category translation itself. Some scholars prefer to limit research and scholarly discourses to highly restricted definitions of translation, such as translation as it is practiced by contemporary professional European translators or translation as it is used commercially (both of which in different ways represent hegemonic versions of translation). Adopting such limited classifications as the basis of research entails acknowledging the ensuing limitations in the applicability of conclusions resulting from the research undertaken on this basis. Others argue for broader definitions, including literary translation, past historical practices, community interpretation, and the like. Increasingly translation scholars from countries outside Eurocentric areas are also objecting to the limitations of classifications and theorizations based principally on Western data and Western histories and practices of translation. As a consequence of the controversy in the discipline about classification – often attributable to the unrecognized nature of *transla- tion as a cluster concept – individual scholars generally must address questions of classification and stipulate the definition of translation being used in a given research project. They must justify what will count as data in the research, be- cause it is not self-evident what should count as a translation process or product in any particular situation or in the current research environment in the field as a whole.

Translation studies is by no means the only discipline that faces problems defining and classifying its subject matter and not all of these problems can be ascribed to dealing with a cluster concept. Definitional problems are endemic in the social sciences, many of the natural sciences, and even mathematics (cf. *EB* 1974:16:384c ff.). Difficulties in defining or classifying objects of study are apparent in cutting-edge research in such fields as cosmology or biochemistry in situations where scientists are aware of a set of phenomena, but do not know the cause of the phenomena or even their full scope. In some cases uncertainties of this kind in physics and astronomy have persisted for decades. Nonetheless, the situation in translation studies regarding definition is somewhat different from those in scientific fields where the objects of inquiry are natural kinds or natural phenomena that have widespread acknowledgment across cultures, because problems of definition in most fields are not usually attributable to the fact that the subject matter constitutes a fuzzy set and that it has blurred boundaries. Trans- lation studies is not unique in facing this problem, of course, because other fields also have cluster concepts as their subject matter – notably linguistics, ethnography, and literary studies, with language, culture, and literature as their (blurred) subjects respectively – and such fields stand out as needing different research protocols from those disciplines with more closely defined subject matter.[10] It would

---

[10] Even biology is faced with blurred boundaries, as in the notorious case of trying to define life and living entities. See also Lakoff (1987:31-37, 118-21, 185-95) on categorization problems related to species and natural kinds.

be interesting to compare research methods in such disciplines with those in translation studies, focusing on difficulties related to establishing classifications in fields based on cluster concepts or concepts with blurred boundaries and attempting to delineate research techniques for coping with the special conceptual features of these disciplines.

Classification is a persistent problem in translation studies because, as we saw in the last section, it has been traditionally held that to recognize a class is the simplest method of science, associated with recognizing the unity of essential attributes in a multiplicity of instances (*EB* 1947:20.129b). In a field that has a cluster concept at its heart, however, where there are no essential attributes nor any simple or obvious form of unity, how is classification to proceed? Conversely, how does a discipline function when there is basic uncertainty and contention about classification and, hence, about the subject matter itself? How can "units of analysis" be identified? Is there a basis for the units of analysis that are commonly accepted by researchers or are such units established in an *ad hoc* or arbitrary manner, relative to every research project individually and based on each researcher's convenience? In such circumstances how can general theory emerge? How do all these questions get resolved across the boundaries of language and culture in an international discipline? These are all questions that will remain essential to discuss in translation studies while it continues as an emerging field; indeed translation studies *will be* an emerging field until some consensus can be achieved with respect to at least some of these questions.

Issues pertaining to classification enter immediately into the activities undertaken by translation scholars in their research. If research *ipso facto* involves repeated observation or experimentation, one must know what should be observed or experimented upon. Because translations constitute a blurred category, translation scholars must stipulate the sorts of translations they will be observing and experimenting with. They must also consider how those translations constitute a coherent group or cluster within local, international, and diachronic categories of translation; how to draw the boundaries between the cluster being studied and other groups; how to relate the group under investigation to other groups of translation; how the specific group is situated within the entire range of translation phenomena; and how the group intersects with various superordinate categories that serve as frameworks for the subject matter. As scholars make these decisions, they must interrogate their pretheoretical dispositions and assumptions about the nature of translation cross-culturally so as to avoid eliminating translation types that could be pertinent to their research.[11] It is always an option to use a

---

[11] For example, descriptive translation studies examining the use of translation in the construction of cultural identity might need to examine some "non-standard" and unexpected types of translation, including perhaps travel brochures or videos at a visitors center. The exclusion of such translations might lead to the omission of important evidence.

limited class of translations in particular research, thus circumventing problems associated with the open nature of translation as a cluster concept, as has been discussed, but if that option is taken, researchers then have the responsibility to recognize and remain cognizant of how such limitations in the research design affect limitations on the validity, applicability, extension, and generalization of conclusions. Such limitations must in turn be indicated in any dissemination of the research results. All of these issues have become more acute in the last decade as the definition of translation has enlarged and the role of translation in the world has expanded, not least because of changing technologies.

A final concern about classification in translation studies pertains to the inductive power associated with classification. If categories whose members are less similar have weaker inductive power (Murphy 2002:244), it follows that in translation studies – a discipline investigating a very diverse category whose members are overall very dissimilar – researchers must engage in inductive reasoning very cautiously. If members of the cluster concept *translation are related by family resemblances, then similarity in translation processes and products will also be characterized by family resemblances, a point worth future examination relative to classification in translation studies. The resulting diverse and dissimilar properties of different members and different clusters of the cross-cultural category *translation, as well as the ability of individual translators to generate new translation types by inventing new strategies or departing from established norms, severely limit the use of induction in the field. This question of induction has direct implications for both research and teaching in translation studies. Goals often seen as paradigmatic of research – including finding regularities, systematicity in investigations, or exhaustive review of data – can be pursued only to a limited extent with reference to a cluster concept. Moreover, because of the diversity in the category, the predictive power of research done on a restricted domain of *translation (say, community interpreting, legal translation, translation for the media, or literary translation) will generally be narrowly limited to a small area of the field or to a very specific context and thus be only weakly applicable to the field as a whole. The limitations of induction in translation studies also have clear implications for pedagogy in the discipline and constitute another reason for avoiding rigid prescriptive teaching methods. The weak inductive power in the field means that prescriptive statements appropriate for one domain of translation may not be at all relevant to many other contexts that students will encounter professionally. Pedagogical prescriptions in translator training or pedagogical instructions based on false induction will lead students astray and do them a disservice in their professional lives. Thus, the seeming recondite question of classification has immediate implications for teaching techniques in the discipline of translation studies.

4.3 Principles of Validation in Translation Studies

A second major concern for research in translation studies pertains to articulating principles of validation. Traces of and appeals to both forms of validation
(the empiricist interest in prediction and the constructivist interest in coherence
and scope) are found in translation studies research to date, but scholars differ
sharply on which principles of validation should be preferred. Gideon Toury and
Itamar Even-Zohar, among others promoting "empiricist" research, have been
interested in prediction, but such scholars have been criticized for this impulse.
Indeed some of the sharpest criticism of the work of Toury and Even-Zohar turns
on their principles of validation: this contention is in essence what the criticism
of their search for "laws" enabling prediction amounts to.[12] By contrast, other
scholars rely chiefly on claims related to coherence and scope to validate their
work. For example, although my own work occasionally evokes empiricist principles of validation, typically I appeal to the principles of coherence and scope
(as well as elegance) in validating arguments.[13] Such contentions and disparities related to principles of validation have become more acute as the field has
coalesced internationally, as it has become more disparate, and as it has included
more parameters in its purview since World War II. In part these contentions
are a function of the expansion of the concept *translation and the consequent
involvement of a broader range of scholars in translation research.

The quality of research and scholarly discourses in the discipline will
be strengthened by more direct discussion about what forms of validation are
generally acceptable and why, what specific types of validation are appropriate
for specific types of research, and similar questions. It should be recognized,
however, that if *translation is a cluster concept, it will be hard to appeal chiefly
to the empiricist tool of prediction as the main form of validation in translation
research, because of the limited inductive possibilities in the field. Insofar as
*translation is an open category, few predictions can hold for all translation
products, for all translation processes, and for all translation situations, because
any assumptions behind the predictions would be tantamount to establishing
necessary and sufficient conditions for membership in the category itself. Thus,
it seems likely that prediction as a principle of validation will normally be useful
only in limited domains where a restricted definition of translation obtains (for
instance, in a particular commercial or government enterprise) or where a class
of translational phenomena has been stipulated by a researcher as the domain
of a research project.

Related to principles of validation in research are protocols of data collection

---

[12] Gentzler (2001:122, 140-44), for example, takes this tack; Crisafulli (2002) offers a useful
assessment of the criticisms of Toury and other objections to "scientific models". See also
Hermans (1999:36, 111-12).

[13] This orientation is apparent in the nature of the argumentation in Tymoczko (1999b).

that ensure the verifiability and replicability of research conclusions, particularly issues associated with sampling techniques and the size and range of data samples upon which conclusions are based. In translation studies these are critical issues because of the open nature of the concept translation, the wide variability of translation types in the cluster category, and the resultant limited power of induction in the field. As the concept of translation is further enlarged, these difficulties in data collection and sampling protocols will become increasingly critical.

We have seen that with respect to the validation of research, sample size is less significant than the variety of data employed, if variation in data exists (*EB* 1947:20.132g). This criterion of variety also causes problems of validation in translation studies. Because of the capacious nature of *translation as a cluster concept, the question of whether the variety of data is appropriate and sufficient relative to the scope of the conclusions reached is a perennial issue translation scholars face. It will not do to investigate oral translation in an unlettered population in South Africa and claim universal applicability of the results to literary translation in Europe or to a professional group of translators engaged in multimodal translation for electonic media. Nor is the converse the case. Conclusions based solely on Eurocentric data from literate contexts have no more privileged claim to universal validity about translation than do conclusions based on data about translation in oral traditional societies. In both cases it is doubtful that conclusions would be verifiable or replicable in the other cultural domain. The variety of data considered is immediately relevant to the domain of the conclusions and the validation possible in translation research.[14]

Several specific features of data collection also problematize validation in translation studies. It is often difficult to deploy standard data collection procedures developed and utilized in other disciplines to ensure replicability and verifiability. One difficulty is achieving sufficient sample size, particularly in descriptive studies dealing with translation phenomena from the past. Because conclusions must be based on a sufficiently large sample in order to justify extensions of the conclusions to other situations, the question of sample size is crucial. Achieving an adequate sample size is not always easy, not only when one is investigating scarce evidence from the past but also when researching a unique translation of a source text, translations of the work of a single author, the output of a single translator or a single translation movement, and so forth. In such circumstances a scholar must look for creative solutions to the problem. Although there are useful techniques for circumventing the absence of large quantities of data – for example, validation of scope based on data external to the translation data themselves (such as paratextual evidence or parallel texts) – the

---

[14] Thus, the domain covered by research is an essential factor in constructing durable theory applicable to the field as a whole, rather than being restricted to the dominant social conventions of specific research contexts. A more detailed consideration of this point in found in Tymoczko (1999b:32 ff.). See also 4.7 below.

problem of sample size is a perennial issue demanding attention in descriptive studies. An insufficient sample size may make it difficult to test and reproduce research results, and the margin of error may be so large relative to the body of data that conclusions remain tentative at best. These are significant problems because adequate research is predicated on the condition that conclusions be testable, replicable, and verifiable.

Even when sample size and variety are sufficient to generate predictions or validation based on coherence and scope, sample size in translation studies may still be insufficient for the use of the strongest class of research validation tools, namely, quantitative methods. Statistically significant quantitative analyses of data are often difficult to achieve in the field because samples can be so diverse. Translated texts are seldom uniform in length, texture, genre, and so forth, thus making quantitative methods difficult to apply. This is a serious limitation because measurement and similar indices of precision are central to research methods in most academic fields, having been standard in many disciplines for more than a century. Partly in recognition of the usefulness of quantification and measurement as forms of validation, corpus translation scholars have worked on structuring corpora that provide large and comparable bodies of data and on developing methods that permit quantitative analyses of the data gathered, thus generating results that can be replicated and tested by other scholars.[15] This is an intelligent response to many of the structural problems of research in translation studies. Nonetheless, even in corpus translation studies there are limitations on the power of quantitative analysis as a consequence of the nature of *translation as a cluster concept and the necessity to limit conclusions to the types of data sampled (cf. Tymoczko 1998). Such difficulties must be faced squarely and acknowledged in evaluations of the conclusions reached in most translation research, even corpus translation studies.

Closely related to difficulties caused by small sample size in many transla-tion research projects is the problem of constructing control samples. The use of a control sample is a classic method of validating results in scholarly research. These are methodological issues that corpus translation studies usually attempt to address; typically scholars who use corpora are careful to construct parallel corpora that provide control samples for use in validating the results of their research. In descriptive translation studies where the data are limited, however there may be scarcely enough data for a sample, nevermind a control sample. This standard of research is also often difficult to incorporate into one's design, because there may be few groups of translations or translators comparable to those one is researching. In certain situations (for instance, when one is investigating a single translation)

---

[15] See Baker (1995), Laviosa (1998), Olohan (2004). One technique that facilitates quantita-tive analysis, for example, is to have all entries in the corpus conform to a standard sample size; in turn this allows other scholars to develop comparable corpora and test their results against published scholarship.

working with a second translation of the same text will offer a control sample, one that is usually more helpful than the source text itself as a reference point. In some circumstances a set of passages within the source text different from those being analyzed can act as a sort of control group: one might choose comparable passages that are neutral with respect to the issues being investigated. In some cases a control group of translations of parallel texts or parallel text types can be used, either from the same source culture or another culture. In certain circumstances the control group for a study might be another textual genre of the source or target culture. Often I have found that for the non-quantifiable research that is common in descriptive translation studies focused on case studies of specific translations and specific groups of translations, it is sufficient to use a sort of virtual control group: to draw comparisons with a variety of parallel translation situations that have already been discussed in translation studies. Such comparisons are threaded through my own published research on translation and they are there in part to compensate for more rigorous experimental control samples. We should note that some descriptive studies focus less on translations as texts than on larger statistical patterns of translation, for example, the perturbations in the number of translations produced in particular languages under conditions of censorship in a particular context. This type of descriptive study is generally amenable to empiricist methods of validation, the use of quantitative methods, and so forth. In such research sample size is usually sufficient and control groups can be defined.

In research on translation processes, as with many descriptive studies of translation products, there can also be problems in establishing control samples that make validation difficult. These issues arise in research on translators' own reports of their translation methods and processes. Asymmetries associated with differences in languages, cultures, and text types also make it complex to establish control samples and other research protocols that permit generalizing the results beyond the language pair or pairs being used in the research project. Questions of validation associated with sample size and control groups are critical in situations where translation materials are fragmentary, sparse, or incomplete, and overt acknowledgment of the problems should be included in the publication of results. By facing such methodological problems directly, the discipline of translation studies may collectively find ways to come to terms more adequately with some of the limitations related to validation, verification, and replicability in translation research.[16]

One of the strongest means of validation available to researchers in translation studies is the interplay between macro and micro methods in analyzing data. If the large translation effects identified and investigated by cultural studies approaches to translation are in fact the result of small word-by-word,

---

[16] Tymoczko (2002) offers additional suggestions for contending with problems related to sample size and control groups.

sentence-by-sentence, and text-by-text decisions on the part of translators – decisions that can be analyzed with contemporary linguistic tools – then research methods in translation studies will normally benefit from connecting those two realms and using the coherence that results as a principle of validation. Frequently it will be helpful and even essential to identify and retrace linguistic specificities of textual construction, so that macro translation effects are understood specifically as the products of textual construction and production.[17]

Durable conclusions result when evidence and arguments constructed on either the micro or macro level are confirmed at the other level, because results that converge from the directions of both macro and micro analyses have a strong claim to validation based on coherence and scope, resonating in both text and context. This is a special case within translation studies of a principle introduced to physics by Niels Bohr; the so-called correspondence principle is a means of extending theoretical formulations. Bohr argued that when a general theory is applied to a situation in which a less general theory is known to apply, the more general theory must yield the same predictions as the less general theory. Alternatively, when theories correspond, the predictions must correspond.[18] One can either view micro and macro approaches to translation as representing two corresponding theoretical frameworks, or one can view the micro levels of textual analysis as a more specific application of macro approaches to language, text, and culture. Either way, Bohr's correspondence principle represents a way of thinking about and formulating the strong validation effects that result from the coordinated deployment in research of both micro and macro approaches to translation phenomena.

Directly addressing the question of validation is essential to strengthen research methods in the emerging international field of translation studies as the concept of translation enlarges and shifts. Progress in this area will also facilitate the interface between translation studies and other fields of inquiry, thus helping to consolidate the role of translation studies within larger research frameworks. This is imperative as translation enters into more spheres of public discourse and public life.

4.4 Interdependence of Data and Theory in Translation Research

We have seen that there is interdependence between empirical elements (or data) and theoretical elements of research. In no discipline can the empirical and the theoretical be kept absolutely distinct: evidence collected loses its pure and theoretically neutral character (*EB* 1974:16.384c ff., 386c ff.). The collection of data itself depends on theoretical assumptions about what counts as data, and

---

[17] Tymoczko (2002) discusses at greater length the complementarity of micro and macro approaches in translation research.
[18] See the discussion in *EB* (1974:14.428a).

description and analysis of data involve interpretive judgments and evaluation that are driven by theory and intellectual paradigms (cf. Crisafulli 2002:32-34).

The interdependence of data and theory is also demonstrable in the fundamental process of hypothesis formation and testing. Research of all types involves the imaginative construction of a hypothesis that in turn is used to interrogate phenomena and, hence, to evaluate data (*EB* 1947:20.128f). But any hypothesis is also constructed within a theoretical framework and presupposes theoretical perspectives and assumptions. Conclusions are formed not merely on the basis of observation, but also on the basis of inferences – both deduction and induction – that follow from the data (*EB* 1947:20.128g). Such inferences, like hypotheses, are in turn shaped by the theoretical framework accepted by the researcher. This might seem like a closed (or even vicious) circle, but it is the interrelationship of theory and data that makes it possible both to generate data and also to interrogate and improve theory.[19]

Because of the reciprocal relationship between theory and data, the entire research system in translation studies will shift as the discipline moves beyond the Western, responding to the internationalization of the research community, incorporating new international data and data related to translation in the context of globalization, and coming to terms with discourses about translation formulated in many parts of the world. Changed conceptualizations of the subject matter and expansion of the purview of the field will lead to the redefinition of what counts as data and the gathering of new types of data. In turn there will be reformulation of old theory (based on Western data) as new data interrogate and shift the theory itself. Conversely, the ascendancy of new international theories about translation will be followed by new hypotheses leading to the investigation of additional types of data. Needless to say, the initiative for many of these shifts in the research system will come from outside the Eurocentric culture area.

In translation studies research it is not always possible to introduce experimental protections to correct for the researcher's bias, including pretheoretical assumptions and theoretical frameworks. In classic scientific experiments researchers often utilize double-blind collection of data and other experimental protocols that mute the role of the researcher's interpretations.[20] There has been little use of this sort of procedure in translation studies thus far, partly because the field has not yet undertaken large-scale experiments that are amenable to double-blind

---

[19] The interdependence of theory, discourses, concepts, objects, and data is discussed perceptively by Foucault (1972:22-76). Toury (1991) investigates the interrelationship between data and theory in translation studies. Cf. Halverson (1997).

[20] In a double-blind protocol, an experimental sample is paired with a control sample, but researchers themselves do not know which sample is which. In a medical experiment, for example, the primary sample of patients is subject to an intervention (say, treatment with a medicine) and the control sample is not. The individuals participating in both groups are themselves ignorant about their status in the experiment, as are the actual researchers who collect the data.

protocols and partly because most research design and hypothesis testing is still undertaken by a single scholar, which makes it *ipso facto* impossible for the re-searcher to be ignorant of the status of subjects or to be restricted from injecting personal perspectives into the research design and interpretation of data.

Although data never have a "pure", "theoretically neutral", or "objective" character, scholars generally attempt to be aware of theoretical presuppositions and to keep in mind biases, perspectives, and partialities, lest they skew the re-sults of the research, thus invalidating the conclusions. This is a topic that merits consideration not merely at the level of the individual but also at the level of the discipline as the conceptualization of the cross-cultural nature of *translation expands. The following pretheoretical assumptions underpinning much current work in translation studies are examples of problematic presuppositions associ-ated with dominant Eurocentric perspectives.

1. Translators are necessary in interlingual and intercultural situations; they mediate between two linguistic and cultural groups.
2. Translation involves (written) texts.
3. The primary text types that translators work with have been defined and categorized.
4. The process of translation is a sort of "black box": an individual translator decodes a given message to be translated and recodes the same message in a second language.
5. Translators are generally educated in their art and they have professional standing. Often they learn their craft in a formal way through schooling or training that provides instruction in language competence, standards of textuality, norms of transposition, and so forth.
6. Because of cultural movements and diasporas associated with globalization and because of the hybridity of the ensuing cultural configurations, transla-tion is currently entering a completely new phase and assuming radically new forms.
7. Translations can be identified as such: translation theory has defined the objects of its study.
8. The parameters of the relationship between source text and translation have been delineated, even though debate still remains on the particulars.[21]

These presuppositions are based on very limited Western perspectives that ignore the widespread existence of multilingual cultures in the world that obviate a great deal of translation, the dominance of oral culture in many places at present and in the past, the wide variation of text types and translation types across cultures,

---

[21] A critique of these assumptions and suggested remedies are found in Tymoczko (2006).

and the fact that translation is often a group enterprise rather than an individual undertaking. The assumptions also rest on historical myopia, ignoring the fact that within a broad sweep of time and culture, translation has rarely been a profession with formal training and that large-scale population movements and diasporas can be traced for thousands of years. These are all the type of presupposition that must be reconsidered as translation studies becomes truly international, moving beyond Western biases and accepting the implications that follow from seeing *translation as a cross-cultural, cross-temporal cluster concept.

The presuppositions listed above merely begin the task of identifying Western, culture-bound assumptions about translation that have been built into the foundation of the discipline and promulgated by scholars in translation studies whose ideas are disseminated internationally. More work is needed to identify other such blind spots that signal the biases built into hypotheses governing research in the field and into translation theory, particularly at this point in the international expansion of the field.[22] It is not problematic as such to hold presuppositions in research, but it is important to know what they are and to recognize how they limit the extension of any conclusions based on them to conditions that do not conform to the initial assumptions. One cannot assume universal applicability of results based on culture-bound presuppositions without engaging in a form of intellectual imperialism.

Aside from these widely held problematic doxa, scholars must also interrogate their own initial premises and pretheoretical assumptions governing specific research projects. Some of these are shared, such as the assumptions above, but others are particular to the researcher. This means, among other things, asking why you believe what you seem to believe with respect to the problem at hand. All such presuppositions must be acknowledged in writing up research. It is also important to be vigilant in looking for and even attempting to generate counterexamples to one's hypotheses at every stage as research progresses. One might continually interrogate one's premises by imagining what the result would be if the contrary of the initial hypothesis were the case and then looking for data that support such contraindications. Such an approach is a humanist analogue to the mathematical technique of proof by contradiction. This sort of skepticism or doubt is characteristic of all research, but investigations of a social cluster concept call for special vigilance. When such interrogations lead to negative results (i.e., no counterexamples are found), the negative results can also be built into the conclusions of the research, thereby contributing to the strength of the validation of the project.

It is not so much that partialities or presuppositions are bad things in translating or translation research. They often lead to very interesting and original translations and to creative scholarly investigations of translational phenomena.

---

[22] Additional interesting suggestions are found in the essays in Hung and Wakabayashi (2005) and summarized in their introduction.

Postpositivist views acknowledge that such frameworks, perspectives, and positionalities are impossible to avoid, and they are essential in translation and translation scholarship that has an engaged, activist, ideological, or ethical dimension (cf. Tymoczko 1999b:278-98; Davis 2001:91-106). Unless interpretive stances are acknowledged in some way, however, partialities can result in research that overextends conclusions and generalizes results to domains in which they do not hold. They can also lead to the suppression of data or skewed interpretations of results. In all of these cases the purely local is then proclaimed as the universal in an imperialistic, hegemonic, proselytizing, or blinkered way.

With regard to the interdependence of data and theory, an important pitfall to avoid is circular reasoning. A researcher must ascertain that the desired conclusions are not built into the premises and protocols of the research. An example of such a circular reasoning would be a research protocol that only attempts to gather and assess data that validate the desired conclusions: clearly the conclusion here has the status of a presupposition. Data collection must always be wide enough to allow for more than the evidence desired and must include attempts to find counterexamples. It sounds self-evident that one would avoid circular reasoning, but a surprising number of research projects in translation studies fall into this trap. For instance, if one begins with the presupposition that translation is transfer and only looks at modern Western data that has strict protocols governing textual fidelity, one will find confirming evidence that translation is a very specific form of transfer; the results of such a study, however, will not offer much conclusive evidence about the actual role of transfer in translations worldwide in the modern era or in the past. We will return to the problems of circular reasoning in the discussion of models below.

In conducting research, therefore, it is essential to adopt a habit of mind in which there is continual interrogatation of the data and self-reflexive scrutiny of one's own interventions, suppositions, interpretations, and theoretical commitments. Questions such as the following are helpful in dealing with the interdependence of data and theory. How does my own (geopolitical, ideological, material, temporal, gender, linguistic) position affect how I look at things? What questions might I ask if I were coming from a different framework (e.g., another position in translation studies, another linguistic or cultural framework, another ideological framework, another time and place)? You could even ask what position you might take if you were another scholar viewing the same data: what might I ask (or conclude) if I were W.V.O. Quine, J.C. Catford, Eugene Nida, André Lefevere, Lawrence Venuti, Mona Baker, Anthony Pym, Michael Cronin, Else Vieira, Theo Hermans, or Jacques Derrida? The importance of articulating one's positionality for oneself and others is one reason I began this book with reflection on how my own views about translation were formed.

A pervasive structural problem pertaining to data in translation studies – as in many other fields dealing with lesser-used languages – is that of exemplification. Michael Cronin (2003:149, cf. 1998:158) and Şebnem Susam-Sarajeva (2002) have discussed this issue astutely, illustrating the difficulties of doing research based on the texts, linguistic structures, and cultural contexts of minority languages. Both stress the burden of description related to linguistic and cultural specifics, history, and ideological background that must be undertaken by a scholar whose subject matter lies outside the dominant languages and cultures of the world. Susam-Sarajeva observes that there is a temptation for a scholar in such a field to be highly selective in case studies and to simplify examples in order to cut the information load for dominant audiences. Both emphasize that language is power and that issues of exemplification are actually pertinent to all languages, because all languages are potentially minority languages (Cronin 1998:151, 2003:87-88, 151; Susam-Sarajeva 2002:204). Scholars of lesser-used languages must also always translate their examples in order to make their materials accessible to readers; although the research material of translation studies is necessarily polyglot, knowledge *about* this material is increasingly produced, circulated, and stored in a limited number of European languages, principally English, French, and German (Susam-Sarajeva 2002:204). The process of translation is not only a matter of linguistic translation; it also involves translation into the dominant paradigms and discourses of contemporary translation studies (Susam-Sarajeva 2002:200). The result, Cronin indicates, is a tendency for translation in minority languages to be "doubly invisible at a theoretical level" (2003:140). Coming to terms with this problem is essential for the health and development of translation studies. It is impossible for any field to thrive unless it is open to all relevant data, particularly divergent data with the potential to stimulate the productive circle of interrogation linking theorization, data collection, and retheorization. Because the subject of translation studies is the interface of languages, texts, and cultures around the world, exemplification cannot be restricted to dominant linguistic materials.[23]

As postpositivist thought has become more articulated, it has been recognized that no research, however "scientific", can actually be objective, as we have seen.[24] Objectivity may be impossible, but interrogating frameworks and attempting to enlarge frameworks are not only possible but at the heart of human learning. One can almost always look beyond and transcend the most extreme limitations of one's own condition and one's own intellectual frame of reference if one tries consciously to enlarge one's perspective. Human beings cannot – nor should they attempt to – escape presupposed frameworks or mental constraints altogether, but we are also creatures adept at counterfactual thinking, at consideration of possibilities that transcend the realm of our experience. We are not trapped within the constraints of what is: we change our environments (including

---

[23] Issues pertaining to research on minority languages are also taken up in the essays in Venuti (1998b) and Branchadell and West (2005).

[24] This point has already been stressed in various contexts but it does not hurt to repeat it because positivism lives on in many areas of popular culture and many people still subscribe to an idea that objectivity is possible.

our mental environments) and enlarge our frames of reference, continually learning and incorporating new perspectives and positions into our thinking. To make these leaps, however, there must be a will to do so, a self-reflexive willingness to query the most automatized aspects of our received thinking. This self-reflexive process is absolutely essential in research, especially in working out questions pertaining to the interdependence of theory and data. We can only hope that as the discipline of translation studies expands, scholars will have the will to enlarge its frameworks beyond those dominant in Western culture.

George Steiner has observed that

> hypotheticals, "imaginaries", conditionals, the syntax of counter-factuality and contingency may well be the generative centres of human speech. . . . It *is* remarkable, to put it soberly, that we are able to conceptualize and embody in language the limitless category of "the impossible", that neither flying azure pigs nor furious green dreams pose any irreducible conceptual or semantic barriers. (1992:226)

This ability to conceive of alternatives and otherness is at the heart of human intellectual life in general, of scholarship and research in particular, and of many other human activities from invention to storytelling. Such cultural generativity is possible, however, only if there is a self-reflexive understanding and awareness of what is already accepted but open to alteration. The activity of translation is a principal means of actualizing hypotheticals, alternative conceptualizations, and otherness across cultural boundaries. As a discipline translation studies is committed to these transfers and transculturations, and it must find ways to incorporate the same commitment to self-reflexivity on the metalevel of theory in the field itself.

In part because translation studies is a relatively young and emerging international discipline, researchers often investigate things that have not been recognized or discussed before. They enact the human ability to imagine otherness, alternatives, and changes to existing frameworks in a field where the subject matter itself – translation – is similarly crossing borders and exploring otherness. Thus, a scholar must often actually define the nature of the data under consideration, enlarging the field in the process. This is a tremendously exciting facet of research in translation studies. The flip side of the excitement, however, is the necessity to justify the importance of new concepts and to articulate the relationship of new data, alternative presuppositions, and changes in theoretical frameworks. Self-reflexivity is essential in all these processes of innovation.

One of the most interesting characteristics of research in translation studies is the accessibility of certain categories of data in the discipline. In descriptive studies especially, because of the concreteness of the objects of study (texts), the data are open to group inspection and common consideration. Similarly interpretation is often open to the commentary and criticism of an audience. In this regard the field is distinct from many other fields, including ethnography and psychoanalysis, where observation itself remains essentially a personal matter, not fully open to general consideration. At the same time certain branches of translation studies share with ethnography the use of the self and the perceptions of the self as primary tools. Sherry Ortner has observed that "minimally [ethnography] . . . has always meant the attempt to understand another life world using the self . . . as the instrument of knowing" (quoted in Chodorow 1999:205). In a similar way, although they analyze concrete objects, many studies of translation, particularly descriptive translation studies, take the form of a personal "reading" in which a scholar attempts to persuade the audience to accept the data selected and the interpretations offered from a rather personal interpretive experience and then to regard these interpretations as signifying particular conclusions that have been inferred. The use of the self is even stronger in the case of translators who, arguing from their own experience of translating, attempt to generalize on that basis about the nature of translation processes. Carol Maier (2006) has written eloquently about such a process in terms of the translator as *theôros* – pilgrim, seeker, searcher for knowledge and wisdom – who undertakes the quest through spiritual and physical journeys.[25]

Cases studies in translation research that rely on personal readings epitomize the interdependence of data and theory. Unless a study has carefully integrated some of the validation methods already discussed, the research relies on a hermeneutic method that is not fully amenable to replicablity. As in literary analysis, such readings can cite specific passages in the texts being discussed for support of the conclusions, but argument rests heavily on personal appeal. When the reading is not validated by corroboratory evidence from the social context or other indices, the argument turns essentially on rhetorical persuasion that the reading is valid, sometimes in the face of very scanty evidence. Data that can be mustered by this sort of reading do not generally speak for themselves or lead to any self-evident conclusion. This is an additional reason for researchers to be careful to assess the strategies of validation in their work, for otherwise the research can be sabotaged by the interdependence of data and theory, leading to vacuous or hermetic conclusions.

As the field of translation studies continues to internationalize and expand, such questions will inevitably become more central to discussions about translation. The self is constituted differently in dominant Western paradigms from the way it is in many other parts of the globe. Moreover, cultures worldwide have very different assumptions and presuppositions about how culture is constituted

---

[25] Geertz (1973:13-28) discusses some of the methodological problems related to these issues of readings, self, argument, and research conclusions, principally as they relate to ethnography. See also Clifford (1988:21-54) on the role of experience in relationship to methodologies in ethnography. Wolf (2002) explores the implications of the role of the self in the constructivist nature of translation and the relationship of self to other in the complexities of cultural translation.

that also bear interrogation in translation research. Western constructions of reality are not the only ones that can lead research into constricted and unpromising avenues.

Unlike the texts of descriptive translation studies that are accessible to the inspection of all, investigations of the process of translation often utilize data that range from personal reporting offering limited transparency to opacity in the extreme. Although scholars are beginning to find ways to investigate what happens as translators actually work, exploring mental processes, decision making procedures, and the like – sometimes with electronic monitoring – to a large extent an individual translator's experience and decision making still remain inaccessible to the researcher. In some respects the individual translator still operates like a "black box" in models of translation.[26] The subjectivity and variation in documents such as self-reported process notes or think-aloud protocols raise questions related to validation, verifiability, replicability, and the interpenetration of data, interpretation, and theoretical frameworks. Attempts are being made to move beyond complete subjectivity in these investigations and they are taking a productive direction; the difficulties, however, should not be underestimated (cf. Gutt 2000a:169).[27] It is likely that in the relatively near future, neurophysiology will be able to investigate phenomena pertaining to multilingualism and translation through direct monitoring and imaging of brain activity, introducing processes that will involve greater verifiability. It will be very interesting to see the results of those studies. Until research tools are developed further, however, the quality of data pertaining to translation processes must continue to be monitored by scholars for the interdependence of empirical data and theoretical perspectives in this branch of translation studies.

Let us return to the point with which we began this section: that theory generates a hypothesis that then defines what will count as data, with both theory and hypothesis influencing how data are collected and evaluated; in turn, data interrogate and potentially modify hypotheses and the larger theories within which hypotheses are generated. This reciprocal relationship between theory and data is essential to use as a guideline in research, for it points to the most powerful potential of research results. Theory informs the hypotheses and data of research, but because the results of research interrogate and refine theory, research can result in the reformulation of the largest frameworks that structure a field of inquiry. The interdependence and reciprocity between theory and data

---

[26] Nida's (1964:145-47) model of the role of the translator essentially treats the translator as such a black box, though the argument of the book as a whole is intended to give the translator a set of considerations to think about and tools to use and though ironically the book itself is aimed at Bible translators who have generally used team methods of translation.

[27] Subjective reports by translators are very valuable in translation studies for many reasons. Nonetheless, research based on such data must attend to questions of validation – including verifiability and replicability – before attempting to generalize the conclusions to other subjects and other situations.

can be expressed in terms of the three forms of logical reasoning discussed by Charles Sanders Peirce: deduction, abduction, and induction.[28] Through a process of deduction, the theoretical framework of the research leads to the initial postulates and hypotheses upon which research is based. In turn data relevant to a hypothesis are gathered, and on the basis of induction from the data, guided by the theoretical paradigm being used, the researcher tests both the hypothesis and ultimately the theory behind the hypothesis as well. When the data do not confirm the hypothesis or the theory, however, then the researcher must use abduction – in Peirce's view the only mode of reasoning to introduce new ideas into intellectual inquiry, and the creative force of research – to retroactively create a new hypothesis that will be compatible with the actual results. Abduction, or retroduction as Peirce sometimes called it, is "the forming and acceptance on probation of a hypothesis to explain surprising facts" (*EB* 1974:13.1109c); such hypotheses formulated retroactively from data collected will obviously in turn be the foundation for the construction of subsequent experiments and research projects. One reason that some systematic and almost mechanical research projects in translation studies seem to issue in "flattened" conclusions may be the absence of room for abduction or retroduction – hence creativity – which allows additional hypotheses (and ultimately theories) to emerge and be tested, thereby recursively impacting on the data collection process itself. Because of the interdependence of data collection and theory formation – particularly when there is room for abduction – a rigorous research program will be inherently self-reflexive. It will recursively seek extension and congruence of both theory and data through the exercise of all three forms of Peirce's logical reasoning.

4.5 Experimentation in Translation Studies

Translation studies is just beginning to deploy traditional large-scale experimental methods to investigate the processes and products of translation. Rather than exploring what is currently in progress or what might be possible in this regard, here we will focus on some philosophical issues pertinent to the nature of experimentation in the discipline. As we have seen, one of the differences between observation and experiment is control (*EB* 1947:20.128c). Beginning with a hypothesis, a researcher devises ways to gather data that test the hypothesis, such as by varying conditions, introducing new variables, and the like. Thus the researcher extends knowledge by proving the hypothesis, by invalidating the hypothesis, or by creating a new hypothesis through abduction, all of which impact on the paradigm within which the research was conceived.

In descriptive translation studies dealing with historical data, one might assume that it is impossible to engage in experimentation because the

---

[28] For a convenient summary of these aspects of Peirce's thought, particularly as they relate to translation, see Gorlée (1994:42 ff.).

data are fixed (generally consisting of preexisting texts from the past). Clearly in descriptive studies the ability to control the material one observes is limited, but nonetheless some elements of control exist and some analogues to experimental methods can be actualized. Moreover, even in descriptive studies, as in more conventional experimental research situations, hypothesis formation is a central feature of the research task. As with any experiment, it is important for a descriptive scholar not merely to attempt to prove a hypothesis by argument, but actually to *test* and *validate* the hypothesis by gathering and assessing data.

In descriptive translation studies a researcher's strategies for testing a hypothesis might include protocols related to the selection of text types, specific texts, and specific passages from the texts being investigated. For example, by selecting textual material relevant in various ways to the hypothesis being tested (text types, texts, and passages that might exhibit predicted effects in view of the cultural and ideological circumstances under investigation, as well as material that would not be expected to show the effects), or by drawing comparisons with respect to parameters relevant to the hypothesis and those that are not, a researcher can interrogate the validity of a hypothesis related to controlled parameters. At the same time, while some texts and passages are selected on the basis of fixed criteria, others might be selected randomly, acting as control samples that also serve to test the hypothesis. If the results are not as expected, it is important to recognize the significance of that divergence, modifying the hypothesis and theoretical paradigm or altering parameters being tested. One then proceeds to look for additional data based on the altered expectations. All these tactics can be thought of as analogues to more conventional experimental techniques used by researchers in most social and natural sciences, who must consider what data to select, what tests to use to confirm or invalidate the hypothesis, what sampling techniques to use, and so forth.

In descriptive translation studies research, one can also simulate certain aspects of an experimental situation by anticipating results. That is, one can make "working predictions" *to oneself* about how translation will be handled in the specific cultural contexts being investigated (on the basis of hypotheses about the cultural systems in interface or knowledge about historical circumstances under investigation). One can then look for symptomatic readings and additional texts or collateral paratextual materials to see if the predictions hold up. When a working prediction does not hold up, the experiment is not a failure. Negative evidence is still evidence, but it is evidence of a different hypothesis or a modified theoretical framework, which will thus be reflected in the conclusions of the research. In a sense such a strategy can be looked at as a way to use prediction as a means of validation internal to the process of the project itself rather than as part of the public presentation of the results. A similar experimental attitude in descriptive studies could be taken toward textual analysis of translation products with respect to controlled parameters (text types, content, linguistic elements, cultural contexts, ideological markers, and the like) decided in advance. A hypothesis can be tested and validation (for the scholar at least) takes the form of confirmation of the scholar's working predictions. In such research the scholar does not arrange for data to be generated, but strategically selects data from preexisting cultural and historical materials (usually translated texts) on the basis of predictions associated with the hypothesis. Here again there is a thin line between hypothesis testing and circular reasoning that must not be overstepped.

In other branches of translation studies, particularly research about translation processes, more classical types of experimentation are possible and are already being employed, including the use of subjects who perform set translation tasks under controlled circumstances. Such experiments can be done with respect to translators at work, varied types of translation tasks, working conditions, priming of translators with different sorts of instructions, types of translation processes (e.g., individual translation vs. group translation), interpretation and its reception, linguistic configurations of translation output, and many more aspects of translation processes. One outcome of greater sophistication about research protocols in translation studies will be increased ingenuity in devising hypotheses that can be tested experimentally and in designing experimental techniques relevant to translation studies.[29]

We should note that in the coming decades technological developments will not merely shift the subject matter of translation research but the experimental methods as well. Such shifts are already apparent, as Graham Turner and Frank Harrington (2000) illustrate with respect to data on interpreting collected and recorded on video tape. Video taping introduces new research opportunities as well as new research problems (such as maintaining confidentiality of the research subjects). Turner and Harrington (2000:257) also point out ethical questions raised by shifts in research technologies and methodologies. Whether the new technologies are video recording or computer tracking of translation choices or brain imaging of translators at work, questions pertaining to ethics must be carefully considered by scholars designing experiments; in many countries the ethics of such experiments with human subjects are in fact regulated by law.

Even when experiment *per se* is not possible, a scholar can maintain a sort of experimental attitude toward research. An experimental attitude includes awareness of theoretical frameworks, deliberation in hypothesis formation, a willingness to seek data that might challenge the hypothesis as well as confirm it, flexibility and breadth in sampling techniques, careful attention to developing control samples, ingenuity about testing and interrogating data, willingness to make predictions and acknowledgment of the implications when predictions are not confirmed, consideration of the quantitative significance of results, and consciousness about margins of error and the limits of generalizing the conclusions. An experimental attitude would also include concern for the replicability of the

---

[29] Olohan (2000) and Hermans (2002) offer a broad range of examples of translation research selected for their typological significance for the field.

results and even perhaps attempts to replicate the results in a slightly shifted research context. All these factors pertaining to experimentation will strengthen research in translation studies and prepare the field for the coming era. It is only a matter of time until neurophysiology turns its attention to translation studies and makes its sophisticated experimental methods available to the field and until the shifting technologies of translation require more high powered experimental procedures than the discipline currently employs.

4.6 Models in Translation Studies Research

The question of inadequate models has been identified as one of the central issues facing translation studies as it expands internationally and interfaces with different disciplines. Crisafulli writes "the predicament of translation studies at the present moment is the lack of an eclectic methodological framework capable of accommodating a wide range of research interests" (2002:26). A first step to achieving such an ecclectic methodological framework is receptivity to varied research models, a goal that many of the essays in the books edited by Maeve Olohan (2000) and Theo Hermans (2002) work toward.[30] Understanding the concept of models, therefore, is important for expanding translation studies to meet current needs in the field, including the demands of globalization. Moreover, there are ideological and ethical reasons for understanding and attending to the role of models in translation studies, because possession, authority, and power are inherent in model development, as Susam-Sarajeva points out (2002:198). All are part of the perquisites of defining how the world is to be viewed, what is to be understood as significant, and what is considered so negligible that it can be ignored.

As we saw in section 4.1, there are five principal phases in creating and utilizing research models: a problem must be formulated and its related system analyzed with respect to relevant variables and constraints; a model must be constructed and articulated; the model must be used to derive a solution; the model and the solution must be tested; and the solution must be implemented. Not all of these steps are involved in every use of modeling. The role of models in translation research varies considerably, depending on what aspect of translation is being addressed (e.g., translation processes or translation products) and what type of problem is being researched (e.g., the role of translation products in cultural change, the role of working conditions in translation accuracy, the development of computer-assisted translation programs). Moreover, the use of models can be explicit and overt on the one hand or covert, implicit, and even subliminal on the other.

---

[30] Productive discussions of models as they relate to translation studies are also found in Hermans (1993) and Williams and Chesterman (2002). Chesterman (2000) contains an overview of general types of models presupposed in the development of translation theory thus far.

In most studies of translation, a partial use of modeling normally suffices; not every stage is always relevant. Nevertheless, it is important to be cognizant of all the stages of model-making because in formulating questions and answers about translation, there are often covert models at work in the researcher's thought processes. One asks a question such as "what contextual factors produce these translation results?", and to answer the question one constructs an implicit social model of translators, translations, and their role in culture. One might consider testing such an implicit model by looking directly for evidence that confirms the model itself. In the case of a descriptive study, one could test the model by looking at paratextual evidence or other historical materials that reveal contextual factors (controlled and uncontrolled variables, as well as constraints) actually at work to see if they are congruent with the model posited.

Overt models are already used widely in translation research, but a number of points related to the development of models, that are useful both for those already experienced in the use of models and for those new to the process, should be examined. First it is essential to be sure that the model matches the conditions being investigated. Although all models involve simplifed representions of the world of experience and, as such, include only those variables with a salient impact on the investigation at hand, it is important to avoid excluding significant variables inadvertently. This can result from untested or inaccurate theoretical or even pretheoretical assumptions. One should also be conscious of the domain covered by the model, ascertaining that the domain is neither too small nor too large. Again, self-reflexivity about personal or culture-bound assumptions is essential in the development of models, as in other facets of research.

Let us consider an example of developing a model that relates to an actual situation that might be investigated. For the role of translation in a given cultural system, a scholar might model cultural interface as a two-language system (excluding as insignificant other languages used in the culture in question) when instead it should actually be modeled as a three- or four-language system. Finland in the nineteenth century offers such a case. Literate people in Finland could almost universally read Swedish, which was the first language of the state and of the educational system. At the same time literacy in Finnish was on the ascendancy, in part as a function of Finnish nationalism. Investigation of translation between Finnish and French in such a context would have to consider not only what French literature was available in Finnish, but also what was available in Swedish translations as well. Conclusions about the pattern of translation of French literature into Finnish could be badly skewed if the translation system were evaluated simply on the basis of a two-language model (French/Finnish). If there were many Swedish translations of French literature, for instance, there might exist a (positive or negative) correlation between what was translated from French into Swedish and from French into Finnish. Moreover, if investigations were to show that French was also widely taught in the educational system and used by educated persons, one might need to build into the model the possibility that many people were also reading French literature in the original, thereby obviating the need for translations of the texts for certain segments of the population. In the latter case the model would have to be more complex, including the availability of texts in French and an investigation of who actually could read French in the receptor system (that is, French would figure as both a source culture factor and a factor in the receptor culture).

Complex multilingual models of this sort would be needed in investigations of translation in Latin America as well, both for the nineteenth century and the twentieth, because the upper classes were frequently educated by nannies in European languages such as French, German, and English. Often people spoke and read these languages in preference to their native Spanish or Portuguese (cf. Larkosh 2002). In such a situation literacy patterns and class impinge on the pattern of translation and would have to be included as significant variables in a model. If most literate people could read French, for example, then a model would have to include some explanation (say, nationalism or language development) for translations from French into Spanish or Portuguese other than simple linguistic comprehension. Although all models simplify the world of experience by omitting variables seen as having relatively little impact, in constructing historical models of translation, scholars sometimes downplay or forget linguistic complexity and multiplicity. This occurs in part because so much research in translation studies is predicated upon or assumes monolingualism in target cultures and focuses on language pairs. Oversimplified models of this type are misleading in many historical investigations, but can be equally misleading in investigations of contemporary translation patterns in multilingual nations such as India. Modeling language in culture is often skewed by Western premises associating language with nationalism (and the norm of one language for one nation) and associating cultural difference with language difference. Such premises must be increasingly interrogated in constructing models for research related to countries beyond Eurocentric areas and certain contexts within Western countries as well, notably those associated with contemporary population migrations (cf. Cronin 2003, 2006).[31]

In constructing a model it is equally important to ascertain that the model corresponds accurately to the largest historical frameworks pertaining to the issues under investigation. Cronin reminds us of the importance of broad historical contextualization as we model contemporary shifting conditions; he quotes the dictum of Stuart Hall who writes "we suffer increasingly from a process of historical amnesia in which we think that just because we are thinking about an

---

[31] The complex multilingual condition of Ottoman culture is discussed in Paker (2002); Paker argues that the modeling of translation in the multilingual Ottoman Empire has been too simple as well. See also the case studies in Hung and Wakabayashi (2005) and Mukherjee (2004). By contrast Kamala (2000:245) observes that there is so much cultural overlap in adjacent languages in India that the idea that each language has its own ethos must be revised in the case of that country.

idea it has only just started" (Cronin 2003:77; Hall 1997:20). Here the example of modeling diaspora in relation to translation is useful. Many scholars writing about diaspora have posited it as a special condition of the late twentieth and early twenty-first century without fully acknowledging existing data on the migration of ethnic groups in earlier periods. That is, they model diaspora as if it were solely a modern phenomenon, correlating diaspora with modernity; they ignore earlier diasporas, including those of Europe in the nineteenth and early twentieth centuries. In fact many of the phenomena of contemporary diasporas existed in previous times. For example, nineteenth-century Irish immigrants in the United States, Canada, and Australia were not cut off from each other or from Ireland. There was considerably more travel between countries than a contemporary scholar might suppose, and emigrants often traveled back and forth between their homelands and their new nations. Moreover, those immigrant groups, like contemporary groups in diaspora, often retained their native languages and aspects of their home cultures in their new countries. At the end of the nineteenth century, for example, there were approximately one hundred Irish-language newspapers published in the State of New York alone. Similar evidence regarding continuity of affiliation and persistence of cultural phenomena across migrations could be evinced with respect to medieval diasporas such as the French diaspora of the twelfth century or the Irish diaspora in the seventh and eighth centuries. It is even possible that archaeological data pertaining to cultural diasporas in antiquity might be of interest. It seems short-sighted to base conclusions about translation in conditions of diaspora on models that treat diaspora solely as a modern phenomenon rooted in contemporary economic and social conditions without testing those models with respect to data related to earlier diasporas.

Although some translation scholars elaborate explicit models for translation processes or for the role of translations in particular contexts,[32] it is more typical in translation studies for researchers to depend on an implicit model, without ever overtly acknowledging the fact, sometimes not even to themselves. This is a problem that can undermine the validity of research in situations where the implicit model does not correspond to the translation conditions under examination, as in the cases of multilingualism and diaspora discussed above. Moreover, when the implicit model is Eurocentric, presuppositions built into the research can restrict the validity of the conclusions to dominant (contemporary) Western notions of translation. Such limitations in modeling translation are particularly compromising if the cluster concept nature of *translation is not recognized in the research. These issues related to the construction of models will move to the fore as the discipline increasingly internationalizes and enlarges its domain.

Wide familiarity with the types of models proposed for translation in descriptive studies and also in investigations of translation processes is useful

---

[32] For examples, see Katan (2004), as well as some of the contributions to Olohan (2000) and Hermans (2002). Other articles in the latter two collections really pertain to methods more than to models in the technical sense of model discussed here.

for any translation scholar. Studies of translation in postcolonial cultures are particularly valuable and stimulating, as we will see in chapter 5, in part because they often present alternate models for thinking about and assessing the processes and products of translation. They also interrogate and challenge old models that approach translation principally from the perspective of dominant cultures. Models of translation based on gender theory offer many of the same benefits, even to a scholar whose own topic is not specifically related to gender. Such alternate models of translation help to pry a researcher away from complacency about hegemonic models of translation constructed on the basis of dominant Western cultures.

An advantage of being conscious about articulating a model for one's research project is that such awareness establishes a more secure foundation for creating hypotheses, for deciding what types of data to collect, for testing data, and for interrogating the validity of the model itself. Though prediction may not be a promising means of validation for conclusions about every facet of translation, within the structure of a model, prediction is relevant to assessing what constraints exist, what variables are significant, what types of data are relevant, what data to expect, what sorts of related social conditions to look for, and so forth. When these predictions are successful, they suggest the strength of the model and its congruence with the world of experience. When the predictions fail, they indicate that the model is invalid as it stands, that additional variables need to be considered, that abduction will be useful in reformulating hypotheses, and that the model must be readjusted so as to accommodate conclusions that are contrary to those expected under the initial hypotheses governing the research.

4.7 Restructuring the Research System

In this chapter I have argued that reconceptualizing *translation as a cross-linguistic category based on many different words and image-schemas for translation products and processes with many specific histories and practices of translation will inevitably have implications for the entire system of research in translation studies. Similar shifts in translation associated with globalization will require basic changes in conceptualizations of the processes and products of translation, as well as in the definition of the roles and identities of translators.

I am hardly the first to make suggestions about changing conceptualizations of translation; indeed we began this chapter with observations to this effect by Wakabayashi and Cronin. A growing awareness of the need to rethink translation because of globalization and current technological shifts is particularly widespread. Anthony Pym (2000:191-92) observes that such rethinking is indicated by the fact that the very names for translation and translator are changing. There are increasing calls for translators to be reconceptualized as "cultural mediators", which Pym (2000:191) observes is already happening at the upper end of the translation profession (cf. Katan 2004, Cronin 2003). Terms such as *localization* and *cultural mediation* indicate a movement away from the old transfer hypothesis that has dominated Eurocentric thinking about translation since the late Middle Ages. Ernst-August Gutt (2000a:166) notes that the term *translation* "has increasingly come to be applied to instances of communication that constitute descriptive rather than interpretive use" of language.[33] The contextual shifts associated with globalization and the growing internationalization of translation studies open new opportunities for and even demand vast efforts in research in translation studies. The result will be new theorizations of translation, new hypotheses to test, and quantities of additional data to gather.

Both the reconceptualization of *translation as a cluster concept and the growing internationalization of translation studies will result in an increasingly decentered discipline of translation studies. A decentered discipline cannot merely operate on a model in which dominant world cultures supply theory which is tested on and applied to the data provided by less powerful cultural systems (cf. Susam-Sarajeva 2002). Rather the entire system of research must be revamped, from data collection through the generation of hypotheses to the articulation of theory. Decentering translation studies will therefore impact on all levels of research and all paradigms of research in the field. It will also require coming to grips with structural problems in the field such as the exemplification issues faced by scholars researching minority or lesser-used languages discussed above in section 4.4.

There are ethical and ideological imperatives for this enterprise, not just pragmatic ones. The process will demand self-reflexivity of all members of the discipline with respect to the subject matter of translation studies and the procedures and protocols of research as well. Such reflexivity is utterly appropriate in a field like translation studies, fitting the very nature of translation as facilitating cross-cultural exchange, communication, and cooperation. Such reflexivity turns on postpositivist understandings of how perspectives related to ideology and subject position are built into theory, methodologies, and research programs in the discipline. Thus, perspective inheres in more than conceptualizations of translation processes and products. Too many researchers in translation continue to assert that their methods are "theory free" or untainted by ideology, and some even continue to arrogate to themselves the powers of "objectivity".

This chapter has begun to outline characteristics that distinguish research methodologies in translation studies, a self-reflexive understanding of which is necessary as the field shifts its research system. In a sense the chapter provides a "snapshot" of the current state of research in the field, not only of what is actually practiced and what is emergent but also what is currently needed in discourses about research and approaches to research methodologies. Even if there were no historical motivations for change at the moment, there would be nothing fixed about research methods in translation studies. It is the nature of research

---

[33] Examples include many forms of advertisements and other types of localizations that do not actually have representation of a source text as their primary goal.

methods to be dynamic, constantly changing as a field evolves, solving some problems and turning to new ones, assimilating data and identifying new areas to be investigated, all the while refining theory along the way. Thus, not only is it inevitable that research methods related to translation will change, they must change if the field is to remain vital.

Change is inherent in a field with a cross-cultural social cluster concept at its heart. Because the subject matter is dispersed and open, in some ways each research project requires its own tools, model, and methodologies. Thus, scholars in such a field must be conscious of the issues raised by research methods and deliberate in thinking through methodological questions anew with each project. Clearly because of the inherent possibility of change and adaptation in translation itself, research on translation will have to remain innovative and inventive in its methods and outlooks. In a context of change, however, it is helpful for scholars to understand what has already been established in the methodologies of translation research if only to innovate more effectively.

In an era of globalization, the discipline needs to foster a balance between encouraging people to value and assert their own local knowledges about translation products and processes on the one hand and mastering established international paradigms about the subject matter on the other hand. Unfortunately, we have seen that it can be argued that to date scholars (and, we might add, translators) have been "educated away" from their own cultures in their thinking about translation (Susam-Sarajeva 2002:199). As a result, the research and pedagogic enterprises of translation studies are at risk of becoming hegemonic. Susam-Sarajeva asserts that even if the researchers' initial goals were "to understand and explain translational – and maybe, therefore, social and cultural – phenomena in their own systems of origin, the more they work *with* central models and tools, the more they are meant to work *for* them" (2002:199). There are ways of making the local and the global mutually nourishing in translation studies as in other domains, but the attempt to reach such a state will require active interventions on the part of translators, translation teachers, and translation scholars, for it runs against the grain of many dominant interests investing in globalization and directing the role that translation plays in the contemporary world.

We have seen that one consequence of the current developments in translation studies is the need to educate translators and translation scholars about more subjects more deeply. An increasing number of fields and skills become intertwined with translation as the world is increasingly networked. Like other professionals in the information age, translators require a broader and deeper general education in order to negotiate the tasks demanded of them during their working lives. More profound understandings of the world and entire fields of knowledge are in turn connected with self-reflexivity and the need for translators and translation scholars to assume greater responsibility in both translation and translation research. It will not be sufficient to carry out assigned tasks and execute existing theoretical formulations in a mechanical way; both translators and scholars will be engaged in the process of interrogating the discipline and reformulating theory.

Perhaps as a consequence of minimal exposure to scientific research in their own education, some readers will find the abstract terminology and links to traditional discussions of scientific research in this chapter intimidating or repellent. Framing research abstractly as it has been here may conjure up stereotypical images of people in white lab coats and other images associated with scientists. It is important to remember that most of the concepts discussed above are related to very ordinary activities that many people in translation studies and the profession of translation engage in daily. Data collection is ultimately observation of the world of experience. It can take such ordinary forms as recording the thoughts resulting from internal reflection on the process of translation by translators themselves, or interviewing ten translators about their practices and attitudes about translation, or reading a number of translated versions of the same source text and analyzing them with reference to a specific issue of interest, or timing translators who work with and without computer-assisted translation programs and then assessing the results.

This chapter (and the previous three) should already have answered a question that often gets asked in translation studies by people who have not been trained in experimental methods, particulary teachers of translation around the world: why do we need translation theory at all? The simplest answer is that all thinking has a theoretical basis; theory cannot be avoided. It is merely a question of whether people are conscious or not of the theoretical foundation of their views.[34]

A theory provides the paradigm (cf. Kuhn 1962) within which whole programs of research, thinking, teaching, and practice proceed. Generally in the evolution of a discipline, competing theories are offered to explain phenomena, constituting alternate paradigms. In translation theory linguistic, functionalist, and literary theories of translation have at times been seen as such competing theories. Such differences are normally adjudicated in the course of time by discrediting some of the competing theories, by a shift of theoretical paradigm, or by incorporating aspects of the alternate views into a broader and more inclusive theoretical approach to the subject matter. The latter is what has happened in translation studies since World War II.

If a researcher or teacher is unaware of theory, it does not mean that no theory is involved in the person's thinking. Rather, it signifies that the research or teaching is being conducted within a dominant theoretical framework or controlling paradigm of which the person is not fully conscious.[35] When the

---

[34] This question is taken up at length from a very different perspective in Chesterman (1997: 42-46) and Chesterman and Wagner (2002). See also the perceptive and critical arguments in Arrojo (1998), as well as sources cited.

[35] Hermans (1999:34) notes that no focused observation is possible without a theory to tell the observer what to look for and how to assess the significance of what is observed; cf. Tymoczko (2002).

theoretical foundation of a field is not recognized explicitly, the defaults of the dominant culture come to the fore. In the case of the emerging international field of translation studies, the cultural default has thus far been Western thinking about translation because many (perhaps most) groundbreaking books on translation theory and practice with international circulation are written in European languages (mainly English). Hence the teaching of translation in many places of the world, both Western and beyond, relies on or is influenced by these materials. Moreover, many jobs for which students are being prepared are funded by multinational corporations that subscribe to Western translation practices and standards. This employment context for translators further pushes the field toward Western conceptualizations. Often under the press to train translators for current markets, translation teachers around the world reinscribe their own cultural knowledge about translation within frameworks of Western intellectual dominance. If there are problems with the implicit assumptions of Eurocentric theory, as I have suggested there are, then there are problems with using those dominant assumptions as the unexamined basis of and default for the emerging international discipline of translation studies. In such a situation the ethical problem of hegemony arises, either because Western scholars extend Eurocentric theory to others or because scholars from other parts of the world internalize dominant Western ideas and promulgate them among their own students. In the latter case local knowledges are eroded and students are educated away from their own cultures, to use Susam-Sarajeva's phrase.

Once the need for translation theory is acknowledged, another question immediately follows: what sort of theory should it be?[36] Because of the complex nature of cross-cultural social concepts such as *translation or literature, art, history, and language, it is very difficult to construct theory in fields that investigate such phenomena, as is evident in the case of translation studies. In some ways it is more complex to theorize a social field than to construct a theory of biochemical processes in human cells or a theory of subatomic particles. In biology and physics the data are extremely complex and require a great deal of difficult observation and testing, but the phenomena do not change from culture to culture. A theory of electrons obviously must hold everywhere – one can't have a credible Chinese theory of electrons, a German theory of electrons, and an Egyptian one; the phenomena associated with electrons are the same everywhere and hence a unified theory is required. In the case of theorizing social concepts, a more complex model of theory is required. One might argue that a local theory of translation is possible as long as societies remain isolated, but once societies (and societies of translation scholars) are in contact, people begin to inquire about how local understandings of the social phenomena in question relate to each other

---

[36] Halverson (1997) takes up some of the epistemological difficulties of theorizing translation, showing that they lead to the nature of knowledge itself and identifying the problem of relativity in conceptualizations of translation as a major issue. See also Arrojo (1998).

and how they fit into larger international frameworks. In such situations local views of social concepts also begin to interact and to shift, as has happened in translation studies since World War II. Although localized practices, concepts, and histories of translation remain, the theory of translation is shifting everywhere. The changes in translation theory are not happening symmetrically, however; instead they are following the flows of power, money, and employment.

Wakabayashi (2000) has astutely discussed the question of the type of theory that translation studies should seek, characterizing the two main camps in the debate as those who promote universalist theories of translation and those who argue for culture-specific or particularist theories of translation. The particularists propose that there is no need for a unified approach to translation theory at all, seeing multiple, culturally specific theories as sufficient and preferable; the universalists aspire to a translation theory that applies to all translators and all translations, regardless of language, culture, or period (Wakabayashi 2000:265). As a strength of universalist theories, Wakabayashi notes the richness in being able to compare translation traditions where likenesses permit perception of relationships between translation traditions and differences enable scholars to "envision translation in new ways, engendering new ideas" (2000:266-67, cf. 259). Wakabayashi (266) observes that one limitation of particularist theories is the small domain they apply to. She attempts to resolve these tensions by calling for "an overarching metatheory of translation that transcends boundaries by accounting for proven commonalities while accommodating culture-specific variations, i.e., a syncretic approach that reconciles different principles and is applicable to all language pairs, perhaps not equally, but in varying degrees" (2000:267). Wakabayashi suggests a decontextualized metatheory and contextualized parameter-specific theories with "constant interaction" between the two (2000:267).

Clearly a theory that delineates commonalities or conditions applicable to all translators and all translations – even in varying degrees – is not the sort of theory that translation studies can aspire to: such a theory would be tantamount to establishing a set of necessary and sufficient conditions for the international concept *translation itself, a futile hope for a cluster concept. By contrast, the idea of multiple theories risks implicit isolation from and exclusion of the other, with the ethical implications that follow (cf. Davis 2001:92; see also the discussion in chapter 2 above). Moreover, the assumptions associated with culturally specific theories of translation would each only be applicable to a very narrow range of phenomena, namely those of the specific culture on which the theory was based at a specific point in time, as Wakabayashi notes, thus having very limited theoretical utility. Such multiplicity by its very nature precludes cross-cultural understandings of the phenomena of translation, yet a theory applicable or restricted to a single culture is almost a contradiction in terms in the case of translation as an intercultural activity, for such a theory could not even explain the reciprocal translation activities associated with cross-cultural interface or international commerce adapted to the needs of two cultures. It is probably best to think of such culturally specific approaches to translation – including Western views of translation as transfer – as *conceptualizations* of translation that both derive from and drive specific practices rather than *theory* as such. If this is so, then the strong Eurocentrism in current cross-cultural thinking about translation (which extrapolates from and generalizes a local Eurocentric understanding and praxis of translation) indicates that the field has barely begun to formulate adequate theory thus far, remaining at the level of Eurocentric conceptualizations in many respects. Because translation varies according to social structure, values, cultural context, historical situation, function, text type, medium, the intervention of translators, and so forth, translation *theory* must be comprehensive and yet flexible enough to deal with these varied parameters through time and space. Only when there are models inclusive enough to account for the practices of many different cultures can we properly talk of translation theory as such.

A way to respond to the paradox delineated by Wakabayashi is to image a type of theory that suits the nature of *translation as a cross-linguistic, cross-cultural, cross-temporal cluster concept. Such a theory requires a new structure – an umbrella or tree structure perhaps – a comprehensive framework making provision for related but very different (and even at times incommensurate) clusters of translation phenomena within it. Such clusters might be culture specific or parameter specific – for example, they might pertain to translation as it has been practiced in China or as it has been practiced in oral literary traditions across a broad range of cultures. Although I am arguing for a comprehensive theory of translation (rather than multiple unrelated theories) suited to a decentered model of translation studies, I do not believe it is possible to construct a rigid, one-size-fits-all theory that claims singular and universal application to all translation situations in however variable the degree. Understanding *translation as a cluster concept pushes us to a different approach to theory, a different model for theory itself. If a field is based on a cluster concept, then that field must have a theory with articulation, flexibility, diversity, and openness corresponding to those features in the cluster concept being theorized.[37]

What I envision when I think of a comprehensive theory of translation, therefore, is not a single set of perspectives or dicta that applies to all translational phenomena, but a coordinated yet differentiated set of understandings that can guide thinking about translation in many different cultural contexts. An example of such a broad and generally applicable understanding would be the proposition that translations are ordinarily context sensitive, with the recognition that such sensitivity can be reflected in myriad ways and that translation metonymics are driven both by cultural norms and translator choice. Translation theory would acknowledge and explore cultural interference that results from translational activity. At the same

---

[37] The logical impossibilities of a closed and totalized theory of translation are argued in Arrojo (1998).

time there would be probabilistic correlates to broad principles identifying more specific phenomena typical of particular cultural configurations. A comprehensive theory of translation would have to grow out of the observation of practice (rather than prescriptively determining practice) because of the pragmatic and *a posteriori* nature of cluster concepts and the necessity to observe (look!) and describe the objects of study. Translation theory must also be open and incomplete in part because new practices of translation are generated in response to changing cultural conditions and technologies; the new practices developed through time in turn need to be theorized. Thus translation theory will continually accrete new branchings.[38]

A theory with an umbrella structure or a tree structure suitable for a cluster concept will also have branchings that allow for two or more alternatives: if a then x, if b then y. This is standard in theorizing many phenomena in the natural sciences and mathematics. The theory governing the basic states of matter (solid, liquid, gas) turns on such a branching structure, making apprehensible such phenomena as the differences in the state of water above and below 0° Celsius: at normal sea-level pressures, if water is above that temperature, it will be a liquid; if below that temperature, it will be a solid. Similar branching structures in theories of animal behavior account for gender variations: if a lion is male, then it will probably behave in such and such ways; if a lion is female, then it will probably behave in other sorts of ways. An example of a branching structure in translation theory might be the following: "if translation occurs in an oral culture, then it will probably have the characteristics m, n, o . . . ; if translation occurs in a highly computer literate culture, then it will probably have the characteristics p, q, r . . .". In the case of cross-cultural social cluster concepts like *translation, however, such branching structures rarely contrast simple binaries as options.[39] Instead the branchings usually lead to multiple possibilities; conceptualizations of such complex situations are often associated with what philosophers call disjunctive theories.[40] Moreover, branching structures in theorizations of cultural phenomena cannot generally be conceptualized in terms of mutually exclusive alternatives that have linear extensions. To the contrary, like many other social phenomena, translation has the complex structuration of culture itself, involving "a multiplicity of complex conceptual structures, many of them superimposed upon or knotted into one another, which are at once strange, irregular, and inexplicit" (Geertz 1973:10).

---

[38] Following Stanley Fish, Arrojo argues for the need to have translation praxis drive translation theory, rather than to image theory as providing an "algorithmic formulation" defining and governing the translator's task (1998:29).

[39] For example, in the case of the concept game, a branching structure might be "if the game is played alone, then w; if the game is played with a single opponent, then x; if the game is played with one player against a group, then y; if the game is played by two opposing teams, then z"; and so forth.

[40] I am indebted here to Elisabeth Camp and Julianna Tymoczko for helping to formulate these arguments.

Comprehensive theories of complex phenomena can also involve indeterminacies, the most famous of which is probably the indeterminacy at the heart of quantum physics: sometimes light seems to act like a wave and at other times it seems to act like a particle. As a result of Erwin Schrödinger's famous thought experiment, this indeterminacy has made "Schrödinger's cat" an icon in popular culture. Like quantum theory, a comprehensive theory of translation clearly will have indeterminacies as well as branching structures, indeterminacies caused by cultural singularities and, notably, indeterminacies related to the agency of translators themselves who can decide to flout rules, invent translation strategies, and inject all sorts of unpredictable elements into translations (cf. Crisafulli 2002:31n4). Despite the workings of norms in translation and the cultural regulation of translation practices, human beings and societies are not fully predictable, so theorization of translation studies like other fields in the humanities and social sciences must entail both uncertainties and indeterminacies. Indeed translation theory must be open in part to provide for new indeterminacies generated by future practices that are initiated by both societies and individuals.

What is not generally characteristic of theories, however, is unexplained inconsistencies or randomness.[41] Theory normally calls for adjustment when such random or inconsistent elements appear in the theoretical structuration itself. That is, a theoretical impetus seeks to develop hypotheses to explain seeming randomness or inconsistency at the level of data and to eliminate inconsistency at the level of theory. In the case of randomness in translation behavior, much can be attributed to (and hence explained by) the idiosyncratic behaviors of translators, as we have already seen.

Let us note, moreover, that even though branching structures and indeterminacies are characteristic of many types of theories, they almost always signal potential areas to be explored further, to be investigated in more detail, to be understood in greater depth. One can always ask "why?" about such points of divergence and often that question can be answered at increasing levels of delicacy.[42] The impetus to investigate more deeply apparent randomness and inconsistency, as well as reasons for branching structures and indeterminacies, in theoretization is usually necessary and productive. All such areas cry out for more explanation, more thought, more research.[43]

---

[41] Here we need to observe the difference between inconsistency at the level of data and inconsistency at the level of theory in the case of social behavior. For instance, in the case of good table manners, data might show that one culture requires that both hands remain visible above the level of the table while another culture requires that the left hand remain below the table at all times. A *theory* of table manners, however, would reconcile these inconsistencies that occur at the level of data by offering a unifying explanation at a higher level than the behavior itself.

[42] For example, questions about difference in behavior related to gender can also be investigated at the level of biochemical differences or at the level of fetal development, which itself involves biochemical effects.

[43] Geertz (1973:24-28) offers a brief but interesting discussion of the role of theory in "an

It is very difficult to delineate the optimal way to theorize in a complex cross-cultural, cross-temporal discipline like translation studies, just as it is difficult to map out a cross-cultural, cross-temporal concept like *translation, a cluster concept that is open and that has shifting and permeable boundaries. Such concepts are not only often expressed differently and inconsistently across cultures, the cultural expressions may even be incommensurate; if the field is to remain vital and to have productive theory, it must be open to those differences. I suggested in chapter 2 that in exploring such questions, the field of translation studies is breaking new ground both with respect to translation and with respect to the understanding of concepts and categories in cognitive science and philosophy. The same is true with respect to delineating the type of theory that is appropriate for complex social concepts and their associated academic disciplines.

Questions about theory in translation studies point to the need for new models of theory. Such models have yet to be fully worked out in any of the humanities and social sciences, in part because so many academic disciplines continue to be structured in terms of cultural enclosure (with a Western episte-mological bias) and in part because people in the human sciences are not always trained to grapple with such abstract questions. Thinking about how we think about the large concepts at the heart of human life takes us into unmapped ter-ritory where scientific and humanistic thought meet. Thus, in addressing these questions translation studies is charting new territory, situating itself at the leading edge of self-reflexive academic inquiry, and beginning to discuss issues that will inevitably occupy scholars from many disciplines in the coming decades.[44]

Thus far I've said very little about the content of future translation research. The arguments in this book, however, implicitly outline important areas of work. The definitional impulse in the field will inevitably continue, particularly as the implications of the nature of *translation as a cross-cultural cluster concept become clearer. Increased attention to international conceptualizations of translation, as well as associated histories and practices, will form another cluster of research interests. Framing translation through international conceptualizations, as well as additional frameworks from current and developing academic disciplines, will open up still other areas of research. Some of these frameworks are already

---

interpretive science"; he concludes that another major function of theory in a field where the subject matter is open is to provide a vocabulary with which the material can be analyzed and discussed.

[44] In trying to image appropriate theory for translation studies, a promising avenue to investigate is the terminology and concepts associated with set theory. The subject matter of set theory includes open concepts (sets), nested sets, overlapping sets, discontinuous boundaries, and so forth. The techniques used to investigate such phenomena in mathematics have potential applications in exploring and theorizing translation. At the same time, some of the standard moves of set theory (including "closing the set" and eliminating "pathological" examples) have been tried in translation studies with dismal and drastic geopolitical consequences, leading to the problems this book is addressing. I am indebted here to Julianna Tymoczko for information about set theory and its possible application to translation studies.

apparent, including questions currently being explored in cognitive science, but the continual growth of academic knowledge will produce frameworks applicable to translation that cannot as yet even be foreseen. Globalization has already begun to raise questions that demand exploration and that have implications for reconceptualizing translation and the role of translators. Questions related to the technologies that enable the networking of the world will increasingly serve as a focus for translation research programs, raising compelling questions that will demand rapid and flexible responses. In all of these subject areas, clarity about the structures of research discussed above will facilitate successful research outcomes.[45]

It is worth reiterating that experimentation in translation studies remains to be undertaken on a large scale. It is likely that this gap will be closed in the near future if only because many young scholars are sophisticated in information technology and research methods. Neurophysiology is also now at the point where it is beginning to be used to investigate particular cognitive tasks that human beings engage in. There has already been a start in mapping brain activities associated with various linguistic tasks and in defining the cognitive centers deployed in linguistic behavior. It is only a matter of time until these technologies are used to research multilingualism and the process of translation in a sustained manner. Other sorts of large scale experiments related to sociolinguistic aspects of translation, employing the methods of the social sciences, will probably be devised even sooner than those associated with the biological sciences. The growing interest in corpora in translation studies is also paving the way for the integration of classic scientific quantitative methodologies into translation studies.

To my mind, however, it is less important to focus on *what* will be researched than on *how* the research is to be conducted. A shift in the research system along the lines indicated in this chapter is the best preparation for the future health of research of all types in translation studies. Indeed reorganization along the lines discussed here is ultimately necessary if any research area is to flourish in translation studies. Unless the discipline of translation studies develops a stronger culture of research, in future some of the most exciting investigations about translation will be conducted outside the field – by neurophysiologists, cognitive scientists, and sociologists.

As new research areas are explored, greater awareness of the particular characteristics of the research methods and the research system of translation studies will help individual scholars strengthen their arguments and make those arguments more convincing, not just to scholars inside the discipline but to those outside as well. Becoming more conscious of research methodologies will also help researchers to perceive their own intellectual and cultural frameworks, to be alert for pretheoretical assumptions, to see the interrelationship between their

---

[45] A more extensive discussion of research trajectories related to the subject matter of translation studies is found in Tymoczko (2005).

data and their theoretical perspectives, to understand the implicit models that inform their research, and to alter those models when necessary. Accordingly, scholars will become more able to discern the balance between valuing their own local knowledge and utilizing broader international frameworks. All such self-reflexivity in research inevitably deepens and broadens scholarly inquiry, and it is utterly necessary in an international field like translation studies, particularly at this historical juncture.

On the level of the discipline *per se*, more discussion of and deliberation about research questions such as those raised here can only lead to greater cooperation and coherence in the field and a strengthening of its position within the academy as well. When differences in the methodologies of translation research are articulated and situated in larger patterns of scholarly research across many disciplines, the differences that exist inside translation studies can be more easily appreciated, valorized, revalued, and readjusted in the emergent discipline. They can be seen as complementary and a source of disciplinary strength, rather than as a source of rivalry and discomfort. Finally, direct consideration of research methodologies reveals areas of strength and weakness in the discipline as a whole, setting a program for future developments and changes in the research culture of the field, as well as its pedagogical enterprise and the praxis fostered. By collectively examining research patterns more deeply and more self-reflexively, translation scholars will see ways to extend the subject matter, improve data collection, propose new hypotheses, sharpen protocols for constructing models, appreciate various forms of validation, and reformulate theory, all leading to an expansion and consolidation of the discipline so that it can meet the challenges of a world in rapid transition.

PART 2: EMPOWERING TRANSLATORS

5. Activism, Political Agency, and the Empowerment of Translators

In the first half of this book, I have argued that reconceptualizing the cross-linguistic, cross-cultural, and cross-temporal concept translation as a cluster concept, thus enlarging translation itself, will result in significant benefits for the discipline of translation studies. The benefits range from the inclusion of all translation products and processes in translation theory to a recalibration of the methodologies of translation research and translation pedagogy, as well as a greater internationalization and a geopolitical repositioning of the discipline as a whole. But the consequences do not stop there. An expanded understanding of translation as it has been conceptualized and practiced around the globe through time also highlights the agency of translators and ultimately leads to greater empowerment of translators in the present age. An appreciation of the capacious nature of translation goes to the heart of empowering translators. An enlarged view of translation highlights the potential and power of translators. Translators can perceive the full range of possibilities of their profession, possibilities that are often stifled within prescriptive notions of translation emanating from a single cultural confine. Such enhanced agency is essential for translators facing the ethical, ideological, and intellectual challenges of the contemporary world.

The agency of translators has been a leitmotif of translation studies since World War II, an intermittent topic of discussion in virtually all branches of the field. This is not surprising in view of the importance of translators to intelligence and propaganda operations during the war. Since the war the perspective has widened. Linguists have stressed the significance of translators' choices and their processes of decision making, indicating that these choices determine meaning itself in the target text and that translated texts are constitutive of the representations of their subject matter. Functionalists ranging from those involved in Bible translation to those interested in commercial translation have stressed the relationship between the effect of the text on the receptor audience and the translator's agency. Poets and other literary figures have promoted translation as part of innovative and creative literary projects, and they have acknowledged the power of translators in furthering the aims of many literary movements. Descriptive translation scholars have documented the role of translation in literary, cultural, and political shifts, showing how the work of translators in shaping texts contributes to fundamental changes in diverse cultural systems.

The interest in the agency of translators intensified during the second stage of descriptive studies. Various approaches converged on the political and ideological roles translators play, with a number of these approaches moving from analysis to programmatics, recommending that translators use translation for particular ideological and activist goals. Thus, some feminist translators advocated "womanhandling" texts so as to shift the target texts away from the patriarchal discourses and male supremacist configurations in the source texts.[1] Working through case studies, other scholars such as Antoine Berman (1992) and Lawrence Venuti (1992, 1995, 1998a, 1998b) promoted translation techniques and strategies that they believed could act as correctives to cultural enclosure and cultural imperialism, as well as other ideological limitations on cultural interface. Arguing primarily from the perspective of their own cultural contexts (France and the United States respectively), Berman and Venuti also attempted to generalize those perceptions to broader social contexts and recommended particular translation strategies that they believed would enhance the role of translators as agents of cultural change. Similarly, postcolonial translation studies focused on the powerful roles that translators have played in ideologically charged situations, either to promote cultural and political change or to consolidate power.[2] Still other scholars have attempted to generalize these various paradigms to additional contexts involving politics, ideology, and power so as to elucidate the agency of translators.[3]

Thus, as the discipline of translation studies has taken shape in the postpositivist climate since World War II, there has been clear movement away from a primary focus on technical questions about how to translate toward larger ethical issues, many of which turn on the agency and power of the translator. It is no accident that postpositivist attention to perspective should issue in discussions of the ethical, ideological, and political dimensions of translation and the empowerment of translators. Perspective is not simply a cognitive matter: it also relates to material conditions and subject position, ideology and values, politics, esthetics, and religion. It follows that questions of perspective inevitably lead to investigations of political and ideological issues on the one hand and to discussions of the agency and power of translators on the other.

With its stress on "facts" and the relations between specific facts, more general facts, and laws, positivism contains an implicit assertion that there is one correct and "objective" way to look at things. It is telling that positivism became the dominant Western epistemological posture at the height of European imperialism, as European empires were consolidating their dominion throughout the world. Empire involves more than physical control: it is also a matter of cultural assertion and control of meaning and knowledge. Positivism contains within it pretheoretical dominant assumptions pertaining to perspective, including perspective on race, gender, class, and culture.

---

[1] Detailed accounts are found in Simon (1996) and von Flotow (1997), as well as works cited.

[2] These approaches are represented in Robinson (1997a); Bassnett and Trivedi (1999); Tymoczko (1999b, 2000); and Simon and St-Pierre (2000).

[3] For example, Pym (1998); the essays on ideology in translation in Calzada Pérez (2003); Tymoczko and Gentzler (2002), focusing on power; and Tymoczko (forthcoming a), focusing on activist translation. See also the discussion of the second wave of descriptive studies and associated bibliography in section 1.6 above.

By contrast, postpositivist epistemologies emerged during the breakdown and rejection of imperialism, and they are associated with the interrogations of dominant assumptions about race, gender, class, culture, power, and nation. Postpositivist epistemologies decenter dominant views and have the potential to open the field of discourse to the perspectives, viewpoints, and values of all peoples and all subject positions. Thus, shifts in an academic field toward post-positivist approaches, as has happened in translation studies, will bring with them considerations pertaining to ethics and ideology, including the perspectives of diverse cultural groups and diverse individuals alike. In the case of translation studies, such considerations converged on the ideology of the processes and products of translation, as well as on the ethical position and the empowerment of translators, the agents of translation.

Postpositivist developments have contributed greatly to understanding many aspects of translation. These gains notwithstanding, the postpositivist trajectory has remained partially blocked by implicit residual positivist presuppositions about the conception of the object of study, skewing the conception of the central subject matter toward Western views of translation processes and products and toward Western notions of the role of the translator. Such premises continue to remain implicitly embedded in the language, discourses, and premises of the field. Writing about the conceptualization of translation as transfer encoded in Western European words for translation, Sandra Halverson observes "regardless of whatever additional surface-level metaphors we may choose to construct, or whatever alternative conceptual metaphors we choose to draw on, we still do not change the conceptual structure that underlies the word we use to identify our object of study, and hence our most fundamental understanding of that concept" ("Forum" 2000:2.359-60). Enlarging the conception of translation along the lines suggested in the first half of the book will thus lead to a reconceptualization of the role and agency of the translator, at least within the discipline of translation studies if not in ordinary language in Eurocentric contexts. By considering the implications of translation as a cluster concept for the role of translators, both scholars and translators themselves can achieve a fuller understanding of transla-tors' prerogatives and a greater appreciation of the full potential of the agency of translators, in part by reflecting upon the roles of translators in cultures beyond the West and throughout time. Liberated from constraints imposed by dominant Western views of their position, translators can in turn view themselves in new and empowered ways, thus potentially allowing themselves to undertake new types of projects, to risk using new translation strategies, to create new types of translated texts, and to engage in new fields of activism and ethical engagement.

In the second part of this book, I focus on the ways that enlarging the concept of translation intersects with empowering translators, beginning with some large questions pertaining to the political and ideological agency of the translator. The brief sketch above indicates that translators exercise many types of agency. Recent explorations of the topic have focused chiefly on ethical, political, and ideological agency, and hence this is where I begin. In the ensuing chapters, however, I also explore other practical and theoretical issues pertaining to the agency and empowerment of translators, discussing in greater depth cultural translation and construction of meaning. By thinking of translation in its largest cross-cultural and cross-temporal sense, we can more easily transcend frameworks based on a single geopolitical perspective or locus, thus setting the question of translators' roles in a broader context than has been done heretofore in translation studies. This broader scope makes it possible to see a greater range of translation possibilities available to an empowered translator.

5.1 Empowered Translators and the Translator's Political Agency: Evidence from Postcolonial Translation Studies

One of the most compelling approaches to the political agency of translators, as well as to the ethics and ideology of translation, has been offered by postcolonial translation studies.[4] Let us begin exploring the political and ideological agency of translators by reviewing what postcolonial translation studies have contributed to these discourses. As Sherry Simon (Simon and St-Pierre 2000:13) has observed, postcolonial translation studies began the process of enlarging translation by enlarging "the map" itself: moving translation studies beyond Eurocentric areas and dominant discourses about translation. Moreover, postcolonial approaches to translation began the process of redefining basic questions related to the politics and ideology of translation.

Postcolonial translation studies *ipso facto* constitute a postpositivist approach, for they engage the question of perspective directly, radically inverting the positivist assumption of a single (objective, correct, dominant, and imperialist) perspective by approaching colonialism primarily from the viewpoint of colonized subjects. Postcolonial studies are considerably broader in their purview than most approaches used by scholars who take up the question of agency in translation, for most scholarly arguments are rooted (often unconsciously) in the perspective of a single culture (for example, in Venuti's case his perspective is that of the United States, despite his wide-ranging case studies; in Berman's case the argument is framed by presuppositions specific to French culture, predicating, for example, a French sense of cultural enclosure). By contrast, postcolonial translation studies, even those focused on a single translator or country, reflect whole classes of cultures, both those of the colonized and those of the colonizers. The intersection between translation studies and postcolonial studies illustrates that questions about the agency of translators need to be recast in more general

---

[4] Note that the temporal scope of the term *postcolonial* varies in postcolonial studies, with some using the term to refer to conditions after the end of colonialism and others using the term to refer to conditions after the inception of colonialism. I use the terms *postcolonial* and *postcoloniality* in the latter sense. Cf. Robinson (1997a:13-14).

ways and answers framed within a broader range of cultures and more pointed political perspectives than can emerge from a single dominant perspective on culture (even when a scholar acknowledges the diversities within single cultures or seeks to challenge those perspectives).[5]

Though subject to extension and generalization, any sort of inquiry about agency in translation, including agency in postcolonial translation studies, must be specific enough in its data and examples to have substance.[6] Thus, a study must either range widely in its muster of data or focus deeply on the data of a specific case study. In the latter case a scholar must show how the conclusions deriving from the study of a single translator or single country relate to the broader sphere of translation in postcolonial situations and the cross-cultural, cross-temporal concept translation in general. In the case of my own work, I chose the latter approach, investigating translation data in Ireland and then generalizing from there. In order to assess the way that postcolonial translation studies shed light on the question of the translator's agency, in what follows I draw on examples from my more extended work on this topic, *Translation in a Postcolonial Context: Early Irish Literature in English Translation* (1999b).

What is immediately striking about the intersection of Irish studies, postcolonial studies, and questions about the agency of translators is that translators in Ireland historically have had and still have a great deal of visibility in their cultural context. Their status as agents of cultural change is well recognized. Moreover, in most cases of translation, particularly translation between Irish and English, there is an overtly political dimension to the translation project; indeed I myself chose an ideological stance in publishing my own translations of Irish texts (cf. the introduction to Tymoczko 1981). Translations of Irish texts into English are almost always acknowledged under the names of the translators. The Irish translators have generally been prominent people in Irish culture, and they have undertaken action for change in their nation and in the world, affiliating their translation projects explicitly with larger cultural and political movements. They have stood out in a variety of ways, not the least being that their texts were often controversial, and most worked actively and successfully for the freedom of Ireland from English imperialism and for the decolonization of Irish culture after English rule ended.[7] The visibility of postcolonial translators

---

[5] Astutely critiquing the positions of both Berman and Venuti, Lane-Mercier argues that they and other contemporary translation theorists "reintegrate the very concepts they wish to reject" (1997:53). Such reinscription can result from attempting to generalize solely on the basis of Western perspectives.

[6] Susam-Sarajeva (2002:198) argues that one of the ways Western theories attain ascendancy and hegemonic power is by being very abstract and and general, thus attaining the aura of "universality" by leaving the local and particular behind. Postcolonial studies have by and large retained the local.

[7] A caveat is in order here regarding the position of translators in Northern Ireland after 1922, many of whom continued to exhibit attitudes associated with colonized perspectives. A detailed analysis of one such case is found in Tymoczko (2000b).

engaged in nation building and opposition to colonial domination is confirmed by case studies included in the anthologies edited by Susan Bassnett and Harish Trivedi (1999), Marilyn Gaddis Rose (2000), Sherry Simon and Paul St-Pierre (2000), Sabine Fenton (2004), Eva Hung and Judy Wakabayashi (2005), and Theo Hermans (2006).

Before continuing, let's make a little detour to consider colonialism in Ireland and the importance of Ireland as a postcolonial nation. As I've written in *Translation in a Postcolonial Context* (287 ff.), although Ireland is a small country, its struggle for independence sent shock waves through the entire British Empire, rocking the foundations of *imperium* and establishing paradigms of textuality and action that inspired the rest of the colonized world. In 1914 Lenin had predicted that a blow against the British Empire in Ireland would be of "a hundred times more significance than a blow of equal weight in Asia or in Africa" (quoted in Kiberd 1995:197), and so it came to pass. The Irish drive for independence was watched and emulated by nationalist movements in India, Egypt, and elsewhere, with tokens of solidarity being exchanged and advice sought from the Irish by other colonized countries. The British authorities saw the direction history was taking as early as 1919, and cabinet minutes reveal the fears that "if the Irish case were conceded, the flames of revolt would be fanned in India and elsewhere"; England would lose the empire and deserve to lose it (see Kiberd 1995:255, 275-76). Marx had been accurate in foreseeing that Ireland was imperial England's weakest point, that with Ireland lost the British Empire would be gone. The history of the translation of early Irish literature into English is, therefore, the history of a translation practice that fired up Ireland, an important country, albeit a small one. The translation movement was central to the Irish cultural revival and from the Irish revival grew the political and military struggle for freedom from England. When we perceive resistance to colonialism encoded in translations of early Irish literature as leading to engagement between Ireland and Britain, then the translation movement investigated in my work must be understood as having contributed notably to shaping the world all of us live in today. It was a translation practice that changed the world, a form of activism as much as a form of writing.

At the same time, the cultural and historical specificity of Ireland – as of any postcolonial nation – must be acknowledged. Ireland is anomalous as a country that endured a protracted period of colonization spanning more than seven centuries, and it is also anomalous because of its close proximity to the colonizing power and to Europe. Independent of its colonizers, Ireland had deep and sustained historical ties to the Continent – both in precolonial times and throughout the period of colonization – that together with its location sustained the country during colonization and permitted the nation after independence in 1922 to sublimate its similarity to other postcolonial nations in a drive to Europeanize, thus obscuring and complicating its profile as a postcolonial nation. Yet Ireland was also the testing ground of the practices and policies of English colonialism and one of the first countries to face the pressing issues of modernity brought on by the adversities of colonialization. By the middle of the nineteenth century, almost a century earlier than most other peoples, the Irish had already become migrants in space and time, facing the reconstruction of their culture, contending with language loss related to the incursions of English, embracing hybridity, reaping the advantages and disadvantages of diaspora. For these reasons and others, Ireland's translation record inevitably shows contours that can only be related to its proper history. Ireland stands as a partial – or metonymic – representation of postcolonial politics and postcolonial translation, illuminating particular aspects of the questions of ethics, ideology, and agency in translation, rather than offering a final word or a comprehensive and definitive scheme. But the same would have to be recognized in any study relying on data drawn primarily from a single nation, whether that nation is large like India or small like Ireland, far away from its colonizers or in close proximity. Indeed, could any different claim be made without imposing a totalizing narrative upon the data, the hypotheses, and the theory that results? The best that can be done is to acknowledge the specificities of the case in question, as well as its commonalities with other postcolonial situations.[8]

The postcolonial context of Ireland reveals a great deal about translation in general, but it is particularly interesting with reference to translating in a highly charged political context where there are gross asymmetries of power and where most cultural production must have a political agenda – regardless of anyone's taste for politics or ideology – because of the inescapable issues of power in the cultural situation. A full consideration of Ireland's translation movement cannot be recapitulated here; the conclusions, however, can be summarized. It is possible to discern politicized patterns of representation both before and after the independence of the Irish state in 1922, illustrating how the politically charged environment in Ireland impacted on translation in an immediate way. Before 1922, for example, the translators privilege – in fact, construct – heroic biography in the translations of medieval Irish literature. They structure their work around internecine warfare and sacrifice, solemnizing Irish heroism and effacing the humor of the early Irish texts. All these shifts can be correlated with cultural resistance to the degradation of Ireland's native people by the colonizers; the translations subvert colonial views of the Irish as brutish, wild, uncivilized, violent, shiftless, drunken, and unheroic. The translators were responding to English mockery and stereotypes of the Irish that had served to justify English rule and made the Irish a butt of English jokes for centuries. Translation of early Irish texts was part of a program to mobilize the Irish against English oppression in a situation that might involve civil war and struggle of brother against brother, which was what in fact came to pass. Working as part of a larger cultural movement that included political, economic, and even paramilitary activists in alliance with literary and

---

[8] A recent overview of how Ireland related to the British Empire is found in Kenny (2004).

theatrical movements, translators were effective in helping to build the Irish independence movement and in bolstering cultural nationalism both before and after the establishment of the Irish state.

Patterns of translation can also be discerned that have to do with the assertion of native Irish culture in a situation where dominant British standards defined culture *per se* using many criteria and applying standards that were diametrically different from those of Ireland's native tradition. A dominant British perspective on culture had been used to argue that the Irish were uncivilized, thus needing government by the imperial power. Here one can see translators' responses that range from the introjection of dominant colonial standards, to polarized resistance against those standards, to the assertion of autonomous native cultural values: the three stages that have been classically identified as the responses of colonized people to colonization (Tymoczko 1999b:178 and sources cited).

Translators combating colonial domination generally choose empowered representations of the colonized group; in this regard they are often less concerned with close transfer or transposition of cultural, structural, and discursive elements in the source texts than with constructivist representations of larger patterns of the source culture that further postcolonial resistance. The representation of Irish literary formalism in the translations is also significant, as is the representation of Irish concepts that signal central cultural values, the material embodiments of those values, Irish cultural paradigms (such as humor), and Irish cultural practices (such as naming patterns). In regard to questions of this sort, it is also interesting to compare the translations of early Irish literature to other types of literary work in Ireland, including the texts of the great Irish writers working in English, such as W.B. Yeats and James Joyce, and the productions of the Irish dramatic movment. Exploring the patterns of representation, transmission, and transculturation of native culture turns out to be a particularly useful way to do symptomatic readings of translations in a postcolonial context, if one wishes to understand the positioning and affiliation of a translator, and the same can be said of Irish literary works as well (see Tymoczko 2003a).

What emerges from the study of postcolonial translation in Ireland and other postcolonial translation studies are challenges to dominant conceptions about translation and to received views in translation theory, challenges that relate specifically to ethics, ideology, and the political empowerment of translators. Postcolonial translation studies point to a paradigm in which translation does not simply or even primarily take place between two equal cultures as a means of free exchange or transfer of information. Instead, differences in cultural power and prestige manifestly affect every level of choice in translation, from large decisions affecting whole texts and groups of texts (including when to translate and what to translate), to the microlevels of translation (right down to the level of the phoneme in decisions about how to represent names). A translator can exercise politicized and ethical agency on all these levels. What follows, therefore, is the complementarity of cultural studies approaches and linguistic approaches to translation and to the empowerment of translators. In fact, what really emerges is the necessity of using both micro and macro approaches in historical and descriptive research about translation, the choices of translators, and the agency of translators, particularly in situations involving radical asymmetries of power (cf. Tymoczko 2002).

Dominant models of translation assume that a translator must "know" the languages and cultures involved in moving between a source text and target text, but translation in postcolonial contexts challenges this view, showing that the work of translators has a fundamental epistemological dimension. The epistemological component is central to the translator's agency and it has an ethical inflection. Translation does not merely reflect existing knowledge: it can precede knowledge and create knowledge. Translation is a translator's mode of discovery used to create, construct, or amass knowledge, and it can be a form of activist dissemination of (hidden or repressed) knowledge as well. In all these roles translation has marked political dimensions, becoming a mode of spying or intelligence gathering used for the purposes of domination or, alternatively, a mode of counterespionage, resistance, and rebellion. As a type of intelligence gathering, translation constitutes one element of the "imperial archive", similar to other forms of knowledge that have been equated with power and embodied, for example, in the British institutions of the Ordnance Survey and the British Museum (see Cronin 2000 and sources cited). Michael Cronin notes that it was impossible to control the British Empire by force, so "information became the dominant means of control. The Baconian equation of knowledge with power gradually became the guiding dictate of imperial policy" (2003:110). In turn knowledge was used to construct representations and social configurations, contributing to the consolidation of power.[9] As a form of resistance, by contrast, postcolonial translation has been a literature of combat and revolt, representing, transferring, and transculturating knowledge and values for strategic purposes benefiting the dispossessed. In certain circumstances postcolonial translation has led to self-definition and self-determination in the fullest sense of the word.[10]

Dominant models also see translation as a form of mediation between two monolingual communities, but the multilingualism and cultural hybridity of most postcolonial contexts challenge this assumption. Translation is not simply a meeting of a self and an other, mediated by a translator. Often it is a way for a heterogeneous culture or nation to define itself, to come to know itself, to come

---

[9] St-Pierre (2000:261-62) argues that in India, through translation *in situ*, British categories of thought were substituted for native Indian ones; citing Bernard Cohn, he observes that in this way the British in India conquered both territory and an epistemological space. Cf. Cheyfitz (1997).

[10] Both the imperialistic use of translation and the resistant use of translation are also illustrated in case studies of translation in China; see, for example, Hung (2005b), Wakabayashi (2005), Wong (2005). Other case studies pertinent to Asia are found in Fenton (2004) and Hung and Wakabayashi (2005).

to terms with its own hybridity, and to construct a national identity. Translators are frequently the agents who set the terms of these discourses. Thus, translators have a potentially activist role in all these areas, an empowered role that has both ethical and ideological parameters.

Moreover, translation in postcolonial situations sets in high relief the fact that translations are not uniform and consistent. Postcolonial translations cannot normally be defined in terms of the binary cognitive structures that translation studies has depended on to describe translations – literal vs. free, formal-equivalence vs. dynamic-equivalence, adequate vs. acceptable, or even domesticating vs. foreignizing – and translations in postcolonial contexts do not generally fall on a continuum between such polarities either.[11] Instead postcolonial translations are complex, fragmentary, and even at times self-contradictory as translators operate within very specific historical and political contexts to position their work ideologically and pragmatically. These features of postcolonial translations are a function of the agency of their translators. Translators use a metonymic process to achieve specific strategic goals, prioritizing particular aspects or elements of the source texts for immediate context-dependent effects and ends. Such metonymies are an essential aspect of the ability of translations to participate in ideological struggles, to be engaged and partisan (cf. Tymoczko 1999b:289-90). Thus, paradoxically, the polarization of postcolonial contexts facilitates theoretical insight into general processes of translation by setting in sharp relief the significance of the featural, functional, and contextual aspects of translators' metonymic choices and the agency those choices reveal.[12]

Postcolonial translations also confirm the necessity of expanding the cross-cultural and cross-temporal conceptualization of translation. Irish translations, for instance, must be viewed within an expanded concept of translation rather than within a dominant contemporary Western view of translation as close transfer. Otherwise many of the most interesting and illuminating translations of early Irish texts into English will be excluded from consideration because of being labeled as retellings, adaptations, summaries, and so forth. Narrow definitions of translation become normative ways of asserting power, excluding recognition and validation of cultural production that challenges dominant powers. These were considerations that I built into my full-length study of Irish translations from the inception and necessarily so. Postcolonial translations – whether initiated for purposes of colonial control or colonized resistance – are often heavily manipulated versions of their source texts; the definition of translation in such circumstances must be broad enough to include divergent translation products which also at times reflect the indigenous translation norms of colonized nations.[13]

---

[11] Additional binaries are inventoried in Wilt (2003:6-7).

[12] Cf. Lane-Mercier (1997) on translations as contradictory, fragmentary, and dialectical rather than binary.

[13] Similar considerations are required in order to understand the types of translations produced by Lin Shu, Yan Fu, and others in China at the turn of the twentieth century (cf. Wong 2005).

Postcolonial translation illustrates that in many cases a translation is not only a text but an act, where the cultural function of the translation can be as important as the product of translation.[14] Hence fidelity may not be of paramount importance in situations involving asymmetry of cultural power, even when a translator's fundamental allegiance lies with the native source culture. As an act, translation in a postcolonial context normally has public dimensions. Far from being invisible, postcolonial translators are often leading cultural figures, highly visible and publicly engaged in the creation and assertion of cultural resistance to oppression.[15] In these ways translation in postcolonial situations epitomizes many of the activist values that have been called for in translation studies, including programmatic valuation of difference, resistance in translation practice, visibility, and so forth.

Finally, even as translation in postcolonial contexts elucidates resistance in translation, it illuminates the barriers to resistance as well, the ways that resistance in translation is thwarted and aborted. Barriers to resistance are often thought of as an immediate function of formal controls, coercion, and oppression, most notably censorship, the form of repression to which texts are particularly subject. Certainly there are instances where censorship is the prime factor constraining resistance, but the postcolonial cases studies I have explored indicate that self-censorship is even more operative than institutionalized censorship in thwarting the agency and activism of translators. Although conformity to dominant norms can sometimes be analyzed as a strategic aspect of the political program of a translator,[16] limitations in resistance can more typically be attributed to the workings of self-censorship resulting from the introjection of dominant norms of the colonizers' or oppressors' regime. Such self-censorship is not always conscious, often turning instead on cultural filters, cultural paradigms, and other sorts of preconscious assumptions. This type of self-censorship in translation can be analyzed as a form of hegemony, where it involves the translator's acceptance of dominant values in hopes of putative benefits (for example, the use and approval of the translation by a dominant audience or an audience not engaged in cultural

---

Other examples from Asian cultures are found in the articles in Hung and Wakabayashi (2005); Ramakrishna (2000:89-91) also documents examples of extreme textual manipulation in India related to liberation movements.

[14] At other times the text and content are clearly of primary significance; see Bastin et. al. (forthcoming) for an important example.

[15] The visibility of translators in other postcolonial situations is apparent in many of the case studies in Fenton (2004), Hung and Wakabayashi (2005), and Hermans (2006), particularly in situations involving nation building.

[16] For example, as an aspect of the metonymics of the translation, certain cultural elements of the source text (e.g., sexual features) might be assimilated to the colonizers' norms so as to facilitate reception of the translator's emphasis on other radical aspects of a resistant representation (e.g., heroism). This is a mode we might call *strategic self-censorship*, to which we will return in the next chapter.

resistance); in such situations the translator becomes the classic subaltern.[17] If these factors of self-censorship found in translations in postcolonial contexts can be generalized as common barriers to resistance, then understanding how the mechanisms of self-censorship can be disrupted is essential to the promotion of agency and activism in translation among contemporary translators.

Even this brief survey demonstrates that postcolonial translation studies reveal many important aspects of the agency of translators, showing that translators can be effective activists and empowered agents of social change, often with highly visible cultural roles. As part of larger resistance movements, translators in postcolonial contexts have engaged in radical manipulation of texts, constructing cultural images and identities, fostering self-definition, and creating knowledge through their work. Representation, transmission, and transculturation are all evident as essential but varying strands in postcolonial translations, indicating the importance of such frames of reference for analyzing the work of empowered translators. Finally, postcolonial translations and the agency of postcolonial translators challenge conventional definitions of translation, breaching the boundaries of standard types of textual transposition in translation and indicating the necessity of demarcating new groupings of translational activities and products. The need for new descriptors for types of translations that emerge in postcolonial contexts also demonstrates the utility of a cluster concept approach to translation in situations where the translator's agency results in improvisational interventions and *ad hoc* creations. A conceptualization of translation as a cluster concept composed of typologies in which characteristics come and go, recombining in unpredictable ways, provides a useful framework for describing the work of empowered translators in postcolonial contexts and confirms the connection between the enlargement of translation and the empowerment of translators.

5.2 Modeling the Translator's Agency: Moving Beyond Postcolonial Translation Studies

As is apparent from this account of empowered translation in Ireland, postcolonial translation studies can contribute significantly to understanding the ethics and ideology of translation, as well as the agency and empowerment of translators in situations characterized by political polarization and asymmetries of power.[18] The efficacy of postcolonial translation is well recognized. In part

---

[17] Gramsci's view of the workings of hegemony and the position of subalterns is summarized in Strinati (1995:160-75).

[18] Many of these same effects are confirmed by activist translation in other arenas as well, such as strategies used and effects achieved by feminist translators (Simon 1996, von Flotow 1997). For example, von Flotow (1997:96) argues that feminist translation draws attention to itself, flaunts its achievements, and exhibits revolutionary fervor. Feminist translators also assume personal responsibility for their texts and declare their positionality toward both the text and the receptor community.

because the agency of translators is so patent in postcolonial translation studies, postcolonial theoretical frameworks have frequently been extended, generalized, and employed as a model for the role of power and agency in other translation contexts. Similar extensions have occurred in literary and cultural studies; the tendency to generalize the theoretical framework of postcoloniality to other situations is not restricted to translation studies. Although postcolonial translation reveals a great deal about empowerment and agency in translation, however, careful attention shows that postcolonial studies cannot function as a model for agency in translation as a whole, using *model* in the technical sense that it had in the last chapter. At the same time because of the utility of postcolonial theory, it is worthwhile investigating how far it is possible to extend the framework in thinking about ethics, ideology, and political activism in translation, and what limitations are discernible in using postcolonial theory as a framework for agency in translation. A place to begin is a brief consideration of what is actually meant by the terms *postcolonial* and *postcoloniality*. Do these terms refer to specific and restricted historical conditions and circumstances, or are they rather to be conceived as referring to more existential or ontological conditions and, hence, as applying to many situations beyond colonization itself? This is an ongoing debate in a number of fields.[19]

I take the position that postcoloniality is best understood in terms of a particular configuration of geopolitical circumstances involving parameters such as conquest and dispossession; the subjection of a local culture within an empire or an imperial network (thus, dominance by a political, economic, linguistic, and cultural "center" of power); the presence and interface in the colonized setting of two languages and cultures at minimum, of which at least one antedates the imperialist conquest; and the absence of self-determination, instantiated not only by imposed leadership and lack of autonomy of the polity, but also by a prohibition against an autonomous army or against bearing arms. I offer this as a partial and suggestive list, not one meant to be definitive or complete: postcolonial situations differ considerably in their characteristics.[20] What becomes clear when we look at this configuration is that postcoloniality is not limited to the circumstances of nations subject to European imperialism, the cases that interest most current postcolonial scholars including myself. Rather, these configurations are traceable in Western antiquity (e.g., Rome), in the Chinese culture area, in the pre-Columbian Americas, and so forth.[21]

---

[19] See Susam-Sarajeva (2002:202) and sources cited for other approaches to the question of extending postcolonial frameworks.

[20] This definition obviously relegates to a marginal position so-called settler colonies, for which adjustments would have to be made. I realize that my views here are contestable and that I diverge in my opinions from a number of postcolonial translation scholars. On these points see also Robinson (1997a:14). Molloy (2005:371-72) discusses the distinctiveness of Latin American postcolonialism and the difficulties of applying postcolonial theory to those cultures.

[21] Robinson (1997a) argues this point at length.

Generalization is necessary and desirable in intellectual work. Indeed it is essential in establishing a field, pioneering a new method or approach, or indicating the significance of data. It must not be overextended, however. Here I want to emphasize how important it is for translation scholars to be scrupulous about the historic contextualization of each situation being investigated. Scholars frequently choose as case studies historical examples that can be generalized, offering transferable knowledge applicable to other situations. This is to the good, but a concern for generalization must be balanced by acknowledgement of the historical specificities and singularities of the materials under consideration. When case studies are compared, they usually present clusters of likenesses *and* differences rather than identical effects. Similarity is not identity, and historical work, like other intellectual investigations, entails the specification of both likeness and difference (cf. Tymoczko 2004 and sources cited).

Moreover, even within a particular situation, history is not monolithic. A country or a people does not have one single history. Instead there is a cluster of related but differentiated experiences that constitute a group history. To write history without acknowledging this heterogeneity is to erase or silence significant aspects of the experiences involved, and conclusions based on such erasures will be problematic and flawed. Almost inevitably the result will be history slanted toward a group in power: whites, men, the wealthy, the politically empowered, the colonizers, and so forth. Such silencing generally involves the acceptance of dominant views, often through the mechanisms of hegemony. Scholars must constantly remind themselves of such presuppositions about the nature of history and interrogate their own pretheoretical assumptions.

For reasons such as these, I believe that it is necessary to carefully define and delimit what is meant by *postcolonial* and *postcoloniality*. If we blur or efface the boundaries associated with colonialism and use *postcoloniality* as a generalized signifier to indicate all oppression, we will not be well served intellectually. The problems of postcoloniality are not precisely those of people in diaspora, of minorities within a pluralistic society, or of women who are oppressed the world around. By lumping such divergent cases together, I believe that people actually learn less about the conditions of oppression and the means of resistance to oppression; specific conclusions about the data are apt to be less reliable, as are the theoretical implications of the analyses, because of the use of faulty premises. Thus, indiscriminately extending postcolonial theory to model the agency of translators does not seem wise to me.

Nonetheless, the question remains: why are we inclined to extend postcoloniality, to treat it as if it were an existential or ontological condition, and to use postcolonial theory to model oppression in general? There are some obvious reasons for this inclination. First, the oppressive conditions of colonialism are so apparent and so manifest – involving not just oppressive physical conditions but mental and cultural inequities and degradations as well – that colonialism serves as a clear case of oppression. It epitomizes broad, systemic oppression that occurs at the level of cultures as a whole. Second, because of the coming together of different languages, cultural configurations, and textual traditions, postcoloniality, in the sense that I have defined it, thematizes issues of cultural production, cultural interface, and cultural power, issues that are of particular interest to scholars in the humanities and social sciences at present, including translation scholars. In postcolonial situations cultural differences are generally highlighted by differences in language, history, geography, and material practices, all of which have significant implications for linguistic, textual, and other cultural forms.

The concept of postcoloniality is also attractive as a paradigm for oppression because it raises in very clear terms questions pertaining to affiliation. Entailed primarily by sharply polarized power gradients and political oppositions between the colonizers and the colonized, the focus on affiliation is also a function of the thematization of culture in postcolonial situations, for culture in turn highlights affiliation with the past, with the history of a nation, with the relationship between the dominant language and other cultural formations, and with the definition of art and the role of the artist, among other things. In addition, the question of affiliation raised by postcoloniality is not alone a question of the existential allegiance and political resistance of individuals, affecting the place of enunciation of each writer or each person involved in cultural production, including translators. Postcoloniality also raises the question of the affiliation of groups of people and the engagement of whole groups in resistance and collective action: in very clear terms it sets out questions of solidarity. These collective aspects of affiliation also include solidarity with other peoples of the world. Postcolonial theory asks how a people stands with respect to the minority peoples of the world and the majoritarian ones, the dominated and the dominating, the conquered and the conquerors. It raises issues pertaining to an artist's – and a culture's – affiliation with power. Thus, postcolonial theory offers an approach to texts that neatly balances ideology and culture, both critical issues in cultural studies and literary studies currently. The nexus of text, language, culture, and ideology is a central concern of translation studies as well, making postcolonial translation approaches of great relevance to the issues before us in this book, particularly the question of the empowerment of translators.

In investigating the attractions of postcolonial theory, let us not underestimate the appeal of the successful cultural resistance associated with postcolonial nations. Virtually all the colonies of Europe achieved independence in the period between the end of the eighteenth and the end of the twentieth century, with the bulk of the success coming in the twentieth century. Postcolonial nations have, therefore, modeled tangible and dramatically successful resistance to oppression, whatever their difficulties and struggles since independence. Significantly, most former colonies have also attempted to address issues pertaining to cultural autonomy, albeit in the difficult circumstances of globalization in the second half of the twentieth century and the beginning of the twenty-first. Therefore, whatever the fragmentary accomplishments and partial results of their political and cultural independence, former colonies exemplify the triumph of resistance, the achievements of activism, the hopes of engagement and agency, and the possibility of success in securing better conditions materially and culturally in all domains.

Still another attraction of postcolonial models is that the condition of colonized peoples and the issues raised by postcoloniality have been relatively well theorized and this theory has by now a long history and an extensive development. Major cultural figures such as Frantz Fanon stand behind the authors of *The Empire Writes Back* (Ashcroft et al. 1989), Gayatri Spivak, and Homi Bhabha. Those who have written about postcoloniality include important writers and leaders ranging across the twentieth century and into the twenty-first, from Léopold Sédar Senghor and Aimé Césaire, to more recent figures such as Chinua Achebe, Ngugi wa Thiong'o, and Salman Rushdie. For all the reasons delineated, therefore, it is no surprise that scholars find it attractive to look at translation and the agency of the translator in the context of postcoloniality.

Indeed translation in postcolonial contexts offers some of the most interesting case studies available for understanding and theorizing the power and agency of translators and questions of ethics and ideology in translation, as exemplified in the discussion of the Irish material above. The study of translation in postcolonial contexts has contributed to a reconceptualization of translation both theoretically and practically, offering insights about the processes and products of translation, and the identity and agency of translators. If this is true – and I hope I have made the case here and in my earlier work – then it follows that more particularized and detailed studies of postcolonial translation movements around the world will enrich translation studies, particularly insofar as they shed light on the empowerment of translators. Fuller and more systematic studies of translation in other postcolonial nations will fill out the differences, for example, between translation movements in the context of nineteenth-century imperialism and those countering twentieth-century neoimperialism. It will also be interesting to tease out the contours of translation in countries such as China and Latin American nations that at different times and in different guises have been both the colonizers and the colonized.

In a postpositivist world, perspective is recognized as an irreducible aspect of any intellectual work and of action in general, and it has become increasingly clear since World War II that translation can no longer be conceived as an objective activity, independent of interpretation. There is a responsibility to be aware of our own frameworks as we ourselves translate, of the frameworks of the translators we investigate, and, recursively, of our own frameworks as we assess the frameworks of other translators and scholars of translation.[22] Postcolonial translations make all such perspectives and frameworks patent, elucidating the agency, the engagement, the effective cultural resistance, and the empowerment

---

[22] On the latter see the example of self-reflexivity in Cheung (2002).

of translations and translators. The study of these translations also makes it clear that the world is such that we cannot merely look and observe, but that we are also called upon to act and to join with others in action.

With my suggestions that *postcolonial* and *postcoloniality* be restricted to a specific domain, I do not mean to eliminate comparisons between translation in postcolonial contexts and other activist translation contexts. Indeed, comparison is one of the strongest cognitive tools that can be brought to bear on any issue, as I have stressed repeatedly. Certainly comparisons can and should be made between various kinds of oppression, and features of postcolonial oppression and resistance, as well as aspects of postcolonial theory, will be highly relevant to other contexts. But comparison is not simply perception of likeness; it involves perception of difference as well. In fact, because similarity is not an identity relationship, it *ipso facto* involves difference. It is therefore important in research of any kind, particularly theorization, to remember the words of Dwight Bolinger:

> Always one's first impulse, on encountering two highly similar things, is to ignore their differences in order to get them into a system of relationships where they can be stored, retrieved, and otherwise made manageable. The sin consists in stopping there. And also in creating an apparatus that depends on the signs of absolute equality and absolute inequality, and uses the latter only when the unlikeness that it represents is so gross that it bowls you over. (1977:5)

Lack of attention to difference results in a great loss of information – loss of as much information as is gained by attention to likeness. Erasure of difference implied in the use of postcolonial theory to model agency in translation as a whole is an example of the problem.

As a concrete instance, let us consider the difficulties of seeing the oppression of women in terms of colonialism in an absolute sort of way. Throughout the course of history the oppression of women has been much more pervasive and much worse overall than colonial oppression. There are also problems with modeling culture across the two domains, in view of the fact that women have no fully autonomous languages or "native" cultures, even though linguistic and cultural patterns are different for men and women. Moreover, it is impossible to use postcoloniality to model questions of affiliation in the case of gender relations, because typically affiliations in postcolonial situations are much more polarized than they can ever be for women and men whose lives as individuals and as groups are inextricably linked. Similarly, there is no transitivity in the model: perspectives on the oppression of women have relatively little use in explaining certain features of the worst forms of colonialism including genocide, something that men cannot inflict systematically on women, however much women are brutalized in specific situations and in general.

Postcolonial theory is also limited in its ability to offer appropriate models for the agency of translators in less polarized situations of power. Thus, the scope of a translator's agency is different and must be theorized differently in the context of globalization, where power vectors interpenetrate to a greater extent than they did in most nineteenth-century situations of colonization.[23] Situations where a translator's affiliation is engaged in more than one direction – such as the case where a translator's immediate financial gains and consciousness of local economic benefits to the community from employment by multinational globalizing corporate interests conflict with larger perspectives on the loss of local autonomy and local knowledge – must be examined with full awareness of the disparities between colonial situations and contemporary conditions of globalization. To do otherwise is to turn the useful tool of postcolonial theory into a universalizing and totalizing narrative.

Such differences between postcolonial situations and others in which power is contested are obvious. Nonetheless, postcolonial theory continues to be extended and deployed as a theoretical framework for situations quite different from colonialism despite asymmetries that make its use inappropriate and despite critical rhetoric about the importance of attention to the specificities of historical and political contexts. It should be clear from the points raised here that it is time to move beyond postcolonial theory as a primary means for modeling the agency of translators. What continues to hinder the adoption of new theoretical models?

5.3 Power and the Agency of the Translator

In part postcolonial theory has become popular for modeling diverse politicized contexts in cultural and literary studies because it has filled a theoretical gap since the fall of the Soviet Union in 1991. The dissolution of the U.S.S.R. resulted in diminished confidence in Marxist theories of power that had served as a default in many academic circles and many political contexts for much of the twentieth century. Marxist theories have not fully sustained themselves in the face of the political and economic developments in socialist countries since 1991, and this failure has been compounded by the complexities of globalization.[24]

The question is, therefore, how to move forward in understanding the ethics and ideology of translation and in developing an approach to the political

---

[23] Of course, in any postcolonial situation there are colonizers who identify with the colonized and members of the colonized group who align their interests with those of the colonizers. Such cases are largely exceptions, however, with most members of each group relatively polarized with respect to the other group. By contrast, the boundaries between local and global are becoming increasingly fuzzy as globalization gains momentum, such that the two are becoming much more difficult to tease apart.

[24] See Strinati (1995:129-76) for a review of Marxist theory, as well as criticisms thereof, in a framework relevant to translation studies.

empowerment of translators? If postcolonial theory does not serve as an adequate model for all politicized contexts involving oppression and if Marxist theories no longer command the assent that they used to, what theoretical framework can ground exploration of the empowerment and agency of translators? The trajectories of translation theory and other fields suggest that new theories of power, ideological resistance, and political activism are needed that are more flexible and more applicable to a broader range of cultural contexts than either Marxist theories or postcolonial theory can be.

If new theories of power are needed, what factors must they address and what elements must they include? Clearly an answer to this question goes far beyond the domain of translation studies and the scope of this study. Nonetheless, it is possible to outline some components that must be part of new general theories of power serving as a basis for exploring the agency of translators. First, the analysis must recognize the materialist bases of power, but the analysis cannot be limited to class struggles alone. It must address issues of production, but also broader economic and social issues including control of trade, markets, and resources. These factors must be related to contemporary phenomena including the informational networking of the world, globalization, multinational corporate culture, the media, and technologies of all sorts from industrial and military to media and information technologies. An adequate analysis of power must include contemporary shifts from accumulating capitalism to consumer capitalism as well. Insights from sociology and political science must be incorporated, yet a useful theory of power must also move beyond the level of single social systems (countries or cultures) to transcultural and transnational considerations (including imperialism, neoimperialism, and diaspora). A contemporary theory must account for power asymmetries on a global scale – rather than primarily in terms of class struggles within cultures – and must also relate global conditions to local ones.

No theory of power can be complete without some account of emerging data about dominance and cooperation from psychology, biology, sociobiology, and evolutionary biology. Such data pertain to gender and other biological attributes, but they also include psychological issues that have social reflexes, including greed, reciprocity, attitudes toward cheating, corruption, deception and self-deception, and so forth. Investigations pertaining to groups and group theory can also be included under this general rubric. In some cases evidence pertaining to biology and sociobiology of different species is essential. It is not that a theory of power should accept biological evidence as definitive, rather a theory of power must take these factors into consideration, integrating them into a framework that allows and accounts for human alteration and transcendence of biological dispositions where relevant. After all, human beings have been one of the most successful species in part because they are skilled in reshaping their own instinctual responses and their own environments. Nonetheless, biology remains a factor to be assessed in the exercise and contestation of power, as well as in other types of political interactions.

A contemporary theory of power should also include input from information theory and related fields. Game theory, for example, has amassed evidence about strategies that enhance success and survival, distinguishing importantly between win-win and win-lose games, zero-sum games and non-zero-sum games.[25] Nor can a plausible theory of power neglect the role of education or the control of meaning and knowledge in power hierarchies. Related questions include decision making, transparency in government, and so forth. Here again the media must be acknowledged as significant factors in the modern exercise of power.[26]

There are also broad linguistic and cultural factors to be folded into a comprehensive theory of power. Human institutions such as religion cannot be ignored, as recent history illustrates, nor can the role of texts in the consolidation of power. Linguistic analyses of modes of signification, relevance, and speech acts are important aspects to be theorized. Even more important is the role of discourse in shaping and perpetuating ideological frameworks that are preconditions of the exercise of power, that act as foundations for power hierarchies, and that maintain and stabilize power gradients that would not be possible if power were based on physical force and resource distribution alone. Discourses are powerful in the construction of meaning and they shape representations of both the self and others. Thus, there is an epistemology of power to be considered in theorizing both power and the decentering of power.

A theory of power is incomplete without a theory of resistance and contestation. Power is not merely something that flows top down: power inheres at all levels of human society. It is essential to avoid simplistic models of power, to avoid seeing power as invested solely or even primarily in political and economic institutions. A comprehensive theory must account for the way that power is exercised by those seeking empowerment and those engaging in activism as well. Similarly it is important to avoid simplistic polarized models of power, in which some have it and some don't. The means and mechanisms for the alteration of power structures must themselves be part of a theory of power: the history of power has shown – whether at the level of the family, the band, the tribe, the nation, or the world – that there is nothing more constant than change in the structure and exercise of power. Thus, a theory of power will include theorizations of conflict and resolution of conflict, both in materialist and discursive terms.[27]

Finally, a theory of power also must intersect with the question of ethics and responsibility. Power can be exercised in all the domains discussed without being necessarily either good or evil. How do questions about what is good and what is right enter into the articulation and exercise of power? How do questions

---

[25] Pym (2000) offers an interesting perspective on translation based on game theory.

[26] Many of the parameters of power are interrelated in multiple ways, as the example of the media illustrates.

[27] On these points see also the discussion in Tymoczko and Gentzler (2002:xi-xxviii). Cf. Lane-Mercier (1997:64-65), quoting Foucault.

of ethics and reponsibility relate to a theory of power? History shows that these questions are inescapable in the maintenance and duration of power structures; thus, they cannot be ignored in theorizations of power.

Translation plays a role in many of these aspects of power and as such the agency of translators is a significant factor to be considered within a theory of power, just as power is a significant factor to be considered in theorizing the agency of translators. Promulgating new theories of power is not the domain of translation studies, but as alternate paradigms of power emerge in the coming years, translation studies must be alert for their implications for the agency of translators. New theories of power will be relevant to many other aspects of the discipline as well, including translation processes and products, the control and commissioning of translation, the dissemination of translation products, translator training, and the structure of the discipline itself. In the meantime, as new theories of power are being developed, discussions of power in translation studies will do well to reflect the complexities of the topic indicated above.

5.4 Two Metaphors for Agency and Activism: Resistance and Engagement

Jean-Marc Gouanvic has suggested that looking at translation from a postcolonial perspective foregrounds essential elements of the practice of translation, showing it to be "a historically determined game of power, imbricated in transnational power relationships" (2000:101). Yet if postcolonial theory only goes a small way to explaining the many facets of power, it can only offer one perspective on the relationship between translation and power rather than an analysis sufficient for all contexts. Nor as yet have the calls for activism in translation embraced the full range of issues that a theory of power must account for and that theorizations of activism demand. Fortunately the theorization the agency of translators is not a necessary precondition for the *exercise* of power by translators themselves. Although it is not necessary to have a fully articulated theory of power in order to have an activist *practice* of translation, a *concept* of activism is useful in selecting appropriate interventions and strategies for action. Thus, whether working alone or in groups, activists frequently invest time and thought in strategizing their actions.

In *Metaphors We Live By* (1980), George Lakoff and Mark Johnson demonstrate the ways in which metaphors permeate languages, structuring how people conceive of common activities and common concepts, often in ways that are implicit and preconscious for speakers. Such metaphors frequently undergird discourses about subjects as well. In translation studies (and elsewhere), there have been two principal ways of conceptualizing activism, both of them based on metaphorical meanings associated with common English words and their counterparts in other European languages: *resistance* and *engagement*. This section explores the implications of conceiving a translator's ethical, political, and ideological agency in these terms, comparing the metaphorical significance of resistance and engagement as modes of activism.

As a concept for politicized activism in translation studies, resistance is associated with the work of Lawrence Venuti (1992, 1995, 1998a, 1998b), who has repeatedly deployed terminology related to this concept to speak about the activist agency of translators. Venuti borrowed the term *resistance* from the common designation for clandestine activist movements opposed to occupying forces, notably those during World War II in Europe that opposed the German occupation and fascist governments. During that period and in similar agonistic conflicts, the enemies of resistance movements were obvious and can still be presupposed in discussions of the events.

In the term *resistance* there is an implicit metaphor about activism: the metaphor presumes the existence of a specific powerful opponent that exerts force in particular ways or in particular directions, and the metaphor suggests that it is the role of activists to oppose the opponent's force, attempting to deflect or thwart (i.e., resist) the actions that the force initiates and the directions that the power wishes to take and to impose on others.[28] Despite (or perhaps because of) the popularity of the metaphor of resistance in European languages, it is important to see that this is a reactive view of activism rather than a proactive one: initiative largely rests with the principal power in the situation, and activists attempt to stop those initiatives.

Although widely used, the metaphor implicit in *resistance* seems to be problematic as the foundation for conceptualizing *agency* in translation; it is unnecessarily restrictive with respect to initiative, limiting the translator to a more passive role than is required or desirable. This is not the only problem with the terms *resistance* and *resistant* as applied to translation. By contrast with resistance movements during World War II, there is no default opponent or ideological target in translation studies to which a translator's resistance can be presumed to refer. Case studies generated by Venuti and others at times discuss resistance as if the antagonist or opponent were obvious, but descriptive studies of translations using this terminology ascribe resistance in translation to diverse and highly variable opponents including colonialism, neoimperialism, capitalism, Western domination, specific regimes such as the United States, specific oppressive social conditions, the patriarchy, bourgeois norms, dominant discourses, Christianity, dominant literary conventions, and linguistic norms. Sometimes the object of resistance is unstated and vague in the extreme. No agreement exists among translators or translation scholars as to what can or should be resisted in most translation situations. As the term has been used with reference to translation, resistance seems to be an open-ended enterprise without predefined or well defined targets that either translators or critics delineate.

---

[28] The *OED* (s.v.) offers the following definitions of the word: (1) "the act, on the part of persons, of resisting, opposing, or withstanding"; (2) "power or capacity of resisting"; (3) "opposition of one material thing to another material thing, force".

In translating texts translators must make choices, and emphasis on the translator's choices and decision making was one of the first steps in exploring the agency of the translator, as we have seen. Translators cannot transpose everything in a source text to the receptor language and the target text, partly because of anisomorphisms of language and asymmetries of culture, partly because meaning in a text is both open and overdetermined, partly because a text makes contradictory demands that cannot all be simultaneously satisfied (for example, the demands of complex content and spare form), and partly because the information load associated with a source text is excessive. Translation is therefore a metonymic process, and translators must make choices, setting priorities for their translations (Tymoczko 1999b:41-61, 278-300; Boase-Beier 2006:50-70). What is interesting about the translator's ideological agency is that resistance is also a metonymic process: a translator cannot resist or oppose everything objectionable in either the source culture or the target culture. Translators make choices about what values and institutions to support and oppose, determining activist strategies and picking their fights even as they are also making choices about what to transpose from a source text and what to construct in a receptor text. Resistance in translation stands at the intersection of two metonymic systems: the normal metonymics of translation itself and the metonymic nature of resistance in situations where the social antagonist is not necessarily predefined or well defined. Resistance in translation is therefore a complex act, albeit a seemingly reactive one, and it involves complex social positioning and complex textual constructions.

Calls for resistance in translation have not always fully recognized these complexities. At times they tend to assume that the object of resistance is known and to be very prescriptive about specific textual strategies to be privileged in resistant translations (perhaps because of pretheoretical assumptions about values or about the object of resistance). In *The Translator's Invisibility*, for instance, Venuti promotes a resistant strategy that he calls "foreignization", which "enables a disruption of target-language cultural codes" and registers "the linguistic and cultural differences of the foreign text", exerting "ethnodeviant pressure" on the values of the target culture (Venuti 1995:42, 81). He argues that such a strategy is effective in combatting the cultural enclosure and cultural dominance of readers in the United States. Generalizing such arguments beyond their immediate cultural context is extremely difficult, however. Although at times foreignization may be an appropriate resistant technique in dominant cultures such as the United States, it is not at all suited to subaltern cultures that are already flooded with foreign materials and foreign linguistic impositions (often from the United States or other Eurocentric cultures) and that are trying to establish or shore up their own discourses and cultural forms. Foreignization has also been rightly criticized as potentially an elitist strategy, more appropriate to a highly educated target audience than to a broad readership or a cultural situation in which the normal education level is more modest than it is in Europe or the United States.[29]

Let us turn to a second metaphor for activism that has also been widely used in translation studies, the metaphor implicit in the English-language word *engagement*. The term derives from words meaning 'to be under a pledge' (from Old French *gage*, 'pledge'). The history and usage of the words *engage* and *engagement* imply commitment, involvement, participation, mutual pledges and promises, making guarantees, assuming obligations, exposing oneself to risk, entering into conflict, becoming interlocked or intermeshed, and action undertaken by more than one person (*OED* s.v.). As a metaphor for activism, the concept engagement suggests a much more proactive stance than the concept resistance does. Engagement suggests a wide range of enterprises that activists initiate rather than being restricted to reactions or oppositions to an external powerful force (as in resistance). Engagement also suggests actions based on commitment to (specific) principles, as well as actions involving solidarity with other people. The metaphor seems to lend itself much more easily to forms of activism involving initiative than does the metaphor of resistance.

This conceptualization of activism with reference to textual forms of cultural production such as translation is associated in postwar thought with the concept of *littérature engagée* (engaged or committed literature), widely promoted in the mid-twentieth century by Jean-Paul Sartre and others in his circle, but also advocated by other Marxist writers, particularly those outside the Soviet bloc. Calling for "a literature of *praxis*" and using phrases such as "to speak is to act" and "words are loaded pistols", in the postwar period Sartre advocated using cultural production "to help effect certain changes in the Society that sur-rounds us" (1988:36, 38, 255). Sartre believed these things could be achieved by developing a literature that would disclose the world (1988:65), that would be "moral and problematic" (1988:235), that had the duty "to take sides against all injustices" (1988:229). He argued that "literature is in essence a taking of position" and that a writer's every word "has reverberations", as do a writer's silences (1988:224, 252).

If translators or scholars adopt or advocate engagement as a form of activism in translation, however, I suggest that it is important to envision something much more proactive than the activities touted by advocates of *littérature engagée*. I take this view of engagement in translation for a number of reasons. First, the effectiveness of literature or other texts that aim merely at attitudinal shifts in the receiving audience is very difficult to assess and less certain to achieve actual political or ideological results than the activism of postcolonial translators has been. Attitudinal shifts are notoriously difficult to correlate with social change; attitudinal shifts are also conspicuously volatile and subject to reversals or ironic finales. It seems particularly dubious at present to argue for the transformative

---

[29] These and other criticisms are taken up in Pym (1996), Lane-Mercier (1997), Hatim (1999), Tymoczko (2000a), Shamma (2005), and sources cited.

value of changing the attitudes of a small avant-garde after a century of repression, suppression, and even extermination of cultural elites. From the annihilation of intellectuals in the Nazi death camps to China's Cultural Revolution, from the neutralization of leftists during the McCarthy period in the United States to the massacres of the educated classes in African countries after the end of colonialism, we should understand that such hopes of attitudinal shifts are often sadly misplaced. Pogroms and purges of progressives and of the left as a whole have occurred on virtually every continent in the last century, wiping away gains associated with attitudinal shifts. Such repression continues unabated today in many places in the world, not least in the Mideast, and the freedoms of speech and of the press are currently under general attack everywhere.

When I think of translation as a form of political and ideological activism, therefore, it is engagement that I usually think about, but engagement of a very active sort. I am primarily interested in and impressed by translations that are forms of speech acts associated with activism: translations that rouse, inspire, witness, mobilize, and incite to rebellion. As engaged translations in postcolonial and other contexts illustrate, such translations act in the world and have a proactive dimension. They initiate ethical, political, and ideological actions, rather than being principally reactive. Engaged translators are visible as subjects, and as agents they have political agendas and use translation as one means to achieve those agendas. Moreover, as the metaphorical aspect of the term suggests, engaged translators often, even usually, join with others of like mind in collective action. Activism of this form is not just an individual effort, nor is it restricted necessarily to translation alone. Typically engaged translators join with writers, publishers, political activists, and others for joint actions and coordinated programs. Translations produced in such contexts have illocutionary and perlocutionary dimensions; they actually participate in social movements and aim to be effective in the world at achieving demonstrable and specific material, social, and political change.

Case studies of translation movements that have been successful in effecting social change illustrate these characteristics. If we look at historical movements such as the Irish translators at the turn of the twentieth century (as well as translation movements that have supported nation building in other postcolonial contexts), they offer valuable evidence about the general nature of engagement, empowerment, and political agency in translation. The Irish translation movement demonstrates that the criteria discussed above characterize translation as an effective form of political and ideological activism leading to geopolitical change. Political effectiveness is most likely if there is a group of visible translators with a common project or program and if the translators as a group operate within the context of a larger political and cultural movement, as was the case in Ireland in the period 1890-1916. Such a movement might undertake the production of other textual forms (theatrical scripts for performance, literary rewritings and creations of various types, pamphlets, speeches, manifestos, and so on); all such textualized forms are prominent features of the Irish revival. The production of texts – including translations – will be coordinated with various other activist initiatives. To be maximally effective, engaged translators (and artists) will also be affiliated with groups undertaking diverse forms of direct activist actions and political organization; this too is evident in Ireland at the turn of the twentieth century where literary figures and translators worked jointly with activists of all sorts, even paramilitary movements.

For such a politicized translation movement to be most powerful, it must also have a clear and articulated set of goals and values to which members of the movement assent and in a sense pledge themselves. The writers and translators of the Irish revival were indefatigable in issuing statements about their principles and aims and in defending and arguing for their positions. In order for translation to have an impact in a particular political context, there must also be a target audience large and diverse enough to initiate and carry out the practical, cultural, and ideological shifts that the translations aim at. These features are also illustrated in the Irish translation movment, where common ideals were hammered out in a number of popular periodicals such as the *United Irishman* and in public fora of various sorts. These cultural forms were all aimed at and open to a large integrated audience at the turn of the twentieth century in Ireland, an audience that drew together Catholics and Protestants, intellectuals and common people, artists and workers, urban and rural populations. Building up such a broad and general audience rather than resting content with addressing an elite may itself be a necessary part of the activist translation program, and it may involve devising economic strategies for producing inexpensive publications that can be widely disseminated. An essential for an engaged translation practice is therefore a (patronage) system facilitating the publication and wide distribution of the activist translations.[30] It is not possible for translators to have ethical and ideological force and to contribute effectively to social change unless their translations can be made public, heard, and read. Thus, engaged translators must work with publishers, people who control or have access to the media, and people who can find ways to fund the production and distribution of the translated material; we see here again the value of coordinated activist involvement for translators. This feature of cooperative action is also illustrated by the Irish revival which disseminated translations and retellings through popular periodicals, the enormously popular classes of the Gaelic League, and the Irish dramatic movement which for years met in ordinary halls that were financially accessible to common workers.

The characteristics of such historical examples of activist translation movements are evident in some contemporary activist movements. Mona Baker (2006b) discusses current groups of translators who have banded together in organizations such as Babels, Translators for Peace, and ECOS (Traductores e Intérpres por la Solidaridad). Contemporary politically and ideologically activist

---

[30] I am using *patronage* in the broad sense discussed by Lefevere (1992b), for example.

translators engage in many types of translation that illustrate the points above. Translators for Peace, for example, translates articles and documents that do not appear in the mainline press, and they find ways to publish and disseminate such materials; they also translate documents of organizations involved in peace missions, supply interpreters for conferences, and so forth. A clear activist agenda is apparent in their mission statement, their activities, and their alliances with other likeminded activists. Babels is an activist translation movement with a broader agenda, drawing from translators worldwide to support such groups as the European Social Forum and others identified with the Charter of Principles of the World Social Forum. Again Babels has an agenda, articulating its goal to be a player in the "anti-capitalist debate". Its associations with other activist groups facilitates the wide dissemination of its translations. Many of the translators in these groups have chosen to be visible in their role as activists. Moreover, these twenty-first century organizations of activist translators are finding ways to reach broad audiences, redefining questions of audience and patronage by using electronic resources as international channels of production and dissemination.

Before leaving the question of ideologically activist translation, let us consider for a moment the texts selected for translation and the target texts as well. In politically engaged practices of translation, texts to be translated are obviously chosen with political goals in view. Historical case studies demonstrate that in many circumstances there must be a willingness to manipulate source texts in translation, so as to adapt and subordinate the texts to political and ideological agendas. The Irish translation movement illustrates that the intent to transmit texts closely, in and for themselves, was abandoned in its activist translation programs.[31] Similar textual manipulation is notable in more recent activist movements associated with identity formation in Quebec and Brazil, as well as in feminist translation movements (Brisset 1996; Simon 1996; von Flotow 1997; Vieira 1994, 1999). In other situations such as the case of ECOS or the translation movement that promoted independence in the Hispanic American nations at the turn of the nineteenth century (Bastin et al., forthcoming), fidelity to the text can be a much higher priority, with the production of the text itself the center of the activist achievement. These differences in textual strategies indicate that engaged translators must be ingenious and varied in their approach to translation processes and the construction of the target text. No single translation approach or strategy is likely to suffice – whether it is literal or free, formally or dynamically equivalent, domesticating or foreignizing. Instead, in activist translation multiple strategies are deployed and maximum tactical flexibility maintained, so as to respond most effectively to immediate ideological and cultural contexts and to specific political imperatives. It is not sufficient simply to disrupt received or dominant standards of textuality in a random, generalized, or even totalizing manner. It may even be desirable to have multiple and complementary representations of the same set of

---

[31] The same is true in the cases discussed in Ramakrishna (2000).

texts in translation.[32] Trying to prescribe a single textual or discursive strategy for activism in translation (such as foreignizing) is like trying to prescribe a single strategy for effective guerrilla warfare. What is required instead is a certain opportunistic vitality that seizes upon immediate short-term gains even as the long-term activist goals remain in view (cf. Tymoczko 2000a).

It is important to flag the implications of these characteristics associated with activist political and ideological translation practices, because the radical manipulation of texts and the radical subordination of text to ideology apparent in many activist translation movements are inimical to translators whose primary orientation is to the integrity of texts themselves. Perhaps because of the nature of charged political environments, translators in postcolonial situations – whether affiliated with the colonizers or the colonized – are often willing to forgo such scruples.[33] In these and other political and ideological contexts, activism comes at a price, one that many translators find unacceptable. It is important to look at these costs steadily, for the alternative is to see translators as politically and ideologically engaged when they are not, to mythologize the agency of translators (as the agency of authors has at times been mythologized), pretending that the work of translation must be more political and more activist than it is in fact in order to be considered worthwhile at all. This is a sentimental posture, and in *Ulysses*, quoting George Meredith, James Joyce reminds us that "the sentimentalist is he who would enjoy without incurring the immense debtorship for a thing done" (1986:164).

5.5 Empowerment and Self-Reflexivity in Translation Studies

If a translator can become a traitor, as the Italian aphorism *traduttore, traditore* suggests, without a doubt it is the political and ideological agency of translators that is the most threatening to those in power. The current lack of viable theories of power prevent modeling the empowerment of translators in a comprehensive way. Nonetheless, actual historical examples of activist translation movements make it possible to sketch out some important ways in which the agency of translators expresses itself most effectively in political and ideological assertions.

A translator's ideological empowerment begins with the necessity to make decisions and choices in translation, ranging from the largest to the smallest levels of text – from choices of what to translate to decisions about how to manage the sounds of the source language. Even when a translator is not a political activist, the translator's agency is notable and powerful because of inherent ethical and ideological vectors of textual choices at all these levels. A translator's choices

---

[32] An example of a multiple translation practice is discussed in Tymoczko (1999b:122-41).
[33] Analyses of colonialist translations are found in Niranjana (1992), Cheyfitz (1997), Fitzpatrick (2000), St-Pierre (2000), Fenton and Moon (2002), Kothari (2003), and Fenton (2004). See also the discussion in 7.5 below.

issue in the representations, transmissions, and transculturations of the target text. They determine the outcome of the interface of discourses and meanings inherent in the source culture and those of the target culture. The translator's choices and the ideological weight of a text in turn reflect the translator's affiliations and the translator's place of enunciation; the translator's programmatics structure the discourses privileged in the translation and the meanings constructed in the target text.

Politically engaged translations and translation movements challenge the neat typologies in current delineations of translation types and again underscore the need for expanding the definition of translation as a cross-cultural concept in order to make room for the *ad hoc* innovative types of translations that emerge in response to ideological challenges in specific historical and political contexts. Such strategies can involve the ostensive display of the foreign, the cannibalistic consumption of the foreign, and everything in between. The need to move away from translation typologies based on binaries is evident, as is the necessity to distinguish types of translations that constitute clusters related to political agency within the overall category translation. These clusters might be based on formal criteria such as fullness of translation, or content criteria such as modes of cultural translation and self-definition, epistemological parameters, or indices of constraint including censorship and self-censorship.

We have traced some important continuities in effective political translation movements from the nineteenth century to the present. These examples constitute only a small sample of similar movements that have been the subject of intense exploration by scholars whose work constitutes the second wave of descriptive translation studies. Many activist translation movements illustrate how the empowerment of translators is accompanied by the expansion of the concept of translation itself, as translators push the boundaries of translation norms in pursuit of their ideological goals. The relationship between empowered translators and an enlarged concept of translation is manifest in explorations of the political and ideological agency of translators.

Although all these characteristics persist in contemporary activist translation, there are also differences in the ways that translators exercise their political agency at present. These changes can be broadly related to three parameters: the locus of the action, the nature of the activist community, and the types of textual products involved. Whereas most empowered translation movements in the past have been based within nations, increasingly the locus of translator activism is moving to the international sphere as activists have taken up causes that transcend the boundaries of single societies. Such are the translators organized around specific political agendas such as Babels, ECOS, or Translators for Peace discussed above. In many situations ideological affiliations are more important than localized cultural or political affiliations for contemporary activist translation movements, and the same is true of political agendas that reflect international concerns more than national ones.[34]

A second parameter in transition is the nature of activist translation communities. Increasingly electronic networking makes it possible for translation communities to extend far beyond the local and to link people with common activist interests around the world. This changing dimension of activist translation communities is obviously related to the broader domain of activist interests: the movement away from national, ethnic, or cultural concerns to an international locus of action changes the nature of the activist community itself. People can join in concerted efforts from very different locations, establishing virtual communities and pooling diverse types of expertise and experience. Cronin observes that the local is important "as a basis for the formation of solidary relationships", but that micro-cosmopolitanism allows for "the trans-local spread of those relationships", that is, for "the establishment of solidarities that are not *either* local *or* global but both" (2006:19). Here Cronin points to both the strengths and weaknesses of translocal activism; he indicates the importance of rootedness in relation to the strength of community and signals a vulnerability of activist translation communities that exist *only* at a virtual level. The importance of the local for solidarity suggests that networked international communities that actually come together in concerted action periodically (for example, by interpreting together at conferences), with the virtual community doubled by physical and personal connection as well, will end up stronger and more able to achieve activist successes. They may also be more resistant to cooptation and more consistent in their political narratives because of opportunities to discuss and reaffirm their agendas together in person, where they can exchange ideas and strengthen their identity as a community gathered together at a (temporary but concrete) locus.

The third parameter that is altering the nature of empowerment in translation is the nature of the translations themselves undertaken by contemporary activist translators. As the concept of translation expands beyond transfer, it is possible to project an expanded field of textual output by activist translators. Although traditional interpretation and textual translation focused on information transfer will continue, other types of translation made possible by technological networking and dissemination will also open up to translators. In fact this is already being exploited by activist international groups, not all of them translators' organizations *per se*. Skill in localization allows activist translators to generate new texts in many languages promoting political causes around the world. The results of such activities are already apparent in electronic networking.

If a translator's most threatening social capacity is political agency, then this is the aspect of the translator's role that societies will be most invested in

---

[34] Calzada Pérez (2003:5-6) notes the overlap of ideology and culture, but makes the point that ideological concerns transcend ethnic frameworks and affect more than single societies. They permeate identity groups of the most varied nature. See the other essays in her volume for additional approaches to ideology that relate to current activist translation movements.

controlling. It is noteworthy that current Western practices institutionalize such control in both pedagogical and professional contexts. Statements of translators' professional ethics promulgated in these contexts typically focus on textual fidelity, responsibility to the patron (client, employer), legal responsibilities, and the like. One discerns here a dispersal of ideology, a strategy to turn translators' attention away from larger ideological questions of ethical engagement and geopolitical concerns that might mobilize the translators' independent agency in activist ways. By restricting the notion of ethics in translation to questions about the microlevels of text and contractual or legal obligations related to terms of employment, the profession inscribes its members within dominant ideologies. The institutions training and employing translators distract them from the largest possibilities of their own ideological and political empowerment by focusing on the most minute levels having to do with translation strategies at the linguistic level and social responsibility related solely to the immediate assignment. Conflicts and contestations pertaining to values, ethics, ideologies, and politics are all effaced, as are moral responsibilities to the community as a whole entailed in an existentialist sense of translational agency.

By defining translation in narrow and prescriptive ways, translation pedagogy also closes off possibilities for translator agency inherent in the range of translation types included in the international cluster concept translation – including abridgments, summaries, culturally manipulated adaptations, and so forth. Both the wide range of translation types attested across time and space and the theoretical openness associated with the blurred boundaries of translation are equally effaced. This narrowing of translation models serves to circumscribe the choices translators permit themselves, leading to self-censorship and self-colonization. Possibilities for liberating the self and activist action are equally suppressed by such modes of training, shortcircuiting the agency of professional translators before it can ever be exercised fully. Translator trainees are inscribed within limits that do not permit the creative textual interventions associated with many of the activist translation movements discussed above. Knowledge of the breadth and openness of translation practices is of its very nature empowering to translators, for it provides models that radically expand the activist possibilities dominant in any specific culture or context.

Kathleen Davis observes that in virtue of the necessity of decision making in the process of translating, translations are always "ethical-political acts" (2001:51; cf. Lane-Mercier 1997:60-65, Arrojo 1998, 2003). A translator's empowerment is greatest when the translator is conscious of the implications of the various levels of choice to be exercised in translation and when the translator is self-aware and deliberate about making those choices. Indeed self-awareness is almost a prerequisite for ideological, political, and ethical agency. Self-reflexivity about the translator's place of enunciation and affiliation is the guide to actual choices in translation – from choice of text to transpositions of language and of culture. Self-reflexivity guides the construction of representations, transmissions, and transculturations. Only self-reflexivity can alert translators to the various constraints – internal and external – that they face in pursuing their ethical, political, and ideological goals in translation, making it possible to come to grips effectively and strategically with the complexities of their historical and cultural contexts. It is also essential for a translator to be self-aware about whether or not to exercise political and ideological agency deliberately in activist contexts, and if so, what type of activism to undertake. If an activist path is chosen, self-awareness is necessary in choosing a context or movement within which to undertake empowered translation. These forms of self-reflexivity associated with a translator's personal empowerment are an expression at the level of the individual of the postpositivist focus on frameworks since World War II. As with other postpositivist understandings of perspective, a translator's self-reflexivity opens up new uncertainties, but new possibilities and powers as well.

6. Cultural Translation and Empowerment

Not all empowered translators have translation projects and agendas that are activist in an overtly political way. Although translation – like textual production in general – always has ideological valences, the empowerment of translators is often expressed in ways that are broader than politics as such. Political agency is only one form of activism in translation studies. A translator does not have to be engaged in political activism or to be a political translator in order to exercise agency related to ethical and ideological issues in translation and cultural interface. Translators whose primary goal is to shift literary systems, for example, are not necessarily political activists in a narrow sense (although they may be, as the Irish examples discussed in the last chapter indicate), yet their translations have implications for ideologies and power within and across cultures, and their praxis has often epitomized empowerment in translation history. This chapter and the next will investigate two central topics – cultural translation and the translation of meaning – that are foundational for the empowerment of translators of all sorts, whether political activists or agents for social change more broadly conceived.

The translation of culture is a standard topic in translation studies, generally treated as a complex matter requiring linguistic and social knowledge, discernment, and skill. It is less often discussed as a matter of empowerment, an important area in which translators exercise ethical, ideological, and even at times political agency. This is curious because culture is the domain where human differences are most manifest, and representation of those differences is a primary form of assertion in cross-cultural interface, particularly encounters involving power. Representations of cultural difference take many forms – economic agreements, treaties, legal provisions, ethnographic treatises, documentary genres of various types, films, and literary texts – other than translation. Such cultural representations are second in importance only to the performance and practice of cultural forms for identity formation and group solidarity, as well as for claims pertaining to consideration and recognition in cultural interactions. Performance and representation of cultural difference on the part of ethnic communities and nations are both associated with the insistence upon recognition of distinct cultural identities, social perquisites, and demands for cultural and political autonomy, self-determination, and independence. Although the expression of difference from dominant and hegemonic standards has been a major feature valorized in translation studies analyzing and advocating the agency of the translator (e.g., Venuti 1995, 1998a, 1998b), the pragmatic dimensions of cultural translation have not been systematically explored by scholars promoting the empowerment of translators.

Because human beings everywhere have bodies with similar capacities and brains with similar structures, in most circumstances physical differences that distinguish peoples are secondary to cultural variation as markers of group identity. This is true, notwithstanding racist claims to the contrary advanced by Western imperialism since the period of European exploration and expansion, other imperialist and racist claims throughout recorded history, and even contemporary claims related to ethnic conflict around the world. The same can be asserted with respect to gender stereotyping, both past and present, as well.

There are many cases where human biological commonalities are so powerful that they override cultural formations, subliminally if not consciously. Color perception illustrates this phenomenon. The linguistic fields of color words vary widely across cultures but common "focal" colors are identified perceptually by all humans, despite radical linguistic differences. Thus, some cultures have distinct words for 'blue' and 'green' and other cultures have a single word for the field that includes blue and green. Nonetheless, all human beings distinguish so-called focal blue and focal green, whatever their lexical repertories, and identification of "best case" examples of the field blue/green by members of cultures having only one word for the field usually show a bimodal distribution with peaks at both focal blue and focal green. These findings can be explained by the cross-cultural commonality of human biology, in this case the nature of the visual receptors in the human eye (Lakoff 1987:26-30). Such cases occur in many domains of culture. Even so, without extensive analysis it is the *difference* in the surface forms of culture (color words in this case) that are most noticeable to other humans, rather than the deep-structure commonalities of physical perception (focal colors).

Both representation of cultural forms and performance of culture are an important part of nation building in postcolonial contexts. I have explored the role of translation in such circumstances, discussing some of the difficulties and perturbations in cultural representation that can result in virtue of asymmetries in the definitions of culture on the part of colonizers and the colonized (Tymoczko 1999a, 1999b:163-90). An emphasis on difference in various types of cultural production can be central to marking out the identity of peoples, and postcolonial theory stresses the importance of the representation of cultural differences in postcolonial literature both in the linguistic patterning of the texts and in the imaging of social and material conditions. By contrast translation studies scholars promoting the empowerment and agency of translators have usually stressed the representation of cultural content, specifically ideology and politics. More rarely have they addressed cultural translation directly or discussed translating the whole field of cultural difference as a political act. In promoting empowered translations of cultural difference, translation scholars have also focused on the crafting of textual and discursive strategies in the target text, rather than on translation of more specific features of the source culture, including its social practices and material basis.

Representing the full range of cultural forms of a social group presents complex technical challenges for translators. The technical challenges are compounded by internal challenges because representation of cultural difference

involves confrontation with a translator's tendency to self-censorship and acceptance of hegemony. These challenges are all well worth undertaking because
cultural translation is central to resisting cultural dominance, neoimperialism, and
the effacement of the local by the global. It is all the more surprising that cultural
translation is not well integrated into translation discourses seeking to empower
translators and to use translation as an activist means of influencing target audiences. Insofar as culture is central to identity and insofar as representation of
culture in translation is constitutive of cultural otherness, issues pertaining to
translating culture are paramount in empowered translation practices. Conversely,
understanding the nature of culture and thinking more deeply about cultural
translation can both aid translators in producing empowering translations. These
are the issues to be addressed in this chapter.

6.1 Theories of Cultural Translation

Historically in translation studies the question of culture has been approached in
terms of surface cultural elements operating chiefly at the level where language
and material culture intersect. Even in these terms the complexity of cultural
asymmetries has been widely acknowledged. In his seminal essay "On Linguistic Aspects of Translation" (1959), Roman Jakobson discussed the problems
of translating cultural elements that have no counterparts in the target culture;
such striking asymmetries produce translation conundrums that admit of no easy
answer. Jakobson gives the example of *cheese* in English, the semantic field of
which includes both fermented and non-fermented curds, versus Russian which
distinguishes the two groups with different words (1959:233). He discusses as
well the ways that languages fill linguistic gaps when new cultural concepts and
objects are introduced, and the linguistic bases of the metaphorical significance
of cultural concepts. Jakobson took a relatively sanguine and optimistic attitude
toward the possibility of translating cultural difference, maintaining that "languages differ essentially in what they *must* convey and not in what they may
convey" (1959:236).

   In *A Linguistic Theory of Translation* (1965), J.C. Catford was less optimistic
than Jakobson about cultural gaps. Although Catford argued that translatability is
a cline and that cultural items are more or less translatable, rather than absolutely
translatable or untranslatable, he was inclined to think that cultural asymmetries
could pose problems of linguistic untranslatability strictly speaking if it were
impossible to build functionally relevant features of the source situation into the
contextual meanings of the translated text (Catford 1965:93-94). It is somewhat
amusing to note that his examples include *sauna*, a cultural concept that is hard
at present to think of as untranslatable since saunas have been transculturated
to much of the world (albeit with very different social valences from those in
Finland). Catford's views of cultural untranslatability derive from his view of
meaning as rigorously language specific, from which it follows that the meaning

of cultural artifacts and customs that have no linguistic (or close functional) counterparts in other cultures can only be approximated by transference to the target language or target text rather than by translation *per se*.

Catford's pessimism on these points was closer to the views of W.V.O. Quine than to the position of Jakobson. Quine (1959, 1960) argued for the linguistic, cultural, and cognitive indeterminacies of even everyday elements of the social context. Using the example of a rabbit passing by, he argued that it is not possible to determine whether a cultural reference ("gavagai") to the animal in an unknown language refers to "animal", a rabbit as such, "undetached" rabbit parts, "rabbithood" or even, we might add, lunch (Quine 1959:148-55). Quine's range of interpretations indicates that consideration of culture and meaning in translation must go well beyond the material level to questions of function and the more abstract levels of logical and philosophical conceptualization. Quine uses translation as a metaphor for the tenuousness of communication in general, even intralinguistically, modeling the way that human experience is in some respects essentially enclosed, because shared words do not always mean the same things to different people. The implications of his views for cultural translation still remain worth pondering.

It was in this context that Eugene Nida cut through the problems of achieving one-to-one cultural translations when cultural frameworks are radically divergent. Nida proposed that dynamic-equivalence translations could solve the dilemma of cultural gaps when no formal-equivalence alternative was available. Thus, in the case of a target culture that had no experience of snow, he argued that it was acceptable to translate "white as snow" with the nearest equivalent that had the same cultural function: "white as egret feathers" or "white as kapok down", for example (cf. Nida 1964:171). Nida also moved beyond the level of material culture, taking up problems of translating complex social concepts in the face of cultural asymmetry. In his work are discussions of complex cultural conceptualizations including kinship relations (1964:82-85, 216-17), temporal reckoning (1964:218), number (1964:72), and even values, such as the concepts of "good" and "bad" (1964:78).[1]

These early considerations of cultural translation have been supplemented but not supplanted theoretically by more recent treatments of the topic. The most systematic contemporary survey of cultural translation is found in David Katan's *Translating Cultures: An Introduction for Translators, Interpreters and Mediators* (2004).[2] Basing his views of culture on those of linguists, anthropologists, and cognitive scientists, Katan looks at a wide range of cultural phenomena that a translator encounters, from environmental factors, behaviors,

---

[1] Note that the pragmatism of Nida's approach to cultural translation in dynamic-equivalence methods is related to the use of translation for the purposes of propaganda during World War II.
[2] Other useful treatments are found in Ivir (1987), Mitter (1987), Hatim and Mason (1990, 1997), Aixelá (1996), Hatim (1997), Sturge (1997), Appiah (2000), Wolf (2002), Bachmann-Medick (2006), and Carbonell Cortés (2006).

and social organization to language, beliefs, and values. Invoking techniques well established in translation pedagogy, he then suggests various strategies for translating these different cultural domains. Timothy Wilt (2003:82, 86) observes that the presentation of culture as dynamic rather than static and the emphasis on the necessity to consider cognitive frames when translating cultural elements are particular strengths of Katan's approach. Wilt (2003:87) notes, however, that Katan's approach to cultural translation is limited by his reliance on binaries.

Despite the importance of the work of scholars such as these, cultural translation continues to be treated in translation studies in a relatively simplistic manner. The problems are various. Most fundamentally, as Sherry Simon (1996:137) has argued, the entire question of culture has not been sufficiently problematized in translation studies. Not only is culture itself conceived of simplistically, translation studies has not yet come to grips with problems of perspective and difficulties of transcending one's own cultural frameworks during the translation process, whether those difficulties are articulated in terms of a hermeneutic problematic about cultural knowledge or in terms of postpositivist questions about uncertainty and frameworks. The limitations on discussions of culture in translation studies are exacerbated by the tendency to use examples from Eurocentric contexts, thus avoiding consideration of more radical cultural differences that arise from broader international scrutiny and inspection of the issues.

The broad purview of scholars such as Katan notwithstanding, translation discourses about culture continue to focus on the level of material culture and behavior, even when lip service is paid to the notion that culture goes far beyond such manifestations. In addition, rather than dealing with the translation of culture in a conceptual way (related, for instance, to the processes advocated by functionalists including skopos theorists or Nida), most considerations of cultural translation remain fixated on the lexical and linguistic aspects of cultural translation. A further problem is that the process of cultural translation is imaged as a linear one, in which cultural problems are solved in series as a translator moves through the text from beginning to end. All these aspects of translation practice, pedagogy, and theory mean that discourses about cultural translation remain relatively shallow.

Because culture rarely gets sufficiently problematized, the ethical and ideological implications of cultural translation seldom receive sufficient attention. As a result, the relationship between the translation of culture and the translator's agency is elided. Even in Katan's detailed consideration, the ideological and political implications of cultural translation receive little airing. This dispersal of ideology is again aggravated by the fact that most examples of cultural translation are taken from closely related European cultures and languages. The net result of all these limitations in the way translation studies has conceived of the translation of culture and its discourses about cultural translation is that the power of the translator to shape cultural representations and to form cultural constructions – thus creating empowered and empowering translations through the treatment of culture – has been undervalued, neglected, and even ignored in most discussions. I propose to address some of these gaps in the sections below, looking at the ethical, ideological, and political dimensions of the translation of culture and the translator's agency in constituting cultural representations, transmissions, and transculturations.

It is not possible in this context to develop a theory of culture, and in any case, as Katan indicates, there is no consensus among scholars in the social sciences about how to define culture.[3] We can observe, however, that modern theories of culture stress "things" and "material culture" less than practices and dispositions, including such cultural elements as signs, symbols, codes, beliefs, values, ideas, ideals, and ideologies, all of which form systems and cohesive or networked structures, often stratified or hierarchically organized. In much of what follows, I am using the work of Pierre Bourdieu whose early work offers a broad internationalist framework for problematizing culture that can be utilized in turn for exploring how translators can engage in cultural translation so as to produce empowered and empowering texts.[4]

Bourdieu suggests that the major dispositions of a culture are operative in fundamental practices. These practices in turn are encoded so deeply in the bodies and psyches of members of the culture that they become forms of "history turned into nature", history "denied as such" (Bourdieu 1977:78). Such features of culture are produced by and also reproduce the habitus, to use Bourdieu's language, with the *habitus* being "understood as a system of lasting, transposable dispositions which, integrating past experiences, functions at every moment as a *matrix of perceptions, appreciations, and actions* and makes possible the achievement of infinitely diversified tasks" (Bourdieu 1977:82-83, original emphasis). We will return to this concept below.

Bourdieu (1977:1-30) has discussed the barriers that prevent both insiders and outsiders from comprehending any given culture. The workings of the habitus make it difficult to understand (and translate) the underpinnings of a culture because dispositions are difficult (or impossible) to observe (and are rarely textualized, being "denied as such"). By contrast, a culture's practices alone

---

[3] For a review of proposed definitions of culture, see Katan (2004:24-48) and sources cited. See also Geertz (1973:4-5).

[4] Note that I am using Bourdieu's early theories and trying to work out some of the implications they hold for translation. The application of Bourdieu's work to translation studies has been undertaken in various other ways by the essayists in Inghilleri (2005). His later work is less useful for the arguments being developed here in part because of his own dilution of the notion of the habitus which devolves at some points in his later work to a way of speaking about a single individual's worldview or even about a very immediate and temporary context. These shifts disperse the power and usefulness of the concept for cultural theory and a theory of practice. Moreover, many of his later explorations are extremely culturally restricted, in some cases applicable only to modern French culture since 1800. Often they can't be generalized to European culture as a whole or to the United States, much less to cultural systems further afield.

may seem trivial, unmotivated, disconnected, and random. Bourdieu's concept of the habitus also illustrates the extent to which participants are unconscious of their own culture (it is "history turned into nature"), including those facets of culture constructed by language. Culture is formed of practices that are to a very great extent not consciously understood. People know what is appropriate in a cultural context without being able to explain or even always identify the operative cultural structures, practices, values, or dispositions. The problem of analyzing a culture – one's own or another – is correspondingly acute, as Bourdieu indicates.

Thus, it is as difficult for members of a culture to describe or explain their own practices as it is for external observers to do so. In the case of insiders, the fact that dispositions seem "natural" rather than a matter of history means that explanations have a way of becoming somewhat arbitrary and untrustworthy, at times misleadingly structured by the very questions posed to the informants. In the case of external observers, there is a tendency to see cultural practices and cultural systems as more static, rigid, and deterministic than they are experienced in practice. Observers tend toward theories and constructions of culture that posit rules, failing to allow sufficiently for cultural heterogeneity, creative improvisation, and diachronic shifts. The result is objectification, hypostasis, and false consistency. Observers can also remain locked in the belief that their own cultural practices are "natural" and hence retain an alienated stance toward the cultural other. Bourdieu observes that these difficulties of understanding culture constitute "*two opposing systems of lacunae*" (1977:18, original emphasis).

Moreover, in the case of translation of culture, culture is coded in the body of the translator as well as the body of the subject, so to speak. A translator must not only unpack the embodied and situated knowledge related to cultural configurations and practices in the source text, the source culture, the author or speaker, and so forth, but be able to interpret the embodied and situated cultural practices and dispositions of the translator's own culture and the culture of the receiving audience. Most crucial are those embodied practices that shape the translator personally and the translation process itself.[5] All of these difficulties in perceiving and writing culture are further complicated by particular individual perspectives having to do with values, political commitments, ideological engagements, and self-interest. These complex issues related to perceiving and writing culture as a precondition of translation aimed at promoting (equitable) cultural exchange remain to be widely acknowledged and discussed in translation studies, even by scholars who are most vocal in calling for translators to be activists.

If culture is problematized along the lines of contemporary theories of culture, such as those of Bourdieu, then cultural translation becomes a compelling and complex topic related to the agency of translators, more so than has

---

[5] Cronin (2006:76-79, 111, 119ff.) discusses the embodied agency of the translator, as well as some of the problems that result. Cf. Maier (2002, 2006).

been recognized heretofore in translation studies. Constructivist and interpretive aspects of translating culture become paramount, and the place of enunciation of the translator becomes problematized. In addition the recursive need for self-reflexivity and geopolitical responsibilty on the part of the translator are highlighted. Cultural translation emerges as an area that is central to the ethical, ideological, and political agency of the translator and to the creation of empowered and empowering translations.

6.2 The Impact of Audience on Cultural Representation

In most communicative situations the cultural context of the communication is assumed or presupposed.[6] This is usually the case, for example, when storytellers tell stories and authors write literary texts, as well as in most social, commercial, media, and governmental transactions. Moreover, most texts are produced within a culture for audiences from the same culture. As a consequence there are many common cultural assumptions shared by the speaker or writer and the audience addressed. Usually the speaker or writer can assume that the audience knows the cultural underpinnings of the subject matter and its background. These common understandings are important because most aspects of culture are backgrounded in texts, except when an aspect of the culture itself is the subject and moves to the foreground.

What happens when the audience is larger than the cultural context from which a text emerges or when the primary audience addressed is outside the culture of the speaker or the culture associated with the subject matter? In such a situation the divergence between the perspective of the author or speaker and that of the audience becomes critical with respect to cultural assumptions and cultural representations in the text. This is the situation of most translations, of course, heightened in the case of translations between cultures that are not closely related. In cases where there is disparity of cultural context between the subject matter and the audience, it is rarely sufficient for an author just to transpose cultural material, implicitly presupposing, alluding to, or sketching the cultural background, because the audience is likely to be ignorant of the cultural assumptions in the resulting text and will be unable to make necessary and relevant inferences about meaning. Translation in most situations must contend with these issues.

Postcolonial writers, minority writers, and regional writers are faced with these types of disparity and divergence all the time, and it is instructive to see how they handle the situation. One option is for an author to provide cultural explanation and background in order to compensate for the cultural ignorance and difference in perspective of an audience unfamiliar with the cultural context

---

[6] Relevance theory in linguistics has this feature of communication as a central tenet; Sperber and Wilson (1995) discuss the implications at length and Gutt (2000a, 2000b) applies relevance theory to translation.

of the subject matter. William Faulkner used this technique; he wrote primarily about the South, but addressed a much larger audience in the United States and throughout the world. He usually chose to write into his texts a large amount of explanation about the culture of the South, inventing local histories and local families that would epitomize central issues in Southern history and culture as he saw it. Other writers follow a similar path of cultural explanation, including many postcolonial writers such as Chinua Achebe.[7] Some writers also use paratextual materials (footnotes, introductions) to fill in for differences in cultural knowledge presupposed by the subject and the audience.

Cultural material can also be elided or it can be assimilated to cultural concepts and contexts familiar to the audience. Authors can minimize cultural background, effacing cultural particulars and "universalizing" the text, or they can assimilate cultural patterns to the expectations of the audience. Many medieval writers took one of these paths, including Geoffrey of Monmouth who adapted his Celtic historical materials not merely to the language of his readers (Latin), but to the cultural patterns and values of his Norman French audience as well.[8] A notorious modern example of this strategy is found in the autotranslations of Rabindranath Tagore who shifted the entire speech act of his own Bengali poems, as well as their form and content, assimilating his poetry in English translation to the standards of the late romantics (such as the early Yeats) and constructing himself as the sage from the east (Sengupta 1990, 1995).

There are also other means of dealing with gaps in cultural assumptions separating author, subject, and audience. For instance, an author may choose to present cultural material with absolutely no explanation, taking the position that the audience should be able to understand the material on the basis of general knowledge, absent which it will fall to the readers to do the homework necessary to fill in the cultural background for themselves. Colonized populations are often in this position, needing to acquire enough education about the colonizers' culture to understand "metropolitan" texts whether in the original language or in translation.[9] It is a tactic less used by writers from colonized nations. Ironically James Joyce approached writing in exactly this way: in *Ulysses* all manner of cultural material about Ireland is presupposed, from the history of the country to the geography of Dublin, from religious contestations to cultural habits and demotic speech. The result is a steep learning curve for readers who are not Irish (and for many Irish readers as well). Characterizing such texts from minority, subaltern, and postcolonial cultures, Doris Sommer calls this technique "resistant" writing; she sees resistant texts as marking off "an impassable distance between reader and text, raising questions of access or welcome", and producing "a kind of

---

[7] This means of cultural mediation in postcolonial literature and translation is discussed at greater length in Tymoczko (1999a).

[8] The case study is found in Tymoczko (1990b).

[9] The Chinese writing system effected such an assertion, congruent with Chinese dominance over a large culture area. See section 7.5 below.

readerly 'incompetence' that more reading will not overcome, because a rhetoric of socially differentiated understanding blocks the way" (1992:104-5). Sommer indicates that a resistant textual strategy does not necessarily "signal a genuine epistemological impasse"; rather the impasse is announced so as to position the reader within limits, thus decentering the power and privilege of readers from dominant cultures (1992:105).

As can be seen, the cultural knowledge and values of the audience generally influence the presentation of culture in most cases where there is a disparity between the cultural presuppositions of author or subject and audience. Although the examples I've given are from literary texts, similar cases could be evinced from many other domains, including newpapers, legal documents, and business correspondence. When the presentation of culture is not shifted to take into account the knowledge of the audience (e.g., the case of Joyce, where the author makes no compromises for the audience), the actual speech act of the text itself becomes marked: perhaps as aggressive, as especially assertive of dominant standards, as arrogant, as overly erudite or hermetic, and so forth, depending on the interpretation of the reader who must cope with the opaque cultural material. It should be noted that refusal to make allowance for the reader is often associated with power gradients. In general the texts of elites or colonizers are not adapted to the needs of readers from lower classes or readers from colonized populations. It is left for those with less power to learn dominant standards regarding what "legitimately" constitutes adequate cultural knowledge and cultural literacy. Unexplained cultural assertion is a matter of power. This is why the appropriation of such a stance by writers outside dominant spheres decenters power, as Sommer argues.

All of these issues related to audience and disparities of assumptions about culture and all of these strategies for communicating culture across gaps of cultural knowledge are encountered in translation. The task of the translator is similar to the task of minority or postcolonial writers, but in many respects the work of the translator is more difficult. Not only must the translator contend with cultural gaps, but the translator is constrained by a preexisting (fixed) text. A writer can shape the text as a whole in ways that are congruent with the strategy chosen for dealing with cultural disparities that exist between the subject and the audience. A translator by contrast risks altering the shape of the text by introducing translation strategies to mediate cultural knowledge for the receptor audience. In the simplest case, shifting a cultural concern from the background to the foreground in the translation – for example, by explaining a cultural element and therefore bringing more attention to it than it has in the source text – alters the subject matter of the text as well as the text type. In such a case the translated text becomes more didactic than the source in virtue of the explanations introduced. Adding paratextual materials such as footnotes also shifts the text type in much the same way.[10] By contrast, the tone of a very simple and

---

[10] Cf. Tymoczko (1999a). Paradoxically this sort of shift from background to foreground

intimate text will be disrupted by a resistant strategy of cultural translation that omits cultural information.

We will return to these questions of audience below, but before proceeding let us note that the real power of a translator lies in the ability to communicate across cultural difference. If culture everywhere were the same and if translation were only a matter of switching linguistic codes to express the same cultural conformations, human translators could much more easily be replaced by machines. Indeed such simple tasks are beginning to be performed adequately at present by computer assisted translation programs. The center of a translator's agency lies in the power to adjudicate difficulties caused by disparities and asymmetries in cultural understandings and cultural presuppositions. This power includes the ability to introduce new ideas, to broaden experiential realms, to enrich mental domains. In part because of its role in cultural mediation, Clifford Geertz sees the aim of anthropology as "the enlargement of the universe of human discourse" (1973:14); this phrase might apply equally well to translation. Homi Bhabha hints at this view of the translator's agency in naming cultural translation as the way that "newness enters the world" (1994:212-35).

Of course, a translator's skill in cultural translation can also be used to impose new cultural configurations on an (unwilling) audience, to steal cultural treasures, to despoil a people of their land, to convert a people by force to another religion, and so forth. Case studies of this sort have been documented by many scholars including Tejaswini Niranjana (1992), Vicente Rafael (1993), Eric Cheyfitz (1997), Sabine Fenton and Paul Moon (2002), and those who have contributed to the anthology edited by Fenton (2004). Such acts are tantamount to cultural warfare and are paradigmatically associated in translation studies with nineteenth-century European imperialism, but similar cultural impositions are documented in the Chinese culture area and elsewhere outside Eurocentric domains. Moreover, such moves occur every day currently in commercial translations for multinational corporations and the localization industry. Power is not always exercized "for the good": as in any other domain involving power, there are always contestations over how a translator's agency should be directed in cultural translation.

Paradoxically a translator's power to introduce newness, to communicate across cultural differences, is ultimately made possible by the powers of the audience. In a sense all human beings are latent translators. They are able to learn new concepts, to acquire new words (from their language or other languages), to borrow new cultural patterns, to communicate with more than one language or fragments thereof, to construct hybridities. Audiences themselves have the capacity to receive translations and to translate the translations for their own uses. These are all related to Jakobson's (1959:236) contention that languages differ in what they must convey, not in what they may convey, for humans can

---

could also result from *lack* of explanation for then a perfectly ordinary aspect of culture may become marked by its opacity.

manipulate and expand language to accommodate new ideas and new cultural forms presented to them. Contrary to Quine's skepticism about communication and his thesis of the indeterminacy of translation, translators and their audiences have astounding abilities to learn from, make sense of, and assimilate new and even fragmentary communications that mediate and convey cultural difference. Translations transform receptor languages and cultures because it is through translation that "different, incommensurate signifying systems interact, and because the translated foreign text necessarily *performs* new meanings in the target system" (Davis 2001:41; cf. Toury 1995:27). Although audiences are inherently able to receive and assess such performances, assimilating newness, a translator's skill in cultural translation lies in large measure in inducing an audience to be willing to learn, to receive difference, to experience newness.[11] Thus cultural translation is at the heart of a translator's agency and empowerment, ultimately grounding politically, ideologically, and ethically empowered translations.

6.3 A Holistic Approach to Translating Culture

Translation across cultural difference is not only the center of a translator's power and agency, it is where the translator demonstrates the greatest skill. This is no doubt why Katan (2004) repeatedly emphasizes that a translator must actually be seen as a cultural mediator (cf. Pym 2000:191, Cronin 2003). Nonetheless, exactly how cultural translation is achieved is somewhat mysterious and not always well analyzed. To some extent the problematic of cultural translation is obscured because much of the literature on the topic is written with reference to closely related cultures, stressing cases of translation between modern European languages and cultures where the degree of cultural difference is actually quite small. When greater cultural difference obtains, difficulties in cultural translation become correspondingly large. Theoretical and practical consideration of cultural translation, like the conceptualization of the concept translation itself across time and space, is an area of translation studies where the field will benefit greatly from moving beyond Western data.

If it is difficult for both insiders and outsiders to perceive the nature of a culture, as Bourdieu suggests, how is it possible for translators to achieve an understanding of the cultural elements of source texts? Assuming such understandings can be reached, how do translators know how to adapt the cultural elements in the source texts to the needs of the receiving audience? How do translators shape representations that will allow the target audience of a translation to comprehend the source culture and the source material? Such questions have no clear answers within a postpositivist epistemology, and the difficulty in resolving them is one reason that ethnographers and anthropologists have experienced a

---

[11] Nord (1997:93) also discusses the way that readers of translations are willing to accept new, original, or foreign ways of presenting old and new ideas.

crisis regarding the representation of culture in their own disciplines.[12] Just as there is no easy resolution of the crisis of representation in ethnography and anthropology, there are no simple solutions to the problems raised by cultural translation in translation studies. Nonetheless translators must translate. It is essential to have translation practices that provisionally address the deepest issues about mediating culture, even if the practices do not provide ultimate or final answers to theoretical questions that are currently being debated extensively in many of the social sciences.

Translation studies has generally approached representing culture in a linear fashion, with translators being taught to direct their attention to specific locations in texts where cultural problems are embodied in surface elements of the text: unfamiliar words referring to elements of the material culture, behaviors and practices that are unknown to the target audience, culture-bound symbols, sociolinguistic conventions such as politeness conventions that vary across languages and cultures, alternate institutions and social structures, and so forth. These questions are then resolved one by one in serial fashion until the translation is achieved. The problem with such approaches is that they don't acknowledge and address the mainsprings of cultural difference – the largest frameworks of culture or the habitus – in any systematic way, nor do they provide adequate means for coordinating, integrating, and giving cohesion to cultural representations across whole texts. They also efface problems of interference from the perspectives and frameworks of the translating agent. Approaches to cultural translation must be developed that fully validate and attend to underlying systemic disparities of culture as well as differences in particulars and that consider problems of perception on the part of the translating agent. There is a need for a holistic mode of conceptualizing cultural translation that moves beyond paradigms currently operative in translation studies.

Note that I am using the term *holistic* differently from Doris Bachmann-Medick (2006:36-37) who criticizes the term as suggesting a general and undifferentiated approach to culture which is viewed as responsible for a unified conception of tradition and identity. My usage follows current terminology in the United States in the fields of education and medicine. In education and medicine *holism* indicates attention to all facets of a child or patient respectively, rather than just attention to the cognitive or the physical well-being of the subject. It is in this latter sense of the term that I am arguing for attention to a broader field of cultural phenomena, as well as additional specific facets of culture, than has been the practice in translation studies thus far. I take the view that a holistic approach to cultural translation rather than a selective focus on a limited range of cultural elements enables greater cultural interchange and more effective cultural assertion in translation, allowing more newness to enter the world.

---

[12] Essays on this topic are found in Clifford and Marcus (1986) and Clifford (1988:21-54). See also Sturge (1997), Wolf (2000, 2002), Bachmann-Medick (2006), and sources cited. Cf. Staten (2005).

In a holistic approach to translating cultural difference, as I conceive it, instead of focusing primarily on the surface aspects of culture in a text, particularly the material aspects or customs of a culture as they occur in a localized and linear fashion, a translator begins by considering (however briefly) the entire scope of cultural underpinnings that come into play in the specific source text being translated. In a sense a translator attends first to the field or system of cultural formations that must be negotiated in translating a source text within which the specifics of the text can be situated; this field or system is antecedent to and encompasses any cultural specifics in the text. No doubt many translators do this on an intuitive level (especially in commercial translation), but for others it may be helpful to begin by making an explicit mental or written inventory of the principal features of the cultural field in question that are relevant to the text being translated and that present difficulties for the receptor audience. One goal of such an inventory is to think about how the specific cultural context of the source text can be presented to the target audience in such a way as to allow the audience to understand or receive the dispositions and practices of another people in a cohesive or integrated fashion consonant with and framed by the text itself and the purposes of the translation.[13] Such an integrated framework will not only serve to locate the surface features of the culture of the source text being represented for the target audience, it avoids a piecemeal translation process that inevitably disperses the substance and ideological implications of cultural differences.

It is important to recognize that the cultural interface in any translation project is complex and may indeed be more complex than the model outlined in summary fashion below. The cultural underpinnings of the subject matter might be different from those of the culture of the author and of the original audience both. In turn the translator's culture and the culture of the target audience might be different from each other, and also from those of the subject matter, the author, and the source audience. Depending on the number of cultures in interface, a translator's cultural analysis will accordingly increase in complexity and the model below will be expanded. Similarly the model will be modified if the translator is a member of the source culture and is translating for a different target culture; in such a case communicating cultural difference will require a somewhat different process of self-reflexivity.

---

[13] Obviously if the text stresses the inconsistencies or incoherence of a culture, as do Flann O'Brien's *At Swim-Two-Birds* and Ionesco's theater of the absurd, then the inconsistencies themselves must be the focus of the cultural representation. Similarly if a text stresses the contestations and fractured faultlines of a culture, as does Kiran Desai's *The Inheritance of Loss*, then the cultural representation must also capture these features. Note that these challenges are not restricted to literary translation: many advertisements play with such cultural inconsistencies and faultlines to make their products memorable. Although a culture and a text to be translated may well have inconsistencies, a translator needs a coherent *plan* for approaching cultural issues in the translation itself.

Accounting for the material culture and social patterning of any source culture[14] is obviously important in a holistic approach to cultural translation. Constraints set by climate and geography and relevant historical frameworks must also be part of the translator's awareness as the cultural translation takes shape. But in a holistic approach to culture, there are other cultural aspects that have textual reflexes that in a sense take precedence over specific material, physical, and historical manifestations of cultural difference. In the rest of this section and the next, I offer a partial repertory of cultural elements that a translator might consider in a holistic approach to translating culture, incorporating them either explicitly or implicitly in the translation process and taking them into account in making choices that determine the cultural representations of the target text.

Let us return to Bourdieu's concept of the habitus. Bourdieu suggests that culture involves homologies between dispositions and practices, with such practices becoming "history turned into nature"; these dispositions and practices are at the core of the habitus which constitutes a system of lasting, transposable dispositions, integrating past experiences and functioning as a matrix for perceptions, appreciations, actions, and tasks (1977:78, 82-83).[15] As a starting point for a holistic approach to translating culture, therefore, a translator might do worse than to think about the habitus of the source culture as it relates to the translation project, considering the cultural matrix presumed within the source text but not necessarily expressed. Reflecting on the relevant unstated but interconnected dispositions and practices presupposed in a text offers a broad way to frame specific decisions involved in cultural translation as the text is translated. That is, a holistic approach to translating culture will begin with the largest elements of cultural difference that separate the source culture and the target culture as a framework for coordinating the particular decisions about culture that occur as the text is actually transposed into the target language.

Such analysis is not, of course, easy, in part because of the effacement of these large aspects of culture, their unspoken character, and the tendency for members of a culture to view them as "natural" or "real" in an essentialist sense. A translator who has been immersed in the source culture may have problems perceiving the culture that are similar to those of native members of the culture. If a translator has studied a source culture, there may be some existing foundation for the translator's analysis, though again perceptual problems of outsiders and the tendency toward hypostasis must be taken into account. Whatever the position a translator has with respect to the source culture, translators should remember that as a group they are in an advantageous position to undertake cultural analysis. Most translators have an interest in, sensitivity to, and training about cultural

---

[14] Or source cultures in cases where the culture of the subject matter and that of the author differ, for example.

[15] Bourdieu (1977:96-158) exemplifies the interconnectedness of these various cultural levels in his analysis of Algerian culture. Note especially the diagrams where many relations are made graphic.

differences in general. More important, experience in dealing with more than one language and more than one culture in interface elicits implicit and explicit comparison, hones skills in comparison, and inculcates a sense of self reflection. As has been discussed, comparison is one of the most powerful cognitive tools at the disposal of human beings. In the case of cultural translation, comparisons are put at the service of cultural understandings. Despite such skills in negotiating cultural difference, however, difficulties in perceiving cultural difference are always entailed in the positionality of a translator, no matter whether the translator is an insider or an outsider of the source culture in question. Either way the inquiry involves self-reflexivity because one cannot attempt to perceive or analyze cultural difference without renewed attempts to be aware of the culture of the self, the way history has become nature in the case of the self, leading to all sorts of dispositions, perspectives, presuppositions, and practices that are a function of one's own habitus (including dispositions about cultural translation).

I have stressed that the analysis of the habitus of the source culture should be undertaken *as it relates to the text to be translated and to the translation project*. Cultures are not monolithic, undifferentiated, or static. Similarly no habitus is uniform or static: there will always be variations related to specific location and positionality, for example, and cultures are dynamic, continually exhibiting diachronic shifts. Strictly speaking there is no single set of dispositions in any culture, but a set of related dispositions linked by family resemblances, many of which can be correlated with such factors as class, religion, gender, generation, and so forth. Indeed a habitus produces different and sometimes complementary subject positions: male and female, young and old, master and servant, dominant and subordinate, and so forth. Moreover, all cultures have dissidents, subversives, and counterdiscourses. The concept of the habitus serves as a means of conceptualizing the way a culture produces related but differentiated effects (and differentiated subject experiences) both synchronically and diachronically.[16] A translator must take into account positionality inscribed in and mobilized by a text, factoring variation and heterogeneity into an analysis of elements of the habitus that relate to the specific translation task at hand. Cultures like languages are open, heterogeneous, and marked by generativity and performativity. Translation of culture requires sensitivity to all those factors.

Scholarship in translation studies has been at pains to stress the dynamism and heterogeneity of culture in the last two decades. Simon (1999:58) has argued that the idea of culture as an envelope that binds members of a community within the same coherence of meaning today belongs to the realm of myth;

---

[16] Mills argues that the structures of discourse ensure that "the knowledge produced within a particular period has a certain homogeneity. This is not to suggest that all of the individuals existing within a certain era agree on a particular view of the world, but simply that all of the sanctioned utterances and texts are produced within similar discursive constraints" (1997:75). Though she frames this argument in temporal terms, similar claims can be made about cultural or territorial units as well.

instead, citing James Clifford, she indicates that the idea of culture as a set of coherent values, behaviors, and attitudes has given way to the idea of culture as negotiation, symbolic competition, and performance. In a similar vein Jean-Marc Gouanvic (2002:182-88) maintains that the cultural turn in translation studies demonstrated that culture is not a stable unity but a dynamic process implying difference and incompleteness; he laments that despite this shift of perspective, cultural translation generally continues to use methods that presuppose the existence of stable cultural units. Similarly Bachmann-Medick (2006:37) asserts that cultural translation should be antiessentialist, uncovering counterdiscourses and resistant actions within a culture, thereby shifting inquiry toward a dynamic notion of culture and cultural difference. It follows that a holistic assessment of the cultural dimensions and cultural context of a text to be translated must consider questions about the heterogeneity of the larger cultural system and its dynamism through time rather than slip into essentialist postures.[17]

Let me give a concrete example of how thinking about the habitus of a source culture might help a translator. In translating early medieval Irish texts into English, I find it helpful to articulate to myself that the culture was a warrior culture, organized around and holding values along basic Indo-European lines.[18] At the same time, this Indo-European matrix was shaped by the history of Ireland itself: the prestige associated with knowledge, learning, and the arts inherited from common Celtic culture; life on a relatively small island where travel by land was difficult (because of bogs); a thousand years free from external invasion or aggression; a peaceful (and assimilative) conversion to Christianity; and so forth. We should note that from within the culture such statements would have seemed to be both truisms (how could a culture be anything but heroic?) and also overstatements (almost everyone would have knowledge of exceptions to those structural analyses, including powerful women, wealthy peasants who

---

[17] In English thinking about the habitus as a system rather than as a field may be helpful in perceiving the dynamism of cultures. This may reflect a linguistic anisomorphism (and hence a translation problem) between English and French (as used by many cultural critics, including Bourdieu). In English *field* is more inert and inanimate than *system*. Although English has the locution "field of battle" that certainly indicates movement and contestation, *field* has as its primary meanings associations with agrarian constancy (empty stretches of land, meadows, a cultivated expanse dedicated to a single crop), where French *champ* has more primary associations involving human activity. The opposite is true of *system*, because in English a system almost always involves moving parts, where French *système* has as its first meaning the fairly inert "ensemble organisé d'éléments intellectuels" (an organized collection of intellectual elements) in the *Petit Robert* (s.v.).

[18] Indo-European culture is characterized by a tripartite social division into the priest-king, warrior, and agricultural classes (and also slaves) and exhibits a fundamental division between male and female (or, to be more precise, between male and non-male, where children of both sexes are classified as non-male). Traditional Indo-European culture had a primary pastoral orientation, with secondary agricultural practices introduced through contact with other (conquered) cultures.

had attained aristocratic status, and pacifist clerics). Many of the singularities of Irish history also made class strata somewhat permeable, and actual practice in war had atrophied to a large extent before the Viking period because of the relatively peaceful and prosperous nature of the culture. The culture was also in transition along a number of lines during the period 600-1000 C.E. Thus I find it important to think about the likely dating and provenance of a text I am working with so that I can reflect possible historical, regional, and authorial variations in my assessments of the cultural background, and I also try to remain alert for counterdiscourses in the text. These basic elements of and approaches to the habitus serve as a guide for interpreting the source text and for determining the overall representations of the culture in my translation, and they also remind me of blind spots in my own cultural assumptions, of conflicts with my own values, of potential conflicts with the cultural assumptions of my target audience, of problems in achieving any ideological goals I might have, and so forth. Moreover, by comparing the habitus of the (part of the) source culture reflected in the text with that of the target audience, I begin to think about cultural assumptions not explicitly indicated on the surface of the text that must be mediated in some way (for instance, in paratextual materials) for the receptor audience so that readers can make appropriate inferences about meaning.[19]

6.4 Elements to Consider in Holistic Cultural Translation

In holistic medicine a physician cares for the physical body of the patient, but attention does not stop with the physical. The patient's mental and emotional health are also considered, as are the patient's family, occupation, and environment. Holistic cultural translation is similar: material culture is not forgotten, but it is contextualized within larger frameworks and supplemented by attention to many aspects of culture that are less tangible on a physical level. We have already discussed how thinking about the habitus sets a context for cultural translation. Here I discuss more specific features of culture that are not always noticeable on a physical level but are often particularly significant for an assessment of the cultural implications of language and text.

A translator must make special provision for translating what I call the signature concepts of a culture. By "signature concepts" I mean cultural elements that are key to social organization, cultural practices, and dispositions constituting the habitus of a culture. Such signature concepts are central to a culture's universe of discourse and to the horizon of expectation shared by its members. Signature concepts are intimately involved in the discourses of a culture as well as its practices. Concepts such as freedom, progress, wealth, shame, purity, and bravery are emblematic of signature concepts of different cultures in the world

---

[19] See the discussion in section 7.1 below for additional material related to the habitus of early Irish literature.

at present, but not all signature concepts are so abstract or oriented to values. They might involve cattle, hunting, ships and sailing, and so forth.[20] The signature concepts of a culture are related to whole sets of cultural assumptions; they reflect economic and social structures, as well as material features of the culture, in addition to being repositories of value, meaning, and significance related to the ways the culture is thought about and organized by its members. Language is partially productive of these concepts, and words denoting signature concepts are dense with cultural associations and connotations. Obviously signature concepts of a culture also figure in and even drive many of the metaphors a culture lives by, thus entering into the linguistic matrix of a culture in fundamental ways. Note that by definition signature concepts relate to several levels of culture at once, serving as nodes where dispositions, practices, discourses, and social organization intersect. Thus, the signature concepts of a culture that appear in a text demand a translator's careful attention, particularly if the translator is intent on conveying cultural difference or, in the case of a colonized culture, communicating an indigenous cultural perspective rather than simply adapting to or reproducing global or dominant cultural contexts. At the same time, however, literal translations of a culture's signature concepts can be meaningless or even ridiculous to a receiving culture because of fundamental conflicts with how *culture* itself is defined in the target system.

Again, an example will be useful. In early Irish texts words pertaining to heroism (including concepts of honor, shame, and taboo) generally fall into the category of signature concepts. Similarly words pertaining to cattle and cattle raiding are frequently signature concepts, reflecting the Indo-European pastoralism that shaped multiple dimensions of Irish life and defined concepts of wealth and status. These pastoral words also signify the direction that heroism took (petty raiding, tribal rivalries) in a contained and relatively peaceful insular setting that had experienced no invasion for a thousand years. Translations that flag such signature concepts by marking them in some way, such as by using reserved terms for the concepts – either by borrowing terms from the source language or by inventing defamiliarized locutions in the receptor language – will signal (and usually validate) cultural difference by pointing to the signature concepts as distinct and by making them memorable. Translations that use ordinary receptor terms, varying the translation of the signature concepts by using different target words for specific source terms, will sublate cultural difference and disperse the distinctiveness and ideological implications of the culture of the source text.

Let me stress that a holistic procedure for translating culture is a partial one. Even in a complex text, a translator is only faced with a limited aspect of the habitus and a limited range of the signature concepts of a source culture. Only part

---

[20] An extended example of translating signature concepts of a culture is found in Tymoczko (1999b:163-90). There I look at the signature concepts *síd*, *riastrad*, *táin*, *ces*, and *geis* (respectively, commonly translated as *the other world*, *cattle raiding*, *distortion*, *debility*, and *taboo*).

of the habitus will be mobilized as particularly relevant to any given text. I am not suggesting that a translator undertake total cultural analysis and representation (even supposing such things were possible). Indeed some of the most interesting results of the sort of cultural conceptualization that I am suggesting are the gaps and mysteries that it turns up. Clifford Geertz observes that "cultural analysis is intrinsically incomplete. And, worse than that, the more deeply it goes the less complete it is" (1973:29). Within translation studies these themes have also been sounded, with Michael Cronin writing that cultural knowledge presents an "infinitely receding horizon" (2006:135; cf. Staten 2005). At the same time Cronin suggests that the harder a culture is to see, "the more profound the vision" and that paradoxically another culture is never closer than when we fail to understand it and when we are confronted with a blockage of interpretive mastery (133-34). He sees awareness of cultural complexity as producing a distancing effect that results in closeness rather than familiarity (135).[21]

The metonymies of translation, the heterogeneity of cultures, and the limitations inherent in cultural interpretation notwithstanding, in specific cultural contexts the dispositions and practices of a culture are related, resulting in cohesive cultural formations.[22] It follows that in a translator's work there is an important dialectic between thinking about the large-scale dispositions and practices related to the habitus that are presupposed in a particular text and identifying more specific elements that embody or relate to those larger frameworks. When that dialectic between relating specifics, such as signature concepts, to the broader cultural system is productive, the result is the possibility of a more cohesive cultural presentation that furthers the translator's goals for the translated text. At the same time attention to the cohesive nature of culture must not obliterate the fact that cultures are not monolithic, homogeneous, or static. They are dynamic, heterogeneous, and varied in many respects, thus having a centripetal aspect as well as a centrifugal one, so to speak. Holistic cultural translation can be responsive to both impulses, finding ways to mark both as occasion arises.

Clearly some translators are alert to signature concepts intuitively, but others can profit from strategies that make the signature concepts of the source text more perceptible during the translation process. Here again self-reflexivity is essential, for it is impossible to perceive cultural difference and to be attentive to the habitus and the signature concepts of another culture if one has little self-awareness about the habitus and signature concepts of one's own culture. Translators must constantly attempt to interrogate the way "history has become nature" in their own cultural framework, as well as in other cultural situations, and to ask about concepts that serve as points of reference for dispositions and

---

[21] This sort of satisfying infinite regress in interpretive mastery is especially true of cultural analysis of the past where the cultural horizon is *de facto* not fully perceivable.

[22] Geertz (1973:17) observes that cultural systems must have at least a minimal degree of coherence or else they would not be called systems.

practices of their own habitus, lest those concepts interfere with their ability to perceive and represent other cultures effectively in translation. It might help for translators routinely to ask such questions as the following. What are the signature concepts of my own culture with respect to the issues under consideration? How do they compare to the signature concepts of the source culture of the text I am translating? How do they compare to the signature concepts of the target culture? Imperfect answers to questions such as these are usually better than no answers at all – or than no awareness that such questions should be asked.

Closely related to the translation of the signature concepts in a text is translation of key words and conceptual metaphors. Conceptual metaphors that structure cognition and are built into language itself – the "metaphors we live by" – are also indicative of the mental furnishings and basic orientations of a culture and its perspectives on the world (Lakoff and Johnson 1980). Conceptual metaphors are fundamental elements of the linguistic exponence of culture and they are also elements that reproduce culture.[23] Contrasting with conceptual metaphors are key words, "loaded" words that at times signal signature concepts of a culture but that at other times point to more idiosyncratic or thematic cultural elements chosen by an author (or speaker) to structure a particular text. Through iteration in a specific textual context, such key words convey the author's themes or viewpoint, and they can contribute to the formal structure of the text as well.[24] In the case of both metaphors we live by and key words, consistent linguistic representation – that is, stability at the rank of the word or phrase or even literalism – is essential to distinguish and highlight these elements in a cultural representation, while varied translation of the terms will tend to disperse their significance.

In a holistic approach to cultural translation, attention is also paid to discourses

---

[23] An example from Old Irish is the verb *maidid*, 'breaks', used of a wave breaking on the shore but also used to signal a defeat in battle. Thus, *ro-mebaid for Connachta* (literally, '[the battle] broke against the Connachtmen') means 'the Connachtmen were defeated'. Although students are normally taught to translate such a locution idiomatically (here, 'to be defeated'), the metaphorical import might in this case be worth signaling by some literalism in translation. The seas to the west of Ireland are some of the wildest and most dangerous seas in the world, and there can be enormous waves breaking against cliffs and rocks around the island. The native Irish boat is a woven boat with no keel, covered with hides, flexible and normally well adapted to the seas in the area. If such a boat were swamped by a breaking wave, however, the result would be disastrous; it would be much less bouyant and hence less apt to stay afloat than a boat made completely of wood, and it would be much more difficult to bail out also. Moreover, the earliest medieval texts (and their associated metaphors) come from a period when the Irish warrior class had settled down as agrarian gentry, before the Vikings necessitated a reinvigoration of the Irish facility in combat. To me the metaphor suggests the terrible nature of defeat in battle, sounding a cautionary note to accounts of war and battles rather than glorifying warrior activity as most other medieval European heroic traditions do.
[24] For example, the metaphor of blue eyes, representing racist hegemony in the United States on the eve of World War II, is used to structure Toni Morrison's *The Bluest Eye* (1970). Thus, the word *blue* is a key word, with multiple exponence in the book, including musical reference to the blues.

in a text, another aspect of culture that is revealed primarily through language. Discourses are related to dispositions, including ideological dispositions, and they also motivate actions and practices, many of which have ideological implications. Discourse analysis has become an important topic in translation studies, and most translators are aware that discourses are essential elements to consider in textual transposition, particularly if a translator wishes to attend to the structure, function, and ideology of a text. The importance of discourse analysis for cultural translation, cultural representation, and cultural mediation, however, is less generally discussed. In many texts discourses are sporadically distributed: that is, they are often represented by isolated or even fragmentary elements rather than recurrent and extensive articulations. The importance of such seemingly disconnected discursive formations emerges in the context of a holistic approach to translating culture, because the significance of isolated discourse fragments and their relation to larger cultural patterns that have other types of exponence in the text is more evident in a holistic approach than in a linear approach to cultural translation.[25]

Another element that commands attention in a holistic approach is the translation of cultural practices. By translation of practices I do not simply mean descriptions of actions in other cultures, though such descriptions are important of course. The translation of cultural practices goes beyond representation of physical and social practices encoded or alluded to or even presupposed in a text; it includes translation of linguistic practices that are written into the fabric of a text. Naming practices stand as an example; they vary from culture to culture and are central to the question of personal and social identities, as well as to social cohesion (cf. Tymoczko 1999b:222-47). How such cultural practices are represented is a significant aspect of the ideological and pragmatic positioning of a translated text and hence an important aspect to be determined in any strategy of cultural translation. Attention to and transposition of such practices can in some cases produce a radically different target text than does domestication of these elements to target culture norms.

A holistic approach to translating culture also includes the translation of cultural paradigms. In *Translation in a Postcolonial Context* (1999b:191-221), for example, I have discussed humor as a cultural paradigm; paradigms of humor are in turn connected with the dispositions and practices of a culture. Because asymmetries in paradigms of humor exist between cultures and because paradigms of humor shift over time within single cultures, such paradigms are intertwined with many other broad cultural patterns. They require a significant level of cultural discernment and choice on the part of a translator. The significance of the divergence of paradigms of humor is illustrated by the Muslim riots that occured around the world in 2006 in

---

[25] The discourses in a text lead as well to significant cultural narrativities that a translator should not sublate. Cf. Baker (2006a, 2006b).

response to cartoons published in European newpapers. Rioters probably had no idea (or interest in the fact) that in Western cultures Christian figures including Jesus, God, and the saints are frequently the subject of jokes and cartoons, nor did publishers of European newspapers foresee the cultural response in the Islamic world caused by divergences in paradigms pertaining to humor.

Humor is not the only type of paradigm that translators confront in texts. Very significant paradigmatic differences also occur in the making of arguments and in logical sequencing from culture to culture, differences that affect the production of discourse itself as discussions in translation studies have begun to recognize (Hatim 1997:35-53, Bandia 2000:147). Similar divergences are found in paradigms pertaining to the use of tropes (such as metaphor or hyperbole) and cultural expressions of basic forms of human interaction such as affiliation and dominance. Difference in such paradigms is more the rule than the exception from culture to culture, yet because cultural paradigms are so basic, so pervasive, so diffuse, and so unspoken in cultural fabrics, it can be hard to perceive them and articulate them as patterned elements of culture. Even translators are apt to forget that cultural paradigms are examples of history turned into nature.[26]

A holistic approach to translating culture will also include attention to the translation of overcodings. By *overcodings* I mean linguistic patterns that are superimposed on the ordinary ranks of language to indicate a higher-order set of distinctions in language practices. Such overcodings range from literary overcodings signaling genre to the ordinary overcodings in spoken and written language pertaining to such things as politeness conventions. Overcodings have commanded attention continuously in the development of translation studies but they are less generally discussed in the context of cultural translation and cultural representation. Perhaps the most widely discussed category of overcodings treated in translation studies is the translation of conventions associated with literary forms: poetry, narrative, theater, film, and other types of media productions. Within each of these literary types, one can also distinguish overcodings appro-priate to specific genres (e.g., within narrative, the overcodings specific to novel, epic, romance, folktale, or fable). Other sorts of artistic and literary overcodings including intertextuality, quotation, and allusion have also been widely discussed. As translation scholarship has demonstrated, literary overcodings vary radically across cultures, and there is no simple decision procedure for the treatment of asymmetries in overcodings. At the same time failure to attend to such literary conventions shifts the translated text considerably. The same is true of overcod-ings having to do with politeness and other forms of ordinary speech.

Many other types of textual structuring also fall under the category of over-codings. Thus, certain aspects of register, dialect, and technical languages can

---

[26] Boothman (2002) offers a detailed and perceptive analysis of translation between ideologi-cal paradigms.

be thought of in terms of the cultural translation of overcodings, as can general constraints affecting the translation of most government, medical, legal, and business documents. It is hard to think of forms of translation that can avoid the question of overcodings altogether, and hence specific types of overcodings are widely discussed though not necessarily grouped together in the way I am doing here. It is somewhat puzzling that these issues have seldom been related to larger questions of cultural translation, applying what is known and theorized about cultural translation to questions of overcodings. Similarly, the cultural implications of various strategies for translating overcodings with respect to the ideological positioning of translated texts also bears more sustained investigation.

A group of overcodings that has commanded extensive attention in translation studies has to do with appropriate forms of social interaction, particularly in their verbal (rather than non-verbal) manifestations. Thus, overcodings having to do with politeness have been well analyzed in the literature of translation studies.[27] There are overcodings of this type that remain to be investigated, however, such as overcodings having to do with persuasion, respect, deference, acknowledgment of social hierarchies, and gender. As translation studies becomes more internationalized and moves beyond Eurocentric perspectives, more attention will be given to these issues because there are many languages that encode semiotic information such as social rank and gender in the structure of the languages themselves, as, for example, Japanese and Korean do with respect to gender or Javanese with respect to social rank. This distinction will inevitably turn attention to forms of social address that in many languages take the form of overcodings rather than structural features of language. It is likely that the international variation in exponence of such particulars will lead to more adequate theorization of overcodings in general.

These various elements of cultural translation call for heightened attention in translation studies at present because cultural difference itself is currently so polarized, serving as a basis of contention around the world, resulting in wars between countries, civil wars, and ethnic conflicts that end in genocide. Many of my examples have been deliberately taken from medieval Irish texts so that the points about cultural translation could be introduced with reference to a culture that at present has relatively little ideological and symbolic value and relatively little resonance for most readers. Words and cultural concepts bring with them charged cultural associations and potentially charged cultural assertions that have political implications. Some of those implications have a life-or-death magnitude in the current geopolitical context, and they are implications that translators ignore at their peril. Cultural wars are currently being waged between nations and within nations in part because contemporary media have made cultural differences more perceptible and hence potentially more objectionable than ever before.

Thus, it is not possible to discuss translating words such as *freedom, de-*

---

[27] See, for example, Hatim (1997:139-56), Katan (2004:302-18).

mocracy, faith, choice, family, religious fundamentalism, oil, car bomb, martyr, victim, or *nuclear program* without running into, invoking, and mobilizing whole fields of cultural, ideological, and political responses related to both source and target cultures. Just to have used such concepts as the primary examples in this discussion of cultural translation would have made the text so charged ideologically that it could hardly have been written or read as a document primarily about theorizing translation. It would have required an introduction establishing my place of enunciation not just with respect to language and translation but also with respect to my nation, cultural values, religion, political history, and sexuality, among other things. Cultural differences have become the most explosive issues on the planet, and they cry out for more attention from translators, translation scholars, and teachers of translation in the ways I have been outlining in this chapter. Almost any culture but an ancient minority culture used as a source of examples would be interpreted as a weapon of some kind – and even the fact that I have chosen here to discuss examples other than current ones will be interpreted by some readers as a political statement (which is probably the case: a statement about peace). At present in virtually every translation assignment, translators are faced with some charged cultural elements that have had relatively little discussion in translation studies. The discipline will profit from finding ways to talk about these issues in deeper and more systematic ways. My choice here to use relatively few politicized examples is an attempt to begin the conversation about cultural translation *per se* without immediately and simultaneously ending the conversation by shunting the topic to contemporary politics.

The importance of cultural translation at present is one reason that the words for both translators and translations (in English and other languages as well) are shifting. Cultural mediation is moving to the center of concern in translation studies. The term *localization* also points to the centrality of culture in the activity of translation: it signifies a concept of translation in which there is an effacement of the cultural differences between the culture of the producer of a product and the culture of the consumer. Localization appears to preserve the cultural singularity of the receptor society, leveling the privilege of certain source culture formations, even as it obscures or hides cultural difference. Ironically, although localization buffers cultures and seemingly protects one culture from the impositions of another, it makes other sorts of fundamental cultural assertions and impositions (about modernity, "progress", consumerism, and materialism, for instance) on cultures across the board. Thus, localization strategies for translating culture ostensibly preserve receptor cultural forms even as they construct a uniform market for globalized consumer and media products.

The parameters considered here as useful for a holistic approach to cultural translation are by no means exhaustive, but they serve to indicate the general approach I am advocating.[28] As aspects of the "stratified hierarchy of meaningful

---

[28] There are many more cultural parameters that could be considered, including, for example, symbols and icons (e.g., having to do with the identity of an individual, family, class, nation, or deity).

structures" of a culture (Geertz 1973:7), these parameters – the signature concepts, metaphors we live by, key words, discourses, paradigms, overcodings,
and so forth – can also be imaged as a tree structure with the habitus as the root
stock, so to speak. Although the metaphor cannot be reified such that the habitus
becomes conceptualized in a rigid manner, the idea of a tree structure offers a
helpful analogy for conceptualizing holistic practices of translating culture. Most
of the groupings discussed above are related to both dispositions and practices;
specific surface forms of culture such as elements of the material culture or social
activities are typically related to these various large-scale cultural manifestations
as terminals at the ends of the branches of the tree structure. Paradoxically, some
specific cultural elements can be analyzed as terminals of more than one branch,
because of the cohesive nature of culture itself. Moreover, cultural forms (whether
linguistic, material, or behavioral) normally have multiple meanings and their
motivations are overdetermined. Hence, they can be interpreted in many ways
within the overall patterns of a culture and thus assigned equally to different locations in a tree structure. Depending on context, specific words can simultaneously
indicate signature concepts of a culture, encode metaphors we live by, function
as key words, and signal literary overcodings in a specific text. As a consequence
when translating culture, a translator may actually be called upon to find ways to
situate and contextualize a particular cultural marker within more than one type
of cultural pattern. A translator like an ethnographer is faced with "a multiplicity
of complex conceptual structures, many of them superimposed upon or knotted
into one another, which are at once strange, irregular, and inexplicit, and which
he must contrive somehow first to grasp and then to render" (Geertz 1973:10).
A holistic approach aids in those tasks.

     A method of translating culture in which a translator looks at the cultural
matrix or cultural system of a text being translated and models it holistically
before starting to translate the words of the text itself challenges linear practices
of translating culture where localized cultural elements are translated word by
word and sentence by sentence as they appear in the text. A holistic approach
responds to Sherry Simon's call for translation scholars to problematize culture
(1996:137) as well as to her insistence on the ethical nature of translation as "the
materialization of our relationship to otherness" and the experience of "what is
different" (1992:161). A holistic approach to culture models a large range of
cultural differences that can be potentially represented, transmitted, and transculturated before the translation process actually begins. It moves well beyond
material culture and it accommodates views of culture that are dynamic and
heterogeneous rather than unitary or essentialist. Such an approach allows for
the incorporation of varied subject positions into cultural translation, as well.

     At times I think of a holistic approach to cultural translation as "translating
from the inside out". That is, holistic cultural translation is not content with
considerations pertaining solely to the observable surface or textualized manifestations of culture in a source text; it attends as well to the (unseen) dispositions

at the center of the habitus, the logic of practice, and the internal dynamics of social systems (cf. Blommaert 2005:226-27). Yet here again we must remember the problems that face any interpreter of culture, whether one is a cultural insider or an outsider looking in, namely, the opposing sets of lacunae related to understanding culture that Bourdieu discerns (1977:18). No matter what the translator's subject position is, there are difficulties in attempting to perceive the dispositions of a culture and the workings of the habitus. The ambiguity of the metaphor "translating from the inside out" thus suggests the risks of undertaking cultural translation from either perspective. Moreover, even if a translator begins as an outsider, by the time the translator becomes bicultural, the second culture also begins to seem self-evident and to become part of the world of the translator, taking on some of the status of "history turned into nature". One must remain aware of these complexities, at the same time seeking to have one's bicultural perspectives mobilize cognitive powers associated with comparison; comparison can heighten self-reflexivity and serve as a guide for the holistic cultural mediation being undertaken.[29]

Although earlier scholars have suggested looking at culture in a large framework, with Susan Bassnett and André Lefevere even going so far as to call for "the culture" to become "the operational 'unit' of translation" (1990:8), such a broad purview is not actually feasible as a working method. Translation studies must define practical ways to approach the task of translating culture. Christiane Nord observes that translators need smaller segments than the whole text to focus on (1997:69); a whole culture is even less practical as a unit of translation than a whole text in developing a concrete strategy for translation.[30] The tree structure discussed here suggests the beginning of a pragmatic approach to translating "a whole culture" as it is reflected in a "whole text", indicating units for approaching the task.

A holistic process of thinking about the large and profound cultural strata reflected in a text that can set the groundwork for translating the cultural strand of the text has affinities with the concept of "thick description". The term was first used by Gilbert Ryle in teasing out aspects of the philosophy of meaning, and it was borrowed by Geertz (1973:3-30) as a way of characterizing the activity of ethnographers. By analyzing and relating cultural components of a source text in a holistic manner, in a sense a translator constructs a thick description of the

---

[29] Wolf (2002) offers a valuable discussion of problems caused by translators' positionalities with respect to the construction of cultural representations in target texts, having to do with cognitive interference from their own languages and cultures (e.g. categories), as well as asymmetries of power. She calls for a model of cultural translation that attempts to escape from essentialist bias (190). Sturge (1997) also investigates several translational strategies employed by ethnographers, looking at the ideological implications of those strategies and their relationship to the translator's place of enunciation.

[30] Fawcett (1997:64) also discusses problems of conceptualizing the text as the appropriate unit of translation.

cultural dimension of the text for the self, preparatory to making the decisions that will actually constitute the cultural representations of the receptor text. Clearly a "thick" conception of the cultural patterns to be transposed rather than a "thin" one enables a translator to be both more effective and more responsible as a cultural mediator.

Kwame Anthony Appiah has applied the ideas of Ryle and Geertz to translation and has argued for the value of a particular type of academic translation "that seeks with its annotations and its acompanying glosses to locate the text in a rich cultural and linguistic context" (2000:427). Appiah's call is more strategy specific than the holistic approach I am advocating, perhaps because he takes it as a given that a translator can and will be able to perceive cultural significance in a source text. The model outlined here, by contrast, problematizes the understanding of culture and is not proposed in terms of a specific discursive strategy that determines the textual characteristics of a translated text. Rather, it is antecedent to the choice of translation strategy: it forms the conceptual basis for the network of decisions about cultural representations, transmissions, and transculturations that the translator will elect to enact and that can be realized in any number of specific translation strategies or textual constructions.[31]

A holistic approach to translating culture facilitates cohesiveness in the cultural representations, transmissions, and transculturations of the target text. The goal of such an approach is not so much to translate a source culture "fully" or "accurately" (though a holistic analysis is effective for documentary purposes, as Appiah indicates), as to empower the translator in deciding *how* to translate culture. Holistic cultural translation facilitates the translation of culture intelligibly and effectively within the larger framework of the goals that the translator has for the translation. A holistic approach to cultural translation is particularly advantageous for strategically conveying cultural difference, but it can also be used to strip a text of cultural markers that could interfere with the translation's reception. In creating empowered and empowering translations, holistic cultural translation permits greater self-awareness in translation choices and greater control in constructing the cultural representations and performances in the target text that support the translator's specific aims and goals. These characteristics of holistic translation enhance the agency of a translator, opening possibilities for translations with an activist edge derived from their cultural positioning. The approach serves as a potent tool for an empowered translator to exercise political and ideological agency. Thus, holistic cultural translation meets many of the goals of translation discourses about agency developed during the last two decades. In part this is true because a holistic approach to cultural translation focuses attention

---

[31] Muhawi (2006:2.370-72) takes the question of thick translation in still another direction, arguing that there is a distinction between thick translation and thick description of culture. He sees thick translation as unfolding over time and through history as a consequence of multiple translations of specific source texts, endowing translators with visibility as they interrogate both source and target texts.

on deep and systemic cultural differences, rather than on surface manifestations that lend themselves to exoticization. Political activism is only one of many possible goals for cultural translation, however; it is to the broader question of goals and strategies related to cultural translation that we now turn.

6.5 Strategizing Cultural Translation

In theorizing cultural translation, as in other facets of the discipline, translation studies must aim at approaches that have wide applicability internationally, approaches that can be useful in many different cultural contexts. They should be relevant to translating between various types of cultures: closely related cultures and those with extremely different cultural configurations, large cultures and small, rich cultures and poor, dominant ones and the marginalized. Theories of cultural translation should be able to account for Eurocentric cultures and other cultures around the world, cultures that are more and less powerful in geopolitical hierarchies, cultures that are relatively homogeneous and cultures that are highly heterogeneous. There should be means of dealing with the very diverse textual practices in highly literate cultures and in oral ones. The ability to account for translating culture across asymmetries of power is essential.

Theoretical approaches to cultural translation should also be flexible enough to be useful for many different translation tasks and many different purposes: introducing new cultural perspectives and practices, as well as preventing cultural infiltration; transmitting cultural material explicitly and providing cultural background for other foregrounded materials; representing and asserting cultural difference and resisting cultural imposition. Broad theoretical approaches to cultural translation should also be transitive: they cannot be predicated on culture flowing in a single direction or unidirectional cultural interface, for example, from dominant cultures to subaltern ones. In sum, useful theories of cultural translation must be applicable to and functional in many different cultural and ideological contexts, relevant to many text types, adaptable to many subject positions and geopolitical interests, and relevant to a culture whether it is the source or the receptor.

One of the weaknesses of approaches to cultural translation thus far has been insufficient attention to theorizing the ideological implications of cultural interface in these diverse situations. A particular deficit in some of the most interesting approaches to cultural translation has been the lack of transitivity. In this regard, although the positions on cultural translation of Antoine Berman (1992) and Lawrence Venuti (1992, 1995, 1998a, 1998b) have been extremely stimulating to and valuable for the discipline, as well as productive of assertive and activist translations, they are also limited. Strategies advocating the experience of the foreign in cultural translation are quite relevant to France which has been resistant to forms of cultural otherness for centuries; French attitudes to the foreign are probably attributable in part to French cultural dominance in Europe for hundreds of years lasting well into the second half of the twentieth century.[32] Similarly, foreignizing translation might be salutary for the United States because of the country's melting-pot ethos and its rising geopolitical prominence and cultural dominance since World War II. Nonetheless, we have seen that foreignizing strategies cannot be recommended for subordinate or minority cultures that are flooded with materials from dominant cultures and that thus find their own local forms of knowledge and culture being eroded. In short, theoretical and pragmatic approaches to cultural translation should be transferable knowledge: they should account for and enable translation in situations where either foreignizing or domesticating techniques are applicable, serving the ideological needs of dominant and marginalized cultures equally.

Holistic methods of cultural translation outlined above have the flexibility to be useful in the many and diverse cultural situations translators are faced with. It should be recognized, however, that thinking holistically about cultural differences and using a holistic approach to cultural translation are both only antecedent to selecting a decision-making procedure for cultural translation and devising an actual translation strategy to serve the translator's larger goals. A holistic approach to culture prepares a translator conceptually to develop a heuristic that guides translation choices, allowing the translator to decide which cultural differences to convey and which to adapt to target norms or even which to suppress. It gives a basis for establishing a hierarchy of values that determines the elements to transpose from the source text and elements to construct in the target text. It guides the metonymic process involved in the strategy and specifics of cultural translation, offering a framework for determining which cultural elements (including those that are presupposed) to convey or stress and which to subsume or assimilate. Thus, a holistic approach to cultural translation is a foundation for developing a translation strategy that shapes the cultural representations, transmissions, and transculturations of the target text, not the strategy itself.[33]

An analysis of the cultural matrix of a text approached holistically does not provide answers to the questions that must be asked in order to develop a translation strategy. Why is the translation being made? For whom? In the service of what? In part there is a disjunction between a holistic approach to cultural translation and actual strategies of cultural transposition because the cultural information in a source text is overdetermined. A translator cannot represent or transfer all the cultural materials in or presupposed by a source text, nor all the elements that a holistic analysis identifies as significant, a topic we will return to in the next chapter. A translator must therefore develop a purposeful strategy guiding

---

[32] Arguably French cultural ascendancy continued into the 1960s and 1970s, when it was generally replaced by U.S. cultural dominance in Western Europe.

[33] Holistic approaches to translating culture can be compared to certain functionalist views of translation. Nord (1997:67-68), for example, discusses the preferability of holistic approaches to bottom-up processes that begin with language transformations and emphasize code-switching.

choices that construct and emphasize particular representations, transmissions, and transculturations of cultural content in the receptor text. Paradoxically translation strategies generally also involve suppression of certain cultural elements because of the overdetermination of cultural information (and because of cultural incompatibilities). Specific decisions relating to cultural transposition are guided by a strategy developed for each particular project based on the cultural elements involved, the purpose of the translation, and the nature of the two cultures the translator is mediating between, but any such strategy is facilitated initially by approaching the question of cultural translation in a holistic way.

To reiterate: a holistic approach to cultural translation is antecedent to choosing a strategy for translation, not the strategy itself. This distinction can be illustrated by considering different ways that holistic approaches can be used by translators to create different types of translations where power and agency are patent: holistic cultural translation can be used for literary purposes or ideological ones, activist political purposes or scholarly ones, the cultural assertions of a colonized people and the rule of colonizers. Legal and commercial translations normally involve holistic considerations of culture, and some form of holism is probably used in the cultural transpositions of almost all forms of localization.[34] This sort of versatility in holistic cultural translation is apparent with reference to the three forms of cultural interface used as frameworks for translation in chapter 3, that is, the cultural representations, transmissions, and transculturations found in a given translation.

When people think of the function of cultural translation (especially in the West), they often think first in terms of the representation of the source culture for the audience of the translated text. In representations of culture, holistic cultural translation generates an extensive inventory of elements to be assessed by the translator, resulting in a much more thorough consideration of cultural factors that become candidates for representation than is the case in an approach based on linear apprehension and transposition of textually localized cultural markers. A thorough consideration of the cultural field of the source text gives a translator much greater power to choose and control the representations being aimed at. This is particularly true in an ideological sense. Linear translation of culture privileges the unspoken but dominant cultural dispositions, values, conceptual structures, and ideological orientations instantiated in the translator's unconscious internalized norms, which by default become the cohesive basis of the cultural translation. As a consequence these dominant default norms *de facto* become the larger but unspoken controlling framework of the cultural representations of the source text. A holistic consideration of culture, by contrast, involving self-reflexivity about cultural translation, tends to disrupt the translator's conditioned dispositions in favor of more deliberate strategizing about representation.

---

[34] Legrand (2005) implicitly supports a holistic approach to translating law, arguing against the possibility of simply translating a law linguistically from one legal system to another, because the meanings of *law* and *rule* themselves differ from culture to culture.

Similarly, holistic approaches to cultural translation facilitate strategies aimed at transmission or transfer of cultural material in a source text. Whether cultural translation has as its goal transmitting scientific, commercial, legal, medical, or literary materials, a holistic consideration will promote the development of effective strategies for assessing the range of cultural materials predicated in the source text and the reception constraints that govern the translated text. One might contend that accurate and adequate representation of culture is a prerequisite of transference of cultural knowledge in translation, but this is not necessarily the case. For example, one could suppress certain cultural elements in translating advertisements for or instructions about products produced in one country and marketed in another. Successful transfer of cultural knowledge might even stand in inverse relationship to accurate representation of all the cultural elements in specific source texts (as in the case of information about particular uses of a product in the source culture that might be anathema in the receiving culture). This sort of inverse relationship is also seen in postcolonial translation, where representation and transfer at times conflict.[35] Judgments of this type are difficult or impossible without a holistic view of the cultural translation being undertaken and without a strategic plan for the transfer of the cultural material as well.

If the goal of cultural translation is ultimately transculturation of certain features of the source culture, many of the same considerations obtain. In this case cultural representation might also be skewed or manipulated because representation would be secondary to the primary goal of effecting uptake of cultural elements marked for transculturation. Again examples abound in localization practices for advertisements of products and services of many multinational corporations, where differences in sexual mores between the source and target cultures might motivate radical restructuring of the source text in order to focus on making the product saleable in a country where sex is not used as a promotional feature. In much the same way Irish nationalist translators at the turn of the twentieth century attempted to transculturate the heroic spirit of medieval Irish texts in order to construct a new revolutionary ethos of heroism in the twentieth century; history demonstrates the effectiveness of their results, but the actual representations of the medieval texts in translation involved extreme manipulations of the cultural configurations of the source texts (Tymoczko 1999b:62-89).

Beginning with a holistic approach to cultural translation does not, therefore, determine the type of strategy a translator uses nor does it delineate the type of translation that results. These disjunctions are apparent from the brief examples given above, including those pertaining to representation, transfer, and transculturation. A holistic approach to cultural translation facilitates a translator's

---

[35] An example is the selective transmission of information about early Irish culture in translations into English during the Irish revival: humor and free sexual mores were reguralry omitted because they would have interfered with representations of early Irish heroism in an English-language context (Tymoczko 1999b).

agency in choosing a translation strategy and in executing that strategy effectively. It heightens a translator's ability to achieve desired results by taking into
account a wide variety of parameters in constructing a cohesive and well-knit
cultural strand in the target text in accordance with the translator's purposes and
goals. Holistic cultural translation increases the translator's understanding and
conceptual control of the cultural materials in the source text to be translated,
as well as the translator's power to develop effective translation strategies and
achieve specific translation results appropriate to the receptor culture, all the while
cautioning the translator about interferences from the translator's own cultural
dispositions and practices.

Observe that the agency that results from holistic cultural translation – as in
any effective translation method – may be powerful but not necessarily ethical.
The complexities of cultural translation illustrate that focusing on the power of
translators is not sufficient for promoting responsible agency in translation. A
translator's sense of agency as such will not issue in a will to translate a source
culture to a target context in an ethical or responsible way. Because holistic
cultural translation precedes but does not constitute a strategy for translation as
such, it can facilitate cultural transpositions of all sorts, from the radical cultural
manipulations of colonialist translations (such as those of William Jones[36] or Edward Fitzgerald) to the activist translations associated with nationalist movements
fighting colonialism (such as those of the Irish revival), to the ideologically
motivated translation program of the Soviet Union before 1989. Some translators engage in cultural translation to support or even incite imperialist wars, to
further economic exploitation, to support terrorist agendas for organizations that
kill civilians, and to back up data-mining surveillance operations that control
domestic populations.

This disjunct between effective methodologies of cultural translation and the
ethics of cultural translation may explain some of the features of the arguments
about agency put forth by both Berman and Venuti. Both are concerned to link
cultural assertion to ethical translation interventions. Yet ironically the challenges
to dominant cultures that they argue for and the strategies they espouse are ethical primarily because of the nature of cultural enclosure in the specific contexts
each is responding to. The problem in the work of both authors is the attempt
to generalize and universalize the strategies each proposes. It may be precisely
a sense of the dangers of discussing a broader range of specific situations that
results in their offering a fairly general and somewhat fuzzy notion glorifying
the foreign and foreignizing. By picking valorized vocabulary and deploying
that vocabulary to discuss situations where *ipso facto* the strategies they promote
will result in clear progressive and ethical postures, each can suggest in language
that is at once strong and vague that other translators should follow suit. Here
Venuti's use of the term *resistance* is of particular value, for it allows readers to

---

[36] Niranjana (1992:12-19) discusses the translations of William Jones.

image an indeterminate and virtually unlimited range of ideological opponents. The principal limitation in both efforts to join agency in cultural translation with responsible activism narrows their vision to specific translation strategies that are not at all transitive or transferable to a wide range of other contexts, including minority or marginalized cultures where the foreign is in flood.

Thus, to say that a holistic mode of cultural translation is powerful and that it facilitates the agency of translators is not to claim that it is necessarily good. Both the necessity to look more deeply and broadly at a culture in assessing the cultural elements of a text to be translated and the need to understand and acknowledge one's own cultural predispositions and biases add new dimensions to a translator's engagement with the culture of the self as well as the cultures of others. Even as the approach to cultural translation proposed here enhances a translator's agency and empowers a translator's ability to be a cultural mediator, it also indicates the importance of an augmented concept of the translator's responsibility in cultural translation. Motivations other than power as such are required to promote a sense of heightened participation and responsibility in the contemporary world and to make the agency of translators ethical as they undertake cultural translation. Neither promoting effective approaches to mediating cultural difference nor prescribing specific discursive strategies for constructing target texts suffices to ensure ethical translation results. For those purposes translation studies as a discipline will have to engage ethics and questions of responsibility directly in a sustained manner.

6.6 Cultural Translation, Ideology, and Self-Censorship

For more than a quarter century, it has been generally agreed that translation is a text about a text or, to put it another way, a form of metastatement (cf. Holmes 1994:23-33; Lefevere 1985, 1992b). If we put this seemingly innocuous observation in an ideological context, we must recognize that the ideology of translation is quite complex. A translation's ideology is determined only partially by the content of the source text – the subject and the representation of the subject – even when the content itself is overtly political and enormously complicated as a speech act, with locutionary, illocutionary, and perlocutionary aspects of the source text all contributing to the ideological effect in the source context. The ideological value of the source text is in turn complemented by the fact that translation is a metastatement, a statement about the source text and its content that constitutes an interpretation of the source text. This is the case even if the metastatement is seemingly only a form of reported speech (cf. Jakobson 1959:233) or quotation uttered in a new context, because in quoting a source text, a translator in turn creates a text that is a representation with its own proper locutionary, illocutionary, and perlocutionary forces determined by relevant factors in the receptor context.[37] Thus, even in a simplified model, the ideology of a translation will be an amalgam of (1) the subject and content of the source text and their representation in the source text; (2) the various speech acts instantiated in the source text relevant to the source context; (3) the translator's representation of the source content and the source text; (4) the purported relevance to the receptor audience of the translation; (5) the various speech acts of the translation itself addressing the receptor context; and (6) any resonances and discrepancies that exist between the two "utterances" of source text and translation.[38]

The ideological power of cultural translation potentially inheres at each of the levels distinguished above. The ideology of translation is intertwined with the translation of culture because cultural translation is a prime means of engaging in cultural assertion, conveying and valorizing difference, undertaking activist translation, affirming identity and autonomy, and claiming or decentering power. It is also a means of asserting dominance, deprecating or suppressing other cultures, manipulating representations so as to enhance power hierarchies, preventing cultural infiltration, and the like. Implicated in most cultural assertions of dominant nations, the various levels discussed above are also significant in developing activist strategies of translation.

Cultural translation is not only an important expression of the translator's ideological agency, it is also a prime locus of censorship and self-censorship in translation. Censorship and self-censorship can be exerted at any of the levels at which ideology enters the process of translation. As a consequence it is obviously useful to explore and understand how and why official censorship impinges on the representation, transfer, and performance of cultural materials in translation, and the topic of censorship has in fact begun to be explored in descriptive translation studies.[39] Nevertheless, how translators silence themselves seems to me even more critical to investigate than how official censorship silences translators, partly because there are so many documented cases of translators finding means to foil formal and informal forms of censorship. This history of circumventing

---

[37] On speech act theory see Austin (1975) and Searle (1969); it has been criticized in Sperber and Wilson (1995). The ideological aspects of reported speech have been discussed by Vološinov (1971:149 ff.) and Parmentier (1993). A comprehensive study of translation as reported speech is found in Folkart (1991); see also Gutt (2000a, 2000b); Tymoczko (2003b). An interesting analogy between the translator's role in reported speech and the translator as an actor who performs a recreation of the voice of the author of the source text is found in Mayer (2000).

[38] This is a very schematic model of the ideological dimension of translation; one would also have to consider various contextual aspects such as patron, geopolitical relations between source and target culture, the function of the translation or the use to which it is put, and so forth. The essays in Calzada Pérez (2003) explore additional perspectives on the intersection of ideology and translation.

[39] Discussions of censorship and translation are found in the essays collected in Merkle (2002) and Ní Chuileanáin et al. (forthcoming), as well as Bastin (forthcoming) and Merkle (forthcoming). See also Cronin (2003:92-103).

censorship is one reason that Cronin calls all translators "escape artists" and sees translation studies as "a branch of escapology" (2003:93).

Andrew Chesterman (2000:26) has stressed the crucial role that a translator plays in the final shape of any translation. He observes that in answer to the question "why did the translator make this decision?", explanatory hypotheses may be offered, but that ultimately,

> insofar as explanatory hypotheses appeal to situational factors such as the skopos or socio-cultural factors such as translation norms, it must be borne in mind that these only actually affect the translation via the translator's own mind. This realization places the translators at the centre of a causal model. If we exclude alterations made to a translation after it has been submitted to the client, there are no causes which can bypass the translators themselves. They themselves have the final say. It is their attitudes to norms, skopos, source text, translation theory, etc. that ultimately count, rather than these external factors *per se*. (2000:26)

Absent a group process of translation (with an ideological controller, as in China after 1949, for instance), Chesterman's analysis is astute. Gillian Lane-Mercier also stresses the individual translator's responsibility, despite the fact that translation is a "culturally determined discursive activity" (1997:65). Clearly censorship is one of the external factors that can be added to Chesterman's list, but in the end many translators are not thwarted by censorship, finding myriad inventive ways to subvert it instead.

What is harder to circumvent is self-censorship. In my experience self-censorship is more pervasive and ultimately more responsible for limitations in translation than official censorship itself. It is interesting to see how people stop themselves from translating what they profess to want to translate in the manner they profess to want to translate it. This is never more apparent than in cultural translation where translators who claim to love the source language and the source culture restrict and censor their own representations, transmissions, and transculturations of the distinctive cultural aspects of the source materials in their translations, even though no overt external power controls or censors them.

The tendency to self-censorship in translation can be analyzed as a classic example of hegemony.[40] Antonio Gramsci explained that hegemony is secured through processes in which dominant groups constantly negotiate with subordinate groups to win their active consent to a political and ideological consensus that favors the dominant group. If ideological and political processes and discourses institutionalized in civil society do their work, subordinate groups need not be forced to consent but will do so in the belief that their interests are to some extent included in the dominant culture. This belief is not necessarily false and often

---

[40] A good overview of hegemony and the ideas of Gramsci from a perspective relevant to translation studies is found in Strinati (1995:160-75).

arises, Gramsci suggests, "because concessions are made by dominant to subordinate groups" (Strinati 1995:166, cf. 167). Through such mechanisms translators introject and promote dominant interests by means of their translations as a result of believing, for example, that their way of translating will benefit themselves personally (such as through professional advancement) or that it is the only way that their source texts can find an audience in a dominant receiving culture.

Alternatively, the tendency of translators to buy into dominant views and to stop themselves from textual production suggesting difference or dissent can be analyzed in terms of norms. Under many circumstances translators freely subordinate their work to the dominant social, ideological, and textual norms of their culture. Some scholars have even claimed that adaptation to norms is the mark *per se* of a professional translator (Merkle 2002:15-18, Brunette 2002). Yves Gambier notes that the absence of firm directions leaves translators to their own judgment about how to translate, the result often being adaptation to normative pressures (2002:217). Whether we think of the acceptance of cultural constraints as a result of hegemony or the adaptation to norms, it is the tendency to conform willingly to dominant discourses and standards that lies at the root of self-censorship, particularly in cultural translation. Thus, if for no other reason than to be self-aware about norms and hegemony, it is useful for translators to have in mind the sort of broad inventory involved in holistic cultural translation outlined here. Holistic procedures can remind translators of their agency in cultural translation, itself an important factor, for, as Cronin notes, "translators, potentially primary actors in the current changes affecting the planet, must not accept the most damaging form of self-censorship, an indifference to their own importance" (2003:102).

A more constructive aspect of self-censorship impinging on cultural translation is the decision of translators to suppress facets of a source text to further their own programmatics in translating. We have seen that a holistic approach to cultural translation enables translators to give broader, deeper, and more cohesive representations of a source culture. The approach can also be used to facilitate strategies that produce effective fragmentary representations of a source culture so that translators can pursue goals other than documentary translation or representation as such: artistic, ideological, or commercial goals; clear transference of certain cultural information; transculturation of specific cultural forms or values; activist programmatics; and so forth. In such cases the balance between selection and suppression of cultural information might be viewed as a form of *strategic self-censorship*, a form of self-censorship in which some cultural elements of a source text are given zero translation because of goal-driven decision-making procedures consciously chosen by the translator.

Strategic self-censorship is not limited to cultural translation, but it is often easier to track in the translation of culture than in the translation of other aspects of a source text. It reveals how the work of translators is shaped by ideological and politicized forces, and attention to these matters can be invaluable in descriptive translation studies. Strategic self-censorship usually involves both resistance to and complicity with oppressive cultural norms simultaneously. The characteristics of strategic self-censorship fit with the metonymic nature of translation, reflecting a translator's decision that not all aspects of a source culture can be translated in light of the translator's goals for the translation. Strategic self-censorship is an important phenomenon to understand, because its mechanisms indicate that empowered translation does not fall into a binary mode – on the one hand translators as submissive victims of censorship and on the other hand heroic resistors against external oppressors and internal collusion; on the one hand faithful translators of the source culture and on the other hand cultural manipulators. More typically translators accept and acquiesce in some norms but oppose and challenge others, setting priorities and undertaking some cultural self-censorship for what they see as a greater good (for instance, empowered or activist use of translation for a particular purpose).[41] Clearly there is a fine line between strategic self-censorship and hegemony.

Self-reflexivity is essential for translators in assessing their tendencies toward self-censorship, particularly in cultural translation. Because of the importance of cultural differences in situations involving geopolitical power, sovereignty, autonomy, and cultural identity, it is not a trivial matter when translators efface cultural difference and assimilate the cultural patterns of a minority source culture to dominant receptor norms. Some self-censorship in cultural translation is probably almost always necessary, if only because cultural meaning in the source text is overdetermined, but the question is where to draw the line. There can be no *prima facie* rule in this regard, for such translation decisions are context specific. What is clear, however, is that translators often compromise cultural translation much more than they need to, vitiating their own agency and empowerment in the process. They are also often more timid in their representations than is required, undertaking less cultural transfer than they might and underestimating the ability of their audiences to tolerate, learn from, and engage with cultural difference and newness.[42] Such (preconscious) inclinations and assumptions should be interrogated and even resisted whenever possible or else *de facto* translators construct themselves as subalterns.[43]

---

[41] Cf. Lane-Mercier (1997:60-65).

[42] The translation procedures of Seamus Heaney in *Sweeney Astray* stand as a cautionary example; see the discussion in Tymoczko (2000b).

[43] Ironically the same is true of many postcolonial writers, particularly those writing in one of the languages of the former imperial powers, chosen as a mode of reaching a more international audience. It is significant that relatively little postcolonial literature written in the national languages of former colonies is translated and read internationally. The precondition of reaching an international audience is therefore usually implicit autotranslation into a so-called metropolitan language, a process that involves cultural translation as well. The result is that postcolonial writers are in effect required to do a form of pre-screening of their cultures,

Let me conclude this discussion of self-censorship with a fable for translators, postcolonial or minority writers, and others who are faced with dilemmas related to cultural translation. In *Huis clos* (*No Exit*)[44] Jean-Paul Sartre offers both an insight and a warning. It is very easy for human beings to become their own torturers and to construct their own prisons, as in the case of the characters in Sartre's play. The great moment in Sartre's drama occurs when the door to the room where the characters are enclosed and confined suddenly springs open: it springs open and the characters choose not to leave their prison. As translators and writers we must look for the moments when the door opens so that we can embrace the liberty before us; indeed we must attempt to pry the doors open ourselves. In some ways this is more true in cultural translation than any other domain of translation. Kathleen Davis (2001:93) calls for translations to answer to the "singularly other" within the source text, seeing the respect for singularity as central to the conceptualization of ethics and justice. Such singularities and otherness – and hence the ethics and justice of translation – are overwhelmingly intertwined with cultural translation. In constructing ethical translations, cultural translators have not only censorship and norms to contend with but also the prison of their own fear and their own self-censorship.

6.7 Cultural Translation and the Agency of the Translator

The translation of culture requires awareness of perspective, minimally a recognition that the source culture has (at least) one view of culture and the receptor culture another view. The postpositivist development of translation studies since World War II, however, has problematized the understanding of all such perspectives. There has been a steady move away from the positivist contention (built into early anthropology and nineteenth-century humanist disciplines) that one can determine the "facts" of a culture that one is observing or the "facts" of one's own culture in any simple way. Postpositivist understandings have also undermined the developmental view of cultures associated with the imperialist contention that some cultures are "primitive" and that there is an evolutionary progression leading to the "modern" cultural paradigms associated with the (powerful) Westernized countries of the present, exposing such developmental discourses as a tool of power associated with the assertion of specific sets of interests. The

---

affecting both cultural representation and cultural transmission, in order to reach international audiences. This form of cultural translation inherent in postcolonial writing in a language such as English is subject to the same temptations and perils of self-censorship that translators face, as described above. It follows that the comments about cultural translation made here are to a large extent applicable to the writing of postcolonial writers as well as translators.

[44] Literally 'closed door', where *huis* for 'door' is an old-fashioned and formal term used in locutions related to secret negotiations held behind closed doors.

consequence has been much more complex assessment of cultural perception, an appreciation of the varied ways culture can be approached in translation, and a greater awareness of the importance of the translator's agency in the process. Bhabha underscores the importance of undertaking cultural translation and of executing it with specificity, asserting that "cultural translation desacralizes the transparent assumptions of cultural supremacy, and in that very act, demands a contextual specificity, a historical differentiation within minority positions" (1994:228).

Cultural questions have been moving toward the center of translation studies since the cultural turn that began during the 1980s associated with the rise of cultural studies, the movement that marks the beginning of the second wave of descriptive translation studies. Ironically, however, translation studies has missed opportunities to match its ideological interest in cultural questions with the theoretical reconsideration of culture evident in most of the social sciences during the same period. The social sciences have explored postpositivist implications of cultural construction in their own disciplines – notably in responses to the crisis of representation in anthropology and ethnography – but this intersection remains to be fully realized in translation studies.

This gap in translation studies is worth reflecting upon. It is particularly strange in view of the interests of scholars associated with the second wave of descriptive translations studies, beginning with the cultural turn, for such studies have almost uniformly valorized cultural difference and promoted activist strategies for expressing cultural difference. One might have expected that the translation scholars who were part of the cultural studies branch of the discipline would have already theorized cultural translation on both the micro and macro levels more extensively. Instead the focus has been principally on ideological reflexes of culture rather than on cultural configurations as such.[45]

The failure to theorize the translation of culture and to articulate its praxis more adequately may be connected with an invidious suspicion about culture in many quarters of academe. Michael Cronin (2006:14-20) has suggested that culture *per se* has become associated with cultural particularisms and has been condemned as connected with the most retrograde forms of nationalism. Cronin argues that the "withering scepticism about the particular", noticeable in the work of Benedict Anderson (1991) and Eric Hobsbawm (1983) and amplified by many others, is "damaging to a genuine openness of cultures" (2006:18).[46]

---

[45] Calzada Pérez (2003:5-6) has a useful discussion of the difference between ideology and culture germane to this point.

[46] A criticism of Hobsbawm's view of tradition is found in Cronin (2006) and also in Tymoczko and Ireland (2003). Cf. Legrand (2005).

Presumably conjuring up such things as folk celebrations and ethnic food, the concept of particularism in culture has been devalued as backward-looking in some cosmopolitan circles, including translation studies, where scholars have often been at pains to undercut the notion of cultural traditions altogether. Cronin suggests that in this paradigm cultural identities are seen less as creative constructions than as inheritances from an older order; culture itself is imaged as immutable, bound to the lifeways of racialized or ethnic groups (2006:32, 46). The hostility to cultural particularism is especially debilitating for small ethnic groups and small nations concerned with the preservation of cultural identity (Cronin 2006:12-13). If Cronin is right in these arguments, as I think he is, then these pretheoretical dispositions require reconsideration if translation studies is to have an adequate theory and practice of cultural translation.

Ironically, cultural differences are not at all restricted to traditional societies or those engaged in identity politics, nor are they insignificant in distinguishing contemporary nations. Indeed cultural differences among powerful nations and blocs of nations motivate some of the most significant geopolitical tensions of the present. Moreover, one need only think of the different ways that language politics, multilingualism, and cultural difference are configured within contemporary nations – for example, Japan, India, France, Egypt, Mexico, and the United States – to see the importance of traditions in contemporary nations. Obviously religious traditions are also central to current national and international identities and conflicts. Such basic cultural premises might well color the content of an entire text being translated, calling for cultural mediation in a very deliberate way on the part of the translator. That is, the complexities of holistic cultural translation are not reserved for translating material from traditional societies: in many ways they are even more significant in translating cultural configurations characterizing "modern" societies.

It is possible that the tendency to be suspicious of culture, to efface discussion of significant cultural distinctions in translation studies, and, hence, to theorize cultural translation in a relatively shallow manner is also related to the homogenizing impulse of one strand of globalization. Inattention to the theorization of the complexities of cultural translation and a relatively simplistic praxis of cultural translation reify an implicit hegemonic acquiescence of segments of the discipline of translation studies in the cultural practices of the powerful patrons of much contemporary cultural interface, despite lip service paid to politically correct appreciations of cultural specificities.

Whether for these reasons or others, the implementation of current understandings of culture and cultural construction in terms of concrete and practical translation techniques remains to be worked out and detailed in translation studies. Although Katan (2004) has addressed many important issues, his achievements are limited by his relatively narrow range of examples, as well as his scant attention to the ethics, politics, and ideology of cultural translation. He has also given limited attention to the problematic of "knowing" any culture – whether one's own or another – and to the necessity for self-reflexivity in cultural translation.[47] It is also essential to move beyond the Eurocentric world in formulating the theory and praxis of translation, and this necessity to enlarge translation studies is nowhere more acute than in discussions of cultural translation. Here I have offered suggestions for addressing the complex issues that impinge on cultural translation and for responding to the ethical imperatives about culture commanding current concerns in both academic and ordinary life, imperatives that are epitomized by the interface and mediation of cultural difference in translation.

If translators, like ethnographers, are constructors of culture through their representations, transmissions, and transculturations, they obviously play a very powerful role in cultural interface and cultural mediation. Conversely cultural translation plays a central role at every level of a text, from the largest levels of content and form to the smallest linguistic levels, right down to the phoneme. All of these levels have ideological and ethical significance as well as implications for cultural construction, as we have seen.[48] In a similar vein Nord (1997:69-70) indicates that function can be expressed at all ranks of a text; she argues that a function can be seen as a vertical unit bringing together features at various ranks. The same might be observed about cultural translation which also acts as a vertical feature of a translation, bringing together elements expressed at all ranks of the text. It follows that cultural translation must be considered as important at all levels, from the smallest to the largest, because every level or rank of a text contributes to the cohesive construction of culture in a translation. Just as a single function of a text can be expressed at a number of levels of the source text, so can specific aspects of a culture be expressed at every textual level as well. Similarly, the various levels of a translated text express the translator's strategy of cultural translation and contribute to the construction of the cultural significance for the receptor audience. Culture can thus be represented, transferred, or transculturated at all textual levels consonant with the translator's program. Silences or assimilations at all the various levels of a text are also significant for cultural translation functionally, ideologically, and ethically. These facets of

---

[47] For example in Katan's final chapter on becoming a cultural mediator (2004:329-40), the emphasis is on understanding and adaptation, positing that students can achieve competence at cultural translation and mediation in three or four years. There is almost no problematization of the ability to achieve knowledge of one's own or other cultures.

[48] Examples can be found in my earlier studies. I've discussed the ideological implications of cultural representation at the level of the phoneme (an issue in the translation of names) in Tymoczko (1999b:222-47) and argue that translation of the article is associated with colonialist representations of the Irish as prescientific in Tymoczko (1985).

cultural translation remain to be amplified in translation studies, but the holistic methods I have explored here are a good starting point for future work.

Attention to the power of translators as cultural mediators can easily get overwritten or even obliterated by attention to other metonymies of translation. Poetry has traditionally been identified as what gets lost in translation, but in fact many aspects of culture can more justly claim that distinction, being totally effaced in translation. Such effacement is a political and ideological act, yet it is often accepted as inevitable almost unconsciously and automatically by translators, scholars, and critics alike. Even in situations involving asymmetries of power and conflicts of ideology, it seems easier to notice modes of constructing politicized content than to perceive the ideological significance of cultural constructions in translations. This blindspot is paradoxical because culture remains the prime source of difference in texts and in the human world, and it is probably the most important aspect that translators attend to in constructing representations in their work, in transmitting and transculturating new ways of being in the world, and in framing ideological and ethical interventions.

In many ways cultural translation is at the root of all translator empowerment: political, ideological, and ethical empowerment as well as other forms of agency to a large extent follow from cultural translation. Thus, expanding and emphasizing methods of cultural translation give more responsibility to translators and simultaneously enhance the quality of their agency. A deeper engagement with culture and the necessity of self-reflexivity in cultural translation make translation more complex, but also highlight the skill and action of the translator. Enlarging the understanding of cultural translation gives translators more choices and those choices become indicators of new ways to conceptualize translation as such.

Reconceptualizing cultural translation by using frameworks from the social sciences facilitates new ways of perceiving the role of cultural representation, transfer, and transculturation in translation theory and practice. In turn a holistic approach to cultural translation based on such frameworks makes possible deeper and more layered perceptions of a culture and of the cultural elements to be considered in the process of translation – even as it brings awareness of the hubris inherent in any claim to understand a culture. Reappraisal of cultural translation (as would be the case with any other fundamental strand of translation theory and practice) will subtly change the entire field. A disciplinary change driven by shifts in cultural translation beckons at present because cultural interface and cultural representation have moved increasingly to the forefront as a result of greater international cultural interchange, more networking associated with globalization, and the intensity of cultural conflicts in the contemporary world. Cronin (2006:30) argues that a commitment to appropriate culturally sensitive models of translation is central to any concept of global citizenship in the twenty-first century. By committing to deeper theoretical explorations and better practical articulations of cultural translation, we enlarge translation, empower translators, and move the field of translation studies toward greater ethical awareness all at the same time.

7. Liberating Meaning, Legitimating Translation

After posing the question "in what respects must a translation be similar to its original?", Stephen David Ross observes that the most natural answer is "a translation ought to have the same meaning as the original" (1981:8). Indeed many teachers of translation and many instructional books on how to translate begin with that very premise. Anthony Oettinger gives an articulate statement of this classic view of translation: "If the originals have some significance, we generally require that their images also have the same significance, or, more realistically, as nearly the same significance as we can get. Keeping significance invariant is the central problem in translating between natural languages" (1960:104). Despite the widespread repetition of this view of translation, it has been contested throughout the postpositivist development of translation studies, from Quine (1959, 1960) who early on initiated discourses that challenge fundamental presuppositions about language assumed in this view of translation to contemporary deconstruction scholars such as Derrida and his followers who reject the idea that meaning can be safely transferred from one linguistic system to another.[1]

A central problem with this view of translation, as Ross goes on to indicate, is that "neither meaning nor similarity of meaning is a clear notion" (1981:8). Probably the most empowering activity translators can undertake, therefore, is to explore and reflect upon the nature of meaning in general and the nature and role of meaning in translation in particular, thus liberating their translation practices from the false dictate to preserve meaning. This is not an easy task because meaning is treated by many translation scholars and teachers, as well as translators themselves, as if it were a straightforward and obvious thing, a simple and unproblematic concept. This disposition diverges sharply from the views of meaning in linguistics, philosophy, and literary studies, as well as many other academic disciplines, where there is both puzzlement and contention about what is meant by meaning.

Rather than attempt to define or delimit the nature of meaning here – an enterprise that has turned out to be inconclusive and futile in other disciplines – I intend to problematize simplistic concepts of meaning prevalent in translation studies, demonstrating the constructivist nature of meaning in translation. Because translators are the ones who construct meaning in translated texts, it follows that translators are meaning makers and that in this capacity they wield considerable power, have great responsibility, and exercise important agency. An understanding of translators as meaning makers is a good starting point for exploring the intersection

---

[1] Cf. Davis (2001:17-18), Arrojo (1998:41-42), and sources cited. Appiah (2000) also gives a very interesting critique of the view of translation as the transfer or preservation of meaning. Almost all studies of translation discuss the question of meaning at some point, but the relationship between various types of meaning to translation is the focus of the articles in Thelen and Lewandowska-Tomaszczyk (1990, 1996) and Lewandowska-Tomaszczyk and Thelen (1992, 1997).

of the nature of meaning and the agency of the translator. The next two sections begin this exploration with practical exercises that problematize the question of meaning in translation and demonstrate the role of the translator in creating and constructing meaning. Following those concrete exercises, I turn to more abstract and theoretical discussions of the nature of meaning in translation.

7.1 The Translator's Decision-Making Process and the Construction of Meaning

A way to begin thinking about meaning in translation is to look at how translators approach a text and to observe translators actually translating. Any text can serve as an example, provided that it involves some linguistic anisomorphisms, cultural asymmetries, and formal challenges with respect to the target culture, as well as some questions about the meaning of the source text itself, whether for linguistic reasons (having to do with lexical field or multiple exponence, for example) or historical and contextual ones. These are in fact features of most texts, and the text selected does not have to be long.

A good example is the following very short poem in medieval Irish. Probably dating from the ninth century, the poem survived because it was quoted in an eleventh-century metrical manual (Murphy 1956:174). Translating such a poem is not only a good exercise for students, it is also a good exercise for teachers and scholars, encapsulating many of the basic challenges of translating meaning or significance for experts as well as novices.[2] The task is to translate (indirectly via English for those who do not know Irish) the following short poem into whatever language you wish, using whatever translation strategy you deem best.

> Int én bec
> ro-léic feit
> do rinn guip
>   glanbuidi:
> fo-ceird faíd
> ós Loch Laíg
> lon do chraíb
>   charnbuidi. (Murphy 1956:6-7)

The text reproduces Gerard Murphy's edition in *Early Irish Lyrics*, and Murphy also offers the following facing translation: "The little bird which has whistled from the end of a bright-yellow bill: it utters a note above Belfast Loch – a blackbird from a yellow-heaped branch" (1956:6-7). We can note that Murphy (following earlier editors) has already manipulated the text, marking out the

---

[2] A text of this sort can be given to students as an in-class assignment or it can be assigned as homework to be prepared for the next class meeting, with students responsible for bringing copies of their translations for the other members of the class.

poetic form by lineation and segmenting the text with added punctuation. Thus, two short declarative sentences have been joined by a colon. The following is my own English gloss translation, which provides the lexical meanings of the individual words in the Irish syntactical order.

> the bird little
> has loosed whistle
> from point of beak
> pure-yellow
> it throws cry
> over Loch Laig
> blackbird from branch
> piled-yellow

Here the exercise for readers is to translate this poem (indirectly from English), and you can begin straightaway or do the translation after a little background reading about the text, which follows.

Because few readers of this book know Old Irish, it may help in making decisions about the translation to have more information about early Irish language, literature, and culture.[3] First some background on the (habitus of the) culture, which D.A. Binchy famously characterized as "tribal, rural, hierarchical, and familiar (using this word in its oldest sense to mean a society in which the family, not the individual, is the unit)" (1954:54). Binchy notes that the characteristics of early Irish culture stand in complete contrast to the unitary, urbanized, egalitarian, and individualistic society of modern Western cultures (1954:54). The political unit was the *túath* (usually translated *tribe* in English, though a túath was not a kin-group), and the society was composed of many of these relatively small groupings of people, each originally having its own king and its own gods. There were no cities as such in early medieval Ireland; the culture was almost entirely rural in the pre-Christian period and even thereafter for centuries. Early Irish culture at the time (ca. 500-850 C.E.) was also a heroic society with a strong class hierarchy; warriors constituted the principal noble class and commanded considerable prestige, second only to the priest-king class. As Binchy indicates, the society (as reflected in the laws) was also organized around families, with the family responsible for the legal and social conduct of individuals and their well-being. Land was owned by the family as well and it was inalienable.

When the poem was composed, Irish society was in transition. The Celts had come to Ireland around the third century B.C.E. and had lived there in relative

---

[3] Note that an exercise in which almost all students have to do an indirect translation has the advantage of leveling the playing field, so that some students do not have access to privileged knowledge unavailable to the others. The difficulty of using an example of this type, particularly an ancient text, is that the text is decontextualized, which makes inferences about meaning more difficult but which also highlights the role of the translator as meaning maker.

peace, unconquered by the Romans. As a result many of the warrior aspects of the culture had become muted in the thousand years before the Viking raids began at the end of the eighth century. The warrior class had settled down as a sort of rural gentry, with their special social role as fighters exercised only sporadically or somewhat ritualistically. This shift was furthered by the Christianization of the island that happened gradually and peacefully from the fourth century onward. By the end of the sixth century, the Christian church had become monastic in Ireland, abandoning its early diocesan structure to adapt to the rural conditions of the island. Paradoxically, however, many of the great monasteries began to take on some of the functions of cities, acting as population centers that fostered learning, the arts and crafts, and certain forms of economic activity. Most of the monks probably wore black robes, typical of early medieval orders, while secular individuals wore more colorful clothing appropriate to their particular social rank. The society was also in transition to larger types of political units, because the concept of the "great king" had come into the society through contact with Mediterranean ideas of kingship and Christian Roman concepts of empire. At least two competing centers claiming "high kingship", one in the north and one in the south, were coalescing by the time the poem was composed.

The poets in Ireland descend from the pre-Christian Celtic learned classes, which had originally included the druids. The native learned classes were originally associated with augury, keeping the calendar, announcing the festivals and the seasons, and knowing "natural philosophy". They also had ritual functions, including special roles related to the inauguration of kings. There was a formal education system for the poets that involved many years of study, and this system remained intact until the seventeenth century. During their apprenticeship poets were expected to master many complex metrical forms, because formalism was extremely important in the literary and social system, a mark of the poet's professional status. One should note that there was little need for "nature" description or "nature" poetry of the sort associated with European romanticism, because the culture was entirely rural and constantly in touch with "nature".

Early Irish culture practiced bird augury. Black birds (especially crows and ravens) were connected with inauspicious augury, especially when the birds cried from above; they were at times associated with the prophecy of death, associations that persist in Ireland to the present. In general black birds formed a single native taxonomy (Tymoczko 1990a). Thus, blackbirds, crows, ravens, rooks, and cormorants (among others) were seen as related conceptually. The black birds were connected with battle (especially crows and ravens, as carrion feeders), and several of the war goddesses were conceptualized as crows or thought to be able to metamorphose into the form of crows. The bird in the poem seems to be the European thrush called in English *blackbird* (*Turdus merula*), the only small black bird with a yellow beak in Ireland. It is a male bird, because the young and females of the species are brown. Nonetheless the bird is associated with the other black birds because the Irish term *lon* (blackbird), though proper to *Turdus merula*, also clearly refers in some passages to crows, the war goddesses, and so forth. For all these reasons, the imagery here is polyvalent.

Moving from the cultural background to the literary as such, we can note that the poem has two stanzas. It uses a syllabic meter of three syllables per line, with lines 1-3 and 5-7 ending in monosyllabic words and lines 4 and 8 ending in trisyllabic words. The rhyme scheme is aaabcccb. Irish rhyme is distinct from English and European rhyme; in this poem, rhyme *a* is actually imperfect rhyme, constituting consonance rather than normal Irish rhyme. Rhyme *b* is homonymic rhyme, which involves repetition of the same word or the use of homonyms to carry the rhyme. Rhyme *c* is perfect Irish rhyme, requiring vowels to be identical and the final consonants of rhyming words to be members of the same phonemic class (here voiced palatalized spirants) rather than being identical as would be the case in English, for example. Notice the rich alliteration within some lines and linking lines as well.

A few lexical notes are also in order before you begin to translate. We should note the use of *fet*, 'whistle, alarm signal'; the word is not restricted to birds, but it is relevant that the blackbird has two calls, the first the blackbird's famous melodious song and the second an alarm cry. The term *rinn*, 'point, tip', here used of the bird's beak, is frequently used metonymically to refer to weapons. Another significant word is *glan*, 'pure' (cf. the related verb *glanaid*, 'purifies'), which may suggest an implicit comparison between the blackbird's beak and the "impure" beaks of the scavengers in the same native taxonomy, the crows and the ravens. There may be a subliminal pun in the use of the word *faíd*, 'outcry', which could here bring in associations involving word play on *fáith*, 'prophet'. Similarly *buide*, 'yellow', is a homonym of *buide*, 'thanks', and that second meaning might have relevance in the poem. Finally, I have translated the word *carn*, 'cairn', compounded with *buide* in the last line, as "piled" (cf. Murphy, "yellow-heaped"), but a cairn is literally a pile of stones that generally marks a grave or has some other funerary or memorial association. The semantic meanings of these words clearly have some surprising and dissonant associations.

I suggest the following protocol at this point. Readers should set the book down for 20 minutes or so and prepare a quick translation of this short poem. (Should you be a technical translator, the fact that you may feel you know little about literature is not relevant: the poem is composed of two simple declarative sentences and the problems the sentences pose are similar to virtually any two sentences you translate in a technical document.) After translating the poem, note your decision-making procedure. What elements of the poem have you attempted to capture in your translation? When there were conflicts between translating specific aspects of the poem, what elements did you privilege? Where have you made choices? How have you handled dissonances? Make some brief notes about your choices and process.

If you decide to skip over preparing an actual translation of the poem, please stop for a few minutes to consider the problems faced by a reader or a translator of this poem. Ask yourself what problems of interpretation the poem raises, where I use the term *interpretation* advisedly. What questions does the poem raise that the translator needs to address? What choices and decisions must a translator make to translate this poem? What decisions would you be inclined to make in order to translate the text? Make a few notes to record your thoughts.

Compare your translation (or your assessment of the factors to be considered in a translation) with the following examples generated by translation students at the University of Massachusetts.

> The bird's shrill
> whistle pricks,
> yellow glints
>   forewarning:
> Here atop
> Loch Laig rocks,
> war cries talk
>   this morning.
>   Tamsen Merrill, 1996

In this first version the translator interweaves themes pertaining to prophecy, warning cries, and war, resulting in an ominous tonality. Ms. Merrill suggests that the prophetic note foretells the possibility of war and that war is the cause of the foreboding. There is ambiguity as to whether the "yellow glints" refer to the color of the branch or to the bird's beak, and thus the imagery here is very condensed. She also privileges the Irish form, holding the lines to three syllables each and uses English off-rhymes to mirror some qualities of Irish rhyme and the rhyme scheme aaabccb. She has chosen to privilege these formal elements of the poem over the color imagery or even the identity of the bird as a blackbird.

The following Spanish version has a very different configuration.

> Avecita negra
> Que desde el ramaje dorado:
> una melodía entonas.
>
> Avecita negra
> una señal entonas
>
> De tu piquito dorado
> sobre el lago encantado?
>   María Twardy, 2003
>
> [Black little bird
> you who from the golden branches

> sings a melody.
>
> Black little bird
> is it a signal that you sing
>
> From your golden little beak
> Over the enchanted lake?]

In notes on her version, Ms. Twardy says that she replaced the color bright yellow with golden because in Spanish *dorado* (golden) provides a good collocation and *amarillo brillante* (bright yellow) is too wordy and "sounds awful" because the phrase constitutes two long words both with "ll", thus undermining "all the magic the original has". Her version reflects her sense that "the bird represents something else, a religious representation maybe" and that "what the bird is really doing with its note is sending a signal, but we don't know for sure what kind of signal it is". Moreover, instead of using Loch Laig, which is local to Ireland, she decided to keep only the word for lake (*lago*), replacing the proper name with the adjective for enchanted (*encantado*); she imagined Belfast Lake "as a mysterious, isolated, and beautiful place". Interestingly enough, unbeknownst to Ms. Twardy but a testimony to her literary sensibility, there are many supernatural legends associated with Belfast Loch (Loch Laig) in Ireland. Here a different set of thematics is chosen from those of the previous translation, and the form shifts considerably (in part because words are longer in Spanish than in Old Irish), yet the translator builds rhyme into the translation, including homonymic rhyme in a scheme abcacbb.

Murphy imagines the bird on the yellow-heaped branch as singing from a flowering gorse-bush presumably in spring (1956:174). Here he is probably influenced by the appearance of the blackbird in other early Irish poems, notably epigrams and other poems associated with the arrival of spring and good weather, because the blackbird's beautiful call is characteristically heard in Ireland in May and June. It also may be that Murphy did not know about the existence of the blackbird's alarm cry and that he was only familiar with the song that has made the blackbird famous as one of the world's most melodious songbirds.[4] It is possible, however, to read the "branch piled-yellow" in other ways, and some translations image the bird calling out amid the golden leaves of autumn rather than the yellow flowers of spring. These images may reflect the superb autumn colors of the New England landscape in October, the month many of my students translated their versions. The ominous tone in some of their translations also captures the foreboding that New Englanders feel just before our harsh snowy

---

[4] See Murphy (1956, numbers 2, 6, and 52) for more poems featuring blackbirds; in number 6 the song of the blackbird is called *cas* (literally 'curly', i.e., 'trilling'). We don't know how much of an ornithologist Murphy was, nor do we know whether he considered that the poem might be a counterdiscourse to the other blackbird poems intertextually related in the medieval Irish poetic corpus.

winter sets in. These are, of course, readings that are compatible with autumn in Ireland as well, which shares the golden leaves of New England, though not so many of the fiery reds and oranges, and also brings foreboding of winter, though more for penetrating damp and dark rather than snow.

Here is an example of such a translation.

> From perched atop
> an autumn branch
> a little bird
>   is waiting.
> 'Cross Belfast Loch
> through yellow bill
> he sounds his call
>   of warning.
>
>   Erica Pasqualucci, 2000

In Ms. Pasqualucci's poem the cause of the foreboding is quite different from that in the Merrill version above. Winter is suggested more strongly than war as the cause of the apprehension, yet it is interesting to note that the end of autumn (the end of harvest, the return of the livestock from the upper pastures) also marked the beginning of one of the two seasons of war in medieval Ireland, as some legal and literary texts indicate.[5] Thus, unknown to both Ms. Pasqualucci and Ms. Merrill, their translations converge on what is plausibly a central node of the poem's thematic concerns: a foreboding about the return of the season of war (whether associated with the dismal season of winter or the flowery season of summer). In this reading the return of war is signaled by the blackbird's alarm cry, where the blackbird itself can double for the crows and ravens associated with the war goddesses, and the yellow color signals either the changing foliage of the autumn trees or the flowering of the gorse. In Ms. Pasqualucci's version the formalism of the poem is again emphasized by the short lines with the syllabic pattern 44434443 and by the rhyme and off-rhyme linking lines 4 and 8, 6 and 7, and 1 and 5, as well as by the substantial alliteration in the poem.

A different approach entirely is taken in the following dynamic-equivalence version in Dholuo, a Nilo-Saharan language of which various dialects are spoken by the Luo people in western Kenya, northern Uganda, and southern Sudan. Dholuo is the native language of the translator.

> Tel-tel
> Winyo matin no.

---

[5] Thus, for example, the great military raid in *Táin Bó Cúailnge* commences after Samain (November 1), the start of winter. The other season for war was summer. Significantly in one text with legal import, military service from clients is excluded in spring and fall. I am indebted here to Gene Haley for information on these points.

Dhoge bith.
Oywak kor ka achwich
Gweng Kanjira.
E wi yien ma oti eliel.

Milton Obote Joshua, 2004

[Woodpecker
that small bird
has a sharp beak
pecking on the right hand side
in the village of Kanjira
on the tree growing out of the mound.]

Here the blackbird has become a woodpecker, a bird whose sound is considered ominous in East Africa. The sound itself is represented with onomatopoeia (*tel-tel*) in the poem. Mr. Obote Joshua writes that the sharp beak represents the physical beak of the bird, but it also implies the ability of the bird to forecast a dreadful or ominous event. Moreover, the word *yuak* in line 4 signifies 'mourning' in some contexts. The piled-yellow branch becomes a mound of red earth here, which could be either a jutting termite hill or the mound of earth visible on a newly dug grave; and the tree growing out of the mound has both a physical meaning and a metaphoric one. Finally, the poem is relocated from Ireland to Kenya and set in the village of Kanjira, one of the communities of Dholuo speakers who reside on the southern shores of Lake Victoria in western Kenya. Kanjira is an administrative center that reminds the poet of Amherst, Massachusetts, where the translation was composed. All these cultural readjustments preempt most of the formal qualities of the poem, and yet the translator maintains an oral tone reflective of the literature of his audience (and of medieval Ireland) in his use of onomatopoeia and very short words. In addition, the Dholuo poem replaces the 24 syllables of Irish with a very tight 28 syllables.

A still more radical treatment of the poem is the phonetic translation that follows.

In and beck
row leak fate
doe run whip
    glum-we-thee
foe curd fade
oust Lag Lake
lone doe cried
    cairn-we-thee.

Erik Olmsted, 1997

As in the case of the translations of Catullus by Celia and Louis Zukofsky (1969), here Mr. Olmsted decides that "the medium is the massage" and the meaning itself. Carefully choosing monosyllabic English words whose sounds correspond with those of the Irish words, he closely reproduces the sounds and meter of the Irish poem. Seemingly abandoning semantic meaning altogether, Mr. Olmsted nonetheless manages to suggest some of the thematic content by picking words that indicate a rural setting (*doe*) and augury (*fate*).

The translation strategy is curiously appropriate for a poem from Celtic tradition, which has been characterized by Thomas Parry with reference to Welsh poetry as follows.

> It is important here to recall the critical standpoint which determined Welsh poetry down to the end of the eighteenth century, that is to say, so long as the least element remained of what can properly be called the Welsh tradition. *That standpoint is that sound is as important as sense; that metre and . . . the whole framework of verse, are as much a part of the aesthetic effect as what is said. . . .* The tendency of modern criticism has been to consider primarily the thought expressed in a poem; as for the rhythm, the rhymes, the alliteration, they are desirable no doubt but are regarded as an adornment of the verse, additional elements, so to say, introduced to give beauty to the work. The poetry of today is read with the eye, and the eye is the door of the understanding. The poetry of old was heard with the ear, was recited or sung, and the ear is the gateway to the heart. The complex effect produced by the sound of answering consonants, rhymes floating on the hearing, old words bringing with them a fragment of the past into the memory and uniting yesterday and today . . . that was the way in which poetry gave satisfaction to our fathers. Much the same satisfaction as is got from instrumental music, in which there are neither words nor intelligible meaning at all. (1962:48-49, original emphasis)

Parry continues

> We can easily imagine many a prince listening to the recitation of a poem in his court without "comprehending" it, except that he understood it to be a eulogy of himself. The truth is no doubt that the thing was so much of a tradition, and the prince had heard so much singing of his praises and those of his household ever since he could remember anything that the magical old words and the strange, polished phrases had become like the music of the organ in his ears, or like the Latin sentences in the Mass. Though he could doubtless understand occasional words and sentences, he had no desire to concentrate on following the sense of every line, for it was enough for him to hear the elegance shown in the deft repetition of the consonants and the long string of rhymes, and to enjoy the knowledge that the whole was a eulogy on himself. Indeed there is often but little meaning in the verse; hundreds of the lines are not much more than eulogistic sounds. (1962:48)

Parry is writing about later medieval Welsh poetry, but much the same could be said of most early medieval Irish poetry. Thus, Mr. Olmsted's phonological translation preserving the meter and sounds of the poem while downplaying the sense is not at all amiss for transposing a poem from a culture that valued sound and formal structuring in poetry as much as medieval Irish culture did.

The translations quoted here are a very small sample of the versions of this short Irish poem that have been generated through the years by my students and others who have tried their hand at this poem. There have been classical Chinese versions, where each line has the traditional symmetry of characters and golden imagery evokes associations with the emperor; there have been imagist versions that Pound would have loved; there have been translations that focused on the contrasting color imagery of black and yellow; there have been limericks that signaled "Irishness" to the writer; and there have been many other versions with interesting strategies as well. No doubt, if you have done a translation yourself, your version will have similarities to some of the versions we've looked at here and differences also. Even if you've merely inventoried what would have to be considered in a translation, you will find that the actual versions printed above have introduced possibilities of meaning that did not occur to you. I always find it amazing to see how many different ways people can read and interpret a text that I know well, even a small and rather straightforward text like the twenty-four-syllable poem we have been considering.

What do these radical differences in meaning produced by the translators of this poem signify about translation? Do the differences suggest that these students (many of whom are trained translators incidentally) are bad translators or brilliant translators? That they have an inadequate understanding of the text or the culture or that they are incredibly perceptive readers? That translation is ultimately impossible or able to reach across time and culture? Beyond translation, what do the results say about the meaning of the source text? About how the source audience would have understood the text? What do these translations tell us about textual interpretation? About understanding in general?

Modeled on techniques developed in the North American translation workshops, an exercise such as this is important not merely because it demonstrates the creativity, artistry, and skill of translators, though it does all of that.[6] The exercise takes us to the heart of questions about meaning in general and meaning in translation in particular. It demonstrates that meaning is far more complex than the semantic meaning privileged in translation pedagogy, as illustrated by the poems focused on preserving sound and form. The exercise raises issues about

---

[6] On the approach to translation of the North American translation workshops, see Gentzler (2001:5-43). A virtuosic exploration of meaning and form in translation based on the repeated translations of a single text – reminiscent of the translation workshop approach – is found in Hofstadter (1997).

the plenitude and variability of meaning that need to be discussed and understood by translators and translation scholars alike. It demonstrates in a tangible way how translators determine, construct, and create meaning in their work, illustrating at once the ways that the meaning of any translation is more restricted than the meaning of the source text and yet more inclusive at the same time. In sum the exercise problematizes the meaning of meaning in translation, indicating the necessity to explore the nature of meaning further in order to understand human communication and translation as a special form of communication.

7.2 Where Does Meaning Reside?

Another way to problematize the question of meaning in translation is to ask people directly to brainstorm where meaning lies in the process of translation. One can begin with the hypothesis that is being interrogated in this section. Let us assume for the sake of argument that the task of the translator is to transpose or transfer the meaning of the source language text to the receptor language text, so that the translation "means" the same thing as the source text.[7] Where then does meaning reside in a text? Where should a translator look for the meaning to be transposed?

Asking such questions directly is a good way to introduce a group of translators to the problems of the role of meaning in translation. Brainstorming such questions in a group is a particularly effective way to proceed. The advantage of brainstorming the problematic of meaning is that people will give different answers, thus complementing each other's approaches to the question and supplementing each other's views in cases where they are limited. Moreover, the swiftness of brainstorming gets many ideas on the table quickly without restraint or censure.[8] Because most readers of this book are not likely to have to hand a

---

[7] As in earlier chapters of this book, when I speak of a "text" here, I am including oral utterances as well as written ones.

[8] Brainstorming is a technique in which a group of people freely generates ideas pertaining to a question, an issue, or a problem very quickly and without comment about responses as they are generated. Usually there is one person who keeps the session going by restating the question (e.g., "where does meaning reside in a text to be translated?") and by recognizing people who wish to contribute. Another person records the responses in a place visible to the whole group (e.g., on a blackboard or a large sheet of paper). People are asked to give short responses in quick succession without comment on each other's statements. The object is to generate as many ideas as possible as quickly as possible, some of which will be pertinent, others not necessarily so. After the group winds down or after a specified interval has passed (e.g., "let's brainstorm this question for ten minutes"), the group then considers the results, groups like things together, gets rid of redundancies and things that do not fit, comments on particular points raised, and discusses the overall results. The technique is an excellent non-threatening means of stimulating people to think actively and quickly about an issue and to be participatory.

group of people who can be called upon immediately to brainstorm these issues, it will therefore be useful again for you to put the book down at this point for ten minutes or so and to think about how you would answer the question being posed. Where do *you* locate meaning in a source text? Think in terms of large categories as well as specifics. Make a quick list of your thoughts.

The results of such brainstorming sessions with my students are found on the following pages. The list is both somewhat redundant and also incomplete. The redundancy is partly a function of the way that one textual element can serve multiple purposes in terms of meaning. For example, a metaphor will have lexical meaning, but it can also have structural significance in a text or consti-tute a key word.[9] The list is incomplete of necessity, in part because any given text – oral or written – has its own specific configurations that bring in factors proper to itself; in part because of the self-referential quality of texts; and in part because of contextual aspects of meaning. Meaning is also an open-ended affair, with new types of meanings constantly being generated as cultures change. The incompleteness of the list is also partly a function of the particular limitations that my students and I share, including limitations in our linguistic and cultural knowledge and our positionalities. I am confident that your list will include things that we have not thought of and I welcome suggestions readers have for enlarging and improving the repertory.

---

[9] Cf. Nord (1997:69-70) who explores "vertical slices" of a text, arguing that a single func-tion of a text can be expressed at every rank of the text. Meaning like culture or function is not rank bound, and specific aspects of meaning can operate at different ranks of the text simultaneously.

"WHERE DOES MEANING RESIDE IN A TEXT?"

content
        subject matter
        information
        reference
        logic, truth value
        emotive values
        amount of detail, technicality, accessibility
        what is assumed and unspoken
        author's or text's presentation of the subject
        author's or text's view of or perspective on the subject

narrative elements
        order and temporality of narration
        plot
        characters
        setting
        themes
        point of view
        narrative voice
        focalization[10]
        foregrounding, salience

ideological framing
        ideological and political positioning
        discourses
        values
        overt or implicit narrativities
        suggestions, implications, subtexts
        perspective and point of view
        affiliations and commitments of the author
        relationship to cultural consensus, cultural norms
        relationship to political contexts
        opposition to established discourses

pragmatics
        function of the text
        speech acts (e.g., lie, satire, parody, irony)
        illocutionary and perlocutionary force

---

[10] Bal (1997:142-61) discusses the concept of focalization.

linguistic practices (e.g., politeness, gendered language)
rhetorical structure
cultural paradigms with linguistic exponence
other sociolinguistic considerations
performance markers

form[11]

text type, genre
set forms (e.g., sonnet, business letter)
structural elements (e.g., iteration)
literary "ornament" (e.g., rhyme, alliteration, meter, etc.)
timing, duration, pace, length
sequence
textual segmentation
titles, labeling

style[12]

virtuosity
clarity or obscurity
tone

language variety
dialect
register
technical language
variation in language variety vs. homogeneity

textual or literacy practices and structures
information load
redundancy, noise
pauses, silences, gaps, omissions, blank spaces
"the white of the page"
key words
images, symbols
tropes (e.g., metaphors, metonymies, hyperbole)
dissociated metaphors[13]
controlling metaphors
self-referentiality of the text

---

[11] The relationship between meaning and form at many levels is discussed in Bolinger (1977) and Hofstadter (1997). Form at the level of the text is also related to the elements included below under textual practices.

[12] The question of style in relation to meaning is exceptionally complex; cf. Boase-Beier (2006) for one approach.

[13] This concept is developed in O'Connor (1956).

intertextuality
  allusions
  quotations
  filiation in cultural or literary tradition

iconicity[14]

grammar
  syntax[15]
  word order
  parts of speech, tense
  morphology
  marked vs. unmarked formations and constructions
  emphasis, stress, fronting
  placement of words in a sentence, on the page
  linguistic function

words
  semantic meanings (connotations, denotations, possibly etymological
    meanings)
  idiomatic meanings, idioms
  figures of speech, metaphors
  "metaphors we live by"[16]
  imagery
  ambiguity, word play
  polysemy, shared exponence
  semiosis
  semantic fields
  choice of words (compared with other possible choices)
  contrasts, juxtapositions
  collocations
  repetition, iteration
  deixis
  names, proper nouns

sound
  phonemic associations

---

[14] A good discussion is found in Boase-Beier (2006:138-45). See also Bolinger (1977). Iconicity can exist at every rank of the text, including sound, word choice, syntax, and the macro structures of the text.

[15] Bolinger (1977) discusses the relationship between meaning and form at the level of the sentence, as well as other levels.

[16] Such as those discussed in Lakoff and Johnson (1980).

onomatopoeia
paronymy
rhythm
intonation
voice

performative elements of language
innovation
depletion
defamiliarization
difficulty, frustration, resistance
ambiguities, word play

textual technology
medium (e.g., manuscript, print text, electronic text)
script[17]
textual segmentation
arrangement on the page (e.g., concrete poetry)
punctuation
labels, titles
presentation (e.g., printing quality)
font, typeface, graphology[18]
illustrations
concrete physical qualities (e.g., type of paper, colors, book cover)
publisher
textual context (e.g., series, anthology, other associated texts)
paratexts (e.g., introduction, footnotes, appendices)

historical and cultural context
historical and cultural background and presuppositions
cultural practices
material culture
customs
elements signaling the habitus
signature concepts of a culture in the text
cultural representation
cultural symbolism, tropes, myths, discourses
presence of foreign linguistic and cultural elements
quantity of material transferred or transculturated from other cultural
     contexts

[17] The intersection of script, meaning, and translation is discussed in the article "Script in Translation" by Gordon Brotherston (in Baker 1998:211-18).
[18] Cf. Hofstadter (1997:194).

socioeconomic context
       time and place of production and of publication
       status of the language of the text, the nation it comes from
       identity and fame of the author or speaker
       place in the oeuvre of the author or speaker
       history of the production or ownership of the text
       availability, price, distribution system
       history of the text (e.g., its fame and prestige, its position in the
             literary system and the canon)
       metatexts about the text
       criticism, reviews, interpretive tradition
       intended audience
       reception context
       function of the text

implied user or reader
       initial recipients (e.g., a king, a mass audience)
       accessibility or exclusivity
       patronage (initiator)
       construction of the implied reader

reader responses
       personal responses, personal experiences
       meanings associated with secondary historical and
             socioeconomic contexts

disruptions, violations, or absence of any of the above

Notice that English is a good language for a discussion about meaning in part because the word *meaning* is such a broad-guage term with a large semantic field. There are other words in English that have similar (though more restricted) domains – *sense* and *significance*, for example – but *meaning* is the common word that is most inclusive. It encompasses everything from technical and scientific knowledge to reference and ideology and even emotion. All semiotic systems are covered, text and subtext, verbal substance and materialist context. Meaning is affective and cognitive, surface and symbol, concrete and discursive. Many other languages also have such broad-guage words, but discussions of meaning in some languages employ vocabulary that privileges certain types of meaning – notably semantic meaning – thereby presupposing an answer to what is being questioned here, implicitly asserting very Western perspectives on the role of meaning in translation. By contrast, the question "what is the meaning of this text?" can be partially answered by any of the items on the preceding list. To narrow the meaning of *meaning* in English, one must add some qualifier – *semantic* meaning, *ideological* meaning, *emotional* meaning – for otherwise meaning of any sort can be inferred. Alternatively, one can narrow the domain of *meaning* by designating a word – such as *reference* – to serve as a technical term representing a specialized type of meaning in a particular discursive situation.[19] It should be obvious that in this discussion we are considering the role of meaning in translation in the broadest sense possible.

Let us turn to the results of brainstorming the question of meaning in a text. I am assuming that by now readers have compiled a brief inventory of places where meaning enters the translation process to be considered in translating a text; readers should also have inspected the list on the previous pages. Notice that there are many types of meaning listed above, including linguistic meaning, sociolinguistic meaning, socioeconomic and historical meaning, content, ideological significance, and so forth. The question of meaning is so complex that even the various *types* of meaning that a translator contends with are not all adequately represented in the list.

The process of trying to specify where meaning resides in translation is also worth commenting upon. First, it should be clear that the prompt for the brainstorming, "where does meaning reside in a text?", is a trick question: the meaning of a text does not all reside within the text itself, and students are usually fully aware of this problem in responding to the prompt. Much of the meaning of a text and the meaning that a translator must consider lies outside the text itself, as the list indicates. This includes meaning that the translator as reader brings to the process of translation, including any contextual, material, or functional

---

[19] Note that the designation of this type of technical term for a facet of meaning is reminiscent of Wittgenstein's discussion of drawing boundaries for cluster concepts such as number or game considered in 2.4 above. It is possible to assert such a boundary, but such an assertion only functions in the narrow confines of the situation stipulated.

meanings presupposed. In literary studies a threefold distinction regarding literary analysis is common: the critic must consider text, context, and intertext. That is, to understand the meaning of a text, a person must look at the text, but the context is equally important, as are other texts (the intertexts) to which the text is related.[20] A reader makes inferences about meaning based on all of these factors – text, context, intertexts – and hence the meaning of all of them must be considered in the process of translation. In an astute discussion of the role of meaning in translation, Kathleen Davis (2001:12-30) argues that text cannot be cleanly delineated from context, that there is no clear boundary between the linguistic and the non-linguistic, and that meaning is open and cannot be fully determined. Moreover, she points out that everything meaningful participates in a systematic play of differences (Davis 2001:23). Further, Rosemary Arrojo indicates that "if meaning is social and, therefore, inescapably conventional, it is not intrinsic to texts or to any other form of discourse but is, rather, always ideologically and historically produced" (1998:34). The result, as she concludes, is that "different groups within . . . societies and cultures will always be inclined towards heterogeneity rather than consensus" about meaning (Arrojo 1998:35).

Thus, the blackbird poem in the last section would have a very different meaning if it were discovered to be a modern forgery of a medieval poem. Because the contexts and intertexts would be so different in the two cases – as would questions pertaining to various linguistic and sociolinguistic aspects of the text, including functions, speech acts, and literary genres – the inferences a reader could make about the meaning of the text would be altered considerably. One might, for example, ask about the ideological, cultural, and literary motivation for writing an ersatz medieval poem in the twenty-first century – all of which would be very different from comparable features of this poem dated from the ninth century. This point about the significance of context for the meaning of a text has been made brilliantly by Jorge Luis Borges in "Pierre Menard, autor del Quijote" ("Pierre Menard, Author of the Quixote"). Because a source text and its translation emerge from and function within different contexts, it follows *ipso facto* that they have different meanings. If for no other reason than context, therefore, it is illusory to imagine that meaning preservation or transfer can or should be the goal of translation.

A similar difficulty is presented by reader response as a factor in the meaning of texts. In literary studies reader reception theorists such as Wolfgang Iser have demonstrated that texts are always incomplete and that readers bring their own knowledge and experiences to bear on realizing or filling out the meaning

---

[20] One sees the effect of intertextuality in Murphy's interpretation of the blackbird poem discussed in the last section. He was aware of the other medieval poems associating blackbirds and springtime (having edited them), and hence he interpreted the yellow branch as the flowering gorse in May.

of a text.[21] Douglas Hofstadter observes, "How far a translator can reasonably drift from a literal text has everything to do with the fabric of human associations – with what lies mentally close to what, and what lies far away. Such associations come, of course, from deep familiarity with how the world itself is structured. If one has lived through millions of complex experiences, as we all have – including vicarious ones, from books we've read to movies we've seen to adventures we've heard friends relate – then just a few words can trigger rich imagery at a conscious level, as well as vast clouds of associations at a more subliminal, invisible level" (1997:9a). Different contexts will create different clouds of associations and issue in different meanings.

It goes without saying that authors and translators cannot ever fully anticipate or control readers' responses, and thus it follows that authors and translators cannot circumscribe the meaning of their own textual production. Nor does a text mean the same thing to author and translator or to any two readers. A text elicits different responses depending on the individual reader's (or hearer's) experience, situated knowledge, and affective life, and the meaning of the text is configured differently as a result. The variation of textual meaning across individuals has been discussed by functionalist translation theorists, and Christiane Nord (1997:31) notes that "a 'text' is as many texts as there are receivers".[22] But there is a self-reflexive issue here as well, for a translator as the chief reader in the translation process – and in some ways as one of the most perceptive readers – also contributes meanings that emerge when the translator becomes the writer of the translated text, a point that the translator should remain aware of. The variation in meanings that readers perceive and that translators construct is illustrated by the range of meanings exhibited in the translations of the blackbird poem in the last section.

Reader responses also vary by time and place, often in completely unpredictable ways, as a text moves through history. Thus, James Joyce's *Ulysses* was read in very different ways after Hitler came to power and began persecuting the Jews of Europe; Joyce's use of a "Jewish hero", Leopold Bloom, came to be seen as a more universalist and humane gesture and as a much more politicized act than it was when the book was initially published in 1922. Joyce could in no way have anticipated how his text would change meaning as a result of Nazism.[23] Similar

---

[21] Iser (1974) provides examples of the process. Many of these contextual and readerly factors related to meaning are illuminated by relevance theory as developed by Sperber and Wilson (1995), which indicates that readers must make inferences about meaning on the basis of their situated knowledge. See also Gutt (2000a, 2000b).

[22] Arrojo (2002) offers an excellent discussion of the struggle for control of meaning in translation. From a psychoanalytic perspective Chodorow (1999) explores the affective mechanisms behind the differences of perceived meaning among individuals.

[23] Joyce actually configures Bloom more as an ersatz Jew than as a Jew, and the configuration evokes early Irish mythic patterns and specific Irish political discourses (cf. Tymoczko 1994:24-43). Levin (1941) initiated the modern reading of this figure as a courageous mark of resistance to European (specifically Nazi) antisemitism.

points have been persuasively argued in Walter Benjamin's "The Task of the Translator" (1923), where Benjamin maintains that texts are not stable over time. Thus, rather than preserving or transferring the meaning of a source text, a translator adds new meanings to the text. Benjamin argues that the shift of meaning resulting from translation ensures that the text has an "afterlife" or survival (*Überleben, Nachleben, Fortleben*) in virtue of the added value of the translation itself.

Let us examine in greater depth the meanings of a text related to intertextuality. Imagine again that the Irish poem in section 7.1 were discovered to be a forgery from our era. In that case the literary and cultural reference points would not only be the medieval Irish poetic tradition in general and other medieval Irish poems dealing with blackbirds and "nature" in particular, but would have to include the poetry of the European romantics, the poems of Robert Frost, and the work of other modern poets, including "Thirteen Ways of Looking at a Blackbird" by Wallace Stevens. If we discovered that the forgery had been done by W.B. Yeats during the Irish revival, the poem would have political overtones associated with Irish cultural nationalism; an entirely different set of intertexts would then serve as reference points for the meaning of the poem, including the various revivals of Irish literature in English such as those staged by the Irish dramatic movement during the period 1898-1920. Such intertexts provide frameworks for understanding the meaning of a text related to its form, its themes, and its historical and political grounding, as well as its mobilization of and dissent from established discourses.

These various aspects of the context-driven evolution of meaning that occur in the life of a text and that distinguish a source text from its translation put in question whether it is ever possible to construct a "dynamic-equivalence" text in the sense that Nida (1964) envisions. It is difficult to understand how a translator can fully determine what the meaning of a text was for its "original" audience and even more difficult to see how that meaning could be reproduced for any other audience in a different context. Although we seem to have an intuitive sense of what Nida means by the concept dynamic equivalence, strictly speaking we must recognize that the meanings of so-called dynamic-equivalence texts are significantly different from those of their sources.[24]

Readers will notice that the list above contains still other external sources of meaning associated with a text, including the identity and cultural position of the author, the patron, the textual technology (e.g., oral vs. written, manuscript vs. printed text), and the actual nature of the textual production (e.g., illustrator,

---

[24] Many of the same questions arise with respect to functionalist theories in general. Nord (1997:9, cf. 2003) observes that there are also situations where equivalence in function is not desired: for example, when the target text has a different purpose from that of the source text or when the target audience is different from the source audience. We should note that by definition the target audience is always significantly different from the source audience, if only in virtue of language and culture. On these issues see also Fawcett (1997:58-60) and sources cited.

quality and price, number of texts printed, mode of dissemination). In translating it is not simply sufficient to treat a text as if its meaning were a closed system circumscribed by the words of the text. One must always consider the meanings derived from the material basis of its production, as is the case with any other cultural form.

Aside from the range of meanings that accrue to a text because of context, reader response, and material circumstances, there are still other difficulties with viewing the task of the translator as the re-creation of the meaning of the source text in another language. The very possibility of stability of meaning across linguistic boundaries has been disputed by modern linguists who see meaning as language specific. This argument was applied to translation early in the history of translation studies by scholars such as Roman Jakobson and J.C. Catford, and their arguments have been generally accepted in the field. The result is that most linguists in translation studies – as well as most other scholars in point of fact – agree that shifts of meaning are the usual and normal consequence of translation, if for no other reason than anisomorphisms of language. Although writers such as Jakobson (1959) and Catford (1965:43-48) would agree that it is possible to inject some source language meanings into a translation, translation does not normally follow this trajectory. Difference in meaning is the usual result, with "sameness" of meaning being the exception that proves the rule.[25]

Another interesting aspect of the meaning of texts in the list on pages 278-82 is suggested by the clusters of meanings that lie outside the realm of semantic meaning as such. Semantic meaning is traditionally the type of meaning privileged in (Western) philosophical theories of meaning, as well as in translator training. Some of the types of meaning that lie outside the domain of semantic meaning are well recognized in translation studies, for instance, linguistic meaning.[26] Form, genre, poetics (including sound, rhythm, rhyme, timing, duration, pace, and other literary conventions), and style carry meanings that go well beyond semantic meaning. They have been discussed in translation studies less as types of meaning than as equivalence problems, but it is important not to efface their semiotic significance. From the form of an utterance at the level of the phrase and the syntax of a sentence (Bolinger 1977, Lakoff and Johnson 1980) to the most complex structures of rhetoric and literary form, formal meanings of texts have been a staple of literary analysis.[27] Functional meanings also go beyond

---

[25] Cf. the discussion above in section 1.3.

[26] An early discussion of linguistic meaning is found in Nida (1964:57-69).

[27] A poem like "Jabberwocky", the translation of the blackbird poem by Eric Olmsted in section 7.1 above, and the Zukofskys' translations of the poetry of Catullus all have meaning, but those meanings are not primarily semantic meanings as such. They fuse linguistic meanings and formal meanings, presupposing an understanding of these types of meaning for the recognition of the significance of the text. On the relation of these forms of meaning to translation, see, for example, Hofstadter (1997), Berman (2000), and the discussion of Berman's signifying process of literary works in Munday (2001:149-51).

the level of semantics, from speech acts and the semiotic constructions in advertisements to the complex performative meanings of traditional oral literature (including spells and proverbs) and literary modes such as comedy.[28] Similarly the physical characteristics of a text – whether in manuscript, printed, or electronic form – have material, economic, and sociolinguistic meanings that require both practical and theoretical consideration. These various examples are just a few of the many types of meaning that extend beyond semantics and content, and that command a translator's attention. For hundreds of years translation in Western contexts has privileged close semantic meaning over larger patterns of formal and functional meaning, thus privileging simpler forms of similarity relations rather than analogical forms of translation. Despite the tendency to privilege semantic meaning and even to think of it as meaning *tout court* in Western cultural and pedagogical contexts, brainstorming elicits many other ways of signifying, allowing participants to contemplate the broad range of meanings that translators contend with.

Brainstorming the question of meaning reveals many other difficulties in claiming that preservation of meaning is the goal of translation. What is immediately obvious, however, from an inventory of elements that contribute to the meaning of a text – even a schematized and an incomplete list like the one above – is that it is impossible for a translator to attempt to recreate and transfer all the source text meanings that can be discerned and inventoried. The sheer number of parameters to be considered in assessing the meaning of an utterance, the complexity of determining textual meaning, and the openness of meaning indicate that it is not feasible for a translator to attempt to transfer meaning in a comprehensive way. There is no decision-making procedure that can take into account all the factors surveyed above, notwithstanding the fact that they do not constitute a complete inventory of the types of meaning that are encountered in translation. It should be clear from the brainstorming exercise that describing translation as the transfer or preservation of meaning is not an appropriate way to formulate the goal of translation and the task of the translator. No translator can preserve all the meanings and all the types of meanings that a text encodes and that are indicated by its context and elicited by its reading. There is simply too much information for a translator to attend to and to attempt to reproduce. Instead of actually attempting to transfer meaning, a translator copes with the surplus of meaning in a text by making choices about meaning, prioritizing those meanings, and creating a heuristic for constructing the translated text so as to perform the meanings desired.

This brainstorming exercise on meaning, therefore, returns us again to the notion of translation as a metonymic process. Many functionalists recognize the metonymic aspect of translation. Nord, for example, writes that "a translation is thus a new offer of information in the target culture about some information offered in the source culture and language"; she sees translators as choosing

---

[28] On meaning in traditional literatures, see Turner (1982), Basso (1990, especially 138-73), and Appiah (2000).

"items they regard as interesting, useful or adequate to the desired purposes" and transferring "the chosen informational items . . . to the target culture using the presentation the translator believes is appropriate for the given purpose" (1997:26). Recognition of the metonymic nature of translation also has implications for formulating the role of meaning transmission and construction in translation. Nord observes that the nature of meaning in translation "does not allow us to speak of *the* meaning of *the* source text being transferred to *the* target receivers" (1997:32). Because only part of the meaning of a source text is ever transposed in translation, the meaning of a translation results from the choices that constitute the translator's decision-making process; these choices shape the construction of the translated text which then accretes still other meanings associated with its recontextualization and the contributions of a new readership.[29]

Persuasive as they are, these pragmatic considerations are secondary to even more fundamental issues related to determining and transferring meaning in translation. Kwame Anthony Appiah points out that the sheer volume of meanings is a subordinate consideration in the difficulty in seeing preservation of meaning as the goal of translation. He writes, "the reason why we cannot speak of the perfect translation . . . is not that there is a definite set of desiderata and we know they cannot all be met; it is rather that there is no definite set of desiderata" (Appiah 2000:425). The translator is the one who decides on and creates the desiderata, the one who establishes the criteria that determine which meanings are to be (re)constructed in the receptor text. In view of the necessity of decision making in the task of translation, Appiah argues "that we should give up language that implies an epistemology in which the work has already a meaning that is waiting for us to find" (2000:426). Commenting on this passage, Davis notes that such a reworking of the epistemology of meaning in translation "returns responsibility to the translator, who needs to be aware of the cultural risks involved. Without extractable, transcendent meaning or a neutral reading strategy that somehow exists without implication in institutional, political, social, and economic forces, the translator must take on the impossible but necessary task of decision" (2001:65-66). For these reasons, a reconceptualized and expanded understanding of the role of meaning in translation leads directly to a heightened awareness of the agency and power of translators and to the importance of the ideological and ethical responsibilities of translators as well.[30]

7.3 A Brief Excursus on the Nature of Meaning

The nexus between the epistemology of meaning and the agency of translators indicates that it will be useful to give a very brief summary of thinking about

---

[29] Nord (1997:120) approaches this question of decision making about meaning from a functionalist point of view on translation; cf. Davis (2001:12-30, 91-106) who discusses the question of meaning and decision making from the point of deconstruction.

[30] These topics are also taken up in Lane-Mercier (1997) and Arrojo (1998).

meaning in other disciplines, particularly philosophy, during the last century. It is obviously impossible to give a full survey of the subject in this context, but a brief map of the terrain can serve as a reference point for considerations about meaning in translation. For more than a hundred years, meaning has been the subject of intense and protracted debate, even turmoil, in many domains of Western learning: linguistics, philosophy, religion, most of the humanistic disciplines, the social sciences, and even the natural sciences. The debate affects such questions as whether there is truth, how to interpret evidence, where the boundary of fact can be drawn, and even how statistics should be evaluated.

This sort of contention was not typical of earlier centuries. The so-called Platonic theory of meaning, inherited from antiquity but amalgamated with Christian doctrine at the end of the Roman period and during the Middle Ages, produced a longstanding and relatively stable view of the relationship linking ideas, language, and the realm of experience in the West. This Platonic view of meaning had prevailed for centuries by the nineteenth century. A schematized way to conceptualize the Platonic paradigm is to conceive of the existence of a realm of ideal (abstract, disembodied) ideas or forms (as Plato called them), each of which corresponds to some changeless abstract concept that was seen as universal. These forms (connected with the realm of the divine) were understood as being imperfectly represented in the world of physical experience. Although language was used to speak of the (imperfect) world of experience, the meaning of language was derived from its relationship to the ideal forms and ideas beyond the tangible world. Within such a Platonic framework of meaning, therefore, translation can be looked on as a process of substitution, in which one code for referring to the realm of universal forms is replaced with another code referring to the same realm. In the West the concept of translation as transfer of meaning took shape within this philosophical context for understanding meaning itself.

In translation studies Platonic theories of meaning persist in the idea that translation involves "deverbalization", insofar as deverbalization suggests that translators can refer to an abstract, non-linguistic realm of ideas in moving between one language and another. Platonic theories also are implicit in ideas that translators are located "between" (cf. Tymoczko 2003). The idea of a transcendent realm that serves as an ideal point of reference for the meanings of the world is not limited to Western cultures, but that idea is inflected differently in other cultures. Note that some of the international conceptualizations of translation signaled by linguistic metaphors for translation discussed in section 2.2 suggest that the immanence of meaning makes linguistic substitution possible in translation. Others, however, suggest that meaning can only be mystically reborn, reshaped, reformulated, and revoiced in a new language, rather than being preserved or transferred unchanged. These differences are beyond the scope of the present study but they merit additional investigation.

Platonic views of meaning sustained a major challenge from positivism in the nineteenth century, which stressed observation in assessing the truth of statements of fact and recognized only "positive facts" and the relations between specific facts, more general facts, and laws. Rejecting the Platonic level of ideal forms or ideas, positivists challenged Western religious and philosophical frameworks inherited from antiquity for construing meaning. The philosophical stance of positivism looked back to the empiricist tradition associated with Hume and Locke, in which meaning was rooted in sense impressions and linked to things in the world. Because positivism rejected metaphysical and subjective views as having no claim on truth, the legitimate domain of meaningful language was seen as limited to the realm of facts and laws that could be empirically viewed as universally or objectively true. This is in part why the early Wittgenstein could hold in 1921 that "What can be said at all can be said clearly, and what we cannot talk about we must consign to silence" (1961:2-3, cf. section 1.1 above). Positivism replaced a Platonic sense of universality underlying language and meaning with another universalist criterion to which language could be referred, namely facts and laws that were observable, verifiable, and applicable in all circumstances. In positivism, as in a Platonic theory of meaning, the practicalities of translation entailed in replacing one code with another might be difficult, but in principle translation was straightforward with respect to the question of meaning.

At the beginning of the twentieth century, therefore, meaning was still a relatively simple issue in Western tradition, even though a contested one.[31] Most people either accepted some outgrowth of positivist views of meaning or they adhered to traditional Platonic views of meaning, inherited from the Greeks and incorporated into the fabric of Christian thought, even though Platonic views of language, universal forms, and experience were being brought increasingly into question. During the early decades of the twentieth century, however, positivist views of meaning were challenged by various approaches to language and philosophy (such as hermeneutics) and then further destabilized in the 1920s and 1930s by new thinking in the natural sciences that resulted in the decline of scientific positivism. These shifts in science were driven principally by developments in physics and mathematics that brought into question basic positivist understandings of facts and certainty, necessitating a reappraisal of the centrality of perspective and the importance of the position of the observer or knower. The fact that these shifts occurred in physics and mathematics was particularly damaging to positivism, which had seen meaning in those disciplines as the most certain of the certain. Scientific challenges to positivism also coalesced with challenges about meaning coming from many other directions, including psychology, cognitive science, literature, and various artistic movements (cf. above, sections 1.1 and 1.4).

---

[31] This is, of course, a very schematized narrative of meaning in Western philosophy. Cronin (2006:104 and sources cited) indicates that the beginning of the shift toward understanding semantic meaning as language specific can be discerned as early as the Renaissance.

Ever since that time Western philosophers, linguists, and others have tried in various ways to shore up the concept of meaning. They have sought to redefine the relationship between concepts or ideas, experience, and language, so as to ground the notion of meaning once again. Within philosophy, for example, the impetus to understand and recuperate meaning has been played out in most philosophical movements, from hermeneutics to the Anglo-American schools of logical positivism and the philosophy of language. The result, however, has not been a new consensus about meaning; rather, the twentieth century passed and the twenty-first century has begun with increasingly divergent approaches to the topic and a growing repertory of elements that must be considered in any theory of meaning.

Three approaches to these questions serve as examples of attempts to rethink the concept of meaning, illustrating the difficulties in the endeavor. In hermeneutics inquiry about meaning begins with the primacy of individual perspective and personal experience, in part to circumvent the positivist focus on "facts" and to reinscribe other aspects of human life – including art, religion, and individual experience – within the notion of meaning and the meaningful. Because of the focus on individual perspective, however, the difficulty in hermeneutic theories of meaning has been to match individual perceptions with the external world and to make perceptions of different individuals commensurate with each other. These issues of connection continue to be a challenge in hermeneutics and have not led to a widely accepted formulation of meaning or resolved the problematic of meaning to the satisfaction of most philosophers.

By contrast the Anglo-American school of logical positivism attempted to recuperate the notion of meaning from a more positivist starting point (as its name suggests), seeking to connect meaning with truth, certainty, universal applicability, and verifiability. Various attempts have been made to reframe meaning in terms of such things as sense data, reference, propositional logic, and truth values. Each of these concepts was the subject of intense excitement and debate for a period, but each turned out to have limited utility as a vehicle for grounding meaning as a whole (for instance, finding a way to model the complexity of ideas sufficiently, to connect meaning with language, to deal with contextual meanings, and so forth). Thus, each formulation led to some impasse, such that no agreement could be reached on its usefulness in contributing substantially to discourses about certainty in meaning.[32]

---

[32] Logical positivism is only one of many modern analytic approaches to philosophy to take up these issues. A full overview of the approaches of contemporary Western philosophy to meaning is obviously beyond the scope of this discussion, but we should note that the founder of modern analytic philosophy, Gottlob Frege, attempted to continue the Platonic tradition of meaning within the context of logic and modern views of truth. Much of the inquiry about meaning in the last 30 years has been devoted to investigations of how context or external interactions with the world determine meaning. Stanley (forthcoming) offers a brief but comprehensive overview of investigations of meaning in the philosophy of language. I am indebted to Elisabeth Camp for suggestions on this overview of meaning and philosophy; all shortcomings are my sole responsibility.

Standing somewhat outside the philosophical schools, though influencing many of them, is the work of Charles Sanders Peirce who posited a tripartite relationship linking experience, ideas, and language. Peirce's theory is couched in terms of firstness (immediate unanalyzed feeling), secondness (an occurence that results in knowledge of the factual world),[33] and thirdness (the command of feeling and action by general principles that can be correlated with continuity and projected into the future). One can see even from this schematic account that Peirce attempts to move beyond the positivist focus on facts and to make room for personal experiences and perspectives that go beyond the rational, while at the same time he attempts to make provision for more universalist perceptions of the world, including scientific and mathematical knowledge. Although firstness is a matter of unmediated affect, Peirce stresses that secondness and thirdness are mediated by signs (language in particular). That is, the knowledge of both secondness and thirdness depends primarily on signs, and he emphasizes that we think about signs in terms of other signs. Although Peirce's ideas continue to command high interest, they lead to no circumscribed notion of the nature of meaning. This is the case in part because of the problematic for meaning posed by the centrality of signs and semiotics to secondness and especially to thirdness, the locus in Peirce's scheme where laws and generalizable statements about the world are formulated. We will return briefly to the question of signs and meaning below.[34]

There are of course many other other Western philosophical schools whose inquiry has focused on the problematic of meaning in the last century; in certain respects, for example, deconstruction can be looked at as a long meditation on the meaning of meaning. The most radical recent contribution to the investigation of meaning is relevance theory, stressing the necessity for any recipient of language to make inferences based on contextual information in order to decide the meaning of an utterance (Sperber and Wilson 1995); we will return to this approach to meaning below in section 7.4.

Several points can be made about this search for the meaning of meaning and a theory of meaning. First, despite the attempts of philosophers, linguists, psychologists, cognitive scientists, and others to recuperate and ground a theory of meaning, the trajectory of thinking about meaning since the beginning of the twentieth century has revealed more and more diverse types of meaning to be accounted for. In addition to material, conceptual, and linguistic meanings, one must also now acknowledge sociolinguistic meanings, cultural and historical meanings, ideological meanings, embodied meanings, emotional meanings, cosmological meanings, and many others, only some of which are reflected in the list generated in section 7.2 by brainstorming the question of meaning in translation.

---

[33] Involved, for example, in orientation, decisions, and actions. Secondness takes place in the here and now, but involves comparison with the past.

[34] An exposition of Peirce's thought and its application to translation is found in Gorlée (1994) and Stecconi (2006).

Throughout the last hundred years, there has been a steady broadening of the concept of what must be considered with regard to meaning and significance. The result is an increasing sense of indeterminacy about how to establish the bounds of meaning or to relate truth and certainty to meaning.

Second, there is widespread agreement (even though contested in its particulars) that however one thinks about the question, meaning is something that is less objectively "out there in the world" than it is something constructed by agents, most notably by individual human beings and groups of people (namely, cultures). This widely shared view of the role of human agents in making meaning implies that most contemporary theories of meaning are constructivist in nature.

Third, virtually every theory of meaning stresses the central role of signs in constructing meaning. Because language is the most important human sign system, language itself therefore plays a fundamental role in constructing and establishing meaning. But there are problems in consequence. The relationship of language to context (including personal experience) is significant insofar as context itself shifts meaning. Moreover, because language is always in flux, if meaning is tied to signs (language), meanings cannot be stable. The current meaning of a sign looks back to earlier meanings and forward to future meanings: there is no originary, foundational meaning for any sign. In addition, signs can only be explicated in terms of other signs; for any theory of meaning, the result is a sort of infinite regress, in which again there is no stable originary or ultimate point that grounds certainty of meaning. Because signs can only be explicated in terms of other signs, the phenomenon of unlimited semiosis (involving endless chains of signs) results in semiotic associations potentially having wide variability across time, populations, and individuals. Perhaps most important in terms of the implications for translation of the link between meaning and signs are semiotic anisomorphisms and asymmetries across languages. If languages are the chief human sign systems and if languages are asymmetrical and anisomorphic, then strictly speaking the meanings of signs cross-linguistically cannot be the same or fully commensurate, nor can they be completely determined in moving across linguistic boundaries.[35]

These various aspects of contemporary Western views of meaning in other disciplines are applicable to and consistent with what is known about meaning in translation. As the results of brainstorming the role of meaning in translation indicate, translators must take into account a very diverse and wide-ranging set of phenomena in translating textual "meaning". Constructivist theories of meaning are consonant with the data that have been gathered about translation

---

[35] Davis (2001:14-19) discusses issues of meaning from the perspective of deconstruction, particularly questions related to the instability of signs. She observes that "the meaning of any text is undecidable, since it is an effect of language and not something that can be extracted and reconstituted. Translators must therefore make decisions in this strong sense. The decision-making process is one of the reasons that translations are performative events rather than replays of events that have already happened" (2001:51).

since translation studies coalesced as an academic discipline. This congruence is particularly apparent in data from descriptive studies of translation products and from observations showing that translations have a one-to-many relationship to the source text, that contextual factors (including ideology and politics) impinge on translators' constructions of meaning, that translations of the same source text can differ radically in different languages, in different contexts, and so forth. Translators construct meaning in translated texts by transposing and reformulating a selection of the wide range of diverse meaningful elements that they perceive in source texts. There is no uniformity in what different translators see as meaningful and in what they choose to construct as meaningful for their receptor audiences. Moreover, because languages differ in their patterns of semiosis and their semiotic associations, translations never have the same meaning as their source texts. Note that constructivist understandings of meaning in translation are not limited to Western thought. An appreciation of the asymmetries and differences involved in translation and the need to reformulate the source text rather than transmit it unchanged are implicit in many of the metaphors and image-schemas underlying the international terms for the cross-cultural concept translation discussed in section 2.2 above.

Because the nature of meaning continues to be contested at present, almost all theoreticians of translation acknowledge the problematic of meaning in some way, but people approach the problem from different directions, depending on their disciplinary orientation and their allegiances to specific schools within those disciplines. The problematization of meaning in translation theory reflects the problematic of meaning in other intellectual and academic domains, from linguistics and philosophy to literary studies and history, from anthropology, sociology, and cultural studies to the natural sciences and mathematics. The debate about meaning reflects fundamental changes during the last two centuries in the West about the relationship between language and experience, as the understanding of meaning has shifted from a Platonic norm to (contested) positivist views to postpositivist constructivist views of meaning. It is probably no accident that this seismic shift occurred during the same period that Western cultures had contact and contestation with so many other cultures and languages beyond the West, the period that spans the height of European imperialism through World War II to the present. The independence of most colonized territories around the world was accompanied temporally and historically by the postpositivist recognition in Western culture of the importance of alternate perspectives throughout the world, not just politically but linguistically and culturally also. The result has been a fundamental decentering of meaning itself.

What is interesting to me about an exercise like brainstorming the locus of meaning in translation with a group of students is that even a relatively small group of students reveals a broad recognition – even if in a subliminal or poorly articulated manner – of the problematic of meaning in our time, as well as an understanding of the diverse and varied ways in which a text or an utterance can have meaning. Students recognize that meaning is language specific, that it is context dependent, that it shifts depending on receptor or reader, and that it is constructivist in nature, even if they can't state those realizations in abstract language and even if their own words have to be translated into standard academic discourses. Moreover, in the specifics of their suggestions for where meaning resides, they recapitulate many of the intellectual debates pertaining to meaning that have occurred in the last half century. They generate suggestions that encapsulate embryonically the insights of diverse fields that have grappled with meaning or even coalesced in response to questions about meaning – fields such as sociolinguistics. Students also generate theoretical insights about textual reception and contextual effects related to those that are foundational to reader response theory and relevance theory. In addition students often exhibit a sophisticated awareness of the role of discourse and ideology in text, even if they have never used the word *ideology* and remain unacquainted with the term *discourse analysis*. Students also indicate awareness that meaning is not stable over time and space, thus recapitulating some of the points of Benjamin. In part students can encapsulate and recapitulate these diverse approaches to meaning by brainstorming the subject because these questions about meaning have become part of the fabric of contemporary culture. Knowledge of the basic contestations about meaning is part of cultural literacy, gained not just through formal education but also through informal sources, paradigmatically the media which have disseminated these ideas around the world. In fact, although these views began as Western discourses, the problematic of meaning has become an issue worldwide, in some ways most acutely realized in postcolonial countries where the relationships between power, privilege, signs, and constructivist meanings are so clearly apprehensible. It is the job of teachers of translation, whether through brainstorming sessions or the course of general instruction, to help students consciously understand the implications of these complexities of meaning and to give them vocabulary for their latent perceptions.

To sum up, because of the complexity of how things mean, as well as the complexity of thinking about meaning during the last century, it is not at all appropriate or helpful to tell translators and students of translation simply to discern the meaning of a source text and then transfer that meaning to the target text, as many textbooks and teachers continue to do. Such an instruction constitutes a double bind for translators, and double binds are a classic form of undermining the agency of individuals and groups as well. Presenting translation as a practice of transfer of meaning obscures the problems a translator faces instead of opening up those problems for inspection; it impedes the development of effective strategies of translation instead of leading to productive discussions of how to develop strategies for transposing, constructing, and performing meaning; it disempowers translators instead of empowering them. Because students and translators are aware – however subliminally – of the complexity of the nature of meaning, an implicit or explicit denial of the problematic of meaning turns the question of meaning in translation into an impossible burden for translators, a labyrinthine trap, an insolvable puzzle. The only solution that many translators can devise is to subordinate their own agency to prevailing norms, dominant ideologies, and prescriptive translation protocols. Such forms of translator training construct students and translators as subalterns.

It is liberating for translators, students of translation, and translation scholars alike to be given exercises that raise significant and difficult questions about meaning, that validate their sense of the problematic of meaning, that increase their experiential understanding and awareness about the difficulties of constructing meaning in translations, and that connect the construction of meaning in translation with ideological and ethical agency. Through such exercises, issues about the constructivist nature of meaning in translation become concrete and lived realities for translators and translation scholars rather than remaining mere abstractions that can be set aside and bracketed during the actual process of translating or analyzing translation data. To connect the problematic of meaning in translation with larger frameworks of intellectual inquiry about meaning during the last century also enlarges the purview of translation and validates the agency of translators, for translators come to see themselves as significant players struggling with important issues that have been central to intellectual inquiry in many disciplines for decades. These understandings turn the construction of meaning from a furtive gesture to an empowered assertion. Making such connections is perhaps the most significant way that the discipline of translation studies can empower translators and promote empowering translations.

7.4 Overdetermination and Underdetermination of Meaning in Translation

One of the most challenging aspects of translation is that meaning in a source text is always both overdetermined and underdetermined; even empowered translators find it a central problem in the construction of their target texts. These features of meaning – overdetermination and underdetermination – have been standard topics in the pedagogical and theoretical literature of translation studies since the field was formed, though not generally named as such. They are inescapable features of translation, if only for linguistic reasons: the anisomorphisms of language are such that obligatory features of one language do not usually match the obligatory features of another language. Thus, if the source language makes a linguistic distinction not found in the receptor language, the meaning of the source text is overdetermined and has supplementary information that the translator cannot easily capture or reproduce in the receptor language. By contrast, if the receptor language requires distinctions that the source language does not make, then the meaning of the source text is underdetermined from the point of view of the receptor language and culture. Similar phenomena of overdetermination and underdetermination are also recognized and discussed with respect to higher levels of the text such as culture (for example, cultural gaps that can exist either in the source culture or the receptor culture).[36] Linguistic and cultural asymmetries can be found on every level of a text, from the level of the word to more complex levels, including the cultural parameters discussed in chapter 6. On the levels of culture, they take the form of asymmetries in practices, signature concepts, discourses, text types, literary genres, and overcodings of many types.

Approaches to translator training tend to discuss these issues but downplay the implications of such asymmetries for the role of meaning itself in translation and for the agency of the translator. Questions of overdetermination and underdetermination of meaning are rarely explored with reference to their implications for the ideology of translation and rarely taught as sites of the agency of the translator as a meaning maker. More typically they are treated as technical (linguistic) questions that translators must learn to manage. Here by contrast we will explore the broader significance of translators' choices when facing overdetermination and underdetermination of meaning, so as to understand how such decisions relate to an expanded concept of translation and the empowerment of the translator.

Let us begin with the question of the overdetermination of meaning in translation, which is palpable in the list generated by my students in section 7.2 (and no doubt supplemented with your own additions, if you did the exercise suggested), indicating where meaning is to be found in the analytic or reading phase of the translation process. There are so many factors that impinge on the meaning of a text – related to language, content, culture (including history and textual practices), and context (temporal, spatial, pragmatic), as well as personal associations and perspectives the translator brings as reader – that any source text is supersaturated with meaning. As a consequence no one person can "know" or "perceive" all the meanings of a text, not even the author, much less a translator. This state of affairs is obviously related to the insights of reader response theory. It also may explain the habits of canny writers like James Joyce who steadfastly refused to comment on, validate, or refute interpretations of *Ulysses* proffered by friends and critics (thus leaving a very open text still more open to the meanings seen by readers). He recognized that there were elements in his own texts or ways of reading them that he had not necessarily constructed deliberately or knowingly anticipated.

Nor is meaning even fixed in time, as we have seen. It is open-ended, expanding and retracting as time passes, as history unrolls and culture alters, as signs change significance. The meaning of a text also shifts each time a new audience is opened up by translation and a new set of associations for the text begins to grow; this follows from Benjamin's insight in "The Task of the Translator" that translators give a text an "afterlife", that a text cannot survive without such alteration and expansion of meaning. There can be amazing developments

---

[36] Linguistic and cultural anisomorphisms resulting in overdetermination and underdetermination of meaning are canvassed in Jakobson (1959), Nida (1964), Catford (1965), Bassnett (2002), and Katan (2004), for example, as well as in most translation textbooks.

in this regard: the largest potential audience in history – estimated at the time at a few hundred million readers – for Joyce's *Ulysses* was made possible when the book was translated into Chinese in the 1990s; it is an audience that will generate surprising new interpretations of the text, taking Joyce's work in unforeseen directions.

Exciting as all such developments are, the resulting accretion of meanings contributes to the overdetermination of meaning of a text and complicates the task of the translator even further. Textual meaning becomes a palimpsest of readings from different times and different cultures. This is not merely a feature of literary texts: in some ways it is even more obvious and more problematic with reference to political and legal documents. The Declaration of Independence of the United States offers an obvious case where one reads the words, "We hold these Truths to be self-evident, that all Men are created equal, that they are endowed by their Creator with certain unalienable Rights, that among these are Life, Liberty, and the Pursuit of Happiness". In the twenty-first century these words have quite different meanings than they did for the framers of democracy in the United States, including those who actually signed the Declaration of Independence. Collectively the men who ratified the document did not include women or people of color in the phrase "all men are created equal". Yet subsequent political developments expanded the eighteenth-century meanings of the text, causing it to be read in different and much more expansive ways. Any comprehensive assessment of the Declaration of Independence, therefore, would have to recognize several layers of historical interpretation and meaning; a translator facing this complexity would have a task far surpassing the difficulty of any similar passage in a work of literature.

Still another factor that contributes to the overdetermination of meaning is unlimited semiosis. Semiotic meanings lead from sign to sign; associations form endless chains of meaning. Such meanings can only be pragmatically or arbitrarily bounded by a given individual (or by cultural conventions). Theoretically, however, the phenomenon results in any utterance being subject to overdetermination of meaning, and this form of overdetermination varies from person to person, group to group. Writing about the phenomenon of overdetermination, Dan Slobin points out that "any utterance is multiply determined by what I have seen or experienced, my communicative purpose in telling you about it, and the distinctions that are embodied in my grammar" (1996:75).

Paradoxically textual meaning is also underdetermined. Jerome Bruner argues that meaning is ambiguous and that reference rarely achieves singular expression; not only are utterances polysemous, he maintains that there is an unlimited number of ways that expressions can be related to one another (1986:64). As a consequence of the underdetermination of meaning, David Olson indicates that language always requires an act of disambiguation (qtd. in Bruner 1986:64).

The most extensive exploration of and statement about the underdetermination of meaning in language has been made by Dan Sperber and Deirdre Wilson in *Relevance* (1995), one of the most radical contemporary reconceptualizations of the nature of language. Turning away from the view of language as code, Sperber and Wilson argue that any utterance has ambiguous elements that must be interpreted with reference to context, supplemented by associations and inferences relevant to the specific situation in which the utterance is produced. Even so, an utterance has multiple determinants and leaves the interpretation ambiguous; thus Sperber and Wilson invoke a principle of efficiency as a primary principle of disambiguation of linguistic performance.[37] The inherent incompleteness of decontextualized language in and of itself is often the root of the underdetermination of meaning in language as we encounter it in texts and even as we deal with it pragmatically in daily communication. These factors are critical in the process of translation where language is often at least partially decontextualized.

Although the primary cause of the underdetermination of meaning can be attributed to the nature of language and communication, such effects can also be seen at the macrolevels of textual meaning. The underdetermination of meaning in literary texts, for example, entails the necessity for readers to supplement the text with their own interpretations. Any literary sign can be problematized by a quest for greater and greater delicacy (cf. Iser 1974). If an author writes, "bread and cheese were on the table", a reader can always ask what sort of bread and what sort of cheese are to be imagined. Is the cheese cheddar, gouda, or stilton? And if it is gouda, is the gouda a slice, a wedge, or a whole wheel? The same process can be applied to the bread, the table, and so forth *ad infinitum*. We see here the wisdom of Wittgenstein's observation that imprecise language is often far better than precision, being in fact "exactly what is called for" (1953:section 71). In many situations, however, translators cannot merely recreate underdetermination in their target texts.[38]

Again this question of underdetermination goes far beyond ordinary language and literary texts; it includes political and legal documents, as well as texts generated by the media. A good case of underdetermination of meaning in important political and legal documents is the Constitution of the United States, where the meaning of the original document has been supplemented with legal precedents and Supreme Court decisions established over a period of more than two hundred years. These precedents stipulate how the Constitution is to be interpreted in instances where the meaning is controversial because of ambiguity and underdetermination. In many cases underdetermination of political or legal texts results from changes of culture over time: new technologies, new attitudes, and

---

[37] On the principle of efficiency in processing effort in relevance theory, see Sperber and Wilson (1995:123-32, 260-79).

[38] For example, because the receptor language and source language may have different levels of specificity required in certain domains. Translation of English *cheese* into Russian would require at minimum a determination of whether or not the curds had been fermented (cf. Jakobson 1959:233).

new practices all raise questions about the meaning of political documents that the framers of those documents could not have anticipated. Does freedom of speech, for example, cover the dissemination on the Internet of electronically generated pornography featuring children? Fortunately it is judges and lawyers, not usually translators, who decide meaning in such radical cases of underdetermination.

Difficulties related to the underdetermination of meaning are particularly acute in the case of texts from very different cultures, texts from the past, and texts of dead languages (cf. Tymoczko 1999b:146-62). Often most difficult to construe are texts that are radically decontextualized in some way, for instance, by having uncertain authorship, provenance, or dating. Scholars of antiquity, medievalists, and translators of the Bible and other scriptures struggle with underdetermination of meaning all the time, but translators who work with any textual material from a culture that is significantly different from their own are likely to face similar questions. Meanings can be lost over time, as is seen in the case of the anonymous texts that have come down from the past, whose origin in time and space is mysterious. Many sacred texts fall into this category, and scholars try to determine their historical evolution in part so as to better interpret (and translate) them. The decontextualization of the blackbird poem discussed in section 7.1 is an example of these types of underdetermination of meaning: it would help readers and translators considerably in understanding the meaning to know where, when, why, and for whom the small poem was composed.

Although linguists and philologists have been most articulate about the underdetermination of meaning, it is deconstruction scholars who have most (in)famously stressed the overdetermination of meaning. Paradoxically these are complementary not antithetical perspectives on the problematic of meaning in translation. The implications of both overdetermination of meaning and underdetermination of meaning in texts to be translated are suggested by Theo Hermans, who observes that "prejudice, the recipient's horizon of expectations, is a prerequisite for interpretation. For this reason interpretation can never hope to exhaust the meaning of a text, but remains partial and open-ended".[39] The problem is acute when the horizon of expectation of the original audience in the source culture is significantly different from that of the translator or when it is unknown. In such cases meaning is even more radically underdetermined in the translation process, with the translator never able to compensate confidently for many of the contextual assumptions framing the source text, some of which can be perceived only by their absence. For reasons such as these, translation operates between two problematic indeterminacies, the underdetermination of meaning and the overdetermination of meaning, both of which require choices on the part of the translator as the meaning of the translated text is constructed.

Clearly translators must make decisions as they come to grips with both

---

[39] "Translation and the Relevance of Self-Reference", unpublished paper delivered in Salamanca in November 2000.

underdetermination and overdetermination of meaning in the translation process. On the one hand they cannot capture all the meanings suggested by the
source text. Conversely there are choices that must be made to compensate for
underdetermination of meaning having to do with contextual presuppositions,
ambiguities, and gaps that affect the meaning of a text on its linguistic, cultural,
and ideological levels, among others. Unlike critics who can comment on the
existence of multiple possibilities of meaning and suggest alternate interpretations without committing themselves to a decision about one interpretation over
another, a translator cannot simply list putative choices: a translator must actually make decisions.[40] Translators must act, creating texts for receptor audiences
that encode specific determinations of meaning, concrete representations, and
performances of (some of) the meanings of source texts. Such choices involve
responsibility and power, and to make such choices effectively, a translator
must feel empowered. That sense of empowerment must go beyond the level of
language to include the configuration and construction of meaning at all levels,
the representation of culture, forthrightness in asserting cultural difference, and
responsibility for ideological and ethical positionings.

Any set of choices related to overdetermination and underdetermination of
meaning is ideological and ethical. Thus, any narrowing of the range of overdetermination will have ideological and ethical motivations and implications. We
see this, for example, in the case of Bible translation, where a biblical translator
might decide to "focus" on "the good news" of the Gospels when faced with
overdetermined meaning. This focus will lead to choices that exclude other meanings that might have as much or more significance to readers, such as literary or
poetic meanings that might be of interest to a poet, or historically contextualized
meanings with ancient political, social, and cultural implications that might be
of interest to a historian. In a similar way any decisions about filling in for underdetermination of meaning will also have ideological and ethical motivations
and implications. One might think about the problems of interpreting the "branch
piled-yellow" of the Irish poem discussed in section 7.1. Is this yellow branch
a sign of spring and an indication of supposed Celtic sensitivity to nature or is
it a reference to fall indicating supposed Celtic melancholy? Does the branch
refer to the onset of a season of war and, if so, does the poem express an antiwar
sentiment? All these choices create charged representations of medieval Irish
culture and construct Irish identity in significantly different ways; in turn those
constructions have ideological signficance.

Decisions about how to translate underdetermined and overdetermined
aspects of a text result in specific representations, transmissions, and transculturations in the target text. In turn these features become operative in the receptor
culture, not merely characterizing the translated text but also acting as metonyms

---

[40] Of course, in some types of translation a translator can give alternate readings in footnotes
or other paratextual materials as a form of hedging the choices in the translation.

for the author, the source culture, and so forth. In that sense they entail responsibility and ethical commitment on the part of the translator. They at once reflect and reveal the position, perspective, and place of enunciation of the translator. Translation is never a neutral iteration, whether that iteration involves partiality or augmentation in response to overdetermination and underdetermination of meaning in the source text.

There is no way to short-circuit these ethical processes of decision making and choice in translation with respect to overdetermination and underdetermination of meaning. Insofar as a translator follows an established protocol for filling in textual underdetermination or for narrowing overdetermination, a translator is adopting a predetermined ideological agenda motivated by the interests, position, and power of those instituting the protocol. Those interests might be commercial (capitalist, globalizing, multinational) business interests, governmental policies,[41] or established sectarian interpretations of how to translate specific words in a sacred text. In adopting any such externally regulated protocol, a translator's agency will be subordinated to and confined by the powers that dictate the decision-making procedure. This happens all the time when translators accept conditions of employment. Nonetheless it is essential that translators be aware of the implications of such protocols and hold themselves ultimately accountable for their work.[42] For many translators such subordination poses no problem, because their values are consonant with the framework within which they work. Insofar as there is dissonance, however, by consenting to the protocols, the translator incribes himself within an inconsistent narrativity (cf. Baker 2006a). These are paths by which censorship and self-censorship enter the translation process.

In disregarding the ideological and ethical implications of their own translation choices relevant to the construction of meaning, translators collude in the effacement and dispersal of the ideology of translation. Imagining that meaning can be transferred in an unproblematic manner ultimately circumscribes and confines translators within their own cultures and the (dominant) perspectives of those cultures (or worse, within hegemonic subordination to the dominant values of another culture commissioning the translation). Such a posture toward translation dismantles self-reflexivity about the translator's perspective, positionality, and place of enunciation, thus eroding not only openness to difference but also responsibility, agency, and the ability to engage in activist translation. Collusion of this sort can also entail alienation from the material being translated and the cultural mediation being performed.

Any simplistic belief that the primary job of the translator is to transfer meaning, therefore, is problematic for multiple reasons. It runs counter to the

---

[41] For example, goverment policies in the European Union might dictate the translation equivalents of specific words or the way to frame "the same" legal documents.

[42] See Davis (2001:97-98, 106) on the relationship between protocols, translators' choices, and ethical responsibility with reference to professional translation, no matter how technical. Cf. Chesterman (2000:26), Cronin (2000:43).

postpositivist trajectory of translation studies since World War II. It undermines the understanding of translation as a form of cultural production that powerfully changes societies. It negates the responsibility translators have for mediating and shaping culture. It eviscerates the possibility for translators to act in the world.

The two systems of overdetermination and underdetermination of meaning in translation are significant reasons that translation cross-culturally is a cluster concept. Decisions about what constitutes meaning in translation take many forms, and negotiating the challenges of overdetermination and underdetermination of meaning is central to those processes and the types of products that result. The results can range from emphasis of political meaning to a focus on formal meaning (such as genre, or prosody, or even sound patterning), from minute lexical transposition intended to expand the lexical repertory of a receptor culture to emphasis of the cultural strand in a text. These orientations in turn form the basis of the many types of transfer, representation, and transculturation that we have considered at various points in this volume. All these are potential centers of distinct clusters of translation within the larger concept. Methods of transposing and constructing meaning in translated texts take potentially unlimited forms involving creativity, invention, and engagement. The result is an infinite variety of translation processes and products that as yet translation studies has scarcely begun to inventory in a comprehensive manner.

In this chapter reflections on the process of production and construction of meaning in translation have taken us back to the utility of seeing translation as a cluster concept. We began the book with the enlarged conceptualization of translation as a premise for exploring the empowerment of translators. It is signficant that beginning with the translator's agency and empowerment in making meaning brings us full circle to an enlarged concept of translation.

7.5 Beyond Meaning to Generativity

No matter how we come at the question of meaning in translation, whether by analyzing the construction of actual translations and the practices of translators, by brainstorming the meaning of meaning in ordinary language, by investigating philosophical discourses and debates about meaning, or by considering the overdetermination and underdetermination of meaning in the interface of languages, the implications for translation converge: translation cannot be conceptualized as a process in which "the meaning" of a text is simply transferred and preserved across languages, nor can the task of the translator be defined as the preservation of meaning. Textual meaning is open-ended, not fully determinate, and subject to change; meaning is at once underdetermined and overdetermined. There is no predetermined circumscribed meaning in any translation task for a translator to transfer. Translators must make choices about where meaning lies in the source text and its context and what meaning to invest in the target text. Translators both define the meaning of the source text and construct the meaning of the target text. In both roles translators are meaning makers.

Translation has traditionally been thought of as a metaphoric process: the process of replacement of an element in one text by an element in another text, consisting chiefly of the selection of target language choices. Word for word, sentence for sentence, trope for trope, cultural field for cultural field, genre for genre, form for form, and function for function, translation is often presented as a metaphoric process. Replacement fails as a model for the treatment of meaning in translation, and it is particularly problematic in accounting for overdetermination and underdetermination of meaning, which call upon the translator to omit or to supply meanings. A metonymic approach to translation, by contrast, fits with modern theories of meaning and is congruent with views of meaning in translation as multivalent, as constructivist, and as both overdetermined and underdetermined, thus taking many potential forms in target text renditions.

The role of translators in making meaning is frequently effaced, in some cases systematically so. There are strong cultural determinants in how meaning is constituted in translation and it is always in the interest of those in power to deny and disavow the constructivist nature of meaning. This institutionalized disavowal impinges on how translation is viewed and how translators are trained and supervised. Those in power have an investment in attempting to limit, define, and regulate meaning, in large part because power rests on the way meaning is controlled and constructed as much as it does on physical coercion. This is true at every level of human society, from the global to the level of nations and cultures, from the local to the level of intimate groupings such as families. At all levels those in power attempt to define and stipulate meaning, to establish and regulate discourses, and to circumscribe expression.

We have already seen in chapter 5 that imperial conquest and control are much more than a matter of physical coercion or force: indeed because it was impossible to control nineteenth-century European empires by force alone, information became the guiding dictate of imperial policy (cf. Cronin 203:110). Conquest involved dominance of both territory and epistemological space (St-Pierre 2000:261-62 and sources cited). Michael Cronin (2006:112-16) argues that we are moving into an age in which information and force are again becoming increasingly intertwined. Epistemological supremacy does not turn merely on dominance through control of information and knowledge, but on dominance through control of meaning. Thus, the epistemology of power goes beyond acquiring information and amassing knowledge, despite the fact that knowledge has been a priority of imperial powers – an interest made tangible in surveys, maps, census-taking, ethnographic observations, histories, collections of artifacts, and the cultivation of flora and fauna of conquered territories, all of which have been part of the imperial archive.[43] Epistemological control extends to the imposition and regulation of meaning as well. We see this control of meaning in the creation of discourses and the (re)definition of words and concepts imposed in imperial

---

[43] Cf. Cronin (2000), St-Pierre (2000:262), and sources cited.

domains. In England's colonies from Ireland to North America and India, British categories of thought were substituted for native ones. The phenomena are nowhere so clear as in the domains of land tenure and law.[44]

By controlling meaning (semantic and conceptual meaning, but also meaning embodied in cultural practices), conquerors make known and knowable territory that is physically and mentally strange and unknown (cf. Bernard S. Cohn, quoted in St-Pierre 2000:262). A hierarchy is established in which the imperial language takes precedence over vernaculars and imperial meanings are superimposed upon native ones, even as imperial rule is imposed upon native rule; native concepts and meanings are translated into the meanings of the imperial power (cf. St-Pierre 2000:262). Discussing Western imperialism, Sherry Simon indicates that the result is a set of "interpretive activities whose final meeting [rests] exclusively within the colonizers' language", such that colonized cultures are "contained within the hermeneutic frames of Western knowledge" (2000:11). In all these processes translation is central and translation serves not just to transmit information and knowledge but to construct meaning itself. As a consequence translation can become a set of practices aiming to "compact and reduce an alien reality into the terms imposed by a triumphant Western culture" (Simon 2000:11), where the terms serve not merely as linguistic passwords between cultures but also engender new meanings among the conquered. A postcolonial space thus constitutes "a power-knowledge nexus" (Dasgupta 2000:294), a nexus that involves meaning as much as knowledge, in which there is "daily exposure to the conflictual aspects of language exchange" (Simon 2000:13). In such an environment, meaning is both dislocated and constantly contested.[45]

These patterns of control and stipulation of meaning are not restricted to Western imperialism; they are evident in Chinese imperial contexts also. In section 2.2 we saw that the nature of Chinese writing led to the effacement of differences in meaning among its subaltern cultures and that such effacements constitute powerful ideological vectors. Charles Holcombe observes that "to the extent that . . . [Chinese characters] are tied to a particular set of ideas – to a specific vocabulary – [the characters] bring with them the vocabulary of Chinese higher civilization . . . [creating] an 'empire of ideas' . . . which simultaneously circulates and reinforces Chinese concepts and excludes other ideas or at least makes their expression difficult" (quoted in Wakabayashi 2005:19). This means of extending an imperialistic and hegemonic worldview through the use of an invariant writing system based on ideograms across differences of language, forcing the use of imperial concepts and "mental translation", is an obvious imperialistic

---

[44] See the arguments in Cheyfitz (1997), Tymoczko (1999b:165), St-Pierre (2000:261-62), and sources cited; cf. Gouanvic (2002:182-88). Both the imposition of and resistance to epistemological conquest are explored in Rafael (1993).

[45] See also the discussion in section 6.2 above. The lack of accommodation to colonized audiences and the stipulation of what "legitimately" constitutes adequate cultural knowledge and cultural literacy are significant factors in the control of meaning in imperial situations.

tool for regulating meaning.[46] Coupled with the Chinese refusal to translate into other languages and the insistence on using Chinese as the language of diplomatic communication in China, this imperial history manifests clear policies intended to impose and control meaning, similar in intent to those documented in Western imperialism.[47] No doubt, systematic investigation would show that control of meaning can be traced in other imperial systems as well, from Rome and the Mughal empire in India to the pre-Columbian empires in the Americas.

Translation is a central cultural domain where control of meaning is imposed and regulated because of the potentially transformative power and the constructivist nature of translation. Raylene Ramsay notes that translation foregrounds "another way of being in the world", thus exposing "the fictitious creations of meaning" in one's own language (2004:167-68). Similarly Gouanvic argues that translation "necessarily is involved in the struggle of cultural productions for legitimation and recognition" and that it can "dislodge hierarchies of legitimation" (2000:106). The potential to unmask and subvert the epistemological authority of a receiving culture and the possibility of disrupting cultural legitimations are yet other motivations for controlling the way that translators import meaning into a culture, for such subversions and disruptions can have momentous consequences for any society. The dimensions of meaning surveyed here are merely illustrative of the immense ideological and political import of the role of meaning in translation and of translators as meaning makers in cultural interface and domestic change. It is no wonder that the intent to govern meaning is materialized in the systemic controls and sanctioned protocols associated with translating documents connected with power in particular, whether those texts are business contracts, government documents, legal texts, treaties, sacred religious books, monuments of cultural identity and cultural nationalism, or the great works of a literary canon.[48] Only by being aware of their own ability to

---

[46] Wakabayashi (2005) notes that Chinese epistemological control, facilitated by the use of characters, was triumphal in constructing meaning across languages deriving from at least three major linguistic families.

[47] The Chinese insistence on communication being conducted in Chinese and the associated difficulties foreigners had to overcome in the process of communication were explicitly seen as symbolic of China's prestige and cultural dominance. See Hung (2005a:148-49, 2005b:74-75). It is telling that after the wars between the two imperial systems (which the British won), the Treaty of Tientsin between China and Britain included the provision that the sense expressed in the English text would be the correct sense and the English text the legally enforceable one (Hung 2005a:159-60). The British also stipulated that China establish a cadre of translators who could communicate in English.

[48] Descriptive translation studies have documented that it is not simple, for example, to re-translate a canonical literary text and find either a publisher or an audience for it. Moreover, central texts and genres in a literary system show signs of more regulation and less variation in translation than do peripheral ones, particularly when those works relate to cultural nationalism. On these issues see Helgason (1999); cf. Bassnett and Lefevere (1990:1-13) and Hermans (1982).

construct (and deconstruct) meaning – as well as ways that societies attempt to control meaning – can translators fully exercise their agency as meaning makers. Decentering power is not just a matter of politics, ideological struggles, ethics, and values: it is also an epistemological matter related to meaning and knowledge. Translators play key roles in these domains. The issues raised here about translators as meaning makers take on new urgency in contemporary contexts and conflicts; they are reasons that the lives of translators are in peril once again in our world.

There is inevitable loss and gain of meaning in moving between languages because of obligatory features of languages and anisomorphisms across linguistic boundaries. Similarly there is loss and gain of meaning in moving between universes of discourse, cultures, systems of poetics, and ideologies. But loss and gain of meaning are not necessarily terrible things. They are inevitable, in the very nature of meaning itself as it shifts across time and space, across language and culture, across societies and persons. The openness of meaning is consistent with the openness of translation as a cluster concept, and realizing this plenitude in translation is empowering for the translator. Contemporary theories of meaning legitimate translation by acknowledging that shifts of meaning, multiple interpretations, and constructivist interventions by translators are not only inevitable but ultimately desirable.

Nonetheless, the ethical dimension of the loss and gain of meaning demands attention. Decisions related to meaning in translation require that translators invent strategies for executing their choices deliberately and that they monitor the ethical implications of those strategies. Gillian Lane-Mercier observes that "translation is a 'violent', decision-oriented, culturally determined discursive activity that compels the translator to take a position with respect to the source text and author, the source culture, the target culture and the target reader, thus engaging, over and above socially imposed norms and values, the translator's agency together with his or her responsibility in the production of meaning" (1997:65). The invention of strategic modes of choice is central to translation processes that acknowledge responsibility for the construction of meaning, with the ethical implications that follow. In turn strategic innovations of this sort have the potential to create new types of translations for new translational purposes, including activist ones. Thus, the openness of meaning in translation is related to the possibility of generating new and different forms of translation processes and products that in turn testify to the power of translators to change cultures and the world. At the same time the possibility of increasing the repertory of translation processes and products both reflects and reifies the openness of the cross-cultural concept translation. The recursive relationship linking the empowerment of translators and the enlargement of translation entails the openness of meaning and the role of translators as constructors of meaning as well. Because this is a recursive relationship, the flow between expanding translation and empowering translators can be perceived as starting from either direction.

One can begin with the larger open concept and see that an enhancement of the translator's possibilities and powers results, or one can begin with the translator's full powers – the translator's legitimate, liberated, and liberating construction of meaning – and end up perceiving possibilities for enlarging the boundaries of the concept translation. In either case the role of the translator as meaning maker is central.

When a translator translates, it is not possible to capture all meaning associated with the source text. There is no failing or deficiency here, however, because there is no boundedness to the initial meanings of the source text that the translator is called upon to transpose, no closed circle of meaning, no "all" to be translated. Meaning is open, always in flux, and the nature of meaning in translation is one element in the dynamic. In the abstract these qualities of meaning may seem unsettling, anxiety provoking, destabilizing. But the openness of meaning is woven into the texture of our bodies, our experience, our lives. It is the openness of meaning that allows texts and cultures to change and survive. In every facet of life, meanings alter and adapt, evolve and enlarge. As old meanings are abandoned, new and generative meanings emerge. Empowered translators, empowering translations, and enlarged domains for translation are all part of that process.

8. Enlargement, Empowerment, Ethics

The principal argument of this book is that translation as a cross-cultural concept must be reconceptualized and enlarged beyond dominant Western notions that continue to circumscribe its definition. Reconceptualization is necessary because many types of translations cannot fit into current theorization of translation and are consequently marginalized in or even excluded from contemporary translation studies discourses. Some of the marginalized types of translation are quite old, such as medieval and modern practices typical of oral cultures. Some are new, including emerging practices of localization and multimedia translation associated with the electronic networking of the world. Some are associated with languages and cultures beyond the West; they are excluded theoretically despite the growing internationalization of the discipline of translation studies, because translation theory has thus far been grounded in the Western European metaphor of translation as transfer. The result is omission of many ideas about translation around the world, ranging from those associated with metaphors of birth and turning over to metaphors of following after, biography, and definition. All these ideas have the potential to sustain translators as they strive to meet contemporary challenges.

I have argued that the cross-linguistic, cross-cultural, and cross-temporal concept translation is an open concept with fuzzy boundaries. Its openness is typical of many concepts that are most characteristic of human life: language, literature, art, text, performance, ritual, game, number, family, kinship, history, religion, and social regulation or government, among others. Famously discussed by Ludwig Wittgenstein, cluster concepts such as these are found in most human cultures but generally configured differently in each society. Their blurred boundaries seem specially suited to features of human cognition and human social life, in part because their inherent flexibility allows for approximation, learning, adaptability, change, evolution, and opportunism, all useful to a species that has survived by being able to improvise, to apprehend and conserve innovations, to alter its environment, and to change course strategically when pleasure or pain has dictated swerving away from the tried and true. It is obvious that translation should be such a concept because successful cultural interface is essential to adaptive human life. The forms of interface between different human individuals and different groups must be conceived in ways that are versatile enough to permit productive encounters with diverse types of people. Clearly the flexibility in translation, like that of other important social concepts of human beings, is related to our learning capacities, our extraordinary skill in analogical thinking, and our facility at discerning similarity and difference in multiple, partial, overlapping, and creative ways. By contrast, hardening modes of cultural interface is probably a preeminent indicator of power asymmetries and the assertion of dominance and dominion. Thus, the narrowing of conceptualizations of translation to dominant Western ones since World War II – with the result that Western ideas are triumphal in translation studies no less than in many scientific and technological fields – can be looked upon as such an extension of power. This extension of one form of local knowledge as a universal should not be allowed to efface other local knowledges and should not be taken as a substitute for theory itself in translation studies.

If taken seriously, the reconceptualization of translation will change many facets of the discipline of translation studies, from the perception of its history to the functioning of its research system and its pedagogical practices. The postpositivist trajectory of translation studies in the last half century indicates a definitional impulse in the field consonant with a need to reconceptualize translation. Paradoxically more and more parameters of translation have been defined over the decades, more and more perspectives have proved productive, but fewer and fewer facts or certainties have resulted, and less and less closure has been achieved. The result has been more open definitions of the processes and products of translation on the theoretical level, if not always on the level of praxis. This trajectory will continue, but recognition that it stems from the nature of translation itself as a cluster concept will enable scholars and translators to direct, control, and utilize the enlarging conceptualization of translation more effectively.

The simultaneous expansions and uncertainties in the field and its increasingly postpositivist orientation have brought greater self-reflexivity to translation studies. From such self-reflexive perspectives, the conflicts and competitions of particular schools of translation studies are less significant than their complementarity, facilitating a dialectic about the complex open nature of translation. Postpositivist epistemologies entailing self-reflexivity have also deepened the appreciation of the ethical and ideological nature of translation. A cluster concept approach to translation also explains the special importance of descriptive translation studies in all these shifts and developments of the field. Observation is essential in the case of cluster concepts because the properties of such a concept cannot be predicted *a priori*, they can only be discerned *a posteriori* through observation of actual practices. As a result we must *look at and describe* the variety of translations and translation processes in many different circumstances in order to understand the nature of translation through time in the many cultures of the world. Empirical observation is central to the field of translation studies, and descriptive studies have played an essential role in its development practically and theoretically, moving it rigorously toward expanded conceptualizations of the subject matter.

The history of translation studies reveals ideological, economic, and cultural substrata in the development of the discipline. Beginning with the double impetus for translation during World War II (the importance of cracking codes and the manipulation of populations through textual production, paradigmatically propaganda), the course of translation studies can also be correlated with other historical events including the Cold War, the war in Vietnam, the dissolution of the

Soviet Union, the decline of Marxist ideologies, and the globalization currently fueling translation around the world. The field is also increasingly affected by the emergence of English as an international link language. In Europe the single most important historical development influencing translation studies since World War II has been the emergence of the European Union and its decision to retain all its major languages as official ones rather than to use a melting-pot model of political affiliation or even to choose to transact business in a restricted group of dominant languages. The result is probably the most extensive translational activity in the history of the world, with a consequent demand for translators and translator training that has required the development of an academic field to support the political project.

Although English continues to be the dominant and official language in the United States, English has also increasingly lost its singular status in U.S. culture. With the passage of laws in the mid twentieth century requiring bilingual education and linguistic accommodation for those who are not native English speakers, the importance of translation has soared in the United States. Translation has become institutionalized in businesses, hospitals, courts, and various branches of government (notably schools). Bilingual education is legislated in most states of the union in various modalities, and in the United States multilingualism also continues to be a major facet of the culture in large measure because of continued immigration. In Northampton, Massachusetts, for example, the small city of 30,000 in which I live, the school system serving 3,000 children in 1999 accommodated 90 native speakers of approximately a dozen different languages (with 60 students speaking Spanish and the rest of the bilingual children speaking Chinese, German, Khmer, Polish, Punjabi, Russian, Serbian, Tibetan, and Turkish, among other languages). By 2007 the figures had increased, such that of 2855 students in the school system, there were 217 students whose primary language was not English.[1] The changed view of the importance of serving non-English speakers is partly an outgrowth of the Vietnam War which made clear the strategic necessity for U.S. citizens to know more world languages, a lesson that is repeating itself since the events of September 11, 2001, and the wars in the Middle East. Even more significant, however, is the growing number of Spanish speakers in the United States. The closer cultural, economic, and political connections among American nations north and south since World War II are also driving forces for the retention of Spanish in the United States and the changed status of translation in the Americas in general.

Indeed the whole world has been swept up by the necessity to communicate and to translate. Michael Cronin (2003, 2006) discusses at length how population migrations and globalization make translation a necessity within nations – even small ones like Ireland – as much as across national borders. India is the epitome

---

[1] The languages spoken by these children at home are not available because of changes in legal requirements pertaining to reporting about bilingual education.

of countries in which internal multilingualism thrives. With approximately 30 major languages and perhaps as many as 600 others, India is a leader in this regard, having been multilingual historically and having chosen national policies that nurture multilingualism. In India approximately 30 per cent of the children are currently born to internal "migrants" and hence will grow up fluent in at least two vernacular languages in addition to those serving as link languages for the educated (Hindi and English). In some ways India is a model for linguistic conditions of the future world as global interactions and networking proceed apace and translation becomes ever more complex.

Most of the implications that follow from reconceptualizing translation – including reassessing the history of the field, recognition of the need for more conceptual frames of reference for thinking about translation, and revamping the research system – are in a sense predictable because change in the conceptualization of the subject matter at the heart of any discipline reverberates throughout the structure and practices of the entire field. What is more surprising is that enlarging the concept of translation entails the empowerment of translators. Here I have focused on the translator's agency in relation to ideology, cultural translation, and the translation of meaning. The recursive relationship between enlarging the conceptualization of translation and empowering translators results in part from the greater range of options for translation processes and products legitimated within a broader definition of translation. But a more substantial factor is operative as well. Consciously working within an open conceptualization of translation liberates translators to improvise, invent, elaborate, and perform new translation strategies and new translation types that meet the many needs and goals translators work toward. Seeing translation as an open category removes some of the barriers that constrain translators to perform what has already been approved in their own specific cultural contexts and to remain within the limits of dominant models of translation in their own times and places. Thus, reconceptualizing translation expands a translator's practice in principle to all the options that have been performed heretofore and all future options as yet unforeseen. This greater scope both empowers translators and enlarges the conception of translation once again.

The reciprocity between an enlarged conceptualization of translation and the enhanced possibilities and empowerment of translators has become clearer with each argument of this book. The logic of the relationship is indisputable, of course, but how to turn bare logic into discourses serving as entryways into new dispositions and new practices of translation is less obvious. In the last three chapters of this book, I have attempted to develop these ideas, pointing not just to new theoretical frameworks for thinking about the agency of translators but also to new strategies for actual translation practices. These efforts are merely a hint of new prospects for translators and the discipline of translation studies if the concept of translation is enlarged.

Cognitive scientists have established that "background knowledge affects not only initial acquisition of a concept but also later categorization judgments" and that "people tend to positively categorize items that are consistent with their knowledge and to exclude items that are inconsistent, sometimes even overruling purely empirical sources of information" (Murphy 2002:173). In attempting to understand the complex cross-cultural concept translation, therefore, knowledge of a broad range of translation types and a broad range of diverse local concep-tualizations is an important factor in how people think about the subject and also in how they understand their own creativity, agency, power, and responsibility as translators. Understanding translation will increase proportionately as students are exposed to more types of attested translations and as a broad sample of inter-national conceptualizations of translation is more generally disseminated. Such increased background knowledge of the phenomena of translation will impact on future category judgments, future ways of thinking about the nature of transla-tion as a whole, and future expressions of new dispositions in new translation practices. The presentation of expanded knowledge about the conceptualization of translation and translation types within a normalized context, as occurs when translation is presented as a cluster concept, legitimates a broader range of trans-lational data than can a prototype approach treating materials outside dominant models as marginalized and as secondary in importance conceptually. It is not trivial, therefore, to move data about translation from around the world to the center of discourses about translation, however irrelevant or exotic those data may at first seem to scholars focused on immediate market practices, nor is it trivial to consider what type of category translation actually is cross-culturally.

This relationship between knowledge and category judgment takes us back to the views of Charles Sanders Peirce. As we saw in chapter 4, Peirce understood the scientific method – research in general – as one of several ways of fixing beliefs, and he saw beliefs essentially as habits of action. Research that changes the concept of translation will therefore change how translators, translation scholars, and translation teachers habitually *act* with reference to that concept. Research showing the breadth of translational phenomena has the power to fix belief in new ways of thinking about translation that become expressed as *habits of action* reflecting that breadth as well. If expanded conceptions of translation are recursively related to the empowerment of translators, the result will be more empowered habits of translation, with translations themselves more often taking the form of empowered acts.

Several discourses in this book converge on the conclusion that new beliefs about translation issuing from research will result in new practices of translation. A better understanding of the openness of translation as conceptualized in an international context can foster on the local level a habitual sense of confidence in and performance of translators' prerogatives and responsibilities in making meaning, in constructing culture, in acknowledging ideological aspects of their constructions, in formulating representations, in initiating transculturations, in promoting difference, in taking activist stands, and in introducing newness into the world. In short, conceptual change regarding translation can lead to action on the part of translators. In turn a sense of empowerment is amplified with each such action.

There is an obverse counterpart to the relationship between knowledge and acquisition of concepts and category judgments. Murphy indicates that "using category items can lead to changes in the categorization itself": category use may be "an important variable in how concepts are represented" (2002:135). If the field of translation studies and training programs in translation persist in primarily disseminating Eurocentric conceptualizations of translation and if they primarily promulgate Western types of translation throughout the world, shifts in the cross-cultural category translation will occur throughout the world, with local knowledges about translation giving way to homogenized globalized standards based on dominant Western norms. Knowledge of Western category definitions will lead people in cultures around the world to change their own concepts of translation in hegemonic ways, closing off and displacing knowledge based on local image-schemas and local metaphoric conceptualizations, as well as local histories and practices of translation. The result will be the loss of tremendous conceptual and pragmatic resources, but that is not the only problem. Ethical questions are not limited to the global practices of translation; they extend to the theoretical formulations and conceptualizations of the discipline of translation studies itself.[2]

No field is ever static. Here I have traced the trajectory of translation studies since World War II, showing how it has increasingly valorized otherness and multiple perspectives on language and culture. The extension of these postpositivist developments leads to more acute ethical awareness about the practices of translation and enhanced regard for the agency of the translator. We must stay this course toward a postpositivist ethics of difference (cf. Venuti 1998a); the only alternative is a turn to new forms of epistemological imperialism in which particular local forms of knowledge and local histories are subsumed in a globalized universal. If such a turn were to happen, it might look as if some translators were part of the imperial project and others not. In fact, in this scenario all translators become subalterns, relinquishing their claims to participation in primary forms of cultural production.

The question of enlarging translation is not simply an intellectual or cognitive issue therefore; it also has ethical dimensions. It is not just a matter of going forth and gathering in – or of gathering in and going forth – in terms of acquisition of information, new learning, exchange of knowledge, and the like. It cannot be conceived simply in terms of increased traffic or enhanced exchange, particularly that sort of colonial exchange in which some provide the raw materials and

---

[2] Baker (2006a:39-44) discusses the importance of interrogating disciplinary narratives. If one looks at the concept of translation in translation studies in terms of narrative theory, as she suggests, the narrative of the discipline has clearly been a Western one.

others return the finished goods, a form of trade in which the items and terms of exchange are predefined and stipulated. Such a rigidly defined form of exchange limits transactions all the way round, and paradoxically disempowers everyone involved in the process. *How* the enlargement of translation occurs is as ethical an issue as that it occur at all.

If the definition of translation is enlarged, translators' choices are increased, and the agency, power, and creativity of translators expand, that is not the final desideratum for the development of the discipline. Increased empowerment of translators brings also increased ethical responsibility. Faced with expanding the conceptualization of translation and developing more empowered practices of translation in an era of globalization, what can translators, translation teachers, and translation scholars do to insure that such agency is also ethical? This has been a fundamental question behind the investigations in this book, even though issues pertaining to ethics have only surfaced sporadically. It is time to turn directly to the question of ethics.

Translation does not stand in a neutral space: this is true whether we consider translation agents, processes, or products. All are positioned politically, ideologically, and ethically. Ideological and ethical questions about translation have increased dramatically in the context of globalization, and one of the most noticeable aspects of translation studies since the beginning of the cultural turn in the late 1980s – as globalization began to gather momentum – has been the emphasis on and calls for translators to be visible, audible, and ethically empowered agents.[3] Anthony Pym has observed that the convergence on ethics is only partly a function of the times; an increased awareness of the number of parameters involved in translation also puts the focus on the translator's choices and hence the translator's agency (2001:129-30). In turn ethics must shape that agency. It is not enough, however, to enjoin translators to be responsible, ethical, or activist in their practices, any more than it is sufficient to enjoin them to handle cultural translation or meaning in better ways. As with cultural translation and meaning, questions of ethics in translation need to be approached in a concrete manner and with specificity – a specificity that liberates rather than prescribes fixed and formulaic protocols. What we might hope for is more concrete guidance about how to make empowered, ethical decisions in the most ordinary and daily praxis of translation, as well as how to retain one's independence as an ethical agent.

Gillian Lane-Mercier argues that "what is always already at stake in the translation process is neither the visibility vs the invisibility of the translator nor the ethical aim of translation *per se*, but rather the translator's own ethical code, his or her responsibility and engagement with respect to the choices for which

---

[3] These calls are particularly associated with the work of Venuti (1992, 1995, 1998a). The essays in Pym (2001) take up the ethics of translation, offering multiple contemporary perspectives on the question, as well as a thorough bibliography of related work. See also Lane-Mercier (1997), Arrojo (1998). Cronin (2006:73) stresses translators' audibility, even in preference to their visibility.

he or she opts and the aesthetic, ideological and political meanings these choices generate" (1997:63). Because translators take their places among the principal mediators between cultures, their work has important geopolitical consequences, consequences that entail continual ethical self-scrutiny and self-awareness. Self-reflexivity has been a leitmotif of the discussions in the earlier chapters: it enters into the conceptualization of translation, the frames of reference used to situate translation as a practice of cultural interface, assessments of the history and structure of the field of translation studies, the effectiveness of research in the discipline, the assessment and translation of culture, the perception and construction of meaning in translation, and choices about activist roles. Self-reflexivity related to ethical dimensions of translation constitutes an area where translator training and self-training can profit from significant rethinking. This would be true if only because of the heightened ethical implications of globalization, but the specific moment in the international expansion of the discipline of translation studies also requires such a reevaluation. Let me sketch out a few concrete directions that approaches to ethics in translation might take at the level of individual translators and the field as a whole.

In the context of our rapidly changing world, individual translators can be empowered by becoming more aware of where and how ethics and ideology figure implicitly and explicitly in texts, in translation processes, and in the production and use of translation products. These issues can be made more prominent in translation training, not only by explicitly developing translator consciousness about their own agency but by providing broad exposure to relevant historical examples of ideologically controlled or empowered translations that expose ethical questions and ethical conflicts. For instance, students can be introduced to case studies of translation illustrating ethical manipulation and also ethical agency, including both frankly colonialist endeavors and postcolonial examples of resistance, as well as ethical issues in many other types of translation. Such case studies can include examples from the various strands of the second phase of descriptive studies, as well as work currently emerging as a result of the increasing internationalization of the field.

Ethical empowerment is also intertwined with exposure to contemporary views of ethical action stressing the need for decision making based on an awareness of the subject positions of others in addition to the subject position of the self. I have found that it empowers translators to spend time analyzing their own implicit and explicit ethical, political, and ideological formation and commitments. Expanding the domain of ethics and ethical behavior beyond the level of personal behaviors or religious belief to include geopolitical considerations is crucial in how translators think about making decisions and how they position themselves as cultural mediators. All of this sounds obvious to those in translation studies who have been activists or those who have been thinking for years about ideology and ethics in general, and ethical and engaged practices of translation in particular. Nonetheless, even skilled translators can be surprisingly well served by direct discussions of these questions.

It is also ethically empowering for translators to think about their circles of affiliation and responsibility. What reference points does a translator use for making ethical and ideological choices and, hence, translation choices of all sorts? The larger the frameworks within which translators situate themselves, the broader their ethical awareness and sense of responsibility will be. Thus, thinking about responsibilities to self, family, community, nation, and the world open up wider and wider ethical issues for translators.[4] Such an enlargement of affiliation demands increased ethical sensibilities, but it is repaid by increased spheres of action and empowerment. These considerations seem especially pertinent to translators working on projects commissioned by multinational interests and aimed at globalized contexts.

Like other people, translators benefit from understanding that most ethical decisions are not simple alternatives between good and bad. Sometimes there are no obvious right choices. The hardest ethical decisions are in fact usually choices between two goods or determinations of the lesser of two evils. How does one translate when important values conflict? How does one weigh contributing to the manipulation of a buying public versus losing one's job? How does one make choices faced with the possibility of endangering one's family if one undertakes a translation assignment with an ideological imperative? Rarely is there a simple or closed set of criteria that can be invoked in ethical judgments; globalized contexts with their many interwoven parameters necessitate particularly complex ethical thinking. Translators can mobilize themselves more easily and exercise their agency more effectively when they understand that there are always contradictions and interferences in any ethical, ideological, or cultural system and situation. Thus good reasons may impel translators in two diametrically different directions and require adjudication.[5] Failure to understand that such complexities are *normal though difficult* aspects of empowered action – aspects that admit of no simple resolution – can short-circuit a translator's agency.

Consistency is another central ethical concern, not always something that can be fully achieved, as I have indicated, yet it is an issue that a translator must think about in order to be most effective as an ethical agent. Again globalization with its increased set of relevant parameters makes it imperative for translators to attend to questions about consistency in ethical decisions. One tool in this process is to ask about narrative consistency. What "story" does a translator tell about the self in the world? Is this story consistent with the translator's assignments, the impact of the translator's work on the receiving audience, the actions of the employer in the world, and so forth?[6] Seeing the aggregate of one's choices and

---

[4] Questions of multiple affiliation are discussed and problematized in Cronin (2006:6-17).

[5] Chesterman (2001) discusses adjudicating values and virtues in translation.

[6] Baker (2006a, 2006b) discusses the use of narrative consistency to test ethical positions, decisions, and affiliations in translation.

actions in terms of a narrative can help to adjudicate ethical contradictions and conflicts.

These questions are merely a sample of the concrete considerations relevant to an ethics of difference that a translator can be mindful of on a personal level. Translator training can encourage habits of addressing such questions so as to empower translators and help them be responsible in their complex roles. The concrete examples given here indicate the direction translation pedagogy can take to foster ethical awareness and responsiblity among individual translators as conceptualizations of translation expand in a globalizing world.

When we turn from issues relevant to translators on a personal level to questions of ethics at the level of the discipline, still more issues arise related to fostering an ethical praxis of translation. Pedagogical practices emphasizing the importance of choice in the work of translators and the importance of self-reflexivity teach students to interrogate their own cultural and professional presuppositions, thus enabling them to be more flexible in their practices. Such flexibility is at the heart of ethical practices associated with any cluster concept. Students must learn to assess not only what they are doing in translation but what they are not doing, and to understand the ideological and ethical implications of their choices in both regards. Such questions can be built into translator training more explicitly. The consequence will be greater ingenuity among translators in how to negotiate different types of translational similarities and how to become adept at multiple means of creating similarity, prerequisites for the varied practices translators need to master in the rapidly changing and complex ethical world of the present. It is clear that teachers harm their students by limiting student choices in translation through a rigid pedagogy. By contrast, when teachers are clear about the limitations of their own premises about translation and explicit about their own frameworks for translation, as well as the deepest ethical and ideological implications of translation choices, students are better prepared for a future that will inevitably entail changes in translation canons, translation techniques, and increased ethical responsibility, as translation technologies and the definition of translation are elaborated.

Instead of developing a critical ethical sense, often in translation training and in professional codes of ethics, ethical considerations are framed precisely so as to efface translators' most significant ethical responsibilities and to deaden their ethical sensibilities, thus discouraging their agency and disempowering them in multiple ways. Some pedagogical approaches to ethics even instruct students to be "neutral" in their work and to avoid passing judgment on the materials they translate. This ethical stance is epitomized in the training of court interpreters and medical translators, and it may seem appropriate in those contexts, even

though it is not obvious what "neutral" means.[7] When extended to translation
tasks in general, the injunction to be "neutral" eviscerates the agency of translators. Chesterman, for example, explicitly – and somewhat surprisingly – takes
the position that "the political engagement of the translator . . . lies outside the
realm of professional ethics" (2001:147, cf. 152; see also 1997:169-94). By contrast Gouanvic sees this sort of neutrality as an ethical travesty: "Imagine that a
text with obvious racist connotations ends up on a translator's desk. According
to professional ethics, nothing should stop it being translated in a satisfactory
manner. However in terms of this translation meeting the criteria of a general
ethics, nothing is more debatable. Translation retains a responsibility to the future
of target societies" (2001:209).

Approaches to the ethics of translation that recommend neutrality are
paradigmatic of the tendency to disperse ideology and to efface ethical issues in
translator training and professional codes. Such dispersal of ethics and ideology
in translation studies is manifest in the stance of translation teachers and scholars
who stridently maintain that such things as descriptive translation studies, the
arguments of postcolonial translation studies, and complex ideological analyses
of literary translations are irrelevant to pragmatic translator training. By contrast,
writing about the need for investigations of commercial practices of translation
in the past, Cronin observes that "pragmatic translation is as much in need of a
'cultural turn', a political reading, as the high-culture forms of translation practice
that have, up until now monopolized our attention" (2000:43). Colleagues who
refuse to acknowledge ideological and ethical aspects of commercial translation
become agents of and enact the dispersal of ideology in society as a whole and
in the profession of translation in particular. Such teachers uncritically inscribe
themselves and their students alike within dominant and hegemonic ideologies.

The pressure to undermine the translator's ethical and ideological self-
awareness, as well as the translator's empowered agency, may increase around
the world in the age of globalization as translators are enlisted more and more in
projects with a global reach sponsored by multinational political, economic, and
military interests. One form that the dispersal of ethics, ideology, and translator
agency takes is the focus in professional codes of ethics on the microlevels of
textual fidelity and immediate obligations to the employer, effacing larger spheres
of geopolitical responsibility to communities and the world. Anthony Pym reminds us, however, that "the translator's moral allegiance need not be entirely
to one side or the other, not even if only one side is paying", an argument that
he sees as ensuing directly from viewing translation in most circumstances as a
form of cooperation (2000:190). Quoting documents from ECOS, Mona Baker
also emphasizes that "translators and interpreters must be trained for society and

---

[7] In legal interpreting "neutral" might actually signify ethical allegiance to the court or state,
for example.

not just for the market" (2006b:473).

In the last two chapters of this book, we saw that the ethical and ideological aspects of translation are effaced when translators are told that the task of
translation is the transfer of meaning and when professionals are trained to translate cultural markers in a linear fashion as they occur in the text, rather than as
part of a larger conceptualization of the cultural underpinnings. The ethics and
ideology of translation are also dispersed and even undermined by prescriptive
approaches to translation training and the promulgation of strict protocols of
translation. Arguing against the idea of "meaning as presence" and following
Derrida, Kathleen Davis indicates that paradoxically decision making depends
on undecidability; there cannot be a calculus or mechanics of decision, nor can
there be any "right" decision from among predetermined options, because a
calculable program destroys all responsiblity (2001:50-51). Instead she argues
that "translators must therefore make decisions in the strong sense" (Davis
2001:51). Prescriptive approaches to pedagogy that institute or impose rigid
translation protocols efface the ethics of translation and the agency of translators,
eliminating the necessity of strong decision making on the part of translators.
Such pedagogy is a factor in the disempowerment of translators, and shifts in
these teaching techniques are important at the level of the discipline in fostering
ethical responsibility among translators.

It is no accident that the effacement of ethics occurs in the professional
training of translators, for translators are potentially powerful agents, as has
been stressed throughout this book and in translation studies since the foundation of the discipline. Societies are deeply invested in the allegiance and loyalty
of their translators and develop methods to prevent translators from becoming
traitors. The best way to ensure the allegiance of translators is to undermine their
independent ethical and ideological judgment, to keep them inscribed within
dominant politicized loyalties, and to efface this inscription at the very inception
of their careers. It is dangerous for those in power when translators begin to feel
empowered and to exert their own ethical judgments: in such cases translators
can much more easily assume independent ethical agency that may be judged
as betrayal by those in power.

Many translators and their teachers are actually content to stay inscribed in
dominant frameworks and to be disempowered by the effacement of their agency.
Indeed the profession attracts some people who prefer to follow the texts of others rather than write their own texts; such translators often choose a somewhat
passive orientation to their cultural agency and their lives in general, defining
for themselves small circles of affiliation and disavowing any geopolitical role.
The constraints on translators are internal as much as they are external, as we

have seen in earlier discussions of self-censorship in translation.[8] These issues bear more explicit discussion in relation to translator training, particularly in the context of globalization and the increased interconnection and interdependence of the world. Confronting questions related to ethics, responsibility, and affiliation is antecedent to the ability of a translator to feel empowered – to be heard, to be seen, to be able to make engaged choices, to exercise a full range of translation options, to improvise and invent, to construct meaning, to convey cultural difference, to make interventions, to exert activist agency of any sort.

Clearly one factor in empowering translators is to apprise them realistically of the difficulties they face as empowered agents. In order for translators to facilitate multidirectional cultural exchange rather than unilateral dissemination of Westernized cultural forms that displace local ones elsewhere in the world and in order to play active ethical and ideological roles in cultural interface in general, translators must be realistic about the material basis of translation in the contemporary world. Exchange of culture is never "free": economic and ideological interests always drive decisions about what is worthy of translation and how translation is effected.[9] Translators who wish to promote ethical cultural interface transcending the interests and investments of multinational corporations and other globalized entities may have to engage in forms of activist interventions and associations that go beyond their professional employment as translators. Such activities might take the form of joining voluntary associations that translate materials suppressed or ignored by powerful mainstream interests, helping to establish publishing houses to disseminate translations of texts from smaller cultures and minority languages within dominant nations such as the United States, or working with others to integrate translation with various types of direct activist interventions (cf. Baker 2006a, 2006b; Tymoczko 2000). Ethical and activist interventions are often much more effective and easier to undertake in groups – solidarity is generally more enabling than relying on the self alone in contesting powerful interests and in moving beyond the straitjacket of cultural norms. In any case it certainly does not do to imagine that beauty, truth, and justice alone can prevail in achieving equitable multidirectional cultural exchange in geopolitical contexts involving asymmetries of power and unequal economic resources without direct action and intervention on the part of translators themselves, whether working as individuals or in concert.

Enlarging the concept of translation so that it is open and receptive to all international forms and conceptualizations of translation is connected with the empowerment of the translator and the valorization of the translator's agency. In

---

[8] Similar points have been made by Venuti (1992:1) and Arrojo (1998:42-43).

[9] Such interests – including economic ones – governing translation have been well documented in descriptive translation studies. See, for example, Hermans (1999 and sources cited); Venuti (1992, 1995, 1998a, 1998b); Cronin (2003, 2006).

turn the power of translators relates to the ethical ability to convey cultural difference in translation by moving beyond unexamined cultural presuppositions that constitute dominant cultural frameworks as "history turned into nature". Vicente Rafael contends that "translation lends itself to either affirmation or evasion of social order" and its double nature gives translation its political dimension: "it draws boundaries between what can and cannot be admitted into social discourse even as it misdirects the construction of conventions" (1993:211). Requiring self-reflexivity in how individual translators think about translation, as well as how the discipline constitutes itself, seemingly technical aspects of translation studies such as cultural translation and the translation of meaning are central to the ethical role that translation plays in the world. They are central to whether translation will help to establish a more just world where difference is welcome or a world in which new forms of imperialism take shape. As a discipline, translation studies must make these questions more central to its priorities and its pedagogical methods if there is to be a commitment to an ethics of difference.

It is easy for translators and teachers of translation around the globe to view globalization as a bonanza for their own lives, a way to cash in on the expansion of international commercial and media interests as those interests extend their domains and dominion throughout the world. With tempting self-interests inherent in translating for globalizing markets comes the temptation for translators and translation scholars to anesthetize themselves to questions about equitable cultural exchange and the ethical implications of translation. Yet, ironically, at this point in history, a translator's decision to deny ideology in the processes and products of translation and to disengage from ethical questions pertaining to cultural exchange is a decision to disempower the self: it is a decision not merely to become a passive vehicle of dominant norms but to actively constitute the self as a servant of globalizing powers.

Thus the questions explored in this book have a particular urgency now, at this moment. We are at a critical point in time because of the rapid networking of the world and current struggles for global power. There are two possible directions these forces can take us – toward a homogenized world in which the local is subsumed in a generalized and banalized dominant culture, or toward a world in which there is a meeting of difference and a validation of the local (cf. Cronin 2006:127, 129, and sources cited). Both visions of the future are possible and in both scenarios translation will play a central role. Reconceptualizing translation and translation studies along the lines discussed here shifts translation toward supporting the second trajectory. How these possiblilities actually play out in the future will depend to a large extent on whether the concept of translation is enlarged, whether translators find ways to exert their agency and remain empowered, and whether the ethics of translation is addressed by the discipline as a whole.

Throughout this book I have argued that Western conceptual dominance must be dethroned in the discipline of translation studies. But what does *Western* really mean at this point in time? In many respect Western dispositions and practices no longer have a locus: they have escaped their traditional boundaries and cultures. Certainly what is Western cannot be identified solely with Europe or the United States or countries around the world that use European languages. The *ideas* of Western culture have been loosed from Western geography and Western spaces. It can argued that Japan and Hong Kong are ahead of the rest of the world in Westernization – they point to the future of what has been thought of as the West more than perhaps any other parts of the globe. Certainly the idea of the Western cannot be identified with class; it is not possible to control the spread of Western culture and ideas by suppressing or obliterating educated elites (as has been attempted in some postcolonial countries and in China during the Cultural Revolution). Nor can the Western be escaped by retreating to narrow religious frameworks. In point of fact few people in the world would actually want to back away totally from what has generally been identified as Western culture. Many of the poorest people in the world depend for such well-being as they have on the functioning of so-called Western systems that have been generalized around the globe: vaccination programs, disease control, water management, food production, flood controls, transportation, and communications.

In translation studies so-called Western contributions to translation – from the concept of translation as transfer to many of the translation technologies currently revolutionizing the field – have been equally productive and even essential. I have not been arguing against the view of translation as transfer *per se*, but rather questioning exclusivist thinking about translation in these Western terms. The view of translation as transfer is useful for many cases of translation, but it utterly fails in other situations. It obscures the necessity to take communication apart and recompose it in oral contexts, just as it obscures the affinities of translation with telling a story about a source text. It turns away from the life-giving and birthing nature of translation. It obscures the nature of current practices in media translation that go far beyond transfer. And it totally effaces the relation between translation and power.

Such limitations are not a function of Western European concepts of translation as transfer alone. Any exclusivist view of translation would be problematic and any exclusivist assertion about translation based primarily on only one of the world's conceptualizations of translation would run into very similar problems. What is needed in translation studies is inclusivity and complementarity rather than exclusive assertion or rejection of any particular tradition of thinking about translation. This movement toward greater diversity is required not just for the concept translation, but also for the many other cluster concepts central to human life where diversity and richness are adaptive and even essential to human survival. Thus, the real question before us is not repudiating Western thinking about and approaches to translation but reaffirming difference and variation, and using them to reconceptualize the discipline of translation studies as a whole. It is a matter of valuing local knowledge beyond the West, thus reevaluating the praxis, conceptualization, and theory of translation on a fully cross-cultural basis. What is at issue is the development of a discipline that transcends a monologic, single-sided view of cultural meetings and cultural interchange, that sees the value in every local center of knowledge about translation and other forms of cultural interface.

There are analogues in the biological world to my call for diversity and the survival of the local. The ecological problems and even potential disasters associated with monocultures in agricultural practices are well known. The strength of biodiversity in any ecological context – whether it is a cultivated or natural environment – is well recognized. The importance of preserving species and of maintaining biodiversity in successful ecosystems is beyond argument. Nonetheless, these attitudes about biodiversity have yet to be extended to human beings – to human lifeways, human cultures, human ideation.

The enlargement of translation studies that this book argues for can be thought of in terms of biodiversity – but it is biodiversity of the mind, that special type of biodiversity that is most characteristic of human life and most associated with human well-being. The value of retaining diverse *ideas* about translation that have evolved over thousands of years in different human cultures should be obvious. The value of such diverse ideas regarding ways of mediating between cultures and across languages is particularly adaptive, as much a matter of human survival and human welfare as is attention to the physical environment. The "plasticity, pliability, diversity, and adaptability" (Legrand 2005:34) of local knowledges about translation constitute a cognitive and cultural heritage from the past, a legacy that comes to us from the depths of time. The world's diverse ideas about translation are the reserves for dispositions and practices of the future that human beings will need to meet the demands of communication in a rapidly changing world. If cherished, this diversity of ideas – this biodiversity of the mind – will sustain translators in coping with challenging tasks, help them solve ethical dilemmas, and empower them in situations of sensitive cultural interface. These ideational reserves about translation can help translators to act creatively and powerfully, to be effective intellectual and ethical agents. A commitment to exploring and preserving the great variety of human ideas about translation will put translation studies at the cutting edge of category and concept investigations in humanistic and social studies, and at the frontiers of self-reflexive, equitable reorganization of international academic disciplines. The recursive benefits of enlarging translation and empowering translators will come to full fruition when the many and varied conceptualizations of translation worldwide are recognized as resources in contemporary translation theory, research, pedagogy, and praxis alike.

Works Cited

Abel, Jonathan E. 2005. "Translation as Community: The Opacity of Modernizations of *Genji monogatari*". *Nation, Language, and the Ethics of Translation*. Ed. Sandra Bermann and Michael Wood. Princeton: Princeton University Press. 146-58.

Adab, Beverly, and Cristina Valdés, eds. 2004. *Key Debates in the Translation of Advertising Material*. *The Translator* 10 no. 2, special issue.

Adejunmobi, Moradewun. 1998. "Translation and Postcolonial Identity: African Writing and European Languages". *The Translator* 4:2.163-81.

Aixelá, Javier Franco. 1996. "Culture-specific Items in Translation". *Translation, Power, Subversion*. Ed. Román Álvarez, and M. Carmen-África Vidal. Clevedon: Multilingual Matters. 52-78.

American Heritage Dictionary of the English Language. 1969. Ed. William Morris. Boston: American Heritage and Houghton Mifflin.

Anderson, Benedict. 1991. *Imagined Communities: Reflections on the Origin and Spread of Nationalism*. Rev. ed. London: Verso.

Appiah, Kwame Anthony. 2000. "Thick Translation". 1993. *The Translation Studies Reader*. Ed. Lawrence Venuti. London: Routledge. 417-29.

Arduini, Stefano, and Robert Hodgson, Jr., eds. 2004. *Similarity and Difference in Translation*. Rimini: Guaraldi.

Arrojo, Rosemary. 1998. "The Revision of the Traditional Gap between Theory and Practice and the Empowerment of Translation in Postmodern Times". *The Translator* 4:1.25-48.

------ 2002. "Writing, Interpreting, and the Power Struggle for the Control of Meaning: Scenes from Kafka, Borges, and Kosztolányi". *Translation and Power*. Ed. Maria Tymoczko and Edwin Gentzler. Amherst: University of Massachusetts Press. 63-79.

------ 2003. "The Power of Originals and the Scandal of Translation: A Reading of Edgar Allan Poe's 'The Oval Portrait'". *Apropos of Ideology: Translation Studies on Ideology – Ideologies in Translation Studies*. Ed. María Calzada Pérez. Manchester: St. Jerome. 165-80.

Ashcroft, Bill, Gareth Griffiths, and Helen Tiffin. 1989. *The Empire Writes Back: Theory and Practice in Post-colonial Literature*. London: Routledge.

Austin, J. L. 1975. *How to Do Things with Words*. 2nd. ed. Ed. J. O. Urmson and Marina Sbisà. Cambridge: Harvard University Press.

Bachmann-Medick, Doris. 2006. "Meanings of Translation in Cultural Anthropology". *Translating Others*. Ed. Theo Hermans. 2 vols. Manchester: St. Jerome. 1.33-42.

Baker, Mona. 1992. *In Other Words: A Coursebook on Translation*. London: Routledge.

------ 1995. "Corpora in Translation Studies: An Overview and Some Suggestions for Future Research". *Target* 7:2.223-43.

------ ed. 1998. *Routledge Encyclopedia of Translation Studies*. London: Routledge.

------ 2006a. *Translation and Conflict: A Narrative Account*. London: Routledge.

------ 2006b. "Translation and Activism: Emerging Patterns of Narrative Community". *Massachusetts Review*. 47:3.462-84.

Bal, Mieke. 1997. *Narratology: Introduction to the Theory of Narrative*. 2nd. ed. Toronto: University of Toronto Press.

Bandia, Paul. 2000. "Decolonizing Translation: African Proverbs and Aphorisms". *Beyond the Western Tradition*. Ed. Marilyn Gaddis Rose. Binghamton: SUNY Binghamton, Center for Research in Translation. 147-61.

Barbaza, Raniela. 2005. "Translation and the Korido: Negotiating Identity in Philippine Metrical Romances". *Asian Translation Traditions*. Ed. Eva Hung and Judy Wakabayashi. Manchester: St. Jerome. 247-62.

Bassnett, Susan. 1998. "When is a Translation not a Translation?". *Constructing Cultures: Essays on Literary Translation*. Ed. Susan Bassnett and André Lefevere. Clevedon: Multilingual Matters.

------ 2002. *Translation Studies*. 3rd. ed. London: Routledge.

Bassnett, Susan, and André Lefevere, eds. 1990. *Translation, History and Culture*. London: Pinter.

Bassnett, Susan, and Harish Trivedi, eds. 1999. *Post-Colonial Translation: Theory and Practice*. London: Routledge.

Basso, Keith H. 1990. *Western Apache Language and Culture: Essays in Linguistic Anthropology*. Tucson: University of Arizona Press.

Bastin, Georges L., Álvaro Echeverri, and Ángela Campo. Forthcoming. "Translation and the Emancipation of Hispanic America". *Translation and Resistance*. Ed. Maria Tymoczko.

Benedeit. 1928. *The Anglo-Norman "Voyage of St. Brendan"*. Ed. E.G.R. Waters. Oxford: Clarendon Press.

Benjamin, Walter. 1969. "The Task of the Translator". 1923. Trans. Harry Zohn. *Illuminations*. New York: Schocken. 69-82.

Berman, Antoine. 1992. *The Experience of the Foreign: Culture and Translation in Romantic Germany*. Trans. S. Heyvaert. Albany: State University of New York Press.

------ 2000. "Translation and the Trials of the Foreign". 1985. Trans. Lawrence Venuti. *The Translation Studies Reader*. Ed. Lawrence Venuti. London: Routledge. 284-97.

Bermann, Sandra. 2005. "Translating History". *Nation, Language, and the Ethics of Translation*. Ed. Sandra Bermann and Michael Wood. Princeton: Princeton University Press. 257-73.

Bhabha, Homi K. 1994. *The Location of Culture*. London: Routledge.

Binchy, D.A. 1954. "Secular Institutions". *Early Irish Society*. Ed. Myles Dillon. Dublin: At the Three Candles. 52-65.

Blommaert, Jan. 2005. "Bourdieu the Ethnographer: The Ethnographic Grounding of Habitus and Voice". *The Translator* 11:2.219-36.

Boase-Beier, Jean. 2006. *Stylistic Approaches to Translation*. Manchester: St. Jerome.

Bohannan, Laura. 1966. "Shakespeare in the Bush". *Natural History*, August/September. 28-33.

Bolinger, Dwight. 1977. *Meaning and Form*. London: Longman.

Boothman, Derek. 2002. "Translatability between Paradigms: Gramsci's Translation of Crocean Concepts". *Crosscultural Transgressions: Research Models in Translation Studies II: Historical and Ideological Issues*. Ed. Theo Hermans. Manchester: St. Jerome. 103-19.

Borges, Jorge Luis. 1974. "Pierre Menard, autor del Quijote". *Obras completas*. 3 vols. Buenos Aires: Emecé. 1.444-50.

Bourdieu, Pierre. 1977. *Outline of a Theory of Practice*. Trans. Richard Nice. Cambridge: Cambridge University Press.

------ 1993. *The Field of Cultural Production: Essays on Art and Literature*. Ed. Randal Johnson. New York: Columbia University Press.

Branchadell, Albert, and Lovell Margaret West, eds. 2005. *Less Translated Languages*. Amsterdam: John Benjamins.

Brisset, Annie. 1996. *A Sociocritique of Translation: Theatre and Alterity in Quebec, 1968-1988*. 1990. Trans. Rosalind Gill and Roger Gannon. Toronto: University of Toronto Press.

Broeck, Raymond van den. 1978. "The Concept of Equivalence in Translation Theory: Some Critical Reflections". *Literature and Translation: New Perspectives on Translation Studies*. Ed. James S. Holmes, José Lambert, Raymond van den Broeck. Louvain: Acco. 49-58.

Bruner, Jerome. 1986. *Actual Minds, Possible Worlds*. Cambridge: Harvard University Press.

Brunette, Louise. 2002. "Normes et censure: ne pas confondre". *TTR* 15:2.223-33.

Cacciari, Christina, ed. 1995. *Similarity in Language, Thought and Perception*. Turnhout: Brepols.

Calzada Pérez, María, ed. 2003. *Apropos of Ideology: Translation Studies on Ideology – Ideologies in Translation Studies*. Manchester: St. Jerome.

Carbonell Cortés, Ovidi. "Misquoted Others: Locating Newness and Authority in Cultural Translation". *Translating Others*. Ed. Theo Hermans. 2 vols. Manchester: St. Jerome. 1.43-63.

Carney, James, ed. 1964. *The Poems of Blathmac, Son of Cú Brettan: Together with the Irish Gospel of Thomas and a Poem on the Virgin Mary*. Dublin: Irish Texts Society.

Catford, J. C. 1965. *A Linguistic Theory of Translation: An Essay in Applied Linguistics*. London: Oxford University Press.

Chamberlain, Lori. 1992. "Gender and the Metaphorics of Translation". *Rethinking Translation: Discourse, Subjectivity, Ideology*. Ed. Lawrence Venuti. London: Routledge. 57-74.

Chan, Elsie. 2002. "Translation Principles and the Translator's Agenda: A Systemic Approach to Yan Fu". *Crosscultural Transgressions: Research Models in Translation Studies II: Historical and Ideological Issues*. Ed. Theo Hermans. Manchester: St. Jerome. 61-75.

Chan, Leo Tak-hung, ed. 2004. *Twentieth-Century Chinese Translation Theory: Modes, Issues and Debates*. Amsterdam: John Benjamins.

Chesterman, Andrew. 1996. "On Similarity". *Target* 8:1.159-64.

------ 1997. *Memes of Translation: The Spread of Ideas in Translation Theory*. Amsterdam: John Benjamins.

------ 1998. *Contrastive Functional Analysis*. Amsterdam: John Benjamins.

------ 2000. "A Causal Model for Translation Studies". *Intercultural Faultlines: Research Models in Translation Studies I: Textual and Cognitive Aspects*. Ed. Maeve Olohan. Manchester: St. Jerome. 15-27.

------ 2001. "Proposal for a Hieronymic Oath". *The Translator* 7:2.139-54.

------ 2004. "Where is Similarity?" *Similarity and Difference in Translation*. Ed. Stefano Arduini and Robert Hodgson, Jr. Rimini: Guaraldi. 63-75.

Chesterman, Andrew, and Rosemary Arrojo. 2000. "Shared Ground in Translation Studies". *Target* 12:1.151-60.

Chesterman, Andrew, and Emma Wagner. 2002. *Can Theory Help Translators? A Dialogue Between the Ivory Tower and the Wordface*. Manchester: St. Jerome.

Cheung, Martha P. Y. 2002. "Power and Ideology in Translation Research in Twentieth-Century China: An Analysis of Three Seminal Works". *Crosscultural Transgressions: Research Models in Translation Studies II: Historical and Ideological Issues*. Ed. Theo Hermans. Manchester: St. Jerome. 144-64.

------ 2005. "'To Translate' Means 'To Exchange'? A New Interpretation of the Earliest Chinese Attempts to Define Translation ('Fanyi')". *Target* 17:1.27-48.

------ ed. 2006a. *An Anthology of Chinese Discourse on Translation*. Vol.1. Manchester: St. Jerome.

------ 2006b. "From 'Theory' to 'Discourse': The Making of a Translation Anthology". *Translating Others*. Ed. Theo Hermans. 2 vols. Manchester: St. Jerome. 1.87-101.

Cheyfitz, Eric. 1997. *The Poetics of Imperialism: Translation and Colonization from "The Tempest" to "Tarzan"*. Expanded ed. Philadelphia: University of Pennsylvania Press.

Chodorow, Nancy J. 1999. *The Power of Feelings: Personal Meaning in Psychoanalysis, Gender, and Culture*. New Haven: Yale University Press.

Clifford, James. 1988. *The Predicament of Culture: Twentieth-Century Ethnography, Literature, and Art*. Cambridge: Harvard University Press.

Clifford, James, and George E. Marcus. 1986. *Writing Culture: The Poetics and Politics of Ethnography*. Berkeley: University of California Press.

Compact Edition of the Oxford English Dictionary. 1971. Oxford: Oxford University Press.

Crisafulli, Edoardo. 2002. "The Quest for an Eclectic Methodology of Translation Description". *Crosscultural Transgressions: Research Models in Translation Studies II: Historical and Ideological Issues*. Ed. Theo Hermans. Manchester: St. Jerome. 26-43.

Cronin, Michael. 1998. "The Cracked Looking Glass of Servants: Translation and Minority Languages in a Global Age". *The Translator* 4:2.145-62.

------ 2000. "History, Translation, Postcolonialism". *Changing the Terms: Translating in the Postcolonial Era*. Ed. Sherry Simon and Paul St-Pierre. Ottawa: University of Ottawa Press. 33-52.

------ 2002. "The Empire Talks Back: Orality, Heteronomy, and the Cultural Turn in Interpretation Studies". *Translation and Power*. Ed. Maria Tymoczko and Edwin Gentzler. Amherst: University of Massachusetts. 45-62.

------ 2003. *Translation and Globalization*. London: Routledge.

------ 2006. *Translation and Identity*. London: Routledge.

Dasgupta, Probal. 2000. "The Post-Missionary Condition: Toward Perceptual Reciprocity". *Changing the Terms: Translating in the Postcolonial Era*. Ed. Sherry Simon and Paul St-Pierre. Ottawa: University of Ottawa Press. 289-305.

Davis, Kathleen. 2001. *Deconstruction and Translation*. Manchester: St. Jerome.

Delisle, Jean, and Judith Woodsworth, eds. 1995. *Translators through History*. Amsterdam: John Benjamins.

Derrida, Jacques. 1985. "Des Tours de Babel". *Difference in Translation*. Ed. and trans. Joseph F. Graham. Ithaca: Cornell University Press. 165-248.

Devy, Ganesh. 1999. "Translation and Literary History – An Indian View". *Postcolonial Translation: Theory and Practice*. Ed. Susan Bassnett and Harish Trivedi. London: Routledge. 182-88.

Dictionary of the Irish Language, Based Mainly on Old and Middle Irish Materials. 1983. Compact ed. Dublin: Royal Irish Academy.

Eliade, Mircea, ed. 1987. *The Encyclopedia of Religion*. New York: Macmillan.

Encyclopaedia Britannica: A New Survey of Universal Knowledge. 1947. Chicago: Encyclopaedia Britannica.

Encyclopaedia Britannica. 1974, 2005. See *The New Encyclopaedia Britannica*.

Eoyang, Eugene Chen. 1993. *The Transparent Eye: Reflections on Translation, Chinese Literature, and Comparative Poetics*. Honolulu: University of Hawaii Press.

Even-Zohar, Itamar. 1978. *Papers in Historical Poetics*. Tel Aviv: Porter Institute for Poetics and Semiotics.

------ 1990. *Polysystem Studies*. *Poetics Today* 11 no. 1, special issue.

Faiq, Said. 2000. "Arabic Translation: A Glorious Past but a Meek Present". *Beyond the Western Tradition*. Ed. Marilyn Gaddis Rose. Binghamton: SUNY Binghamton, Center for Research in Translation. 83-98.

Fairclough, Norman. 1989. *Language and Power*. New York: Longman.

Fawcett, Peter. 1997. *Translation and Language: Linguistic Theories Explained*. Manchester: St. Jerome.

Feddersen-Petersen, D.U. 2000. "Vocalization of European Wolves (Canus lupus lupus L.) and Various Dog Breeds (Canis lupus f. fam.)". *Archiv für Tierzucht, Archives of Animal Breeding* 43:4.387-97.

Fenton, Sabine, ed. 2004. *For Better or For Worse: Translation as a Tool for Change in the South Pacific*. Manchester: St. Jerome.

Fenton, Sabine, and Paul Moon. 2002. "The Translation of the Treaty of Waitangi: A Case of Disempowerment". *Translation and Power*. Ed. Maria Tymoczko and Edwin Gentzler. Amherst: University of Massachusetts Press. 25-44.

Fitzpatrick, Elizabeth B. 2000. "Balai Pustaka in the Dutch East Indies: Colonizing a Literature". *Changing the Terms: Translating in the Postcolonial Era*. Ed. Sherry Simon and Paul St-Pierre. Ottawa: University of Ottawa Press. 113-26.

Flotow, Luise von. 1997. *Translation and Gender: Translating in the "Era of Feminism"*. Manchester: St. Jerome.

Folkart, Barbara. 1991. *Le Conflit des énonciations: Traduction et discours rapporté*. Candiac, Quebec: Éditions Balzac.

"Forum: Shared Ground in Translation Studies". 2000. *Target* 12:2.333-62.

------ 2001a. *Target* 13:1.149-68.

------ 2001b. *Target* 13:2.333-50.

------ 2002. *Target* 14:1.137-43.

Foucault, Michel. 1972. *The Archaeology of Knowledge and The Discourse on Language*. Trans. A.M. Sheridan Smith. New York: Pantheon.

Gambier, Yves. 2002. "Les censures dans la traduction audiovisuelle". *TTR* 15:2.203-22.

Geertz, Clifford. 1973. *The Interpretation of Cultures*. New York: Basic Books.

Gentner, Dedre, Keith J. Holyoak, and Boicho N. Kokinov, eds. 2001. *The Analogical Mind: Perspectives from Cognitive Science*. Cambridge: M.I.T. Press.

Gentzler, Edwin. 1996. "Translation, Counter-Culture, and *The Fifties* in the USA". *Translation, Power, Subversion*. Ed. Román Álvarez, and M. Carmen-África Vidal. Clevedon: Multilingual Matters. 116-37.

------ 2001. *Contemporary Translation Theories*. 2nd. ed. Clevedon: Multilingual Matters.

Gladwell, Malcolm. 2005. *Blink: The Power of Thinking without Thinking*. New York: Little, Brown.

Gleitman, Lila R., Sharon Lee Armstrong, and Henry Gleitman. 1983. "On Doubting the Concept 'Concept'". *New Trends in Conceptual Representation: Challenges to Piaget's Theory?* Ed. Ellin Kofsky Scholnick. Hillsdale, N.J.: Lawrence Erlbaum Associates. 87-110.

Godard, Barbara. 1997. "Writing Between Cultures". *TTR* 10:1.53-99.

Gopinathan, G. 2000. "Ancient Indian Theories of Translation". *Beyond the Western Tradition*. Ed. Marilyn Gaddis Rose. Binghamton: SUNY Binghamton, Center for Research in Translation. 165-73.

------ 2006. "Translation, Transcreation and Culture: Theories of Translation in Indian Languages". *Translating Others*. Ed. Theo Hermans. 2 vols. Manchester: St. Jerome. 1.236-46.

Gorlée, Dinda. 1994. *Semiotics and the Problem of Translation, with Special Reference to the Semiotics of Charles S. Peirce*. Amsterdam: Rodopi.

Gouanvic, Jean-Marc. 2000. "Legitimacy, *Marronnage* and the Power of Translation". *Changing the Terms: Translating in the Postcolonial Era*. Ed. Sherry Simon and Paul St-Pierre. Ottawa: University of Ottawa Press. 101-11.

------ 2001. "Ethos, Ethics and Translation: Toward a Community of Destinies". *The Translator* 7:2.203-12.

------ 2002. "A Model of Structuralist Constructivism in Translation Studies". *Cross-cultural Transgressions: Research Models in Translation Studies II: Historical and Ideological Issues*. Ed. Theo Hermans. Manchester: St. Jerome. 93-102.

Grähs, Lillebill, Gustav Korlén, and Bertil Malmberg, eds. 1978. *Theory and Practice of Translation*. Bern: Peter Lang.

Gutt, Ernst-August. 2000a. "Issues of Translation Research in the Inferential Paradigm of Communication". *Intercultural Faultlines: Research Models in Translation Studies I: Textual and Cognitive Aspects*. Ed. Maeve Olohan. Manchester: St. Jerome. 161-79.

------ 2000b. *Translation and Relevance: Cognition and Context*. Manchester: St. Jerome.

Hall, Stuart. 1997. "The Local and the Global: Globalization and Ethnicity". *Culture, Globalization and the World-System: Contemporary Conditions for the Representation of Identity*. Ed. Anthony D. King. Minneapolis: University of Minneapolis Press. 19-40.

Halverson, Sandra. 1997. "The Concept of Equivalence in Translation Studies: Much Ado About Something". *Target* 9:2.207-33.

------ 1999a. "Conceptual Work and the 'Translation' Concept". *Target* 11:1.1-31.

------ 1999b. "Image Schemas, Metaphoric Processes, and the 'Translate' Concept". *Metaphor and Symbol* 14:3.199-219.

Hatim, Basil. 1997. *Communication Across Cultures: Translation Theory and Contrastive Text Linguistics*. Exeter: University of Exeter Press.

------ 1999. "Implications of Research into Translator Invisibility". *Target* 11:2.201-22.

Hatim, Basil, and Ian Mason. 1990. *Discourse and the Translator*. Harlow, Essex: Longman.

------1997. *The Translator as Communicator*. London: Routledge.

Heaney, Seamus, trans. 1983. *Sweeney Astray: A Version from the Irish*. New York: Farrar, Straus, Giroux, 1984.

Helgason, Jón Karl. 1999. *The Rewriting of Njáls Saga: Translation, Politics and Icelandic Sagas*. Clevedon: Multilingual Matters.

Hermans, Theo. 1982. "P. C. Hooft: The Sonnets and the Tragedy". *The Art and Science of Translation*. Ed. André Lefevere and Kenneth David Jackson. *Dispositio* 7, special issue. 95-110.

------ Ed. 1985. *The Manipulation of Literature: Studies in Literary Translation*. London: Croom Helm.

------ 1991. "Translational Norms and Correct Translations". *Translation Studies: The State of the Art*. Proceedings of the First James S. Holmes Symposium on Translation Studies. Ed. Kitty M. van Leuven-Zwart and Ton Naaijkens. Amsterdam: Rodopi. 155-69.

------ 1993. "On Modelling Translation: Models, Norms and the Field of Translation". *Livius* 4:69-88.

------ 1995. "Toury's Empiricism Version One". *The Translator* 1:2.215-23.

------ 1996. "Norms and the Determination of Translation: A Theoretical Framework". *Translation, Power, Subversion*. Ed. Román Álvarez, and M. Carmen-África Vidal. Clevedon: Multilingual Matters. 25-51.

------ 1999. *Translation in Systems: Descriptive and System-oriented Approaches Explained*. Manchester: St. Jerome.

------ ed. 2002. *Crosscultural Transgressions: Research Models in Translation Studies II: Historical and Ideological Issues*. Manchester: St. Jerome.

------ ed. 2006. *Translating Others*. 2 vols. Manchester: St. Jerome.

Hillers, Barbara. 1999. "Ulysses and the Judge of Truth: Sources and Meanings in the Irish *Odyssey*". *Peritia* 13:194-233.

Hobsbawm, Eric. 1983. "Inventing Traditions." *The Invention of Tradition*. Ed. Eric Hobsbawm and Terence Ranger. Cambridge: Cambridge University Press. 1-14.

Hofstadter, Douglas R. 1997. *Le Ton beau de Marot: In Praise of the Music of Language*. New York: BasicBooks.

Holmes, James S. 1994. *Translated! Papers on Literary Translation and Translation Studies*. 2nd. ed. Amsterdam: Rodopi.

Hung, Eva. 2005a. "The Gilded Translator: Issues of Authority, Control and Cultural Self-representation". *Translation and the Construction of Identity*. IATIS Yearbook 2005. Ed. Juliane House, M. Rosario, Martín Ruano, and Nicole Baumgarten. Seoul: IATIS. 148-66.

------ 2005b. "Translation in China – An Analytic Survey: First Century B.C.E. to Early Twentieth Century". *Asian Translation Traditions*. Ed. Eva Hung and Judy Wakabayashi. Manchester: St. Jerome. 67-107.

------ 2006. "'And the Translator Is – ': Translators in Chinese History". *Translating Others*. Ed. Theo Hermans. 2 vols. Manchester: St. Jerome. 1.145-60.

Hung, Eva, and Judy Wakabayashi, eds. 2005. *Asian Translation Traditions*. Manchester: St. Jerome.

Inghilleri, Moira, ed. 2005. *Bourdieu and the Sociology of Translation and Interpreting*. *The Translator* 11 no. 2, special issue.

Iser, Wolfgang. 1974. *The Implied Reader: Patterns of Communication in Prose Fiction from Bunyan to Beckett*. Baltimore: Johns Hopkins University Press.

Israel, Hephzibah. 2006. "Translating the Bible in Nineteenth-Century India: Protestant Missionary Translation and the Standard Tamil Version". *Translating Others*. Ed. Theo Hermans. 2 vols. Manchester: St. Jerome. 2.441-59.

Ivir, Vladimir. 1987. "Procedures and Strategies for the Translation of Culture". *Indian Journal of Applied Linguistics* 13:2.35-46.

Jakobson, Roman. 1956. "Two Aspects of Language and Two Types of Aphasic Disturbances". In vol. 2. *Selected Writings*. The Hague: Mouton, 1971. 239-59.

------ 1959. "On Linguistic Aspects of Translation". *On Translation*. Ed. Reuben A. Brower. Cambridge: Harvard University Press. 232-39.

Jedamski, Doris. 2005. "Translation in the Malay World: Different Communities, Different Agendas". *Asian Translation Traditions*. Ed. Eva Hung and Judy Wakabayashi. Manchester: St. Jerome. 211-45.

Joyce, James. 1986. *Ulysses: The Corrected Text*. Ed. Hans Walter Gabler et al. New York: Random House.

Kálmán, G. C. 1986. "Some Borderline Cases of Translation". *New Comparison* 1:117-22.

Kamala, N. 2000. "Gateway of India: Representing the Nation in English Translation". *Changing the Terms: Translating in the Postcolonial Era*. Ed. Sherry Simon and Paul St-Pierre. Ottawa: University of Ottawa Press. 245-59.

Katan, David. 2004. *Translating Cultures: An Introduction for Translators, Interpreters and Mediators*. 2nd ed. Manchester: St. Jerome.

Kelly, Louis G. 1979. *The True Interpreter: A History of Translation Practice and Theory in the West*. Oxford: Blackwell.

Kenny, Kevin, ed. 2004. *Ireland and the British Empire*. Oxford: Oxford University Press.

Kiberd, Declan. 1995. *Inventing Ireland*. Cambridge: Harvard University Press.

Kothari, Rita. 2003. *Translating India*. Manchester: St. Jerome.

---------2005. "The Fiction of Translation". *Asian Translation Traditions*. Ed. Eva Hung and Judy Wakabayashi. Manchester: St. Jerome. 263-73.

Kripke, Saul A. 1980. *Naming and Necessity*. Cambridge: Harvard University Press.

Kuhn, Thomas S. 1962. *The Structure of Scientific Revolutions*. Chicago: University of Chicago Press.

Lakoff, George. 1987. *Women, Fire, and Dangerous Things: What Categories Reveal about the Mind*. Chicago: University of Chicago Press.

Lakoff, George, and Mark Johnson. 1980. *Metaphors We Live By*. Chicago: University of Chicago Press.

Lane-Mercier, Gillian. 1997. "Translating the Untranslatable: The Translator's Aesthetic, Ideological and Political Responsibility". *Target* 9:43-68.

Larkosh, Christopher. 2002. "Translating Woman: Victoria Ocampo and the Empires of Foreign Fascination". *Translation and Power*. Ed. Maria Tymoczko and Edwin Gentzler. Amherst: University of Massachusetts Press. 99-121.

Laviosa, Sara, ed. 1998. *The Corpus-Based Approach*. *Meta: Journal des traducteurs* 43 no. 4, special issue.

Lefevere, André. 1982. "Mother Courage's Cucumbers: Text, System and Refraction in a Theory of Literature". *Modern Language Studies* 12:3-20.

------ 1985. "Why Waste Our Time on Rewrites? The Trouble with Interpretation and the Role of Rewriting in an Alternative Paradigm". *The Manipulation of Literature: Studies in Literary Translation*. Ed. Theo Hermans. London: Croom Helm. 215-43.

------ 1992a. *Translation/History/Culture: A Sourcebook*. London: Routledge.

------ 1992b. *Translation, Rewriting, and the Manipulation of Literary Fame*. London: Routledge.

Legrand, Pierre. 2005. "Issues in the Translatability of Law". *Nation, Language, and the Ethics of Translation*. Ed. Sandra Bermann and Michael Wood. Princeton: Princeton University Press. 30-50.

Levin, Harry S. 1941. *James Joyce: A Critical Introduction*. Rev. ed. New York: New Directions, 1960.

Levý, Jiří. 1967. "Translation as a Decision Process". *To Honor Roman Jakobson: Essays on the Occasion of his Seventieth Birthday, 11 October 1966.* 3 vols. The Hague: Mouton. 2.1071-82.

Lewandowska-Tomasczyk, Barbara, and Marcel Thelen, eds. 1992. *Translation and Meaning.* Part 2. Maastricht: Euroterm.

------ 1997. *Translation and Meaning.* Part 4. Maastricht: Universitaire Pers Maastricht.

Lewis, Philip E. 1985. "The Measure of Translation Effects". *Difference in Translation.* Ed. Joseph F. Graham. Ithaca: Cornell University Press. 31-62.

Lianeri, Alexandra. 2006. "Translation and the Language(s) of Historiography: Understanding Ancient Greek and Chinese Ideas of History". *Translating Others.* Ed. Theo Hermans. 2 vols. Manchester: St. Jerome. 1.67-86.

Lin Kenan. 2002. "Translation as a Catalyst for Social Change in China". *Translation and Power.* Ed. Maria Tymoczko and Edwin Gentzler. Amherst: University of Massachusetts Press. 160-83.

Lowell, Robert. 1961. *Imitations.* New York: Farrar, Straus, and Cudahy.

Maier, Carol. 2002. "Translation, *Dépaysement*, and their Figuration". *Translation and Power.* Ed. Maria Tymoczko and Edwin Gentzler. Amherst: University of Massachusetts Press. 184-94.

------ 2006. "The Translator as *Theôros*: Thoughts on Cogitation, Figuration and Current Creative Writing". *Translating Others.* Ed. Theo Hermans. 2 vols. Manchester: St. Jerome. 1.163-80.

Malinowski, Bronislaw. 1944. *A Scientific Theory of Culture and Other Essays.* Chapel Hill: University of North Carolina Press.

------ 1947. "Introduction". *Cuban Counterpoint: Tobacco and Sugar.* Fernando Ortiz. Trans. Harriet de Onís. New York: Alfred A. Knopf. ix-xvi.

Man, Paul de. 1986. "Conclusions: Walter Benjamin's 'The Task of the Translator'". *The Resistance to Theory.* Minneapolis: University of Minnesota Press. 73-105.

Mayer, Reinhard. 2000. "Evaluating Competing Translations: 'Sincere Roguery and Deceitful Truth' in the Analects of Confucius". *Beyond the Western Tradition.* Ed. Marilyn Gaddis Rose. Binghamton: SUNY Binghamton, Center for Research in Translation. 175-86.

Merkle, Denise, ed. 2002. *Censure et traduction dans le monde occidental, Censorship and Translation in the Western World, TTR* 15 no. 2, special issue.

------ Forthcoming. "Secret Literary Societies in Late-Victorian England". *Translation and Resistance.* Ed. Maria Tymoczko.

Meyer, Robert, ed. 1977. *Merugud Uilix maic Leirtis.* Dublin: Dublin Institute for Advanced Studies.

Mills, Sara. 1997. *Discourse.* London: Routledge.

Mitter, Partha. 1987. "Can We Ever Understand Alien Cultures? Some Epistemological Concerns Relating to the Perception and Understanding of the Other". *Comparative Criticism* 9:3-34.

Molloy, Sylvia. 2005. "Postcolonial Latin America and the Magic Realist Imperative:

A Report to the Academy". *Nation, Language, and the Ethics of Translation.* Ed. Sandra Bermann and Michael Wood. Princeton: Princeton University Press. 370-79.

Montgomery, Scott L. 2000. *Science in Translation: Movements of Knowledge through Cultures and Time.* Chicago: University of Chicago Press.

Morrison, Toni. 1970. *The Bluest Eye: A Novel.* New York: Holt, Rinehart, and Winston.

Muhawi, Ibrahim. 2006. "Towards a Folkloristic Theory of Translation". *Translating Others.* Ed. Theo Hermans. 2 vols. Manchester: St. Jerome. 2.365-79.

Mukherjee, Sujit. 1994. *Translation as Discovery and Other Essays on Indian Literature in English Translation.* 2nd. ed. London: Sangam Books.

------ 2004. *Translation as Recovery.* Ed. Meenakshi Mukherjee. Delhi: Pencraft International.

Munday, Jeremy. 2001. *Introducing Translation Studies: Theories and Applications.* London: Routledge.

------ 2004. "Advertising: Some Challenges to Translation Theory". *The Translator* 10:2.199-219.

Murphy, Gerard, ed. and trans. 1956. *Early Irish Lyrics.* Oxford: Oxford University Press.

Murphy, Gregory L. 2002. *The Big Book of Concepts.* Cambridge: M.I.T. Press.

The New Encyclopaedia Britannica. 1974. 15th ed. Chicago: Encyclopaedia Britannica.

The New Encyclopaedia Britannica. 2005. 15th ed. Chicago: Encyclopaedia Britannica.

Ní Chuilleanáin, Eiléan, Cormac Ó Cuilleanáin, and David Parris, eds. Forthcoming. *Translation and Censorship.* Dublin: Four Courts.

Nida, Eugene A. 1964. *Toward a Science of Translating: With Special Reference to Principles and Procedures Involved in Bible Translating.* Leiden: E. J. Brill.

Niranjana, Tejaswini. 1992. *Siting Translation: History, Post-structuralism, and the Colonial Context.* Berkeley and Los Angeles: University of California Press.

Nord, Christiane. 1997. *Translating as a Purposeful Activity: Functionalist Approaches Explained.* Manchester: St. Jerome.

------ 2003. "Function and Loyalty in Bible Translation". *Apropos of Ideology: Translation Studies on Ideology – Ideologies in Translation Studies.* Ed. María Calzada Pérez. Manchester: St. Jerome. 89-112.

O'Connor, Frank. 1956. "Joyce and Dissociated Metaphor". *The Mirror in the Roadway: A Study of the Modern Novel.* New York: Knopf. 295-312.

Oettinger, Anthony G. 1960. *Automatic Language Translation: Lexical and Technical Aspects, with Particular Reference to Russian.* Cambridge: Harvard University Press.

Ohsawa, Yoshihiro. 2005. "Amalgamation of Literariness: Translations as a Means of Introducing European Literary Techniques to Modern Japan". *Asian Translation Traditions.* Ed. Eva Hung and Judy Wakabayashi. Manchester: St. Jerome. 135-54.

Olohan, Maeve, ed. 2000. *Intercultural Faultlines: Research Models in Translation Studies I: Textual and Cognitive Aspects*. Manchester: St. Jerome.

---------2004. *Introducing Corpora in Translation Studies*. London: Routledge.

O'Rahilly, Cecile, ed. and trans. 1967. *"Táin Bó Cúalnge" from the Book of Leinster*. Dublin: Dublin Institute for Advanced Studies.

------ ed. and trans. 1976. *Táin Bó Cúailnge: Recension I*. Dublin: Dublin Institute for Advanced Studies.

Ortiz, Fernando. 1947. *Cuban Counterpoint: Tobacco and Sugar*. Trans. Harriet de Onís. New York: Alfred A. Knopf.

The Oxford English Dictionary. 1989. 20 vols. 2nd. ed. Oxford: Clarendon Press.

Paker, Saliha. 2002. "Translation as Terceme and Nazire: Culture-bound Concepts and their Implications for a Conceptual Framework for Research on Ottoman Translation History". *Crosscultural Transgressions: Research Models in Translation Studies II: Historical and Ideological Issues*. Ed. Theo Hermans. Manchester: St. Jerome. 120-43.

Parmentier, Richard J. 1993. "The Political Function of Reported Speech: A Belauan Example". *Reflexive Language: Reported Speech and Metapragmatics*. Ed. John A. Lucy. Cambridge: Cambridge University Press. 261-86.

Parry, Thomas. 1962. *A History of Welsh Literature*. Trans. H. Idris Bell. Oxford: Clarendon Press.

Petit Robert: Dictionnaire de la langue française. 1991. Paris: Le Robert.

Pratt, Mary Louise. 1992. *Imperial Eyes: Travel Writing and Transculturation*. London: Routledge.

Pym, Anthony. 1996. "Venuti's Visibility". *Target* 8:1.165-77.

------ 1998. *Method in Translation History*. Manchester: St. Jerome.

------ 2000. "On Cooperation". *Intercultural Faultlines: Research Models in Translation Studies I: Textual and Cognitive Aspects*. Ed. Maeve Olohan. Manchester: St. Jerome. 181-92.

------ ed. 2001. *The Return to Ethics*. *The Translator* 7 no. 2, special issue.

Quine, Willard V. O. 1959. "Meaning and Translation". *On Translation*. Ed. Reuben A. Brower. Cambridge: Harvard University Press. 148-72.

------ 1960. *Word and Object*. Cambridge: M. I. T. Press.

Rafael, Vicente L. 1993. *Contracting Colonialism: Translation and Christian Conversion in Tagalog Society under Early Spanish Rule*. Rev. ed. Durham: Duke University Press.

Ramakrishna, Shantha. 2000. "Cultural Transmission through Translation: An Indian Perspective". *Changing the Terms: Translating in the Postcolonial Era*. Ed. Sherry Simon and Paul St-Pierre. Ottawa: University of Ottawa Press. 87-100.

Rambelli, Paolo. 2006. "Pseudotranslations, Authorship and Novelists in Eighteenth-Century Italy". *Translating Others*. Ed. Theo Hermans. 2 vols. Manchester: St. Jerome. 1.181-210.

Ramsay, Raylene. 2004. "Translation in New Caledonia: Writing (in) the Language of the Other: The 'Red Virgin', the Missionary, and the Ethnographer". *For Better or For Worse: Translation as a Tool for Change in the South Pacific*. Ed. Sabine Fenton. Manchester: St. Jerome. 134-70.

Robinson, Douglas. 1996. *Translation and Taboo*. DeKalb: Northern Illinois University Press.

------ 1997a. *Translation and Empire: Postcolonial Theories Explained*. Manchester: St. Jerome.

------ 1997b. *Western Translation Theory from Herodotus to Nietzsche*. Manchester: St. Jerome.

Rose, Marilyn Gaddis. 1997. *Translation and Literary Criticism: Translation as Analysis*. Manchester: St. Jerome.

------ ed. 2000. *Beyond the Western Tradition*. Binghamton: SUNY Binghamton, Center for Research in Translation.

Ross, Stephen David. 1981. "Translation and Similarity". *Translation Spectrum: Essays in Theory and Practice*. Ed. Marilyn Gaddis Rose. Albany: SUNY Press. 8-22.

Salama-Carr, Myriam. 2000. "Medieval Translators into Arabic – Scribes or Interpreters?" *Beyond the Western Tradition*. Ed. Marilyn Gaddis Rose. Binghamton: SUNY Binghamton, Center for Research in Translation. 99-105.

------ 2006. "Translation into Arabic in the 'Classical Age': When the Pandora's Box of Transmission Opens . . .". *Translating Others*. Ed. Theo Hermans. 2 vols. Manchester: St. Jerome. 1.120-31.

Sartre, Jean-Paul. 1988. *"What is Literature?" and Other Essays*. Cambridge: Harvard University Press.

Schäffner, Christina. 1999. *Translation and Norms*. Clevedon: Multilingual Matters.

------ 2003. "Third Ways or New Centres: Ideological Unity or Difference?" *Apropos of Ideology: Translation Studies on Ideology – Ideologies in Translation Studies*. Ed. María Calzada Pérez. Manchester: St. Jerome. 23-41.

Searle, John R. 1969. *Speech Acts: An Essay in the Philosophy of Language*. Cambridge: Cambridge University Press.

Semizu, Yukino. 2006. "Invisible Translation: Reading Chinese Texts in Ancient Japan". *Translating Others*. Ed. Theo Hermans. 2 vols. Manchester: St. Jerome. 2.283-95.

Sengupta, Mahasweta. 1990. "Translation, Colonialism and Poetics: Rabindranath Tagore in Two Worlds". *Translation, History and Culture*. Ed. Susan Bassnett and André Lefevere. London: Pinter. 56-63.

------ 1995. "Translation as Manipulation: The Power of Images and Images of Power". *Between Languages and Cultures: Translation and Cross-cultural Texts*. Ed. Anuradha Dingwaney and Carol Maier. Pittsburgh: University of Pittsburgh Press. 159-74.

Shamma, Tarek. 2005. "The Exotic Dimension of Foreignizing Strategies: Burton's Translation of the *Arabian Nights*". *The Translator* 11:1.51-67.

Simon, Sherry. 1992. "The Language of Cultural Difference: Figures of Alterity in Canadian Translation". *Rethinking Translation: Discourse, Subjectivity, Ideology*. Ed. Lawrence Venuti. London: Routledge. 159-76.

------ 1996. *Gender in Translation: Cultural Identity and the Politics of Transmission*. London: Routledge.

------ 1999. "Translating and Interlingual Creation in the Contact Zone: Border Writing in Quebec". *Post-colonial Translation: Theory and Practice*. Ed. Susan Bassnett and Harish Trivedi. London: Routledge. 58-74.

------ 2000. "Introduction". *Changing the Terms: Translating in the Postcolonial Era*. Ed. Sherry Simon and Paul St-Pierre. Ottawa: University of Ottawa Press. 9-29.

Simon, Sherry, and Paul St-Pierre, eds. 2000. *Changing the Terms: Translating in the Postcolonial Era*. Ottawa: University of Ottawa Press.

Slobin, Dan I. 1996. "From 'Thought and Language' to 'Thinking for Speaking'". *Rethinking Linguistic Relativity*. Ed. John Gumperz and Stephanie Levinson. Cambridge: Cambridge University Press. 70-96.

Snell-Hornby, Mary. 1988. *Translation Studies: An Integrated Approach*. Amsterdam: John Benjamins.

------ 2006. *The Turns of Translation Studies: New Paradigms or Shifting Viewpoints?* Amsterdam: John Benjamins.

Snell-Hornby, Mary, Franz Pöchhacker, and Klaus Kaindl, eds. 1994. *Translation Studies: An Interdiscipline*. Amsterdam: John Benjamins.

Snow, Charles Percy. 1960. *The Two Cultures and the Scientific Revolution*. Cambridge: Cambridge University Press.

Sommer, Doris. 1992. "Resistant Texts and Incompetent Readers". *Latin American Literary Review* 20:40.104-8.

Sperber, Dan, and Deirdre Wilson. 1995. *Relevance: Communication and Cognition*. 2nd. ed. Oxford: Blackwell.

Spivak, Gayatri Chakravorty. 1992. "The Politics of Translation". *Destabilizing Theory*. Ed. Michèle Barrett and Anne Phillips. Oxford: Polity Press. 177-200.

------ trans. 1995. Mahasweta Devi. *Imaginary Maps: Three Stories by Mahasweta Devi*. London: Routledge.

Stanley, Jason. Forthcoming. "Philosophy of Language in the Twentieth Century". *Routledge Guide to Twentieth-Century Philosophy*. London: Routledge.

Staten, Henry. 2005. "Tracking the 'Native Informant': Cultural Translation as the Horizon of Literary Translation". *Nation, Language, and the Ethics of Translation*. Ed. Sandra Bermann and Michael Wood. Princeton: Princeton University Press. 111-26.

Stecconi, Ubaldo. 2006. " The Foundation of a General Theory of Translation Built on the Semiotics of C.S. Peirce". Dissertation. University College London.

Steiner, George. 1992. *After Babel: Aspects of Language and Translation*. 2nd. ed. Oxford: Oxford University Press.

St-Pierre, Paul. 2000. "Translating (into) the Language of the Colonizer". *Changing the Terms: Translating in the Postcolonial Era*. Ed. Sherry Simon and Paul St-Pierre. Ottawa: University of Ottawa Press. 261-88.

Strinati, Dominic. 1995. *An Introduction to Theories of Popular Culture*. London: Routledge.

Sturge, Kate. 1997. "Translation Strategies in Ethnography". *The Translator* 3:1.21-38.

Susam-Sarajeva, Şebnem. 2002. "A 'Multilingual' and 'International' Translation Studies?" *Crosscultural Transgressions: Research Models in Translation Studies II: Historical and Ideological Issues*. Ed. Theo Hermans. Manchester: St. Jerome. 193-207.

Thelen, Marcel, and Barbara Lewandowska-Tomasczyk, eds. 1990. *Translation and Meaning*. Part 1. Maastricht: Euroterm.

------ eds. 1996. *Translation and Meaning*. Part 3. Maastricht: Universitaire Pers Maastricht.

Toury, Gideon. 1980. *In Search of a Theory of Translation*. Tel Aviv: Porter Institute for Poetics and Semiotics.

------ 1982. "A Rationale for Descriptive Translation Studies". *The Art and Science of Translation*. Ed. André Lefevere and Kenneth David Jackson. *Dispositio 7*, special issue, 22-39.

------ 1991. "What are Descriptive Studies into Translation Likely to Yield apart from Isolated Descriptions?" *Translation Studies: The State of the Art: Proceedings of the First James S. Holmes Symposium on Translation Studies*. Ed. Kitty M. van Leuven-Zwart and Ton Naaijkens. Amsterdam: Rodopi. 179-92.

------ 1995. *Descriptive Translation Studies and Beyond*. Amsterdam: John Benjamins.

Trivedi, Harish. 2006. "In Our Own Time, On Our Own Terms: 'Translation' in India". *Translating Others*. Ed. Theo Hermans. 2 vols. Manchester: St. Jerome. 1.102-19.

Turner, Graham H., and Frank Harrington. 2000. "Issues of Power and Method in Interpreting Research". *Intercultural Faultlines: Research Models in Translation Studies I: Textual and Cognitive Aspects*. Ed. Maeve Olohan. Manchester: St. Jerome. 253-65.

Turner, Victor. 1982. *From Ritual to Theatre: The Human Seriousness of Play*. New York: PAJ Publications.

Tymoczko, Maria, trans. 1981. *Two Death Tales from the Ulster Cycle: "The Death of CuRoi" and "The Death of CuChulainn"*. Dublin: Dolmen.

------ 1985. "How Distinct are Formal and Dynamic Equivalence?" *The Manipulation of Literature: Studies in Literary Translation*. Ed. Theo Hermans. London: Croom Helm. 63-86.

------ 1986-87. "Translation as a Force for Literary Revolution in the Twelfth-Century Shift from Epic to Romance". *New Comparison* 1:1-16.

------ 1990a. "The Semantic Fields of Early Irish Terms for Black Birds and Their Implications for Species Taxonomy". *Celtic Language, Celtic Culture: A Festschrift for Eric P. Hamp*. Ed. A.T.E. Matonis and Daniel F. Melia. Van Nuys: Ford and Bailie: 151-71.

------ 1990b. "Translation in Oral Tradition as a Touchstone for Translation Theory and Practice". *Translation, History and Culture*. Ed. Susan Bassnett and André Lefevere. London: Pinter. 46-55.

------ 1994. *The Irish "Ulysses"*. Berkeley and Los Angeles: University of California Press.

------ 1998. "Computerized Corpora and the Future of Translation Studies". *The Corpus-Based Approach*. Ed. Sara Laviosa. *Meta: Journal des traducteurs* 43 no. 4, special issue, 652-59.

------ 1999a. "Post-colonial Writing and Literary Translation". *Post-colonial Translation: Theory and Practice*. Ed. Susan Bassnett and Harish Trivedi. London: Routledge. 19-40.

------ 1999b. *Translation in a Postcolonial Context: Early Irish Literature in English Translation*. Manchester: St. Jerome.

------ 2000a. "Translation and Political Engagement: Activism, Social Change and the Role of Translation in Geopolitical Shifts". *The Translator* 6:1.23-47.

------ 2000b. "Wintering Out with Irish Poetry: Affiliation and Autobiography in English Translation" (Essay on and review of *Sweeney Astray* by Seamus Heaney). *The Translator* 6:2.309-17.

------ 2002. "Connecting the Two Infinite Orders: Research Methods in Translation Studies". *Crosscultural Transgressions: Research Models in Translation Studies II: Historical and Ideological Issues*. Ed. Theo Hermans. Manchester: St. Jerome. 9-25.

------ 2003a. "Cultural Translation in Twentieth-Century Irish Literature." *Kaleidoscopic Views of Ireland*. Ed. Munira H. Mutran and Laura P. Z. Izarra. São Paolo: Universidade de São Paolo. 189-223.

------ 2003b. "Ideology and the Position of the Translator: In What Sense is a Translator 'In Between'?" *Apropos of Ideology: Translation Studies on Ideology – Ideologies in Translation Studies*. Ed. María Calzada Pérez. Manchester: St. Jerome. 181-201.

------ 2004. "Difference in Similarity". *Similarity and Difference in Translation*. Ed. Stefano Arduini and Robert Hodgson, Jr. Rimini: Guaraldi. 27-43.

------ 2005. "Trajectories of Research in Translation Studies". *Meta* 50:4.1082-97.

------ 2006. "Reconceptualizing Translation Theory: Integrating Non-Western Thought about Translation". *Translating Others*. Ed. Theo Hermans. 2 vols. Manchester: St. Jerome. 1.13-32.

------ ed. Forthcoming a. *Translation and Resistance*. Amherst: University of Massachusetts Press.

------ Forthcoming b. "Western Discourses Implicit in Translation Theory". *Cultural Transactions in Asia: 'Translation' in India and Beyond*. Ed. Judy Wakabayashi and Rita Kothari.

Tymoczko, Maria, and Edwin Gentzler, eds. 2002. *Translation and Power*. Amherst: University of Massachusetts Press.

Tymoczko, Maria, and Colin Ireland. 2003. "Language and Tradition in Ireland: Prolegomena." *Language and Tradition in Ireland: Continuities and Displacements*. Ed. Maria Tymoczko and Colin Ireland. Amherst: University of Massachusetts Press. 1-27.

Venuti, Lawrence, ed. 1992. *Rethinking Translation: Discourse, Subjectivity, Ideology*. London: Routledge.

------ 1995. *The Translator's Invisibility: A History of Translation*. London: Routledge.

------ 1998a. *The Scandals of Translation: Towards an Ethics of Difference*. London: Routledge.

------ ed. 1998b. *Translation and Minority*. *The Translator* 4 no. 2, special issue.

Vieira, Else Ribeiro Pires. 1994. "A Postmodern Translational Aesthetics in Brazil". *Translation Studies: An Interdiscipline*. Ed. Mary Snell-Hornby, Franz Pöchhacker, and Klaus Kaindl. Amsterdam: John Benjamins. 65-72.

------ 1999. "Liberating Calibans: Readings of *Antropofagia* and Haroldo de Campos' Poetics of Transcreation". *Post-colonial Translation: Theory and Practice*. Ed. Susan Bassnett and Harish Trivedi. London: Routledge. 95-113.

Vološinov, V. N. 1971. "Reported Speech". Trans. Ladislav Matejka and I. R. Titunik. *Readings in Russian Poetics: Formalist and Structuralist Views*. Ed. Ladislav Matejka and Krystyna Pomorska. Cambridge: MIT Press. 149-75.

Vosniadou, Stella, and Andrew Ortony, eds. 1989. *Similarity and Analogical Reasoning*. Cambridge: Cambridge University Press.

Wace. 1932. *La Vie de Sainte Marguerite*. Ed. Elizabeth A. Francis. Paris: Classiques Français du Moyen Age.

------ 1942. *La Vie de Saint Nicholas*. Ed. Einar Ronsjö. Lund: C.W.K. Gleerup.

Wakabayashi, Judy. 2000. "A Japanese Perspective on the Universalism vs. Particularism Debate". *Beyond the Western Tradition*. Ed. Marilyn Gaddis Rose. Binghamton: SUNY Binghamton, Center for Research in Translation. 259-71.

------ 2005. "Translation in the East Asian Cultural Sphere: Shared Roots, Divergent Paths?" *Asian Translation Traditions*. Ed. Eva Hung and Judy Wakabayashi. Manchester: St. Jerome. 17-65.

Weber, Samuel. 2005. "A Touch of Translation: On Walter Benjamin's 'Task of the Translator'". *Nation, Language, and the Ethics of Translation*. Ed. Sandra Bermann and Michael Wood. Princeton: Princeton University Press. 65-78.

White, Jerry. 2003. "Translating Ireland Back into Éire: Gael Linn and Film Making in Irish". *Éire-Ireland* 38:1-2.106-22.

Williams, J. E. Caerwyn, and Patrick K. Ford. 1992. *The Irish Literary Tradition*. Cardiff: University of Wales Press.

Williams, Jenny, and Andrew Chesterman. 2002. *The Map: A Beginner's Guide to Doing Research in Translation Studies*. Manchester: St. Jerome.

Wilt, Timothy. 2003. *Bible Translation: Frames of Reference*. Manchester: St. Jerome.

Wittgenstein, Ludwig. 1953. *Philosophische untersuchungen, Philosophical Investigations*. Trans. G. E. M. Anscombe. New York: Macmillan.

------ 1961. *Tractatus Logico-Philosophicus*. Trans. D. F. Pears and B. F. McGuinness. London: Routledge and Kegan Paul.

Wolf, Michaela. 2000. "The *Third Space* in Postcolonial Representation". *Changing the Terms: Translating in the Postcolonial Era*. Ed. Sherry Simon and Paul St-Pierre. Ottawa: University of Ottawa Press. 127-45.

------ 2002. "Culture as Translation – and Beyond: Ethnographic Models of Representation in Translation Studies". *Crosscultural Transgressions: Research Models in Translation Studies II: Historical and Ideological Issues*. Ed. Theo Hermans. Manchester: St. Jerome. 180-92.

Wong, Lawrence Wang-Chi. 2005. "From 'Controlling the Barbarians' to 'Wholesale Westernization': Translation and Politics in Late Imperial and Early Republican China, 1840-1919". *Asian Translation Traditions*. Ed. Eva Hung and Judy Wakabayashi. Manchester: St. Jerome. 109-34.

Zukofsky, Celia, and Louis Zukofsky, trans. 1969. Catullus. *Catullus (Gai Valeri Catulli Veronensis Liber)*. London: Cape Goliard Press.

INDEX